Myths
of the
World

Michael Jordan has degrees in natural sciences from the University of London and is best known as a television presenter. But his real passion is anthropology and the study of gods. He has researched these subjects for over ten years, and written two previous books, *Gods of the Earth* (Bantam 1992), a detailed and controversial investigation of the history of the Mother Goddess, and *Encyclopedia of Gods* (Kyle Cathie 1992), a comprehensive reference covering over 2,500 deities.

Myths
of the
World

A Thematic Encyclopedia

Michael Jordan

KYLE CATHIE LTD

First published in Great Britain in 1993 by
Kyle Cathie Limited
7/8 Hatherley Street London SW1P 2QT

Paperback edition 1995

ISBN 1 85626 156 5

A CIP catalogue record for this book is available from the British
Library

Jacket photograph 'Nakht Farming the Elysian Fields' from the *Book of
the Dead* 1340–1300 BC; © Michael Holford, collection – British
Museum

Edited by Caroline Taggart
Typeset from discs by York House Typographic
Printed and bound in Great Britain by
Cox & Wyman Ltd., Reading, Berks.

Contents

To the memory of my father, Edward Joseph Jordan

Introduction

The imagery of myth is conditioned, in most of us, from childhood, when we read – and delight in – the romances and adventures of gods and heroes and heroines like Zeus and Herakles, Ariadne and Persephone. But even a treasury such as that of the Classical Age provides us with no more than a narrow vision of the rich store that the wider world has created.

The definition of myth is fraught because the material is, by its nature, viewed subjectively. Generally speaking myth is regarded as being based less on fact than on fiction and romance. It is 'once upon a time' stuff. Such a sweeping assumption is, however, littered with pitfalls.

The word myth derives from the Greek *mythos*, but as it appears in the English usage it was coined in the comparative modernity of the early nineteenth century and in the broadest sense it is defined as being the fabric of popular lore. But myths offer much more than 'soap opera' fiction; they convey profound truths about superhuman and human existence, stories which explain the activities of gods in their various tasks and the interaction between gods and other categories of beings.

A distinction needs to be drawn between myths and legends, since they may appear to parallel and even be synonymous one with another. Myth is essentially lore involving deities and ordinary human beings, placed typically in a non-historical setting, and it reflects the close ties between mortal and immortal worlds. Legend, on the other hand, accounts the exploits of apparently historical personalities, be they real or imaginary. The demarcation between myth and legend and between legend and historical fact, however, is not always easy to discern. In many religious doctrines, including Christianity, humankind is perceived to be the progeny of the gods, moulded in their likeness. In other traditions the gods themselves were once mortal men and women who have since attained immortality through self-discipline and inner strength. Particularly in Buddhist and Daoist mythology, the characters of the stories may well have evolved from actual figures who lived out their lives at some period of early history, but in European culture too the lines can become blurred, leading to some potentially confusing distinctions. The stories of King Arthur and the knights of the Round Table are effectively legendary tales, as are those of Beowulf and Robin Hood, while the sagas of the Welsh *Mabinogion* and the Irish *Book of Leinster*, which involve interaction between humans and deities, are more discernible as myths.

Perhaps the most remarkable aspect of myth is that it *exists*. When did the human mind first perceive its own spirituality, and why? At what stage of development did we first contemplate an unseen but discernible world existing in tandem with that of sight, smell, touch and hearing? The realization must have exerted an incalculable impact on the progress of humankind because, once the idea was grasped of another world populated by immortal beings to whom the soul was guided after death, the human race can no longer have been driven purely by a process of natural selection, but by a strength of will from within. The stories which follow reflect that perception of spirituality.

If ritual permits the formalization of a faith, myth constitutes much of its building material and that which may be cynically regarded as little more than 'fairy story' or 'romance' by one culture may be taken to be an immutable historical truth by another. Some trenchant illustrations can be found. The narrative of the Christian New Testament covering the birth and the latter part of the life of Jesus is believed to be fundamentally accurate by most followers of the Christian faith. In fact, the account is never corroborated outside the pages of the orthodox Bible, much of the story of the Nativity is almost certainly a romance, and many theologians are resigned to acceptance of the likelihood that the narratives concerning Jesus's work and death are flawed and may be constructed from little more than collected disparate sayings. Thus, to a follower of Hinduism or Shintoism, the Biblical stories may appear as mythical as the *Rg Veda* hymns or the *Nihongi* texts seem in the perspective of the Christian worshipper.

Archaeology is sometimes able to confirm that a story which hitherto has been thought of as fictional and mythical actually possesses a germ of truth. Excavation has revealed that the labyrinthine arrangement of the palace of King Minos on Crete, described in mythical tales, is a reality. It is therefore entirely possible that a tribute of young men and women was sacrificed to some sacred beast, the personification of a god, captive in the system (see *Ariadne, Theseus and the Minotaur*, page 157).

A clear record, inscribed on a bronze bowl, confirms the exact date in history of the 'mythical' battle of Mu in China, when Wu Wang, the leader of the incoming Zhou Dynasty, crossed the Yellow River to launch an attack on Zhou Wang, the last emperor of the Shang Dynasty (see *Battle of Mu*, page 189).

It may be said that all myths are different, yet all myths are alike in that they follow remarkably similar patterns. There is thus a peculiar fascination in studying the origin of the cosmos as perceived by a Mesopotamian farmer in the fourth millennium BC and to discover that it parallels, to remarkable degree, the perceptions of a classical Greek philosopher two thousand years ago, or of a Siberian nomad telling his stories in the twentieth century.

This book is not an encyclopedia of *mythology*. There is no attempt to provide a detailed study of the concept of myth other than in these opening pages and in the introductory passage which precedes each section. Textbooks of mythology more often than not concentrate on iconographic descriptions of the deities and other spiritual beings who populate 'otherworldly' regions. The purpose of *Myths of the World* is to offer précis of the actual stories, listing them not under cultural or national headings, but according to subject matter. Thus all the myths of creation may be discovered under one heading, as may those of death and resurrection, or of birth. Within each section, myths are listed alphabetically by 'key word'. For the convenience of the reader who wishes to locate a particular myth under its cultural heading, a cross-referencing system is provided at the end of the book. At the end of some chapters a few 'miscellaneous' myths, usually of minor importance and unknown provenance, are included; similarly, the final chapter is entitled 'Miscellaneous Myths' and contains items of interest which did not find place in earlier sections.

Most mythology has arisen within pre-literate cultures in the form of traditions that are *told* rather than written down. The art of storytelling is of prime importance to such societies, though it possesses a variety of purposes. The origins of myth invariably lie in shamanism, the universal nature religion, in which concepts of animism and the esoteric forces directing all natural phenomena first developed. Such beginnings are true whether one is exploring the sagas of North America, the Near East or China. From that first blueprint, myth evolves into investigations of the origin and foundation of the cosmos; of that which is supposedly historical; of the elements and the living world; and of the activities of the otherworld into which mankind enters in the afterlife.

Generally speaking, the earliest recorded mythology is that of the Sumerians, which dates from about 3000 BC, though its stories were probably in circulation as an oral tradition from much earlier times. The most recent is that of aboriginal tribes in such regions as south-eastern Siberia and Australasia.

A myth may be constructed to give substance to an otherwise rather vague philosophy or even to authenticate it, or it may endorse a custom or tradition that perhaps originated with a very practical and down-to-earth purpose. For example, myths were constructed to explain certain Egyptian funerary practices which had probably been born out of considerations of convenience or hygiene. Myth is generally, though not always, linked with ritual and it may provide the means of remembering and perpetuating the correct procedure of a rite. Whether myth preceded ritual or vice versa is an argument which may never be resolved, but which will give conflicting schools of academic thought ammunition for eternal debate.

At the other end of the scale, myth may provide little more than a source of vicarious entertainment, a means of escape into the exotic or the fabulous. Generally, though, a vein of serious purpose may be detected which, in part, serves to explain that which would otherwise be inexplicable. The search for understanding of natural phenomena taxed the more erudite members of ancient cultures deeply and because, frequently, they came up with no rational explanation of the conundrums they observed, or with results that were incomprehensible or contradictory, they sought refuge in the building of myths.

It is important for us, with our inherently cynical view of the 'quaintness' of myths, to sympathize with the situation as it presented itself to the myth-makers. For the societies which originated myths, they were vital to a considered view of the world – and indeed the universe. The imagery is sometimes poignant, sometimes funny, sometimes crude, but it possesses a richness of spirit and imagination which our modern world has all but abandoned, cocooned as it is by technology and global communication at the touch of a button. The outpouring of myth should never be thought of in terms of banal tales and fables to be recited for the amusement and alarm of children. The minds which conjured the stories may have been simpler than ours, but they were no less wise.

Today many of the puzzles which perplexed those ancient minds are mysteries no more. The precise means by which life first began and by which it is to be replicated down the generations; the formidable powers of nature; even the secrets of the universe, can be explained away tidily and impressively by science. We are bombarded with factual and incontrovertible information which has eroded the mystery. But in the eras before science and technology took away our faith and our fear about the supernatural, myth was the 'science textbook' by which our very existence was explained.

In précising myths into a modern anthology, it is difficult to maintain a consistent narrative style. An account of the passage to the otherworld compiled by a sophisticated Egyptian thinker four thousand years ago may be couched in much richer and more profound language than that of a primitive and illiterate tribesman from Papua New Guinea today. The quality and complexity of a myth is frequently determined by the degree of sophistication of the vocabulary at the disposal of the storyteller. For this reason alone an early Mesopotamian myth may appear more banal than one from the hand of a Greek Homer or Hesiod. In certain instances in this volume it has not been possible to provide a continuous narrative. This is particularly true in the case of Egyptian mythology, where the sources of information are often fragmentary. In such instances explanatory details are interjected. The same may also apply where variations of a myth emerge from separate sources.

Many of the myths teach us lessons of moral and human dignity, of loyalty, courage and enthusiasm in the face of seemingly insurmountable odds. They were, in their day, a guide to rules of behaviour and they detailed a code of morality but, for the modern reader, there is a risk in subjective interpretation. The conditions under which we live in the twentieth century may bear little resemblance to those prevailing at the time of the original composition and thus modern-day notions of what is quaint or boorish, funny or crude, heroic or cowardly, may compare poorly with the views of the society which generated the myth. The stories are strictly the comment of a particular age or culture and it is both difficult and fraught with danger to apply their message to a society living in a different age and social climate, as the Nazis discovered when they attempted to resurrect the mythology of their Teutonic ancestors.

Most myth, irrespective of age and sophistication, offers a rich treasure house of visual images, but the way the personalities and characteristics of gods are portrayed is always strongly influenced by the state of understanding which exists between mankind and the natural world. It is significant, when juxtaposing myths artificially, that the views of contemporary cultures may have been at marked variance with one another. The more vulnerable we are to the caprices and moods of nature, the more whimsical, autocratic and savage are the gods who control our destinies. As the forces of nature are increasingly held in check by advances in skills and technological ability, so the gods themselves become more compliant and democratic. Stark and dramatic contrasts can be seen in the often brutal behaviour of deities known to primitive societies and the sophisticated wiles and seductions of those worshipped by more advanced cultures. Thus the gods of clans eking out an existence in the wastes of Siberia or in the rugged isolation of the Hindu Kush are chauvinistic and appear to treat life with a degree of contempt; set beside them, the classical pantheon of Olympus seems almost tame. The fabric and laws of society among the ancient Celts were based largely on a need for conquest of territory and on cattle rustling. If one's survival is determined by fighting one does not send one's troops out equipped with Mills and Boon stories of love and romance. Celtic mythology often reflects this by appearing brutalized. The Celts were also head-hunters, but their gory interest did not equate with mindless butchery since, for them, the brain was immortal, the place of the soul, and so they attached great religious importance to the skull and the forces contained within a severed head. Such apparent barbarity reads badly to us. Conversely a society which is living through a comparatively peaceful and sophisticated era may give the stuff of its mythology an appearance of being more civilized and less reprehensible.

In almost all cases the gods portrayed in myth adopt certain common characteristics. They possess human traits in that they are obliged to walk on two legs, eat, sleep, fornicate, go to the lavatory and sometimes even die. They experience courage and fear, jealousy and magnanimity, anger and joy, mischief-making and honour, duplicity and loyalty. Yet they are also seen to be superhuman. They may exude strength that can move mountains or deliver thunderbolts; they may be vast in dimension like the Hindu incarnation of Visnu who strides the world in just three paces, or possess multiples of heads, arms and legs; they may enjoy the ability to change shape at will and, of course, to appear in the guise of mortals.

A myth may have originated through an oral tradition, but small details may vary from one place to the next. Thus when it comes to be written down, a single story may be consigned to posterity in several different versions. One source may omit a crucial episode and replace it with another. Myth is also often subject to cultural borrowing and plagiarism when it is adapted to suit the needs and observations of its new custodians.

So what among the texts which have come down to us today is authentic and what is adulterated? Probably all versions have a valid claim to credibility. In this volume, for the sake of convenience, episodes which appear separately in different written texts within a cultural period are incorporated into the same myth.

The gradual elaboration of a myth sometimes occurs across a span of time, when its bare bones are fleshed out by skilled storytellers over many generations. It is also possible to observe the reverse process taking place, where the flesh has been pared down by later scribes to make it more succinct than the original rambling saga. In either event oral traditions are characterized by the fact that they are sustained over great periods of time. In the modern literary world we are used to seeing books appearing on the 'remainder' list after a year or so, but the stories which constitute the mythical heritage of humankind have survived and have been retold almost unchanged over centuries and perhaps sometimes millennia.

The mythological store reveals much about the culture which spawned it, about the degree of both material and spiritual sophistication, the aspirations, the strengths and weaknesses. But there exists a *caveat* against reading too much into a mythological legacy. The old polytheistic cults, by their very nature, were marked by tolerance, while the monotheistic religions of modern times – Christianity and Islam in particular – are strongly resistant to adulteration by, or recognition of, other faiths, and even sectarian differences within their own broad churches create agonized debate and censure. The evangelical Christian movement, in particular, has exerted a powerful influence on the traditions of faiths it has superseded. The extent of its interference has ranged from the almost total obliteration of such ancient literary traditions as those of the Aztecs by the Catholic Church under the aegis of the Spanish conquistadors, to the subtle manipulation of Irish mythological store by Christian monks who reduced Celtic deities to the level of boorish and often mindless objects of ridicule. The myths of the Celts all too often appear distanced from serious meaning, but it is difficult to believe that a people with the eloquence and pride of the Celtic races would have tolerated the clownish antics which sometimes emerge in what has come down to us and we have to wonder if the ancient prose has been recorded accurately. The Celtic authority Myles Dillon comments that Christian clerks 'deprived the gods of their original prestige as objects of cult and relegated them to an artificial setting fitting them to a scheme of pseudo-history which was quite foreign to their origin.'

The Middle Ages in Europe were not renowned for tolerance, and Christianity was administered more through the language of the sword and the stake than the tongue. Sometimes the rescue of a literary tradition from zealous Christian hands has come about through the flimsiest of chances. Almost all we know of the religion of the Viking forebears of the modern English peoples is contained in one volume, the *Codex Regius*. During the ninth century AD a group of Norwegian *émigrés* settled in Iceland precisely because they resented the suppression of Nordic traditions and they wished to preserve the remnants of the faith which their ancestors had pursued. They wrote and assembled books relating to the traditions of their ancestors and some of the literary works found their way, through a broad-minded monarch, Frederic III, to the safekeeping of the Danish Royal Library in Copenhagen. Had the Icelandic *émigrés* not rescued their cultural heritage with quite such determination, working against the tide of Christian fervour, the great epics of the gods of Asgarth would have been lost forever. The *Codex Regius*, with its forty-five handwritten sheets of parchment dating from the late thirteenth century, was, nonetheless, saved only by the pragmatism of one Danish ruler and the unusual tolerance of his bishop in Iceland.

A similar story can be told for the mythological traditions of the aboriginal clans living in south-eastern Siberia. In the early years of the twentieth century these scattered groups of nomadic hunters, which had hitherto been protected from Christian adulteration by their sheer remoteness and inaccessibility, were experiencing cultural assault through 'Russianization' and the activities of the Orthodox Church, with the result that myths and legends were commencing the irreversible slide into confused tales and fables often incomplete or remembered barely more than in name. In 1900 an American-Swedish ethnologist, Waldemar Jochelson, spent a year in the region of the Kamchatka Peninsula and he, fortuitously, possessed a passionate interest in recording the legacy of the tribes which lived there. He did so accurately and earnestly and the pages of his massive diaries represent another strictly unique archive.

The rescue of the gnostic Christian texts, which include some of the most sophisticated and provocative accounts of creation, provides an even more extraordinary story of chance discovery and fate. In December 1945, at Nag Hammadi in Upper Egypt, a large earthenware pot was unearthed by two brothers digging out fertilizer in the mouth of a cave. The vessel contained a set of twelve leather-bound codices composed in Coptic and dating from the third and fourth centuries AD. The widowed mother of the two brothers began to burn the manuscripts in a bread oven until those which survived were noticed lying on the kitchen floor by a local itinerant history teacher who realized their potential worth. Even so it was not until thirty years later that they found their way into the safekeeping of the Cairo Museum, where they were translated and published. Such heirlooms are rare.

Myth has always been gathered on an arbitrary and chance basis. The first 'histories' to be compiled were largely based upon a mythological store and the monks or other scribes merely collected together what they could obtain from diverse literary or oral sources, some of it immature, some in a process of active decay, some of it remembered only as a vestige of what it once was. The same process has taken place in this volume and so the myths selected have been through one more in a succession of layers of sifting, editing and discrimination.

If a future holocaust depletes our literary store, both on computer file and sheets of paper, the human survivors will not benefit from the safeguards of an oral tradition. All they will know of myth will be whatever is contained in the few scorched and tattered remants which survive. Without the benefit of a consciousness and a training in memory that our ancestors learned so well, the mythological heritage will be well and truly lost.

To provide a fully comprehensive view of the world's myths would be a gigantic task and the result would fill the shelves of a library. No single work can hope to do more than scratch the surface; the selection of what is, and is not, included will therefore largely be an arbitrary one based on personal preferences and available source material. *Myths of the World* offers a broad cross-section ranging from the best-loved stories of classical Greek myth to small and unfamiliar cameo fragments from remote Siberian tribes. Collectively, though, it reveals the remarkable common patterns of thought which characterize myth, irrespective of time or place.

Chronology of the Principal Religions and Cultures covered in this Book

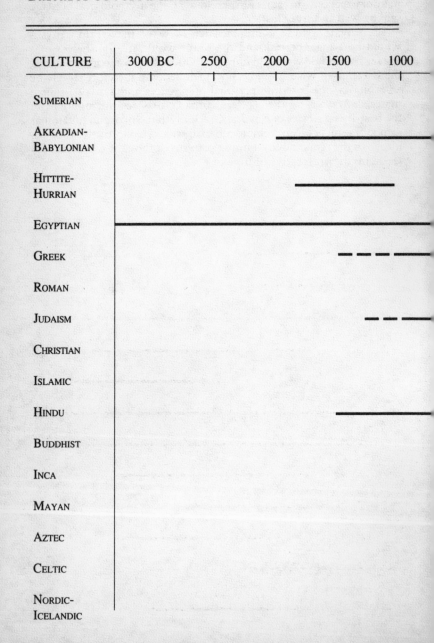

CULTURE	3000 BC	2500	2000	1500	1000
SUMERIAN					
AKKADIAN-BABYLONIAN					
HITTITE-HURRIAN					
EGYPTIAN					
GREEK					
ROMAN					
JUDAISM					
CHRISTIAN					
ISLAMIC					
HINDU					
BUDDHIST					
INCA					
MAYAN					
AZTEC					
CELTIC					
NORDIC-ICELANDIC					

1

Myths of Animism

The religious concepts of nomadic hunting societies whose priesthood is based on shamanism are encapsulated in this section and they may generally be regarded as the most primitive forms of myth.

The philosophy at the core of shamanistic belief is that of animism. It operates on the assumption that before the human intellect recognizes the essential fact that our individual personalities separate us irreversibly from the rest of the world, everything is part of a huge and constantly shifting chain. Each familiar object, no matter whether living or inanimate, is a link in the chain. The links, however, are fluid and can merge one with another. Thus a bird or an animal can equally well become a rock, a cloud or a human being. Likewise a tree can take on human or beastly proportions. The power to produce these changes emanates from the spirit world and thus a spirit can turn, in an instant, into objects of daily life. It can become a log, a stone, a bear, an eagle or even the swirling mist. In other words, at the behest of its spirit guardian, everything in nature can adopt another guise.

Whether, in origin, myth precedes ritual is a chicken and egg dilemma. The myths of animism may, however, serve to keep the procedure of ritual in a precise and established fashion. The mythology provides a mechanism for placing the mysteries of life in a familiar and structured framework. It is particularly important when reading the myths in this section to understand the parlous state into which, all too often, the societies which told them had descended. When, for example, Waldemar Jochelson recorded the myths of the Kamchatka region of south-eastern Siberia, the clans there were in a state of cultural stagnation, if not active decay. Their shamans, who told the stories, were few in number, often little respected, and on the fringes of society. It is very clear that the sense of the stories is frequently muddled or that their endings are incomplete. No attempt has been made here to interpret the stories beyond that which is readily understandable. They are offered very much as they were told and written down. One also has to accept that the atmosphere of colonization and Christian evangelism under which some of the stories were told did not encourage the primitive societies under observation to be wholly forthcoming with the intimate secrets of their beliefs, to which the so-called ethnologists were often overtly hostile. The mythology of the Irish Celts provides an excellent illustration.

Notwithstanding the cautions about interpretation, apart from signalling responses to the forces of nature, myth at this base level also offers a dimension of pure entertainment. Stories involve the raw ingredients of faith, but they are drawn in such a way that there is an overlay of vicarious romance and adventure.

One finds various levels in the spirit cosmos overseen by an illustrious but shadowy and remote being, the supreme creator spirit. Below him there exist guardians of virtually everything which occurs in nature. Often, however, the spirits involved in animistic myth are poorly defined and may only go by the name of an animal or plant or natural phenomenon. Thus, in Siberian mythology, one discovers Big Raven and Cloud Man, Grass Woman and even Diarrhoea Man, while one of the most popular native American deities is Coyote.

Out of the animistic pantheon there often emerges a special figure who is less a god than an immortalized super-hero. Thus one finds Maui in Polynesian myth and Big Raven in the stories of Siberia. He or she (in Eskimo tradition it is a female character, the Old Woman of the Sea) tends to be seen as the first all-powerful shaman of the tribe who has been responsible for the gelling of everyday objects from the ether. This figure also oversees the immediate needs of the temporal world, sorts out its practical wants and acts as an intercessor between the creator god and humankind.

The myths of animism are often laced with sexuality and it is important to understand that in primitive hunting societies the act of procreation among animals and people alike assumes far more pressing urgency than it does as society becomes less vulnerable to the environment and its forces.

The hunting tribes do not generally recognize the concept of a heaven and a hell, though an offended spirit must be placated or it will bring calamity through illness, starvation or death. They do, however, perceive various levels of otherworld from that above the earth to that below. Generally speaking that which is in the sky above, though it may be capricious, is fundamentally benign, while that in the dark realms beneath the earth is to be feared.

THE BEAR MAN

CULTURE OF ORIGIN: native American – Pawnee [Oklahoma and North Dakota]

PROVENANCE: recorded from oral traditions. Principal sources include *The Pawnee: Mythology* G.A. Dorsey. Carnegie Institution of Washington. No 59. 1906. The myth accounts for the relationship between the native

American and the bear which he regards as sacred and it also explains the origin of the Bear Dance of the Pawnees.

A warrior on the warpath comes across a little bear-cub, picks it up and ties some tobacco around its neck to show that he means it no harm. He tells the cub that he hopes when his son is born the bears will help the boy to grow into a wise man. He returns to his wife, who is pregnant, and relates the story, but in doing so he puts the thought of a bear into her mind and when the baby is born it grows into the ways of the bear. The young boy always makes believe he is a bear and he imitates it so well that he comes to resemble the animal. As he grows into manhood he often goes to the forest to commune with the bears and develops a great rapport with them.

One day, when he has become a chief, he and a war party are ambushed by Sioux and all are slaughtered. The bodies lie in a ravine beside a pathway frequented by bears and when one of the she-bears passes by she recognizes the Bear Man. She and her companion use their magic to revive him and he manages to reach the bears' den, where he makes a full recovery apart from his hair, which never grows again because the Sioux have scalped him. He remains with the bears for many years and they teach him great wisdom. Eventually the great spirit, Atius Tirawa, tells the Bear Man to return to his tribe where he will become a great chief but reminds him that he is never to forget the bears or to stop emulating them. Atius Tirawa gives the Bear Man a cedar tree to protect him and a cap to hide his baldness. When the chief returns he is greeted with astonishment, he and his people take gifts out to the forest and he dances a ritual dance for the bears.

BIG KAMAK AND TATQA'HICNIN
(Big Kamak and Root Man)

CULTURE OF ORIGIN: Siberian – Koryak

PROVENANCE: from an oral tradition among the Koryak reindeer hunters living on the Kamchatka Peninsula of south-eastern Siberia. Modern authorship is that of the Swedish ethnologist Waldemar Jochelson, who recorded the tale during the Jesup North Pacific Survey of 1900, sponsored by the American Society for Natural History [Memoirs of the American Museum of Natural History, 10, 1905].

Siberian folklore is often littered with prurient or scatological humour, often with sexual or fertility connotations. In many instances the original message of the myths has been lost or confused and although this myth illustrates the principles of animism whereby every object in nature is controlled by a spirit being who may merge with the identity of that object, the story has become largely nonsensical. One of the underlying features is a ritualized marriage ceremony. Another fringes on the belief that bodily emissions from the spirit world represent the rain which falls on earth. There is possibly also a hierarchical message in that Big Kamak is swept aside in the marital contest in favour of the son of Quikinna'qu, who is second only to the supreme being in ascendancy.

A *kamak* in Siberian culture is a guardian spirit, often symbolized by a carved wooden post. The whaling clans set these up on the seashore, allegedly to attract whales.

Tatqa'hicnin (Root Man) has a daughter called Veai (Grass Woman) who enjoys the attentions of many suitors. She is courted by Big Kamak, who offers to marry her. He tells Tatqa'hicnin that he is going to urinate in his chamber pot and that Veai may carry it outside. Big Kamak places both Veai and the chamber pot on a shovel and carries them off to the house of Quikinna'qu (Big Raven). Big Kamak urinates again, but now it is the turn of Quikinna'qu to put him and his chamber pot on to the shovel and throw them out.

Veai marries not Big Kamak but Eme'mqut, the son of Quikinna'qu, and she bears him a son. When Eme'mqut and Veai go to visit Tatqa'hicnin he does not recognize her and protests that, in any case, it was Big Kamak who married his daughter. The couple stay with Tatqa'hicnin for some time and eventually they go home, accompanied by Tree Trunk Man, Veai's brother. Tree Trunk Man then marries Quikinna'qu's daughter and everyone lives happily.

BITAHATINI

CULTURE OF ORIGIN: native American – Navaho [New Mexico and Arizona]
PROVENANCE: recorded fron oral traditions. The myth was related to Washington Matthews and recorded in the Memoirs of the American Museum of Natural History, 1902. Bitahatini is an archetypal Navajo shaman.

Bitahatini, the third of four brothers, has special shamanistic powers which enable him to hear the songs of the spirit world. His brothers, however, ridicule his abilities. One day the other brothers and their brother-in-law set off on a hunting trip. Bitahatini follows at a distance. That night he rests in a cave and watches as a large number of crows gather to roost in his and in a neighbouring cave. They quieten down, but in the middle of the night he hears voices passing between the two caves saying that the hunters have killed twelve fine deer:

They have killed enough. It is well. Begin the dance now!

The crows, who appear in human form, dance and howl the night away, only ceasing at dawn when they fly off. Bitahatini catches up with the hunting party and relates what he has heard to the brothers, but they scorn his warnings. The brother-in-law, however, tells Bitahatini that yesterday they killed twelve deer and a crow. He tries to persuade the eldest brother that they are destined to kill no more deer, but the latter argues that it is nonsense and that they will have a successful day in the hunt. The two older brothers set off but after four days they remain empty-handed and even the eldest begins to wonder about Bitahatini's powers.

Later the whole party stop to shoot some Rocky Mountain sheep. Bitahatini is told to head them off, but when the moment comes to loose off his arrows he is unable to do so and the sheep pass by unharmed. They throw off their masks and reveal *ganaskidi* or holy men, who ask Bitahatini to discard his clothes and put on a sheepskin. Then they lead him to the edge of a cliff and step off. When the brothers search for Bitahatini all they find is a pile of clothes by the path, so they return home and make up a basket of sacred offerings to the spirits. This is laid at the edge of the cliff where the tracks disappear and the brothers pray to the spirits for Bitahatini's safe return.

Ni'ltsi, the wind, tells them to perform a certain ritual upon which their brother will come back to them. So they sing and pray as instructed for five nights, after which Bitahatini reappears.

He tells them that when he jumped from the cliff edge he landed on a narrow ledge which led to the home of the twelve chief gods who had sent their younger members to capture him. Messengers brought the sacred basket left by the brothers and the gods then showed Bitahatini many secret things, including the means to cure diseases. A rogue spirit absconded to the sky with Bitahatini and the other gods had to go searching for him while the supreme spirit demanded his safe return. He was rescued and the gods taught him their mystical songs which he was, in turn, to teach to his people.

When he is sent home no one can learn the songs except Nakiest-sahi, his youngest brother, who has quietly memorized all he has heard while pretending to be asleep. He also learns all the rituals. After four days a stranger comes to the camp with a blind boy, asking Bitahatini to cure the child. Bitahatini explains that Nakiestsahi knows what to do and when the stranger presents Nakiestsahi with twelve fine buckskins he sings and performs to restore the boy's sight. The fame of Bitahatini and Nakiestsahi spreads and they perform many magical cures.

MASTER-CARPENTER AND SOUTH-EAST

CULTURE OF ORIGIN: native American – Haida [British Columbia and Queen Charlotte Islands]

PROVENANCE: recorded from oral traditions. Principal sources include *Haida Texts and Myths* J.R. Swanton. Bulletin 29, Bureau of American Ethnology. Washington, 1905.

On the southern coast of the Queen Charlotte Islands the spirit being Master-carpenter is in conflict with the spirit of the wind South-east, intending to punish him for his violence. Master-carpenter builds a war canoe, but it splits and each one which he constructs subsequently is a failure. He is about to admit defeat when Greatest-fool arrives and shows him how to do the job. Despite such an unlikely instructor, the work is successful and Master-carpenter sets off in search of South-east. When he thinks he has arrived at the right place he calls out a challenge, but there is no answer until the current brings a large mass of seaweed alongside in the midst of which Master-carpenter sees the head of South-east. He seizes the head and South-east cries to his nephews for aid. Red-storm-cloud responds by turning the sky red. Now the wind begins to rise and, with the help of Taker-off-of-the-treetops, it increases to storm force so that the treetops smash down around the canoe of Master-carpenter. He uses magic powers to defend himself while a succession of other malevolent spirits come to do their worst. The wind, Pebble-rattler, is summoned, followed by Maker-of-the-thick-sea-mist and many others. All are thwarted until South-east summons Tidal-wave, who succeeds in swamping Master-carpenter's boat. The myth has an ambivalent ending. Master-carpenter struggles to the shore, down but not out, and South-east retires back to his own abode.

MIDAS AND THE ASS'S EARS

CULTURE OF ORIGIN: classical Greek, but subsequently adopted into Roman culture

PROVENANCE: recorded from oral traditions

Midas, the king of Phrygia, is one of the judges of the musical competition between Apollo, playing his lyre, and Marsyas with the double flute of Athena. Midas is the only judge to vote in favour of Marsyas, and for his impudence Apollo gives him a pair of ass's ears.

So embarrassed is Midas that he is forced to hide his ears under a hat. Only his barber knows the secret; he is sworn to silence, but is unable to contain himself and digs a hole in the ground where he whispers his knowledge into the earth. Eventually some reeds grow on the place and from that day hence they tell the world, when the wind stirs them, that 'King Midas has ass's ears!' See also *Marsyas and the Flute of Athena*, page 156.

QUIKINNA'QU, EME'MQUT AND TENANTO'MWAN
(Big Raven, Eme'mqut and Existence)

CULTURE OF ORIGIN: Siberian – Koryak

PROVENANCE: from an oral tradition amongst the Koryak reindeer hunters living along the Chaibuga River on the Kamchatka Peninsula of south-eastern Siberia. Modern authorship is that of the Swedish ethnologist Waldemar Jochelson, who recorded the tale during the Jesup North Pacific Survey of 1900, sponsored by the American Society for Natural History [Memoirs of the American Museum of Natural History, 10, 1905].

In the mythology of a primitive animistic society Quikinna'qu (Big Raven) is the founder of the world, perceived not only as a deity but also as the first man and a powerful shaman. Tenanto'mwan (Existence) is a more remote, shadowy figure, out of touch with the affairs of mortals but occasionally lending a hand to tip the balance of things. The myth incorporates several important principles in the shamanistic beliefs of primitive hunting societies. All objects in nature are transmutable and may also conceal spirit beings who have the power to reveal themselves in human form. In this instance Quikinna'qu and his son transmute into birds and then into reindeer-hair mats. The myth also explains the widely held belief that rain represents a bodily emanation from the sky spirits, sometimes semen, sometimes saliva or urine. It further suggests that certain carefully prescribed rituals are necessary before engaging in the hunt.

Quikinna'qu (Big Raven) and his son Eme'mqut are disgruntled that it has been raining for a long time, so they decide to visit Tenanto'-mwan (Existence) to find out what is happening. They put on their raven coats and fly upwards. Standing outside Tenanto'mwan's home, they hear the sound of a drum and when they go into the house they find Tenanto'mwan with his wife Rain Woman. He has dismembered his wife's vulva and attached it to the drum. He has also cut off his own penis and is using it like a drumstick to beat the vulva, from which pours the water that is falling on the earth below. As soon as Tenanto'mwan sees the visitors he stops beating the drum and puts it away, at which point the rain ceases.

Quikinna'qu and Eme'mqut pretend to leave the house, but instead transmute themselves into mats made of reindeer hair and lie down on the floor. Now that Tenanto'mwan thinks he and his wife are alone he takes out the drum again and renews his rainmaking.

From their disguised vantage-point Quikinna'qu tells Eme'mqut that he will make Tenanto'mwan fall asleep and that Eme'mqut must watch where the drum and drumstick are put. Soon Tenanto'mwan and Rain Woman become sleepy under Quikinna'qu's magic and the instruments are put aside.

Quikinna'qu takes the drum and drumstick and roasts them over a fire until they are dry and crisp; then he replaces them. When, however, Tenanto'mwan awakens and starts to beat the drum again the weather turns fine. The longer he beats the drum the longer the weather remains dry.

Quikinna'qu and Eme'mqut return home but, as the cloudless skies continue, the hunting becomes so poor that everyone begins to starve. Eventually Quikinna'qu is obliged to return to Tenanto'mwan and relate the problems on earth. Tenanto'mwan is contrite about his lack of attention and promises that the hunting will become successful. When Quikinna'qu gets home he pulls a post, to which the camp dogs are tethered, from the ground and a herd of reindeer spring from the hole. He makes the necessary sacrifices and the tribe prospers once more.

QUIKINNA'QU AND THE STONE PINE GIRL

CULTURE OF ORIGIN: Siberian – Koryak

PROVENANCE: from an oral tradition among the Koryak hunters living on the Bering Sea coast of the Kamchatka Peninsula in south-eastern Siberia. Modern authorship is that of the Swedish ethnologist Waldemar Jochelson, who recorded the tale in the village of Tilliran during the Jesup North Pacific Survey of 1900, sponsored by the American Society for Natural History [Memoirs of the American Museum of Natural History, 10, 1905].

Like the previous entry, this myth underlines the primitive hunting belief that all objects in nature are transmutable and may also conceal spirit beings who have the power to reveal themselves in human form. The ending, like that of many Siberian stories recorded at the turn of the century, is confused and suggests a partially remembered oral tradition of a society whose culture is in a state of serious decline.

Quikinna'qu (Big Raven) goes to the woods, where he finds a cone that has fallen from a Stone Pine tree. This he smashes with a stone and from it emerges a girl with a head like a copper tea-pot. Quikinna'qu tells her that she is pretty. She replies, 'Do you say that I am pretty? Mama says come into the house.' The house is the twisted trunk of the Stone Pine whose sleeping room is in the hollow of a big branch.

When he enters the house, Quikinna'qu complains that he is hungry and he is told to open the stomach of the girl's mother. This he does and, peering inside, he discovers that it is filled with the nicely fatty meat of a mountain sheep. He eats, chokes himself and dies.

QUIKINNA'QU AND VAK'THIMTILAN

CULTURE OF ORIGIN: Siberian – Koryak
PROVENANCE: from an oral tradition among the Koryak reindeer hunters living on the Kamchatka Peninsula of south-eastern Siberia. The myth was related by an unnamed shamanka in the maritime village of Kamens-koy. Modern authorship is that of the Swedish ethnologist Waldemar Jochelson, who recorded the tale during the Jesup North Pacific Survey of 1900, sponsored by the American Society for Natural History [Memoirs of the American Museum of Natural History, 10, 1905].

The myth underscores the notion held by many shamanistic societies that animals and birds can be possessed by spirit forces who have the ability to appear in human form. The ending of the story seems confused and lacking in point.

Quikinna'qu goes out to collect willow bark and his wife Miti busies herself with feeding the puppies. While Quikinna'qu is away, Vak'-thimtilan (Magpie Man) arrives at the dog shed and eats with the puppies. He also pecks, in amorous fashion, at Miti's face.

When Quikinna'qu returns, he immediately asks what has happened to his wife's nose. She replies that the sharp ends of the dog shed scratched her and so Quikinna'qu cuts off all the rough projections. Next morning he sets off again in search of willow bark and while he is away Vak'thimtilan returns. On this occasion Miti takes him into the house and they begin to make love until they are interrupted by the sudden return of Quikinna'qu. He shouts for Miti to take the load of willow from him, but she calls back that she is busy trampling a skin! Quikinna'qu calls again and this time she hauls the load into the house with one mighty tug.

Quikinna'qu's suspicions are aroused; he enters the living quarters and builds a fire. Then he stops up the smoke hole so that the bedroom fills with smoke. Vak'thimtilan comes out coughing and escapes with some difficulty. He has, however, made Miti pregnant and in due course she delivers two eggs which hatch into human-like children.

Time passes and one day, while everyone is busy storing away a fish catch, one of the twins complains to Miti that he is hungry. Quikinna'qu gives each child a whole dried salmon, but the pair are still not satisfied. He remarks that he is hardly surprised, since they are two thieving sons of a magpie, but the children only cry, so Miti puts them into a grass travelling bag and takes them to the house of

Vak'thimtilan. She flings them down on the floor and chooses to stay with their father.

Quikinna'qu becomes lonely and goes to visit Miti. He eats some food and then goes home.

THE SMOKING OF THE SACRED PIPE

CULTURE OF ORIGIN: native American – general
PROVENANCE: recorded from oral traditions principally in *Illustrations of the Manners and Customs and Condition of the North American Indians* G. Catlin, London 1841 (2 vols).

The mythology of the native American pipe varies from nation to nation but essentially it follows the same principles. The pipe is a sacred object, with a man throughout his life and laid beside the deceased at his burial. It is a common practice among many shamanistic tribal societies to smoke narcotic substances and so facilitate varying degrees of trance-like experience.

In the beginning one of the great and good spirits is walking in a forest when he becomes tired, makes a fire and lies down beside it to sleep. One of his rivals, an evil spirit, comes along and discovers him thus. Taking the opportunity for mischief, the villain of the tale gently rolls him over until his hair is set alight in the red hot embers. At this juncture the good spirit awakens and, in fright, runs away through the forest, his hair blazing. Burning pieces of it are carried away on the wind and where they settle to earth tobacco plants grow.

At a later time the great spirit assembles his people by the Red Pipe-stone Rock [Pipe Stone Quarry – a sheer cliff face of red quartz about two miles in length and thirty feet high] where he breaks off a piece of stone and fashions it into a pipe. He explains that the red rock is their own flesh and the pipe symbolizes peace among them. He smokes the pipe and when it is finished he disappears into the rock, which becomes a sacred place for the native American nations.

TENANTO'MWAN AND MITI

CULTURE OF ORIGIN: Siberian – Koryak
PROVENANCE: from an oral tradition amongst the Koryak reindeer hunters living on the Kamchatka Peninsula of south-eastern Siberia. The myth was related by a shamanka named Ty'kken in a hunting camp on the Tapolovka River. Modern authorship is that of the Swedish ethnologist Waldemar Jochelson who recorded the tale during the Jesup North Pacific

Survey of 1900 sponsored by the American Society for Natural History [Memoirs of the American Museum of Natural History, 10, 1905].

The feuding between creator and consort, with the latter playing the part of the shrewd but vindictive wife, is well recorded in Siberian mythology and the bizarre account of Tenanto'mwan entering his wife's anus is a common theme.

Tenanto'mwan, the creator being, and Miti his wife, live together fairly peacably until one day Tenanto'mwan throws Miti out. She decides to take revenge on the creator for his ill-treatment, so she cuts off her breasts, buttocks and vulva, turning them into four male human beings. She takes the four men into her confidence and suggests that they play a trick on Tenanto'mwan. Miti proposes that she shall go home and the four will follow her, after an interval, saying that they are her brothers who have come to take her away.

Miti slices a little piece of skin from her leg and turns it into a bird, which she orders to fly home. Miti returns home herself and when the bird begins to twitter on the roof she tells Tenanto'mwan that it is announcing the arrival of her relatives. The four 'brothers' complain that, according to Miti, her husband beats her and generally treats her badly, so they are going to take her with them to where she will be in better hands. As soon as they have all departed Miti restores the four to their original form, but she puts them back in the wrong places so that her breasts are on her back, her buttocks are at the front and her vagina is at the rear. Now she returns home again and pretends to play the part of the loving wife.

In bed Tenanto'mwan begins to fondle Miti, but when he complains that all her parts are in the wrong places she snaps back at him and tells him not to touch her. Next morning, in a contrite mood, Tenanto'mwan suggests that they give up quarrelling and playing tricks on each other. He asks Miti to make him a pudding but she refuses, saying untruthfully that there are no edible roots in the store. At this Tenanto'mwan threatens to throw her out for good and find a better wife who will make him decent meals. He goes off in a bad temper.

Left at home Miti cooks up all kinds of delicious puddings; then she runs after Tenanto'mwan and lies on the ground a little way ahead on the path with her legs up and her head buried in the snow. She makes herself grow so large that she blocks the way and Tenanto'mwan walks through the opening of her anus as if it were the door of a house. Once he is trapped inside she closes the entrance and goes home, where she hauls the creator being out and gives him some pudding. Whilst inside her anus Tenanto'mwan has lost all his hair and become permanently bald.

TENANTO'MWAN AND THE REINDEER

CULTURE OF ORIGIN: Siberian – Koryak

PROVENANCE: from an oral tradition among the Koryak reindeer hunters living on the Kamchatka Peninsula of south-eastern Siberia. The myth was related by a shamanka named Ty'kken in a reindeer hunting camp on the Tapolovka River. Modern authorship is that of the Swedish ethnologist Waldemar Jochelson, who recorded the tale during the Jesup North Pacific Survey of 1900, sponsored by the American Society for Natural History [Memoirs of the American Museum of Natural History, 10, 1905].

The story combines elements of animism, the high value placed upon reindeer herds and an object lesson in the status of the true shaman.

Tenanto'mwan, the creator being, possesses three herds of reindeer, including many animals which are the envy of both the Chukchee and the reindeer Koryak clans. The clans agree to join forces, slaughter Tenanto'mwan and steal his reindeer; accordingly they all set off towards Tenanto'mwan's house. On the way they meet Nipai'vaticnin (Envious One), who joins them, saying that he knows the way and that he will go on ahead scouting the route.

Nipai'vaticnin reports back that Tenanto'mwan is only accompanied by two sons and a nephew. Tenanto'mwan, however, has seen Nipai'vaticnin and realized that this is no friendly visitor, so he gathers together his herds and escapes, leaving his son Illa and daughter Kilu at home with instructions not to reveal their whereabouts. When the Chukchee and Koryak raiders arrive and question Illa they suspect he is hiding the truth and threaten to kill him, but Illa points out that they can see Tenanto'mwan travelling across the sea ice with the herds. A hot pursuit commences and when Miti, the wife of Tenanto'mwan, sees the attackers she shouts a warning. Tenanto'mwan puts snow in his mouth and spits it out to melt away the ice between the herds and the shore. He then takes more snow, spits it out and causes reindeer moss to grow so that the herds can feed. Meanwhile the attackers on the shore get hungry and return to Tenanto'mwan's house, where they propose to kill Illa. First, however, they agree to a contest in shamanism to see whose powers are stronger. If Illa is stronger his life will be spared.

Meanwhile Tenanto'mwan tells his eldest son, the hero Eme'mqut, to go and rescue Illa. Eme'mqut makes himself invisible and when the contest in shamanism gets underway he raises Illa off the ground pulling him up by his hair. The Chukchee and Koryak are deeply impressed by this apparent levitation and agree not to kill Illa. When they have gone Eme'mqut reveals himself and points out that it was he, a true shaman, who saved Illa's life. Tenanto'mwan and his herds are henceforth left in peace by the Chukchee and Koryak peoples.

VEAI AND POQA'KO
(Grass Woman and Diarrhoea Man)

CULTURE OF ORIGIN: Siberian – Koryak

PROVENANCE: from an oral tradition amongst the Koryak reindeer hunters living on the Kamchatka Peninsula of south-eastern Siberia. The myth was related by an unnamed shamanka in the maritime village of Kamenskoy. Modern authorship is that of the Swedish ethnologist Waldemar Jochelson, who recorded the tale during the Jesup North Pacific Survey of 1900, sponsored by the American Society for Natural History [Memoirs of the American Museum of Natural History, 10, 1905].

Siberian folklore, like that of many primitive societies, is littered with what the reader might identify as 'prurient' material. Legends are often focused on bodily emissions of one sort or another and, in general, emissions from the spirits are considered to have powers of genesis. In the myth of Veai and Poqa'ko there is a specific and rather disgusting intent which makes it unusual. The powers of animism, in which the most mundane of inanimate objects may possess a spiritual identity which can reveal itself in human form, are clearly identified.

Eme'mqut, the son of the creator being Tenanto'mwan, decides to take a wife and he selects Veai (Grass Woman). She, however, cares little for him and her parents cannot persuade her to consent to the marriage. Meanwhile Acicena'qu (Big Grandfather) has an idea about how to resolve the problem. He goes outside to the lavatory and after he has wiped himself he throws the rag on the ground and kicks it, commanding that it turns into a man. Thus Poqa'ko (Diarrhoea Man) is engendered.

Acicena'qu places a chamber pot in Poqa'ko's travelling bag and tells him to visit the parents of Veai, requesting her hand in wedlock. He is not to go through with the marriage but merely to repel her with his conduct and appearance. As soon as Poqa'ko arrives at the house he sits on the chamber pot in the middle of the floor, at the same time introducing himself to Veai, and announces that he has come to woo her! He points out that she has probably been waiting for someone just like him since she has rejected Eme'mqut as a suitor:

'Now take my chamber pot and empty it outside!'

Veai takes the chamber pot outside as commanded, but she hurls it away and runs to a neighbour's house for protection.

When Poqa'ko goes outside to look for her and finds his chamber pot broken, he picks up the pieces and asks for a drill, a request which is immediately refused to him. So he grows in stature until he can sit over the door of the house and he starts to defecate. This activity persuades the parents of Veai to lend him the drill without further delay. Poqa'ko repairs the pot and goes off in search of Veai. When he finds her he orders her out of her hiding place, but she promptly flees from him again. Unfortunately she runs, by chance, into an underground house where two of Poqa'ko's sisters live and when she asks the women to hide her they join in the chase.

As she runs along Veai takes off her earrings and drops them in the path so that Poqa'ko's two sisters begin to fight over them. Eventually Veai runs into Eme'mqut's house, crying that a repulsive man has been chasing her and she promptly agrees to marry Eme'mqut. Meanwhile Poqa'ko, angry with his sisters for losing their quarry, enters Eme'mqut's house where Veai identifies him as her pursuer.

His plan having succeeded, grandfather Acicena'qu kicks Poqa'ko once more, reducing him to the inanimate rag from which he was created.

VEYE'MILAN (River Man) TRANSFORMS HIMSELF INTO A WOMAN

CULTURE OF ORIGIN: Siberian – Koryak
PROVENANCE: from an oral tradition amongst the Koryak reindeer hunters living on the Kamchatka Peninsula of south-eastern Siberia. The myth was related by a shamanka named Yutaw in the maritime village of Talovka. Modern authorship is that of the Swedish ethnologist Waldemar Jochelson, who recorded the tale during the Jesup North Pacific Survey of 1900, sponsored by the American Society for Natural History [Memoirs of the American Museum of Natural History, 10, 1905].

Illa, a nephew of the creator being Tenanto'mwan, decides to transform himself into a woman. So he and Yine'ane'ut, the daughter of Tenanto'mwan, begin to do some needlework together. One day Yine'ane'ut sends him to see Veye'milan (River Man) to ask for a dog skin with which to trim her coat. She disguises Illa as herself by dressing him in her own reindeer skin, but when she views the result she feels that Veye'milan will see through the ploy; accordingly, she dresses Illa in another woman's outfit and this time is satisfied. Even she takes him for a woman!

Illa arrives at the house just as Veye'milan is coming in from the forest with a load of wood. His wife asks who is out there and he says that Illa is coming (disguised apparently none too successfully) and that he is to be invited in as a guest. Veye'milan offers Illa food and the wife gives him a dog skin, but her husband will not lie down for the night anywhere near Illa lest he too turns into a woman. When everyone is asleep Illa throws himself upon Veye'milan, who tries to push him off and eventually gives such a mighty kick that Illa lands on the floor. With that Illa takes the dog skin and his bag and goes home.

Yine'ane'ut asks him if anyone recognized him and when Illa admits that they did Yine'ane'ut tells him to stop dressing up in women's clothes and to go to Khi'gilan (Thunder Man) where he will find himself a wife.

Next day Veye'milan goes again to the forest for wood, but the straps of his bundle start breaking and he sits down in a place where Illa sat the day before. His wife asks why he is sitting there and he replies that he too will become a woman. He begins to do women's work, but when Illa and his new-found wife come visiting Veye'milan asks how he can return to being a man again. Illa, however, keeps silence and Veye'milan, unable to break the spell, insists that his face must be tattooed and then screams with pain while Illa looks on with some disdain, commenting that tattooing was something he never lowered himself to while being a woman.

Veye'milan is destined to stay with Quikinna'qu (Big Raven) as a servant and his brothers never call there because they are so ashamed of him.

YINA'AGIT AND YINE'ANE'UT
(Fog Man and the Daughter of Big Raven)

CULTURE OF ORIGIN: Siberian – Koryak

PROVENANCE: from an oral tradition amongst the Koryak reindeer hunters living on the Kamchatka Peninsula of south-eastern Siberia. The myth was related by a maritime shamanka named A'yuna'ut in the village of Kamenskoye. Modern authorship is that of the Swedish ethnologist Waldemar Jochelson, who recorded the tale during the Jesup North Pacific Survey of 1900, sponsored by the American Society for Natural History [Memoirs of the American Museum of Natural History, 10, 1905].

Yina'agit (Fog Man) wishes to marry the daughter of Quikinna'qu (Big Raven) whose name is Yine'ane'ut. She has a daughter, Ce'ipine'ut (Yellow Woman) whom she carries around hidden in a glass bead among her ornaments. The three of them go off to Yina'agit's mother where they settle down until one day, when Yina'agit goes hunting, his younger brother stays at home and seduces Yine'ane'ut while she is busy scraping reindeer skins. She defends herself with her knife and accidentally stabs her brother-in-law. Alarmed, she drags the body into the storeshed where she wraps it in a reindeer hide and then conceals it in a sealskin bag.

Yina'agit returns and asks where his brother has gone, but Yine'ane'ut protests that she does not know. When, however, Yina'agit goes to the shed to hang up his bow, a drop of blood falls on him and his investigation finally leads him to the sealskin bag. Realizing who the culprit is he kills his wife, but when he returns to the storeshed he finds his brother alive. Upset, Yina'agit demands to know why his brother has been playing dead when he has just killed his wife in summary justice.

Yina'agit wraps the body of Yine'ane'ut in a white reindeer hide, hangs it up and leaves. Meanwhile a wolf, who has been out hunting, decides to investigate the empty house and discovers the shroud hanging from the rafters. He drags it outside and opens the bundle, but the body rolls downhill so fast that he cannot catch it and as it goes he sees two women emerge and flee. They are Yine'ane'ut and her daughter. The women ask some reindeer for food to give them strength and they run on until they see a ladder let down from the clouds with Ya'halan (Cloud Man) standing at the top. He hauls them up and hears their story, then admits that he is responsible for everything that has happened. He tells Yine'ane'ut that he will marry her and her daughter marries Ya'vac, his son. Ya'halan announces that he must visit Yine'ane'ut's parents to inform them that she is no longer living with her former husband, so they set off towards the house of Quikinna'qu (Big Raven). When they pass Yina'agit's house he demands to know who is there and when he recognizes Yine'ane'ut's voice he begs her not to be angry. She retorts that he has killed her and that a wolf would have eaten her save for a lucky escape.

Eventually they reach the house of Quikinna'qu and tell him all that has happened. His son, Eme'mqut, accompanies them on their return journey and wooes Ya'halan's sister Ya'halna'ut (Cloud Woman). They all live happily.

THE YUSH

CULTURE OF ORIGIN: Prasun Kafir (Hindukush)
PROVENANCE: oral traditions recorded chiefly by M. Elphinstone (1839); G. Morgenstierne (1951); G.S. Robertson (1896).

The demonic Yush live in the mountain meadows, where they have their own sacred fields, generally appearing in groups of seven. Their society is crude and archaic, thus they cultivate millet and hunt, badly, with bows and arrows. A demon may be destroyed with a single blow and the most effective threat to them comes from an arrow smeared with faeces. Should a second strike be administered, however, the demon will be restored. If it dies then its spirit emerges through a hole in the crown of its head. If it is cut into pieces, the pieces will grow into new demons (like the heads of the Lernaean Hydra in Greek mythology). Female demons cook using their bodies as a source of heat, placing one hand under the body and stirring inside the belly with the other hand.

The demons and their consorts frequently appear in the guise of other creatures. One demoness appears in the shape of a pretty girl with whom a mortal youth falls deeply in love. He sleeps with her and, to avenge the outrage of the demons, her brother-in-law transmutes himself into the shape of a bear which begins to devastate the maize crop around the man's village. The mortal youth fires an arrow at the bear and the couple part.

MISCELLANEOUS

JAPANESE: during a storm a young man, Kadzutoyo, comes across a beautiful woman sitting by the wayside. She asks for his assistance, but he is suspicious that her beauty is supernatural and responds by decapitating her when he sees that her clothes remain dry, even though it is pouring with rain. She instantly disappears and in her place lies a dead badger.

NEW GUINEA: at the beginning of the world, before mankind has been engendered, some cassowary birds arrive at the edge of a lake called Tuumbamuuta, where they discard their feathers and take the form of naked women who begin to bathe. One of the gods who is passing by watches the scene and notices that the last of the birds to enter the water is particularly beautiful when it discards its feathers; so, quietly, he steals her garment. When she emerges from the water she cannot find her feathers and she is left behind when the other cassowaries leave at dusk. The god comes out of his hiding place and tries to perform intercourse with the womanly form but, since she is in reality a bird, she has no vagina. She sits upon a rock, however, which cuts her open and she menstruates for the first time, after which the god has intercourse with her and she bears many children, the progenitors of the human race.

PHILIPPINE: a magical bird, the Adarna, is known to have curative powers and a sick king sends his three sons to search for it. The protective magic of the Adarna turns the first two brothers to stone, but the youngest gives aid to a leper and because of his kindness the leper reveals the secrets of combating the bird's magic. The successful sibling returns to his father with the bird and a cure is effected.

2

Myths of Sun, Moon and Stars

The sun and moon are generally regarded as the most significant astral deities and are often created through great violence. Thus the deity of Aztec myth, Nanahuatl, is forced to become a victim of self-immolation so that he may ascend to become the new sun god.

There is no notion of the earth orbiting the sun. When mythologies arise such scientific evidence is not available to the storytellers, so the sun always travels from horizon to horizon. The orb of the sun does not necessarily represent the deity. He may conceal himself behind the solar disc or he may ride in a solar chariot or barque. The latter imagery is well represented in Egyptian mythology, where the sun god Re emerges from the mouth of the earth goddess Nut at dawn to travel across the sky and to re-enter her body at dusk. He then continues his journey through the underworld by night.

Cosmic events including eclipses are often reflected in myth during which the sun or the moon falls to earth in some traumatic event before being restored to the heavens.

Stars are usually seen as fairly inconsequential objects placed whimsically in the heavens to light the night sky, though sometimes they are also perceived to be one-time mortals, or lesser deities who have been placed there to protect them from a worse fate on earth.

AMATERASU–O–MI–KAMI AND THE DIVINE MIRROR

CULTURE OF ORIGIN: Japanese Shinto
PROVENANCE: recorded in various texts and art from oral traditions, including the *Nihongi* and *Kojiki* sacred books.

Through her grandson, Prince Ninigi, Amaterasu is seen as the ancestral mother goddess of the imperial dynasty and the central figure of Shintoism. As sun goddess, she lends her image of the rising sun to Japanese national symbolism. She may have evolved from the Buddhist god Vairocana and the shrine at which she is chiefly worshipped is the Ise Jingu (Ise Naiku) sanctuary at Uji-Yamada.

Amaterasu is the favourite daughter of the primordial god Izanagi having been engendered from his left eye (see *Izanagi and Izanami*, page 50). She has three brothers: Tsuki-Yomi, the moon god, born from the right eye of Izanagi; Susano-Wo, the storm god, born from Izanagi's nose; and Hi-No-Kagu-Tsuchi, the god of fire, during the birth of whom their mother Izanami is burnt to death.

Amaterasu's parents find her brilliance so great that she blinds them and she cannot remain on the earth. She is sent to reign as the Queen of Heaven while her brother Susano-Wo takes dominion over the physical and material world on earth. Amaterasu lives in the sky as a powerful though not omnipotent deity: she is obliged to live in some kind of harmony with her siblings in order to survive. She is at first betrothed to Tsuki-Yumi, but she quarrels with him and dispatches him to the night sky in order to avoid seeing his face. There he rules over the moon with a court of thirty princes, half dressed in white and half in black. Susano-Wo, however, proves a more formidable adversary. Through his own powers he ascends into the heavens with Amaterasu but, having established himself, he invades the sanctity of her house with his storm clouds and tries to commit various excesses with her. She resists his advances and, in a fit of pique, decides to hide herself away in a cave the entrance to which she closes with a boulder.

The world is now plunged into darkness and chaos and the other gods are obliged to think up ways of enticing the sun goddess back into the heavens once more. They call upon the services of the one-eyed god of smiths, Ama-Tsu-Mara, to help them fashion the 'perfect divine mirror' with which they will show Amaterasu her immaculate and dazzling reflection and persuade her, through flattery, to come out of the cave. The gods of carpenters, Hiko-Sashiri and Taoki-Ho-Oi, then build a new palace of exceptional beauty and splendour for her to live in. It is up to the rest of the pantheon to create an entertainment spectacular which will appeal to Amaterasu.

The space in front of the cave is filled with song birds; the god of jewellers, Tama-No-Ya, creates a superb string of curved jewels nearly ten feet long for Amaterasu's apparel; and the goddess of dancers, Ame-No-Uzume, whose realm is the floating bridge of heaven, dons a special head-dress and, carrying a spear, performs her whirling dance, the *uzume*, before the cave. The ancestral deity, Futo-Tama, assembles various magical objects and pushes the mirror forward so that it catches the sun goddess's reflection. He recites the sacred liturgy and begs Amaterasu to come forth, never to hide her face again.

Eventually Amaterasu is encouraged to move the boulder just a little so that a ray of dawn light emerges. Then she is persuaded to come out of her dark hiding place and return to the heavens. Susano-Wo is banished forever to the earth where, at first, he has to beg food from the goddess O-Ge-Tsu-Hime. He is also confronted by the eight-headed dragon of Izumo [a small town on the west coast of Japan] which he kills, taking from its body a magic sword, the Kusanagi-No-Tsurugi (grass-cutting weapon). Susano-Wo yields this sword to Amaterasu in acknowledgement of her superiority and she in turn gives it to her grandson, Prince Ninigi, when he descends to earth.

The divine mirror, the Jata-Kagami, is given as a gift to the first emperor. It stands as one of his sacred symbols.

THE BIRTH OF DUDUGERA

CULTURE OF ORIGIN: Papua New Guinea
PROVENANCE: recorded in recent times from oral traditions

The cosmos is in perpetual darkness because there is no sun. A woman is swimming in the coastal waters when a dolphin comes towards her and rubs itself against her leg. As the subsequent days go by the woman's thigh begins to swell. It continues to enlarge until her father cuts it open and she gives birth to a child called Dudugera.

The child grows rapidly and becomes extremely strong, to the extent that the other children persecute him. In order to protect him his mother carries him back to the beach where he was conceived and the dolphin takes him into its mouth. It swims away with him towards the eastern horizon and then opens its mouth, throwing the boy up into the sky. As soon as he is released he starts to climb, becoming brighter and brighter until he hangs suspended as a brilliant orb in the heavens. He is the new sun god and day has dawned for the first time upon the earth.

Dudugera's form becomes stronger and stronger until his heat is so great that mankind has to shelter from his rays during the daytime. Dudugera's mother is concerned that her son may be causing suffering, so she searches for pieces of limestone in a dark cave. These she hurls into the sky where they become clouds that soften her son's heat.

KAŠKU FALLS FROM HEAVEN

CULTURE OF ORIGIN: Hattic or pre-Hittite – Anatolian
PROVENANCE: cuneiform text derived from an oral tradition and discovered on tablets at the site of Boghazkoy in Turkey [Tablet ref. KUB xxviii.5 translated by Albrecht Goetze (*Ancient Near Eastern Texts* ed. J.B. Pritchard)].

This is one of a number of mythical fragments which offer less a story than a simple explanation of a natural event. Either the myth explains the disappearance of the moon on its daily orbit or, specifically, it accounts for the more dramatic eclipsing of the moon.

NOTE: the myth predates the Hurrian introductions to the pantheon and where Hurrian titles are recognized they are included in brackets.

Unseen by anyone except Kamrusepa, the goddess of healing, the moon god Kašku (Kušuh) descends from heaven to the place beneath the earth. To frighten him into returning to his proper place in the skies the storm god Taru (Tešub) sends a rainstorm, while the god Hapantalliya tries a more subtle approach. He merely goes to keep Kašku company and use his powers of persuasion.

KASTOR AND POLYDEUKES
(Castor and Pollux)

CULTURE OF ORIGIN: classical Greek, but subsequently adopted into Roman culture
PROVENANCE: recorded from oral traditions by the epic Greek poet Hesiod in the *Hymn to the Dioskuri*, the *Catalogues of Women* and the *Epic Cycle*.

The Dioskouroi twins, Kastor and Polydeukes, are strongly associated with horses and probably derive from the Indo-European model of the Asvins in Vedic mythology. They are also strongly associated with a Spartan cult from which they may have originated. The myth involves a complicated 'soap opera' cast of characters and an unusual feature lies in that one brother is mortal while the other attains immortality.

Kastor and Klytemnestra, Polydeukes and Helen, are pairs of twins, offically the offspring of the Spartan king Tyndareos and his consort Leda but, in reality, the illegitimate children of a liaison between Leda and Zeus. The two brothers, Kastor and Polydeukes, the Dioskouroi, wed the daughters of Leukippos, named Hilaera and Phoebe, but at a festival in Sparta, organized in honour of Aeneas and Paris, one of Tyndareos's brothers, Aphareos, drunkenly accuses Kastor and Polydeukes of not having paid the proper dowry for their brides. The insult cannot go unanswered and a brawl ensues with Aphareos's sons, Lynkeos and Idas, during which Kastor is slain.

Zeus intervenes and dispatches the murderer, Lynkeos, with a thunderbolt, taking back the surviving Dioskouroi twin Polydeukes to Mount Olympus.

Various alternative versions of the cause and effect of the fight exist, but the outcome remains essentially the same. Hesiod, for example has the brothers stealing cattle belonging to Lynkeos and Idas which causes the fatal fight. Polydeukes is reluctant to accept the boon of immortality without his slain brother who now resides in the underworld. A compromise is reached whereby Zeus grants Kastor one day out of every two in the company of the gods.

MANDI AND THE ECLIPSE OF THE MOON

CULTURE OF ORIGIN: Prasun Kafir [Hindukush]
PROVENANCE: oral traditions recorded chiefly by M. Elphinstone (1839); G. Morgenstierne (1951); G.S. Robertson (1896)
    The myth provides an explanation, in a heroic confrontational setting between gods and giants, of the phenomenon of the lunar eclipse.

In a rock suspended between earth and sky lives a giant named Guro who, from time to time, transforms into a serpent and descends to earth. The heroic god Mandi and the god of war Gish decide to confront Guro and they instruct a lieutenant, Pegaileamund, to change himself likewise into a serpent so that he can spy on the giant's activities. In his disguise Pegaileamund is able to slither into the giant's fortress unobserved and he discovers the giant engaged in sexual intercourse with his own mother. Later Guro realizes that the gods are ridiculing him for his incest and believes, erroneously, that he has been betrayed by the moon. In a towering rage he attacks the army of deities and only Mandi is prepared to face him. Mandi slices the giant in half with his sword, upon which the upper part of Guro's body ascends into the sky where he waits to capture the moon. His patience is tested for a long while (during the eclipse), but eventually he succeeds in swallowing the moon. It stays within his torso for a while but eventually emerges from his anus and the cosmic balance is restored.

MANDI AND THE RESCUE OF THE SUN AND MOON

CULTURE OF ORIGIN: Prasun Kafir [Hindukush]
PROVENANCE: oral traditions recorded chiefly by M. Elphinstone (1839); G. Morgenstierne (1951); G.S. Robertson (1896)

The world is cold and dark because the giant Espereg-era has caught the sun and moon and hidden them in his golden fortress. Inside the castle is a waterfall and he places the sun to its right and the moon to its left.

In order to rescue the sun and moon the god Mandi transforms himself into a child and presents himself to Espereg-era's mother. When the giant sees the child he decides to adopt Mandi and so each day Mandi is locked in the fortress with a supply of food while the giant goes out to hunt goats. Mandi tries to escape by pushing the door of his room but it opens only by a finger's width and he achieves no more than a golden finger. Espereg-era's mother is concerned that the escape attempt will be discovered and so she bandages the finger, offering the story that the child has cut himself. The next day Mandi manages to open the door a little more and this time his whole arm needs to be bandaged to hide the gold. The giant is apparently duped into believing that Mandi has injured himself trying to make a chair which he is to offer to the giant as a gift.

On the fourth day of captivity Mandi restores himself to his full stature, kicks down the door and discovers the sun and moon standing beside the waterfall. He picks them up, jumps on a horse which is standing nearby, and asks it which way to go to escape the giant. The horse tells him that there is a sword in its right ear; Mandi takes this and they gallop away. As the world becomes light and warm with the power of the sun in Mandi's grasp, the giant gives chase and attacks him, but the god cuts off his head with the new-found sword. Hydra-like, seven more heads grow in place of the original, which again Mandi severs and the giant falls down. Having been dragged across to the right side of the valley, Espereg-era requests that Mandi remove a mountain so that the sun will shine on his burial place and warm the earth. To this dying request Mandi agrees, but he then goes in search of the giant's mother, whom he also slays. Before she dies, however, he agrees to bury her in a place of honour and she expires happily.

Mandi is still clutching the sun and moon, a situation which is causing problems for the world, so the supreme god Imra takes them and hurls them into an orbit in the sky. Other gods create mankind and show people how to live, make tools and weapons, and grow crops. They also provide dogs to wake people up in the morning!

MAUI CATCHES TAMA NUI-TE-RA

CULTURE OF ORIGIN: Polynesian Maori
PROVENANCE: recorded in recent times from oral traditions, including *The
   Ancient History of the Maoris, Mythology and Traditions* J. White 6 vols.
   Wellington 1887.
   The myth is one of several much-loved stories of the exploits of Maui
who may be perceived as a Maori super-hero along the lines of the
Mesopotamian Gilgameš. This particular myth establishes Maui as the sun
god which is perhaps his original role in Maori belief. He evolves from this
into a more general role associated with fishing and the invention of tools
for the benefit of mankind. The myth is correspondingly modified to a
story in which the hair of Maui's sister is exchanged for the ropes used in
fishing.

Maui wishes to catch the sun Tama Nui-Te-Ra because the days are
not long enough to do all the work that is necessary, so he takes some
of the long hair of his sister, Hina-Ika, and he and his brothers braid it
into a strong net. The sun, however, is much too hot and the hair-
ropes merely burn away, so Maui decides to make a new and better
snare by soaking the ropes in water and this time he is successful – the
sun is caught and he pulls it to the surface.
   Maui chastises the sun, telling it that it must travel across the sky
more slowly so that the days become longer and the nights shorter.
Then he hurls the sun into the eastern sky and travels across the world
to catch it and lower it gently into the sea on the western horizon as
night falls.

TECCIZTECATL (TECUCIZTECATL) AND
NANAHUATL (NANAUATZIN)

CULTURE OF ORIGIN: Aztec (classical Mesoamerican) [Mexico]
PROVENANCE: probably worshipped circa 750 AD until 1500 AD and known
   from tradition in the Florentine and other pre-Columbian codices and
   detail on stone carvings. The site of Teotihuacan is at San Juan, between
   Chiconauhtlan and Otumba. The spellings of the names of the two
   principal deities are those which appear in the Florentine Codex, but they
   are not necessarily the most common forms which will be encountered in
   translation.

The world is dark with no sun, no moon and no day until the gods
take counsel together in Teotihuacan to decide who among them will
become the sun and thus bring about the first dawn. Tecuciztecatl
volunteers for the job, but everyone else is afraid and keeps silence.
Nanauatzin, impoverished and physically diseased, is not present in

the meeting but he listens to what is being discussed from outside and eventually the assembly calls on him, ordering him to be the new sun god. Nanauatzin accepts and thus Tecuciztecatl is destined to be the moon.

Both gods enter into a period of penance and fasting during which a sacrificial fire is laid and set alight. Tecuciztecatl brings very costly items for his penance, beating himself with the best fir branches and offering the finest grass balls and the purest incense. Nanauatzin, for his part, brings only inexpensive items including the scabs from his sores to create incense. The two gods subject themselves to four nights of penance, positioned on the summits of two hills built for the occasion [the Pyramid of the Sun and the Pyramid of the Moon at Teotihuacan].

When midnight comes the two gods are decked out in ritual apparel. Tecuciztecatl receives his round, forked, heron-feather head-dress and his elaborate jacket. Nanauatzin has only a paper head-dress, which is tied into his hair, and he is given poor garments to wear. The other gods now encircle the two ordained victims and call on Tecuciztecatl to cast himself into the flames. But the fire burns up mightily and its heat becomes intolerable: Tecuciztecatl retreats in terror. He tries four more times, but at each attempt his courage leaves him. The gods turn to Nanauatzin and urge him forward into the fire. Nanauatzin overcomes his fear and hurls himself into the flames, his body crackling and sizzling. Then Tecuciztecatl, seeing what his companion has done, follows Nanauatzin and is likewise immolated.

An eagle flies into the flames after the two gods and emerges, its feathers browned and blackened for ever more. An ocelot follows, but by now the flames have sunk low and it emerges with only blackened spots on its pelt.

The gods sit around the dying fire for a long time waiting to see who will be the first to emerge from the ashes as the fifth sun. When the sky starts to pale and redden they search the heavens in all directions to try to ascertain where the sun will arise. Quetzalcoatl, Ehecatl, Totec and red Tezcatlipoca look to the east with four of the goddesses and there they see Nanauatzin arise, followed shortly afterwards by Tecuciztecatl. Both, however, have taken the same path and the assembly of gods is at a loss to know what to do, since there are effectively now two suns and the world will burn up.

One of the gods seizes a rabbit with which he whips the face of Tecuciztecatl and, thus wounded, the face darkens. There remains, however, the problem that the two suns are stuck in one position, unable to move; the gods are still faced with imminent death.

It becomes the responsibility of Ehecatl (wind) to blow violently. His action moves Nanauatzin into his proper path as the true sun, leaving Tecuciztecatl stationary in the sky. As Nanauatzin sets in the west, however, Tecuciztecatl starts his own journey across the heavens. Thus they constantly pass each other, the one resting while the other works.

Tecuciztecatl first appears as a very small bow like a bent straw lip-ornament, but he grows larger day by day until he becomes round and disc-shaped; after fifteen days he has completely matured like a large earthen skillet. At first each night he is a bright, deep red, but after he has journeyed a while he becomes paler and the mark of the little rabbit is clear on his face. When he has attained his full brilliance he starts to become smaller until he dies, awaiting his next rebirth.

MISCELLANEOUS

KIRIBATI: the sun god impregnates a mortal woman with a ray of light and she gives birth to a son, Bue. One night Bue sets out in his canoe across the ocean towards the eastern horizon to greet his father and to learn from him. The sun god gives Bue great wisdom and teaches him many skills including the ways to control the winds and to cure sickness.

JAVANESE: the moon goddess Nawang Wulan descends to earth having donned her swan-feather cloak. She lands on the waters of a lake, where she discards her cloak and begins to bathe, but the cloak is stolen by Kyai Agung. When she cannot find her means of returning to the sky she is obliged to stay with the man, so she marries him and they have a daughter, Nawang Sih. The goddess generates rice for the household using her magical powers and Kyai Agung is expressly forbidden to look inside the pot where the rice is stored. One day curiosity overcomes him and he discovers that the pot contains only a single grain of rice. Now the magic will work no more and the goddess is forced to collect and pound rice each day as would a mortal wife. She does, however, find her swan cloak and uses it to fly back into the sky. At night she stays there, but during the hours of daylight she returns to earth to be with her husband and child.

DAYAK (BORNEO): searching for his knife, a young chieftain, Lejo, discovers a group of spirits eating a sacrificial meal which he has left for the goddess of the rice paddies. As they try to escape him, the long hair of one of them, Mang, becomes entangled in branches. When Lejo sees her beauty he falls in love and asks the goddess for her hand. She agrees, but insists that first she must return to the sky to collect her belongings, including some of the darkness of heaven so that she can make herself invisible before all other mortals. She comes back to live with Lejo but, while she is asleep, a little child pries into her travelling bag by making a small hole in its plaited fabric. Immediately the darkness spills out into the house. When Mang awakens she throws the child out of the door, but in doing so releases night into the world for the first time. The people try to catch it, but it spreads everywhere and thus it remains until, through desperate propitiation of the gods, it is caused to fade and disperse. Daylight returns for a while but darkness is never far away.

3

Creation Myths

Since the greatest universal mysteries are those of beginnings and endings, both on the personal and on the cosmic scale, it is not entirely surprising that every culture whose mythology has been recorded has developed notions of the creation process, often highly elaborate ones.

There is a widespread belief that before there can be an ordered cosmos there must be disorganized and antediluvian chaos. This can take the form of a dark, featureless void or it can be a shifting, formless sea, the primal waters of creation. The belief is seen in primitive tribal culture and it possibly reaches its highest evolution in the mythologies of Egypt (from whom it was borrowed by the Greeks) and of the Christian gnostics.

Within the realm of chaos a single being creates itself, frequently out of a cosmic egg, and finds itself alone in a dark and empty space. Through its own immense powers of thought and breath it engenders light in the darkness, followed by the other forms which become familiar in cosmogony – stars, the sun and the moon. The being is often asexual in design, a monad, but through its own parthenogenesis it creates a female counterpart and thus takes on masculinity for itself. This is not always the case: in Polynesian tradition one finds the primordial female Vari-Ma-Te-Takere who lives at the bottom of the world coconut, while the Greeks developed the idea of Gaia, the earth mother, arising from chaos and the gnostics perceived an immense intellect emerging from chaos with a distinct female persona, Sophia or Wisdom. In any event or gender it is this primordial being who also brings into existence the first generation of gods within the pantheon.

The next stage in the process of beginnings is the formation of matter. Material of substance usually arises within the formless and shifting waters of the primal ocean. This *terra firma* may be achieved in several distinct ways – a creator god may scoop up slime from the ocean bed and create a primitive mound, he may haul the land up on a fishing line, the waters may begin to recede under the heat of the newly created sun.

Once the dry land has formed, the primal water is not distinguished as the salty ocean at the earth's surface, but as a separate watery domain which continues to exist under the earth. In Mesopotamian mythology it becomes the Apsu or Abzu. The primal water is, however, often perceived to be a continuing threat to mankind which can burst forth apocalyptically according to the whims of heaven. The drain hole through which it disappeared at the beginning of time is that through which it can surge once more when circumstances dictate.

There is also a fairly universal belief that in the beginning heaven and earth are fused together and that they must be separated to create the air space in which living things may exist. In Mesopotamian mythology, many of the stories begin with the words 'after heaven had moved away from earth'. Sometimes the separation is very cathartic. In Polynesian mythology the sky father and the earth mother have to be forcibly torn apart by their children, while in the Babylonian creation myth, *Enuma Eliš*, the goddess Tiamat is split in half by Marduk to form the earth and sky. In Aztec mythology there is a similarly violent debut wherein the body of the goddess Tlaltecuhtli is sundered by the gods Quetzalcoatl and Tezcatlipoca to create *terra firma*.

In strong contrast, Hindu cosmogony reveals that the god Višnu, in his incarnation as the Trivikrama, takes three giant steps, each of which symbolizes a separation, first of heaven and earth, then of the living things of earth. Very often, once created and separated, the sky or heaven is seen to be kept apart by deities who prop it up at the cardinal points. Atlas has much the same job description in Greek tradition.

The separation having been achieved and sustained, there may then emerge various levels of heaven, in other words a hierarchical progression from the lowest tier staffed by angels or minor deities to the highest plane where the supreme god resides.

Creation is not necessarily regarded as being permanent. Sometimes the belief exists that a constant, albeit highly protracted, process of cosmic genesis and destruction takes place, reflecting that which occurs in the tangible and visible world. Sometimes there is a belief that a deity must be sacrificed in order to achieve creation. In Aztec mythology, where creation has been renewed several times, the self-destruction of gods is necessary to achieve the new and current world. In Japanese Shintoism the creator goddess, Izanami, is burnt to death as she gives birth to the god of fire.

The fashioning of mankind is a distinct feature in the overall process of creation and the first human being, usually male, may be regarded as a demigod. The achievement may again be at the expense of a deity whose personal sacrifice is called upon. Thus, in Mesopotamian tradition, the life of the minor god of intellect, Geštu, is taken so that the mother goddess may mix his blood with clay and sculpt the first human beings. The sundering and scattering of the parts of a deity may also be needed.

ADITI
(the birth of the gods)

CULTURE OF ORIGIN: Vedic Hindu [India]
PROVENANCE: the *Rg Veda* collection of 1028 hymns (Vedas) composed in
Sanskrit circa 1200 BC and based on an oral tradition which was in
circulation among the Aryan immigrants to the subcontinent circa
1700–700 BC. Used as hymns of praise at the time of religious sacrifice,
the Vedas provide less of a narrative than various comments on the
mythology and it is from later works, including the *Brahmanas* (900–700
BC) and the Vedic commentary of Sayana (circa 1350 AD), that a more
coherent narrative emerges.

The Lord of Prayer, Brhašpati, fans the gods into existence from
nothingness, like a smith fanning the flames of a fire. There exists also
a female principle who crouches over the cosmos, legs parted, ready
to give birth to the earth and sky. In a paradoxical and incestuous
scene, the mother goddess Aditi and her father, the sun god Daksa,
are born to each other and from Aditi eight celestial sons, the Adityas,
emerge into the primeval sea causing a mist to arise. Seven Adityas
fashion the world but the eighth, the firebird Martanda, is still-born.
The mother goddess casts out his corpse and from it comes the orb of
the sun.

ALATANGANA AND SA

CULTURE OF ORIGIN: Kono (East Guinea)
PROVENANCE: recorded from oral traditions

In the beginning there exist two creator beings: Alatangana, who lives
in the sky, and Sa, who lives in the dark and swampy primeval
waters. There is no light in the world, so Alatangana sends a cockerel
to Sa with a request to improve the situation. Sa teaches the bird to
sing a magical song at a precise time of day and thus the sun rises on
the first morning.

One day Alatangana decides to create land from the waters and to
clothe it with vegetation. While he is working on the earth he meets
and falls in love with the daughter of Sa. Sa refuses to give the girl in
marriage, so Alatangana takes her far away. They settle down and
raise seven boys and seven girls, some of whom are black and some
white.

As the offspring grow they begin to speak in strange tongues and
when Atalangana mentions this problem to Sa, Sa retorts that it is just
punishment for the abduction of his daughter. Sa, however, provides
the children with appropriate tools and equipment for survival. To

the white he offers pens and paper, to the black he gives farming implements. The white siblings then emigrate to distant parts while the black ones stay and cultivate the land of Africa.

AMEI AWI AND BURUNG UNE

CULTURE OF ORIGIN: Borneo Dayak (inland)
PROVENANCE: recorded in recent times from oral traditions amongst the clans of Dayaks living in the hinterland regions of Borneo.
 In honour of these deities and their traditions the Dayaks perform annual festivals of propitiation and feasting to ensure a plentiful harvest. See also *Tanemahuta*, page 71.

At the beginning of the world, before earth, sky and sea have come into being, a celestial spider hangs upon its web in the darkness of endless space. Into the web falls a piece of flat red coral and slowly the coral grows until it fills the whole of the web. After a long time a slug and a worm fall on to the coral rock and they crawl around on the barren surface until they have covered it with sticky brown trails which become earth. Next a sapling falls to the virgin ground and its roots penetrate the sticky mud. Others join it and soon the forests begin to grow.

 A fourth creature emerges from the heavens, a giant crab, which lands and begins to excavate the flat earth, sculpting it into river valleys, hills and mountains. Rain falls to fill up the river beds and swamps, stimulating other vegetation to spring up, including all the food plants upon which mankind will live.

 A pair of formless beings descend but, although they have the semblance of male and female form, they are unable to procreate. The male spirit fashions tools, including a sword and a loom and, one day, the sword falls upon the loom. From the loom, in the course of time, emerge two wooden human heads and the spirit beings ascend to the place from whence they came. The two wooden heads mate and bear two offspring – heads moving upon necks! These engender another generation of heads, this time born on necks with bodies so that they can crawl about, and they in turn produce two more offspring, Amei Awi and Burung Une, who become the god and goddess of farming.

 Amei Awi and Burung Une produce, initially, twelve children. Four are astral deities, the lunar gods who represent the full, crescent and quarter moons each month, and the remaining eight are human beings. The latter are instructed to ascend a mountain in a test of who shall be the progenitors of the different social classes of mankind. In an ironical twist to the story those who choose to remain at the bottom doing nothing become the first earthly rulers; those who climb halfway to the top before giving up are the ancestors of freemen; but those who labour their way to the very summit are destined to bear the future generations of slaves.

As Amei Awi goes about his tasks he leaves chips of tree bark scattered around his house and these become domestic animals. The pair produce more children but eventually, their job of populating and husbanding the earth complete, they descend below the surface where they continue to oversee the production of crops for successive generations of humanity.

AMMA AND THE CREATION OF THE WORLD

CULTURE OF ORIGIN: Dogon (Mali)
PROVENANCE: recorded from oral traditions

The creator god Amma engenders the sun in the shape of a pot which he sculpts from clay. He fires it until it is white hot; then he binds it with spirals of copper. The moon is engendered likewise, though it is smaller and bound with wires of brass. The stars he forms by smashing pieces off the sun and scattering them over the heavens.

Amma now turns his attentions to the fashioning of the earth itself. He takes a vast lump of clay and sculpts it into the shape of a woman with her head facing north and her legs south. For her pubis he uses an anthill and for her clitoris a termite mound. Having circumcised the clitoris he impregnates the earth and she conceives the first living thing – the golden jackal. Again Amma performs intercourse with earth and this time she produces twins who go to make the green things of the world which will cover her nakedness. The activity of the twins serves to create the wind and with it comes the power of speech.

Amma engenders humankind from clay. In the heat of the sun he creates the black races and in the cool light of the moon he creates white people. The first man and woman are imbued with life and are circumcised. From the man's foreskin is created a lizard and from the woman's clitoris a scorpion. From the intercourse of the first couple come four pairs of twins – first four boys and then four girls; from them descend the tribe of the Dogon.

AMUN AT THEBES

CULTURE OF ORIGIN: Egyptian
PROVENANCE: Papyrus Leiden 1350. New Kingdom period (circa 1567–1085 BC), 18th Dynasty.

The substance of this myth is less a narrative story than an instruction on the nature of the creator god. The god Amun evolved from the Ogdoad, the group of eight primordial forces formulated at Hermopolis. He was recognized in the region of Thebes from the Middle Kingdom period (circa 2040–1783 BC), but his supremacy as a dominant creator god developed in the time of the New Kingdom. His influence was transferred to Thebes when that of Hermopolis as a capital city began to wane.

Amun is the sun god, who fashions and self-creates himself from a cosmic egg in a primal burst of energy. Although at Hermopolis he is merely a member of the Ogdoad, at Thebes he becomes the supreme power, pre-dating the Ogdoad and personifying the sum total of primal matter from which will emerge the cosmos. He is seen in the form of a wind stirring the primeval ooze into a vortex from which emerges the primeval mound of silt. In the Leiden papyrus he is also depicted as a Nile goose which calls the cosmos into existence out of silence, the so-called Great Honker.

In his primordial state Amun is perceived as a snake, Kem-atef, capable of endless rejuvenation. He is more typically depicted in human form, though, transcendent but also strongly ithyphallic because he is the first born of the gods and is therefore the potency by which all the other deities of the pantheon are created. He is described as the 'bull of his mother' and he holds the *ankh* symbol of life and the scimitar of power.

Amun is ubiquitous both in the sky and in the underworld, though he is hidden from the eyes of humankind. Even his true name is a mystery, Amun being a cryptic 'no-name'. Those who attempt to probe his mysteries too deeply suffer instant death.

THE HYPOSTASIS OF THE ARCHONS

CULTURE OF ORIGIN: gnostic Christian

PROVENANCE: the text is contained in tractate II,4 of the twelve codices discovered in 1945 at Nag Hammadi in Upper Egypt where they were buried circa 400 AD [Coptic Museum, Cairo]. The manuscript, written in Coptic probably during the third century AD, may be a translation from a Greek original, but there is some suggestion that the provenance is purely Egyptian. It follows predominantly Christian concepts but with hints of Sethian philosophy. Authorship is unknown and the title has been assigned in modern times. It takes the form of a didactic instruction explaining first the scenario of Genesis and then the origin of Chaos (see also *On the Origin of the World* and *Genesis*, pages 61 and 45). The work opens with short homilies quoted from St Paul's letters to the Colossians and the Ephesians.

The ruler of the primordial beings or Archons has become ignorant and arrogant, believing himself to be the lone authority in the heavens.

A voice reaches him from the void, calling him 'Samael' (god of the blind). Samael utters great blasphemies and pursues these into the abyss of the primordial waters where the material world is made to arise and where Samael's mother, the spirit, Pistis/Sophia, conceives his offspring, the seven so-called authorities who are to rule over the seven heavens of Chaos. The authorities see her image reflected in the waters; they lust after her but cannot reach her, since they are from below and she is from above.

The authorities plan to create a human being modelled out of earth and in the likeness of the form they have witnessed in the primordial waters. Having first made a man they decide to fashion a female counterpart. They breathe into the man and imbue him with a soul, but their powers do not stretch to giving him life.

Pistis watches and when she sees the impotence of the authorities she descends and instils her spirit into the man, calling him Adam. The authorities bring to him all the creatures of the earth so that he may give them names and they place him in Paradise so that he may cultivate and protect it. But they issue a warning to him, telling him that he may eat from every tree save that which recognizes good and evil. Disobedience will bring death.

It is time for the authorities to produce Adam's mate. They place him in a deep sleep, open his side and remove the spirit of Pistis, placing it in the woman. But they are unaware of its origin and they fall into a trap of their own making as the spirit-endowed woman awakens Adam. He at once recognizes her as his mother and the authorities are afraid of what they have done. They decide to impregnate the woman with their semen so as to nullify her powers. Pistis, however, outwits them, merging with the Tree and leaving only a mortal replica of herself beside Adam. Now she instils herself into the instructor, the serpent, telling the couple that they may eat of the Tree and that they have been forbidden its fruit only out of jealousy and fear on the part of the authorities lest the pair learn to know good and evil and become like gods. The woman eats from the Tree and gives the fruit to Adam and they become aware of themselves.

Samael demands to know why Adam has gone into hiding unless he has eaten from the forbidden tree. Adam blames his partner and Samael curses both her and the serpent, throwing the man and woman out of Paradise and consigning them to a life of eternal toil and suffering.

The woman gives birth to Cain and Abel and, as in the Genesis myth, Cain slaughters his brother (see *Cain and Abel*, page 133). The woman is now identified as Eve. She gives birth next to Seth and then to Norea, a daughter, whom the authorities have not managed to defile. From Norea's offspring the human race begins to multiply and improve until it causes the authorities such concern that they decide to create a cataclysmic flood. They attempt to impregnate Norea, as they did the spiritual Eve, but she cries out to heaven for rescue. Eleleth, the great angel, hears her plea and reminds her that, as a mortal woman, the authorities cannot touch her.

Eve now asks the angel to explain the origin of the authorities. Eleleth tells her that incorruptibility, Pistis/Sophia, dwells in the limitless realms where a veil of light separates the visible from the invisible. Once she engendered of herself a force which became projected like a shadow in the light. The force was androgynous and, from itself, it created all matter, but it became very arrogant, believing itself to be the first and only entity to have existed. At this Pistis/Sophia revealed herself and chased the force away into Chaos, where it created seven androgynous clones and again proclaimed itself the only God. When she heard this, Zoe (life), the daughter of Pistis/Sophia, called out, addressing the force as Yaldabaoth and telling it it was a fool. She breathed out an angel of fire who bound Yaldabaoth and hurled him into Tartaros (according to Homer the realm below the great abyss).

One of the offspring of Yaldabaoth, called Sabaoth, observed the power of the angel and decided to switch allegiance to Pistis/Sophia. In return she placed him in charge of the seventh heaven and gave him Zoe to sit at his right hand and to instruct him about the eighth heaven. In his anger at seeing how his offspring had been elevated, Yaldabaoth engendered Envy who, in turn, engendered Death. Death created his own offspring until the heavens of Chaos were filled with them. All this, explains the writer, has been ordained by the father so that the true extent of Chaos can be properly defined.

ATRAHASIS

CULTURE OF ORIGIN: Mesopotamian – Old Babylonian

PROVENANCE: one of the few Mesopotamian epic accounts to which an author is ascribed, Atrahasis is believed to have been written in the late seventeenth century BC by the scribe Nur-Aya during the reign of the Babylonian king Ammi-saduqa.

Atrahasis, whose name means 'extra-wise', is modelled on the Sumerian Ziusudra, one of a mortal couple who survived the flood and who was granted the status of an immortal deity by the great gods. According to the Sumerian King List, Atrahasis was also a historical character who ruled the city of Suruppak [Tell Fara in southern Iraq] in the heroic age before proper records began.

At least two versions of the epic are known – the Old Babylonian version and a Late Assyrian adaptation which was found in the library of Assurbanipal at Nineveh. See also *Genesis*, page 45, and *Gilgameš*, page 179.

The myth describes how the great gods are disenchanted with the hard labour they have to carry out in the creation and maintenance of the world, in particular with the digging and clearing of irrigation canals which were, and still are, vital to the fertility and well-being of the Mesopotamian alluvial plain. One day they lay down their tools and confront Ellil, the creator god and son of the god of heaven, with their grievances.

Every one of the gods has declared war!
We have put a stop to our digging
The burden is too great, it is destroying us
Our work is too hard and the effort is too much.

In order to provide the gods with a convenient labour force, Ellil instucts them to select one of the lesser gods for sacrifice so that, from his blood, humankind can be created. The birth goddess, Mami (Nintu), with the assistance of the god of wisdom, Enki, thus creates humankind out of clay mixed with the blood of the victim, Gěstu, a minor god of intellect. The great gods are called to spit on and trample the clay and Mami pinches it off into fourteen pieces from which she fashions seven males and seven females. She also uses the occasion to lay down certain codes of conduct for earthly marriage and childbirth.

After six hundred years the earth has become over-populated and Ellil is infuriated by the clamour from below. He orders the population to be regulated through judicious balance of nature. The assembly of gods exceed his commands, however, sending drought, famine and disease until, after six years, only a few people survive, and even then the great gods send a flood in order to destroy all remaining life.

Atrahasis is instructed secretly by Enki to build a boat, take on to it the living things of the earth, and prepare for a great flood that will last for seven days. The skies darken with the approaching storm.

There was no visibility
Nothing could be seen in the devastation
Like a raging bull the flood roared in,
Like a wild ass the winds howled
The darkness was complete, there was no sun.

When in spate, the Euphrates can breach its banks and inundate the plain towards the lower-lying Tigris. There are strong similarities in this part of the account with other flood stories which abounded in the ancient Near East, including the Gilgameš epic and the Biblical story of Noah. Whether these all derive from a single universal source, describing some legendary devastation, is unknown.

When Ellil discovers that Atrahasis and his wife have survived the deluge he is infuriated, but Enki reasons with him and the assembly finally agrees that, henceforth, the human population will be regulated sensibly and with compassion.

AWONAWILONA

CULTURE OF ORIGIN: native American – Zuni
PROVENANCE: oral traditions obtained by ethnological investigators. More significant publications include: *Outlines of Zuni Creation Myths* F.H. Cushing, 13th Report, Bureau of American Ethnology, Washington 1896; *The Zuni Indians; their Mythology, Esoteric Fraternities, and Ceremonies* M.C. Stevenson, 23rd Report, Bureau of American Ethnology, Washington 1904.

Awonawilona, the sun god and supreme creator being, is alone in the universe. He first engenders the sea within himself, creating it from his own body through heat. Upon this primeval water, green scum forms and takes shape to become the earth mother and the sky father. These two primal beings create all living things which are destined to emerge from the lowermost and farthest distant of the four caves of the world. The cave is described as becoming so filled with living creatures, some ready to emerge, others unfinished, that they crawl over each other in a writhing mass. The wisest, including mankind, are poised to make their escape while the remainder are less eager. Eventually the leader, and the wisest of men, Po-shai-an-K'ia, finds his way out through a dark and narrow passage. Others try to follow, but they are held back by the sheer crush of numbers.

Po-shai-an-K'ia frees himself into a damp, primitive world of islands and seas. He travels to greet Awonawilona and implores him to liberate the rest of mankind and all the other creatures trapped below.

BELLA COOLA CREATION

CULTURE OF ORIGIN: native American – Bella Coola [British Columbia]
PROVENANCE: recorded from oral traditions by Franz Boas. Memoirs of the American Museum of Natural History, 1898.
The myth accounts for the world inhabited by the Indian tribes of the far north.

Atsa'axl, the Upper Heaven, is ruled by Qama'its (Our Woman), the supreme being, a great warrior spirit whose visits to mankind cause sickness and death. Atsa'axl is like a vast prairie without trees and is reached via a river which emanates from the house of the spirits,

Nusme'ta, in the Lower Heaven. An alternative route is through the hole in the sky, Tslna'lotas. The house of Qama'its lies far to the east in a place where the gale blows continuously, driving everything into the doorway of the dwelling. In the immediate vicinity, however, all is calm and in front of the house is a post carved in the shape of a winged monster whose mouth forms the doorway. The gravel around the building is of three colours, blue, black and white, and at the back is a salt-water lake where the supreme being bathes herself. In the lake lives Si'siul, a water snake which, from time to time, descends to the earth. When it slithers and moves around, the rocks shatter and slide down the mountains.

In the beginning the mountains are very high and are in the form of dreadful human beings who make the world uninhabitable. Qama'its vanquishes them and makes them smaller. When she conquers one special mountain, called Yulyule'ml, she breaks off its nose.

The spirits of the Lower Heaven are the creators of mankind, but they also destroy human beings. In front of Nusme'ta is another post, Nultne'kta, painted with images of birds and with a white crane called Qo'xox perched on the top. The ruler of the Lower Heaven is Senx, the sun, and he is joined by Alk'unta'm, who is of equal importance. In the house the old man who once ruled the cosmos and whose name is Snulk'ulxa'ls stays beside the fire, keeping warm. His mother is a cannibal spirit who inserts her snout into the ears of people and sucks out their blood. In her more familiar form she is the mosquito!

CIPACTLI AND TEZCATLIPOCA

CULTURE OF ORIGIN: Aztec (classical Mesoamerican) [Mexico]
PROVENANCE: probably worshipped circa 750 AD until 1500 AD and known from tradition in pre-Columbian codices and detail on stone carvings.
   The myth adopts a theme familiar from other cultures, particularly among the island races in the Pacific, whereby the earth is hauled, forcibly, from the womb of the primeval ocean.

Cipactli, the great earth mother, is a terrifying hybrid goddess created by the otherworld deities Mictlantecuhtli and Mictecacihuatl in the form of a huge alligator-like monster. So vast is she that the mountains are the scaly ridges of her skin. As she emerges from the primeval waters she is confronted by the sun god Tezcatlipoca. He engages her in a ferocious battle during which he tears away her lower jaw in an effort to prevent her returning to the depths. She, for her part, rips off his right foot.

THEOGONY OF DUNNU

CULTURE OF ORIGIN: Mesopotamian – Akkadian

PROVENANCE: *Theogony of Dunnu* would seem to have grown up as a local tradition around the town of Dunnu, whose exact situation is unknown, but which achieved its chief importance during the early part of the second millennium BC. The authorship is unknown.

One of the many creation myths which arose during the Mesopotamian era, the narrative places the earth and the plough in focus as the primeval powers, the progenitors of the sea. There is a general lack of moral fibre among the gods, with incest, patricide and matricide taking prominent position. In this respect the tone of the narrative contrasts strongly with other creation stories, notably the *Enuma Eliš*, in which conduct is violent, but generally honourable. A problem with establishing the actual intent of the *Theogony of Dunnu* lies in that at least half the textual material has never come to light, and extent and provenance are in doubt.

Plough is the consort of Earth and between them they engender Sea, but now the violence and incest begin. The female earth principle enters a union with her son the Cattle God, who then promptly kills his father, abandons his murderous relationship with his mother and marries his sister, Sea. There follows a series of violent and villainous episodes. The son of the Cattle God, the Flocks God, kills his father and marries his mother, Sea, whereupon she promptly kills her own mother, Earth.

The account continues in the same vein with the son of Flocks God marrying his sister, River, and killing Flocks God and Sea. The Herdsman God, grandson of Flocks God, marries his sister Pasture and Poplar, kills his parents, and so on until the narrative is broken off with nearly forty lines of text missing.

See also *Enuma Eliš*, page 42, and *Genesis*, page 45.

GOSPEL OF THE EGYPTIANS

CULTURE OF ORIGIN: gnostic Christian

PROVENANCE: the text exists as two separate versions contained in tractates III,2 and IV,2 of the twelve codices discovered in 1945 at Nag Hammadi in Upper Egypt, where they were buried circa 400 AD [Coptic Museum, Cairo]. The manuscripts, written in Coptic, are considered to be independent translations from an earlier Greek work. The work relies for its inspiration on a mystical gnostic cosmogony based on Sethianism. Authorship is unknown, though it is traditionally ascribed to Seth, the son of Adamas and father of the gnostic peoples, and the title has been assigned in modern times. The work is intended to account the origins and life of Seth. See also *Hypostasis of the Archons*, page 34.

From the silence of the supreme god, the great invisible spirit whose name is a mystery, come three forces or Ogdoads – the Father, the

Mother and the Son (see also *The Ogdoad of Hermopolis*, page 59). They are preceded by three other primordial principles – the father of the great light who is the archon Domedon Doxomedon, the other archons and the light itself. The Father represents the thought, the word, incorruption and life eternal, will, mind and foreknowledge. The Mother, whose name is Barbelon, presides over heaven. The Son (Christ) is the glory of the Father and the virtue of the Mother. These three sublime beings request power from the supreme silent spirit.

There follows a form of heavenly genealogy (the text is damaged) which accounts the evolution of the other glorious beings through the pleroma (abundance) of heavenly powers and which culminates in the birth of the son of Adamas, Seth, the father of the gnostic race. Adamas, the first man, is born as a shaft of light from Mirothoe, the mother of the holy ones. Adamas, Logos (the word) and the divine Autogenes blend with each other and the word is made man. Adamas begs for a son to be engendered through himself so that he may found an incorruptible race of people and in response the power of light conceives four sons and then a fifth, Seth.

At this juncture a second distinct section of the myth develops which accounts for the origin and fate of the Sethian race. The great archon, Sakla, and the demon Nebruel join forces, first to engender a band of lesser spirits and then to establish the twelve aeons or worlds. The archons are assigned to reign over these aeons. But they become arrogant in their power and threaten destruction through fire and flood. Seth is sent down into the world as its saviour; there he envelops himself in the person of Jesus Christ and thus curbs the power of the archons.

The third section, difficult to interpret, is in the form of a hymn or chant. The fourth and final section details how Seth came to write the Gospel of the Egyptians and tells of its deposition in the mountain of Charaxio.

ENKI, NINMAH AND THE CREATION OF MAN

CULTURE OF ORIGIN: Mesopotamian – Sumerian

PROVENANCE: the earliest inscribed version of the myth dates from about 2000 BC, shortly after the collapse of the Third Dynasty at Ur, but it undoubtedly originates in an earlier oral tradition. The names of the deities appear on inscriptions dating from about 3500 BC. Two copies are known, one held in the University of Pennsylvania and the other in the Louvre. Both, however, suffer from many breaks in the text.

The gods are finding difficulty in obtaining food. Enki, the god of wisdom, is fast asleep so he fails to hear their grumblings until his mother, Nammu, the apotheosis of the primeval waters, brings the problem before him, asking him to fashion suitable servants for the gods.

Enki explains how to engender humankind from river mud and a feast is arranged to celebrate. Enki and the midwife goddess, Ninmah, become thoroughly drunk, but she and her helpers collect a quantity of clay 'from above the abyss' with which to mould six kinds of individuals while Enki decrees their fates. He also gives the individuals bread to eat. The six include one who cannot bend his limbs, a blind man, one with paralysed feet, one whose penis drips semen, a barren woman and an asexual creature without genital organs of any kind.

Enki is tempted to create a seventh individual by his own handiwork, but the exercise fails: he can only engender a sickly and feeble creature which, even though Ninmah is brought in to help, offers no real response. Ninmah curses Enki because he has produced such a travesty, but he eventually appeases her anger.

ENUMA ELIŠ (Babylonian Epic of Creation)

CULTURE OF ORIGIN: Mesopotamian – Akkadian

PROVENANCE: there are two notable versions of this myth, a Babylonian narrative which features the god Marduk, and an Assyrian version which is probably later and derivative and which replaces Marduk with the national god Aššur. The myth seems to have been inscribed as a comparatively late composition: no tablets are found to include it prior to the first millennium BC and those copies which have been discovered show little or no variation. This uniformity suggests that the Epic may not have stemmed from an old oral tradition but may have originated as a literate narrative designed to be chanted as an epic hymn. At least one Babylonian temple tablet instructs that it should be recited on the fourth day of the New Year festival in the month of Nisan (April).

The style is impressively rhetorical and is based on the notion of two opposing forces in the primeval universe – salt water (which the Mesopotamians knew to be detrimental to their agriculture), represented by Apsu, and fresh or sweet water (which was beneficial), represented by Ea.

The title of the myth comes from the first two words of the Akkadian text, of which the opening line translates 'When sky before the earth was formed'.

The narrative opens in the period of chaos before the earth and the ordered cosmos have been brought into being.

When the skies were not yet named
Nor earth below pronounced by name,
Apsu, the first one, the begetter
And maker Tiamat, who bore them all,
Had mixed their waters together, but had not formed pastures,
Nor discovered reed beds;
When yet no gods were manifest,
Nor names pronounced, nor destinies decreed,
Then gods were born within them.

Two primordial beings, Lahmu and Lahamu, are engendered by Tiamat from the silt of the primeval ocean. They beget Ansar and Kisar who, in turn, are the parents of the god of heaven, the begetter of the great gods, Anu.

Anu becomes irritated at the way in which the new generation of gods is disturbing the peace of his great-grandmother Tiamat and himself. The earth mother responds angrily to the suggestion of destroying that which she has created, but Apsu, the god of the underground primeval waters, and his vizier Mummu, continue to plot the destruction of the pantheon of younger gods so that his mother can rest. Ea, the god of wisdom, is aware of Apsu's plotting and puts him into a deep sleep. He then slaughters Apsu, ties up Mummu and lays him over the corpse of the god, building his own house on top of Apsu where he lives for ever with his consort Damkina.

The epic tale, however, has only just begun. Damkina gives birth to the god Marduk.

Anu his father's begetter beheld him,
And rejoiced, beamed; his heart was filled with joy.
He made him so perfect that his godhead was doubled.
Elevated far above them, he was superior in every way.
His limbs were ingeniously made beyond comprehension,
Impossible to understand, too difficult to perceive.
Four were his eyes, four were his ears;
When his lips moved, fire blazed forth.

One gains the distinct impression that Marduk, the Babylonian national god, was no ordinary figure! The epic continues with an extensive eulogy to Marduk's prowess and stature; he is seen to pose an increasing threat to the other gods in the pantheon. They go to Tiamat complaining that, just as in days of old Apsu had plotted against them, so now Marduk is disturbing their peace. Tiamat, their mother, must come to their defence.

But what of us, who cannot rest? Do you not love us?
Our grip is weak, our eyes are sunken.
Remove the yoke of us restless ones, and let us sleep!

Stung by memories of her own fatal inaction against Ea and of the consequential death of Apsu, Tiamat decides to confront Marduk. She convenes a council of war. Terrifying beasts are created to fill the ranks of Tiamat's army and she sets the warrior Qingu at their head, giving him the Tablet of Destinies to hold in his arms.

In the opening lines of the second tablet of the *Enuma Eliš*, Ea listens, angry and dumbfounded, as he learns that Tiamat and the younger gods have lined up for war against Marduk. He goes to his father Ansar and relates details of the fearful forces of opposition. Ansar, afraid of Tiamat's powers, elects to send Anu, the sun god, as an emissary. Anu will try to bluff Tiamat with the formidable strength of arms at Ea's disposal and suggest that she thinks twice before launching an attack. Tiamat is equal to the ruse and sends Anu back empty-handed.

In despair, Ea sends his son Marduk to Ansar and Ansar agrees that Marduk is the only champion of a calibre strong enough to challenge the might of Tiamat. This point settled, Ansar convenes his own war council amongst the older pantheon of gods and, at the opening of Tablet III, he sends his vizier Kakka to spread the word. Marduk puts a high price on the plan, that of supreme autonomy.

Let me [Marduk], my own utterance, fix fate instead of you.
Whatever I create shall never be altered!
Let a decree from my lips never be revoked, never be changed!

Tablet IV begins with a prolonged eulogy to Marduk from the older gods and he, their champion, assembles his own terrible weapons – the four winds, a huge net in which to trap Tiamat, a bow and arrows and a mighty mace.

The Lord raised the flood-weapon, his great weapon,
And mounted the frightful, unfaceable storm-chariot.
He had yoked it to a team of four and had harnessed to its side
Slayer, Pitiless, Racer and Flyer;
Their lips were drawn back, their teeth carried poison.
They know not exhaustion, they can only devastate.

Thus the two adversaries come face to face and the confrontation of cosmic forces begins. Tiamat, however, proves no match for Marduk. He hurls the whirlwind into her open mouth and, as she swallows it, the tempest swells her belly. Marduk lets off an arrow which penetrates and splits her in two, piercing her heart. He throws down her corpse and stands triumphantly over it before stripping the weapons and powers from all the ranks of gods who had dared to side with her.

Tablet V details the creation by Marduk of an ordered world from Tiamat's remains. He places constellations in the heavens, sets the calendar of the year, makes clouds, winds and rain. The great rivers run from her eyes, mountains swell from her breasts. With half of her body he creates the sky, with the other half he builds the earth. The Tablet of Destinies he returns to Anu. Finally he dons the emblems of power and ensures that the rest of the gods, the Igigi, are properly subservient to him.

There then follows an oration by Marduk in which he proclaims his intentions for the future of the civilized world with Babylon at its heart, upon which the other gods proclaim their allegiance.

Tablet VI accounts the trial of Qingu, Tiamat's general, who is put to death and from whose blood the human race is created. Duties are assigned to the gods and the construction of Babylon commences. The epic ends, in Tablet VII, on something of an anticlimax when the so-called 'fifty epithets of Marduk' are detailed in a protracted and laborious list ending with the god of wisdom, Ea, decreeing that his own name shall be the last of Marduk's titles.

ESAUGETUH EMISSEE
(Master of Breath)

CULTURE OF ORIGIN: native American – Muskhogean (Creek and other tribes) [south-eastern USA]
PROVENANCE: recorded from an oral tradition.
    One of the many myths of creation following a cataclysmic inundation, the story in its present form may be the result of Christian missionary influence See also *Genesis* (*The Flood*), page 109 and *Michabo*, page 56.

The creator god Esaugetuh Emissee, whose name sounds like a sigh of breath, rules over the winds from which he breathes life into the world, and over the primeval waters. In the beginning he sends two doves in search of dry land. Eventually one finds a blade of grass. Slowly the waters recede until the globe of the earth takes form and a mighty hill called Nunne Chaha emerges. On this hill the creator god makes his house and from the mud clay around it he fashions the first human beings. Because there is still so much water everywhere he constructs a wall on which he lays the clay people to dry. Slowly the sun turns mud into flesh and bones. Now the god channels the water into rivers and gives the dry land to mankind.

GENESIS
(Creation of the World)

CULTURE OF ORIGIN: Judaic/Christian
PROVENANCE: the *Vetus Testamentum*.
    This account of creation is unusual in that it precludes a female presence in the formation of the cosmos and in that the attitude of the writer towards the creation of woman is strongly derogatory. See also *The Hypostasis of the Archons*, page 34, and *The Origin of the World*, page 61.

The creator god is alone in the void, moving over the dark primeval waters. By the power of his thought and word light is created in the cosmos and it becomes divided from darkness to create day and night. On the second day of his labour the god creates a heaven which separates the waters of the void from those of the cosmos. On the third day, and from the waters of the cosmos, he raises dry land which he names *earth*. Upon this earth he engenders green living things. On the fourth day he places the sun, the moon and the stars in the heavens and on the fifth he engenders animal life in the oceans and birds in the air. On the sixth day of creation he stocks the dry land with animals of every kind and, in his own image, he fashions mankind to rule over the abundance of life he has made. He instructs that he has placed the animal and plant kingdoms at the disposal of mankind. The seventh day he sanctifies as a day of rest.

The second chapter of the Book of Genesis details the creation of man in more detail. The god fashions human form out of earth and breathes life into it to give it a soul. He places this human being, Adam, in a paradise garden in Eden from which the four great streams of the river of life spring. Within the garden the god also plants two trees, the Tree of Life and the Tree of Knowledge of Good and Evil. He forbids the man to eat from the latter tree, though he gives him permission to take freely from elsewhere in the garden. If the man eats from the Tree of Knowledge he will die. The god also allows Adam to give names to all the animals and plants he has fashioned. Then the creator god places Adam into a deep sleep, removes one of his ribs and from it creates a woman.

At this juncture the serpent makes its debut in paradise. It questions the woman about the forbidden tree and persuades her that if they eat the fruit neither she nor Adam will die; rather they will be wise like the gods and know the distinction between good and evil. So the woman eats from the Tree of Knowledge and also gives its fruit to her partner. At once the pair are aware of themselves and they hide their nakedness.

The creator god calls out to Adam and demands to know why he is hiding himself. When Adam reveals that he is afraid, the god asks him if he has eaten from the forbidden tree. Adam points the finger of blame towards his consort. The god curses the serpent and consigns the mortal pair to a life of suffering and toil. The woman he singles out for particular punishment.

> *I will greatly multiply thy sorrow and thy conception; in sorrow thou shalt bring forth children and thy desire shall be to thy husband and he shall rule over thee.*

The god drives the pair out of the paradise garden in case they should be tempted to eat from the Tree of Life and thus gain immortality. To protect the tree he places guardian beasts, *cherubim*, around it armed with flaming swords.

THE SUN GOD OF HELIOPOLIS

CULTURE OF ORIGIN: Egyptian
PROVENANCE: like other Egyptian mythology, this account does not come
   from a single narrative but is pieced together from various religious texts
   and illustrations. At the time of the unification of Upper and Lower Egypt
   (circa 3000 BC) the cosmogony of the Heliopolis [archaeological site in
   north-east Cairo] pantheon known as the Ennead was first mapped out.
   This resulted in a creation myth known from Pyramid Texts dating from
   the fifth and sixth dynasties (2649–2152 BC) and from later Coffin Texts
   (2040–1783 BC).
   The myth reflects a constant fear among the ancient Egyptians that the
   primordial being, Nun, would one day cause a catastrophic deluge on
   earth. The Greek observers of ancient Egypt developed a popular symbolism for the birth of the sun god of Heliopolis. Wall paintings and papyri
   often depict a bird, the *Benu* (meaning 'brilliant arising'), which appears
   either as a heron or as a yellow wagtail. In Greek culture this became
   symbolic of the birth of the sun god and was transposed into an eagle-like
   creature, the Phoenix. See also *Atrahasis*, page 36.

Before the cosmos comes into being, there exists a vast and formless
primeval sea personified as the primordial Nun, one of the eight
deities of the Ogdoad, who is often depicted holding aloft the solar
disc and who may be represented by a sacred lake or cistern. After the
formation of the cosmos, the primeval sea retreats to encircle the
heavens.

Atum, the creator god of Heliopolis (a role shared with the sun god
Re), engenders himself from the primeval ocean as a demi-urge. He is
the supreme being, a totality, monad in form, able to create all the
other deities from within himself. He is perceived thus iconographic-
ally, emerging from a lotus flower and standing on a raised mound,
the *Benben*, which emerges from the waters.

In the surroundings of *Benben*, Atum masturbates himself to
engender Šu and Tefnut, the next two major deities of the Heliopolis
pantheon, the so-called Ennead defined by the Greek historian
Herodotus.

> *He took his penis in his hand and ejaculated to give birth to Šu and Tefnut,
> the twins.*

In an alternative scenario, relying on the use of puns, Atum sneezes to
create Šu from his mucus and he spits out Tefnut. The names of the
two deities can be linked to the Egyptian hieroglyphics for sneezing
and spitting. Šu is the god of the air, typically represented in human
form or, less frequently, as a lion, while his sister, Tefnut, is the
goddess of moisture or dew and is one of the manifestations of the
'Eye of Re' (other authors cite the cow goddess Hathor). Tefnut

appears either as a lion or in human form with a lion's head. She may also be depicted as a snake coiled around a sceptre and in the Pyramid Texts pure water is said to flow from her vagina. Šu and Tefnut become the parents of Geb, the earth deity, and Nut, the most significant creator goddess in the pantheon, who is depicted as a celestial cow held aloft by Šu and stretched across the cosmos to represent the barrier of the firmament beyond which lies the formless void of primordial matter. In later iconography Nut takes human form as a slim, arched figure, naked and poised on her toes and fingertips, which touch the four cardinal points of the compass. Beneath her is Geb, whose erect penis points upwards to her. Nut is often described as consorting with the sun god himself to mother the other deities. It is significant that in Mesopotamian and other Indo-Aryan mythologies, the creator goddess is generally chthonic, symbolized by the earth, while her male partner equates with the sky. In Egyptian cosmogony the sexual connotations are reversed.

According to mythology the sun god emerges from Nut's vagina at dawn and travels through the daylight hours along the underside of her arched body. At dusk she swallows him and he remains within her for the hours of night. This same imagery is incorporated into funeral rites when the deceased ruler is said to be enfolded by the arms of Nut and to pass within her body – thus 'the doors of the sky are opened to him'.

As the consort of her brother, Geb, Nut bears four children – Isis, Osiris, Seth and Nephthys – who represent the 'younger generation' of the Heliopolis pantheon.

HIRANYAGARBHA
(Golden Embryo)

CULTURE OF ORIGIN: Vedic Hindu [India]

PROVENANCE: the *Rg Veda* collection of 1028 hymns (Vedas) composed in Sanskrit and dating from circa 1200 BC, based on an oral tradition which was in circulation among the Aryan immigrants to the subcontinent circa 1700–700 BC. Used as hymns of praise at the time of religious sacrifice.

According to some current thinking, the unknown deity addressed in the hymn is the androgynous primordial being Prajapati, who impregnates himself by fusing elements of mind and speech.

With each verse comes the question, who is the god whom we should worship? The hymn ends with a supplication that this great unknown shall not harm us. A final verse identifying the subject as Prajapati is a late appendage which cannot be confirmed.

The golden embryo arises from the primeval sea. It becomes the Lord of Creation to whom the pantheon of gods owes obedience. It is the source of all life, fashioning the earth and sky and, paradoxically, the waters also come from it. This supreme deity rules over all creatures, everything that breathes and blinks, he owns the mountains, oceans and rivers, he embraces the sky.

IMANA AND THE CREATION OF MANKIND

CULTURE OF ORIGIN: Burundi (West Africa)
PROVENANCE: recorded from oral tradition

The creator god, Imana, decides one day to engender mankind, so he creates a man, Kihanga, who is sent down from heaven to earth on the end of a long silken rope. So elastic is the thread of his descent and so hard does he come down that he bounces several times between heaven and earth.

Kihanga represents the ancestor of all mankind, so his skin is both black and white like a zebra's. Kihanga has many sons and daughters who are the forebears of the African tribes and they include Kanyarundi, his eldest son, and Inaruchaba, his eldest daughter, to whom their grandfather, Imana, sometimes appears in the guise of a young ram.

IMRA

CULTURE OF ORIGIN: Prasun Kafir (Hindukush)
PROVENANCE: oral traditions recorded chiefly by M. Elphinstone (1839); G. Morgenstierne (1951); G.S. Robertson (1896)

The supreme god Imra is alone in the cosmos until he creates the other deities of the pantheon through the power of his own breath. All become subservient to him except the goddess Disani, who sprang from the right side of Imra's body and who occupies a special place (this compares with the account of Athena springing fully armed from the head of Zeus in Greek mythology). The gods collectively own a golden bed and a golden chair and they rule by assembly. Imra claims these items for himself and when the other gods complain, he merely sits down upon the bed. The rest of the pantheon submits meekly and thus Imra usurps the position of supreme god, using the labours and produce of the other gods for his own benefit. He also creates the demons and the more benevolent spirits. Since, as a male deity, he cannot be responsible for farming, he also engenders the 'seven daughters of Mara' to oversee agriculture in the Hindukush.

To create mankind, Imra takes a goatskin, places earth and water inside it and churns the contents. Three women emerge and become the mothers of mortals in three different regions – Kati, Ashkun and Waigal. In an alternative version, the first man is Baba, who settles in Kashmir with an unnamed wife who bears him forty children. They all speak different languages which are unintelligible to their siblings, so Imra orders them to emigrate and populate the world.

IZANAGI AND IZANAMI

CULTURE OF ORIGIN: Japanese Shinto
PROVENANCE: recorded in various texts and art from oral traditions, including the *Kojiki* and *Nihongi* sacred books. The primordial deities, and the mythology surrounding them, are of wholly Japanese origin with no Chinese or Buddhist influence.

Three remote and barely defined primordial beings, illustrious but forever hidden from mortal eyes, come into existence in the darkness of chaos to stand on the Takama-No-Hara (the plain of high heaven). They include Ame-No-Minaka-Nushi-No-Kami (the deity master of the august centre of heaven), Taka-Mi-Musubi-No-Kami (high august producing wondrous deity) and Kami-Musubi-No-Kami (divine producing wondrous deity). These three create the Passive and Active Essences of the cosmos.

The two sibling deities, Izanagi and Izanami, who later become man and wife, are given the responsibility of engendering the material world from chaos, instructed to 'make, consolidate and give birth to this drifting land [Japan]'. All that exists hitherto is a vaguely defined, floating reed bed drifting upon the primeval sea from which is engendered the fourth of the primordial beings, Umashi-Ashi-Kabi-Hiko-Ji-No-Kami (pleasant reed shoot prince elder deity). To assist them in their task of creation Izanagi and Izanami are given a magical and richly jewelled spear. They stand upon the bridge of heaven and use the spear to stir up the primal waters. When they lift it from the sea it drips brine and where this consolidates it forms the first dry land, the mythical island of Onogoro [thought to be Nu-Shima island on the southern coast of Awagi]. This initial place is extended by a further seven islands to make up the Oya-Shima-Guni (Parent-island-country). The dry land is organized and consolidated by the god O-Kuni-Nushi-No-Mikoto, who undergoes a series of ordeals in the process.

Izanagi and Izanami produce many offspring, the eldest of whom is the sun goddess Amaterasu, followed by the moon god Tsuki-Yomi, Susano-Wo the storm god, and Kagu-Tsuchi the god of fire. The lesser deities amongst Izanami's children include O-Yama-Tsu-Mi, the apotheosis of the mountains. From the vomit of Izanami are born gods including Kana-Yama-Biko and Kana-Yama-Hime, the god and goddess of miners. From her faeces she extends the pantheon of lesser deities, including Hani-Yasu-Hime the goddess of potters. From her urine comes Mizu-Ha-No-Me, the most senior among the many water goddesses of Shintoism. Izanami's demise is brought about during the birth of the fiery Kagu-Tsuchi: she is burned to death and the eight thunders spring from her corpse, the most significant being Iku-Ikasuchi. She descends to the underworld, Yomi, where she remains as a deformed corpse. Izanagi follows in search of her but, when he lights a torch to see her, he is horrified by her appearance. He manages to escape by throwing fruit to the demon guardians of Yomi; they pause to eat it while he passes them by.

KAFIR CREATION

CULTURE OF ORIGIN: Prasun Kafir (Hindukush)
PROVENANCE: oral traditions recorded chiefly by M. Elphinstone (1839); G. Morgenstierne (1951); G.S. Robertson (1896)

The universe is built of three components. The upper world of Urdesh is one in which there exist seven heavens (*bisht*), the highest of which is Il-Munj, and the rivers which bound these heavens are the stars, including the north star. The middle world, thought of either as a large disc or as a sleeping giant, is Michdesh, upon which all living things exist. The lowest world is Yurdesh, the underworld, which is a mixture of paradise and hell (*zozuk*). It is reached through one of several holes in the ground, the most significant of which is near the Prasun village of Kushteki. Those who look into the hole die and are immediately transported to the underworld.

In an alternative tradition the transition from earth to the realms of heaven is gradual. It begins deep in the valleys of the Hindukush with the rivers which represent the highway between middle, upper and underworlds. The river comes from the high places and it flows into the realm of the dead at the lowest point in the valley. Heaven begins where the mountain peaks and glaciers touch the sky and the homes of the gods are the sacred mountain lakes overlooked by trees which symbolize the presence of both gods and men.

In a third tradition there exist only an upper world and an underworld. The upper world, covered by a roof of sky, is a place where both gods and mortals move freely, but the real home of both gods and demons is the underworld from which the unborn emerge and to which humankind returns at the moment of death. The lakes are the doorways between worlds and anyone who jumps into a sacred lake makes the journey from one to the other.

In the beginning there exists nothing, neither sun nor moon, and the cosmos is ruled by the supreme god Imra, a deity endowed with great wisdom and cunning. He rules the world at the head of a trinity which also includes Mandi (Mon) as his youthful adjutant and the god of war, Gish. These three supreme gods are equalled in might by the supreme goddess Disani. One other deity occupies a position of high rank, Munjem Malik, the god of the earth who rules the mountain valleys and who also presides over the council of gods. His head appears above ground in the valley of Parun, where it emerges in the form of a vast boulder.

Beneath the highest level of the hierarchy exists a vast pantheon of gods who oversee all of nature. They include Sudrem, the weather god; Zuzum, the god of winter; Wushum, the god of law; Bagisht, the god of waters; and Maramalik, the underworld god of the dead. All the deities are in a permanent state of conflict with the army of demons, the *yush* and the *wechi*, who embody the harshness and dangers of the natural world. It is this endless battle which preoccupies the spirit world.

KHNUM AND THE CREATION OF MANKIND

CULTURE OF ORIGIN: Egyptian

PROVENANCE: principally from hymns and calendar liturgies inscribed in the surviving hypostyle hall of the Temple of Khnum at Esna in Upper Egypt. These compositions date from the Greco-Roman period (circa 700 BC–395 AD) though the concept probably originated in Egyptian antiquity. The hymns and liturgies were intoned during the annual Festival of the Potter's Wheel.

Khnum, a chthonic god usually depicted in human form or with the head of a ram, is sitting before a potter's wheel creating human beings out of clay at the behest of the creator gods. His sacred animal, the ram, signifies the creativity of the natural world and he also creates all the members of the animal kingdom. He installs the respiratory and digestive systems, designs the reproductive organs and supervises pregnancy and labour. He directs the flow of the circulatory system around the newly fashioned body and puts skin on the bones.

In a more specific episode of the mythology, Khnum is directed by the creator god, Amun, to implant two clay figures that he has just made into the womb of Queen Mutemwiya. Amun has impregnated her in a sacred marriage and she is destined to give birth to Amenhotep III. One of the figures represents Amenhotep bodily, the other represents his *ka* or life force.

In addition to his role as the potter, Khnum is seen to control the the vagaries of the river Nile through his supervision of Hapy, the fertility god of the Nile flood, who lives in caverns adjacent to the cataracts. When Khnum allows the inundation to take place each year, it leaves behind a rich layer of silt on which the Egyptian harvest germinates.

MAHATARA

CULTURE OF ORIGIN: Borneo Dayak (maritime)
PROVENANCE: recorded from oral traditions amongst the seagoing clans of Dayaks, the original pre-Malay speaking inhabitants of Borneo.
    The myth affords a moral tone on the importance of matrimony and may have been subject to Christian adulteration (see also *Amei Awi and Burung Une*, page 32).

The supreme god, Mahatara, lives alone in the heavens until he discovers a goddess called Jata who lives in the depths of the rivers and who becomes his consort. They produce fourteen offspring, the other deities of the Dayak pantheon, including the seven Santang goddesses who, in due course of time, will descend to earth on golden brooms and dictate the fates of men. Among their sons, the most significant is the crocodile god Jata.

The earth, although fertile and green, contains no people, so Mahatara breaks a branch from a *garing* tree and whittles one end of it into a sculpture of a man; the other end he models as a woman. He tosses his work of art from the heavens and it falls through the clouds on to a rock beside a river estuary. On impact it snaps into two pieces and the end modelled as a woman remains on the rock where it takes life and becomes a living being called Puteri Bualu Julah Karangan (golden lady of the rock). The portion of branch with the male figure falls into the water and floats away on the current. It is washed up on a small island where it too takes life and becomes a living being. This person is known as Tunggal Garing Janjahunan Laut (the lonely wooden man who comes from the water).

Tunggal builds a canoe and paddles upstream to where Puteri is waiting. They become companions but remain innocent of their sexuality. When it is time for the woman to menstruate she goes into the river to wash herself and her blood is transformed into demonic water spirits. On the second occasion of menstruation her blood falls on to the dry land where it gives rise to earth demons. The third period takes place deep in the forest where the blood becomes tree demons.

Mahatara perceives that a large number of evil spirits have been emerging on the earth so he visits Tunggal and Puteri, advising them how to become properly wed as man and wife and explaining that under these circumstances Puteri will not menstruate to produce evil spirits. The couple do as they have been told, they begin to appreciate their sexuality and Puteri becomes pregnant, her periods thus ceasing. In fact from that moment she is always pregnant! Three of her offspring take special responsibilities: Sangiang, the eldest, is the artisan who makes weapons and tools from a piece of iron which he is found to be holding when he is born; Sangen becomes the farmer, since he is born with seeds in his hand; and Bunu becomes the hunter, having emerged from his mother's womb armed with a bow and arrows.

MANDAN

CULTURE OF ORIGIN: native American – Sioux
PROVENANCE: recorded from an oral tradition of the Mandan tribes

In the beginning the Sioux nation live in an underground village on the shores of a huge lake. Some of the tribe climb up a gigantic grape vine whose roots penetrate their subterranean land, to catch sight of the upper world which they discover to be airy and sunny and plentifully stocked with plants and animals. They bring back such enthusiastic reports that the whole tribe sets out to climb the grape vine. Only half of them manage to climb up the stem, however, because a very fat lady brings it crashing down.

NOTE: according to a somewhat paradoxical tradition, those members of the tribe who are honourable in life will find their way via the lake back to the village after death, but the bad will be unable to make the journey because of the weight of their sins.

MAUI AND THE CREATION OF IKA-A-MAUI

CULTURE OF ORIGIN: Polynesian (Maori)
PROVENANCE: recorded in recent times from oral traditions including *The Ancient History of the Maoris, Mythology and Traditions* J. White 6 vols. Wellington, 1887.

The myth is one of several much-loved stories of the exploits of Maui, who may be perceived as a Maori super-hero along the lines of the Mesopotamian Gilgameš. The notion of the Maori homeland being a vast fish suggests the creation of a land of great plenty upon which the inhabitants can sustain themselves indefinitely.

One day Maui goes fishing with his brothers Maui-Pae, Maui-Roto, Maui-Taha, and Maui-Whao, all of whom he instructs in the art of making hooks and harpoons until one day they decide they can do without him on their trip. He nevertheless accompanies them, disguised as a tiny shrimp hiding in the bottom of the canoe.

The brothers begin to catch fish and soon the boat is full, but then Maui asks them to wait until he himself has done some fishing. The brothers are somewhat scornful of his chances and refuse to let him use their bait. Undeterred, Maui bites himself and uses his own blood as a lure; through his magical powers he allows his line to sink deeper and deeper until it reaches the bed of the ocean, where it is seized by a vast fish. Maui resumes his proper form and begins to haul up the monstrous catch. So vast is it when it breaches the surface that it becomes the land Ika-a-Maui (the fish of Maui), which is the Maori name for the islands renamed by Captain Cook as New Zealand.

MBOMBO AND THE CREATION OF THE WORLD

CULTURE OF ORIGIN: Bakuba (Zaire)
PROVENANCE: recorded from oral tradition

In the beginning the creator god, Mbombo, exists in a dark void filled only with primeval waters. He develops a terrible stomach ache and from his belly emerge the sun, moon and stars. As the days pass by the heat of the sun begins to evaporate the waters and in due course dry land appears. Again Mbombo develops a stomache ache and this time he engenders from his body the plants and animals of the earth. Finally come the people and the tools necessary for their well-being.

In the east the river goddess Nchienge bears a son and a daughter, Woto and Labama, both of whom are white. Woto is destined to become the first ruler of the Bakuba tribe. He takes Labama as his wife, declaring such a liaison to be the exclusive right of kings, and when she bears him children he dyes their skins black since they will need to live and blend in to the forest as hunters of game. One of Woto's nieces conceives and gives birth to a lamb, thus originating the flocks of sheep. Goats also appear, as do their predators, the leopards. The monkey Fumu introduces mankind to the delights of palm wine and thus the world is put on a firm footing.

THE CREATOR GOD OF MEMPHIS

CULTURE OF ORIGIN: Egyptian
PROVENANCE: earliest references to Ptah, the creator god of Memphis, originate in the Pyramid Texts of the Old Kingdom (circa 2649–2152 BC),

when he is envisaged as a craftsman moulding mankind out of base materials. By the end of the Old Kingdom, however, his name is linked and syncretized with that of the primordial god, Tatenen, who personifies the emergence of land from the primeval waters. Ptah's role as the supreme creator god of Memphis is then further elaborated in the Coffin Texts of the Middle Kingdom (circa 2040–1783 BC).

The myth accounting the creation process at Memphis is largely known from the Shabaka Stone commissioned by King Shabaka (712–698 BC) during the Nubian (Sudanese) Dynasty. Memphis, at the southern approach to the Nile delta, was the capital city of Shabaka's predecessor. Having overrun the city, Shabaka discovered that the papyrus accounting the creation of the world by the god Ptah and the rise to supremacy of the god Horus was badly deteriorated. The undamaged portions of the narrative were transcribed, on his instructions, on to a block of black basalt which was erected in the temple of Ptah, but which was later severely defaced when put to use as a millstone in the post-pharaonic period.

The underlying principle of marrying a cerebral creation force with a more physical persona (Ptah with Tatenen) came to be known, under the classical Greek Egyptophiles, as the 'Logos doctrine'. Some authorities argue that the 'philosophies' evolved by the Memphis priesthood constitute an important precedent for certain of the doctrinal arguments raised in the Biblical New Testament.

The creation story runs from column 53 and would seem to be a serious attempt by the priesthood of Memphis to outdo the cosmogony of Atum-Re at Heliopolis (see the *Sun God of Heliopolis*, page 47). The Memphis creation account is an altogether more cerebral affair than the 'spit and semen' story from Heliopolis.

Ptah creates himself out of the formless void. He conceives the cosmos literally in his mind and through his word it comes into existence. He 'steals the march' by engendering all the other individuals of the pantheon, including the Heliopolis sun god, Atum, out of his heart and his speech, having heard and seen and breathed the concept of the cosmos and all things physical in his mind.

From the great void emerge the primordial waters and through the power of the mind of Ptah comes Tatenen. It is he who raises the dry land from the waters.

MICHABO
(The Great Hare)

CULTURE OF ORIGIN: native American – Algonquin
PROVENANCE: oral traditions recorded in *Algonquin Legends of New England* C.G. Leland, Boston and New York 1885.

As in the mythology of many other native American nations, the creator god or *manito* of the Algonquins is perceived both as the creator of the world and as the source of culture who first brings to mankind the skills and refinements of life, including the arts of making fishing nets and of hunting. Michabo, the supreme god, is also ruler of the east wind, constantly at odds with his father, who is ruler of the west wind. Michabo controls the lightning while the mists and clouds are the smoke from his pipe. According to different traditions he resides either on an island in the middle of Lake Superior or far away somewhere to the east in the fastness of the ocean. The title 'Great Hare' is a corruption of the aboriginal root *wah* which means 'the light of dawn'.

There are several creation myths involving Michabo, at least one of which provides less an account of the creation than of the restoration of dry land and living things after a cataclysmic deluge (see also *Atrahasis*, page 36, *Epic of Gilgameš*, page 179, and *Genesis* (*The Flood*), page 109).

Michabo is out hunting when his wolves plunge into a vast lake and disappear. The god wades into the water to rescue the animals, but the lake is stirred up and it overflows to inundate the whole of the earth. Michabo releases a raven, instructing it to search for any dry land and to bring back a speck of soil so that he can construct a new world. The bird seeks unsuccessfully. Michabo now sends an otter but, again, the animal returns without the necessary material. Finally the god dispatches a musk-rat and this time he is brought a portion of matter just large enough to begin the restoration of dry land. There is a further problem in that during the inundation all the trees have been stripped of their boughs, so Michabo looses off his arrows at the trunks as substitutes. In the conclusion of the story Michabo takes the musk-rat as his consort and through her engenders mankind.

In an alternative myth Michabo plucks a grain of sand from the bed of the primeval ocean and creates from it an island which he launches on to the empty waters. The island grows and grows until it is so big that a wolf which manages to stray on to it dies of old age before it manages to reach the opposite shore.

NASADIYA
(creation hymn)

CULTURE OF ORIGIN: Vedic Hindu [India]
PROVENANCE: the *Rg Veda* collection of 1028 hymns (Vedas), composed in Sanskrit and dating from circa 1200 BC, based on an oral tradition which was in circulation among the Aryan immigrants to the subcontinent circa 1700–700 BC. Used as hymns of praise at the time of religious sacrifice.

Nasadiya is a brief and highly paradoxical hymn, posing unanswerable questions about the creation of the cosmos.

When there was no existence, neither night nor day, death nor immortality, what stirred and where? The life force arose through the power of ritual-generated heat and with that force came desire for existence stretching like a cord across the void. Here is another imponderable question. Did creation form itself or was there something which pre-existed?

NOCUMA AND OWIOT

CULTURE OF ORIGIN: native American – Californian (Acagchemem Valley tribes) [San Juan Capistrano, California]

PROVENANCE: recorded from an oral tradition in an extract titled *Chinigchinich; A Historical Account of the Origin, Customs, and Traditions of the Indians at the Missionary Establishment of St Juan Capistrano, Alta California, called the Acagchemem Nation* by G. Boscana. *Life in California* A. Robinson. New York, 1846.

This creation myth parallels that of the mountain clans, but stems from the separate traditions of those living in the Californian valleys (see also *Owiot and Chinigchinich*, page 63).

The spirit Nocuma is the creator of all material things, including the world itself, which he has fashioned from a ball of dirt anchored by a heavy black rock called Tosaut. The sea is limited to a narrow stream so overpopulated that the fish cannot swim about freely and their more adventurous brethren are all for jumping out on to dry land. They are dissuaded by their elders because they have no feet and, in desperation, one or two of the larger fish break open the rock Tosaut. A substance flows out which they find agreeable and which mixes with the stream water to make salt. The water surges up, overflows the stream bank and forms the sea.

Next Nocuma creates humankind from clay, fashioning a man whom he names Ejoni and a woman, Ae. Their children multiply to form the native American nations. Among the offspring are Sirout (Handful of Tobacco) and Ycaiut (Above). They become the parents of Owiot (Dominator), the father of the tribe, who grows into a tyrannical warrior. Owiot becomes so intolerant of all around him that it is decided he must die and a lethal portion of Tosaut is ground up into a potion. Although Owiot receives warning of his fate he is unable to avoid it when some of the rock powder is sprinkled on him whilst asleep and, much to the relief of the nation, he dies. His descendants have to decide what they are to eat instead of the clay they have traditionally consumed, at which point a being called Attajen arrives on the scene, giving them the power to create rain and to stock the earth with plants and animals.

After many years there emerges another spirit being called Owiamot, better known as Chinigchinich (Almighty). He performs a dance before the tribe and then calls the medicine men, whom he instructs to emulate the dance when they wish to entreat him. He prepares to die and the tribe ask if they should bury him. Chinigchinich advises them not to do so lest they tread upon him and he take offence.

THE OGDOAD OF HERMOPOLIS

CULTURE OF ORIGIN: Egyptian

PROVENANCE: various sources, but all in the form of hieroglyphic texts. Literary evidence for the Hermopolis (Egyptian Khemnu) creation account involving the supreme god Amun is very fragmented because of the inadequate excavation of the site of Hermopolis at el-Ashmunein. Some information derives from monumental inscriptions at Thebes, but today the main source is the Papyrus Leiden 1350 (New Kingdom circa 1567–1085 BC). This is one of the funeral papyri which are collectively known as the Book of the Dead. There is also evidence from the Amun temples at Luxor and Deir el-Bahri concerning the role of Amun in engendering the rulers of Egypt through union with the mortal reigning queen. At Luxor there is a description of the fathering of Amenhotep III out of a union between his mother, Queen Mutemwiya, and Amun. At Deir el-Bahri, in the Ipet-Sut temple where, by tradition, Amun engendered the cosmos, one finds a relief identifying Queen Hatshepsut who has been impregnated by Amun.

Eight primordial elements of chaos known as the Ogoad exist before the creation of the sun god and, according to Hermopolis tradition, before the existence of the Heliopolis pantheon, the Ennead. The Ogdoad is divided into four pairs of entities who are personified as frogs (gods) and snakes (goddesses), creatures suitably equipped for life in the primeval ooze. They include Nun and Naunet representing the primordial waters, Kek and Kauket representing darkness, Heh and Hauhet representing infinity, and Amun and Amaunet representing hidden power.

At one particular moment, the eight components of the Ogdoad interact to break the laws governing chaos and out of the new order they generate the primeval mound of silt on which the sun god, Amun, in a new role, is to be born from a cosmic egg. This mound later becomes Hermopolis.

The primordial couples, with one exception, now become redundant. Amun and Amaunet, however, continue to play a dominant creative role at Thebes when Heliopolis is deserted. Amun retains his snake symbolism at Thebes, but is also symbolized by the ram and the Nile goose. He is perceived as being hidden, but nonetheless as pervading the whole universe. He has a strongly ithyphallic form which enables him, as first-born of the gods, to impregnate his own mother.

NOTE: the moon god Thoth plays a significant role in the Ogdoad mythology. The priest of the Ogdoad at the time of the transition from Hermopolis to Thebes in the fourth century BC was also the High Priest of Thoth, who thus became the tutelary god of Hermopolis and the new head of the Ogdoad, titled 'Lord of Khemnu'.

The cosmogony at Hermopolis takes an almost scientific slant when compared with the highly personal and physical method of creation at Heliopolis and the more cerebral or metaphysical process at Memphis.

OLODUMARE

CULTURE OF ORIGIN: Yoruba (Nigeria, West Africa)
PROVENANCE: recorded from oral tradition

The supreme god, Olodumare, lives in the void where there exists only the dark primeval water. One day he decides to create the earth, so he takes the shell of a giant snail and packs into it his daughter Oduduwa in the guise of a pigeon, Aje the goddess of wealth in the guise of a hen, and some earth. He then gives the shell to his son, the god Obatala, instructing him to empty it into the marshes. When the hen and the pigeon are released they begin to scratch at the earth and to scatter it, thus forming the dry land.

Olodumare sends the chameleon to inspect the result of the earth-forming, but the chameleon reports back that the land is not yet firm enough. More earth is scattered. When the chamaeleon, carefully treading the ground, confirms that it is solid enough Olodumare engenders the trees. The first tree to grow upon this newly formed earth is the coconut palm from which Obatala makes palm wine and promptly falls into a drunken stupor, much to the chagrin of Olodumare. Then comes the oil palm to provide food and the kola nut tree.

Olodumare now provides Oduduwa with a bag containing millet and other seed which she is to sow on the earth to produce crops. The earth is now in a fit condition for him to visit, so he descends and holds the first council of gods beneath an old palm tree in the place which is to become the holy city of the Yoruba people, Ile-Ife.

The next task for the creator god is to fashion humankind. He makes sixteen beings, eight male and eight female, equating to the sixteen great gods; he moulds them from clay and breathes life into them. Then he sends the ancestors of the Yoruba people to Ile-Ife to propagate the tribe.

Obatala realizes that the earth needs light, so he first turns a fallen iroko tree into solid gold and then commands the blacksmith of heaven to fashion from it a jar and a boat. A slave then sails the boat with its golden jar up to the top of the sky in the east and down again on the other side in the west. The moon is made from flintstone like a flat disc and sent likewise into the night sky, slowly turning so that sometimes it shows its full disc and sometimes only the curved edge.

To the god of justice, Orunmila, Olodumare gives the responsibility of apportioning the fate of every human being and of acting as intercessor between gods and men through the power of oracles.

ON THE ORIGIN OF THE WORLD

CULTURE OF ORIGIN: gnostic Christian

PROVENANCE: the text is contained in tractates II,5 and XIII,2 of the twelve codices discovered in 1945 at Nag Hammadi in Upper Egypt, where they were buried circa 400 AD [Coptic Museum, Cairo]. The manuscript, written in Coptic, is considered to be a translation from an earlier Greek work. It utilizes various traditions, only some of which are gnostic. Fragments of the myth are known from a separate Coptic manuscript source. Authorship is unknown and the title has been assigned in modern times. The work may have been designed to attract devotees to a particular brand of ideas in gnostic cosmogony (see also *The Hypostasis of the Archons*, page 34, and *Genesis*, page 45). The writer provides a brief didactic preface, indicating that he is about to explain the origin of Chaos.

Among the immortal beings, Pistis (faith) engenders a likeness of herself, Sophia (wisdom), which appears as the primordial light acting as a veil to separate the cosmos from that which lies beyond. Outside the eternal realm of light is a force, the limitless Chaos, described as a shadow which rules over a dark abyss containing the primordial waters. The shadow realizes that something mightier than itself (Pistis) exists, so it engenders from itself another force, jealousy, like an aborted child without a spirit.

Pistis is disturbed at these developments, but she decides that to control the spiritless thing she must give it substance. She makes it as a likeness of herself and she sets it to rule over matter as the primordial authority which she calls Yaldabaoth. It, however, now seems to recognize Pistis only as a reflection of its own omnipotence and assumes it is truly alone. It creates heaven and earth from the waters and then engenders the seven authorities, androgynous clones of itself, to rule over seven heavens of Chaos.

When Pistis/Sophia sees how arrogant Yaldabaoth has become she reveals herself in the light and chides him, calling him Samael (Blind God). Sabaoth, one of the seven androgynous offspring, perceives the evil in his father and turns to Pistis/Sophia. In reward for his loyalty to her she elevates him to champion new forces which have become ranged against Chaos. There follows a cosmic war in which Sabaoth, with forces of archangels, triumphs and is set to rule over Chaos from a new position of power in the seventh heaven. Pistis also sends her daughter Zoe (life) to teach him of the eighth and highest heaven.

Sabaoth builds a palace containing a great throne and creates a multitude of lesser gods (angels). Pistis/Sophia sets Sabaoth on her right (justice) and Yaldabaoth on her left (evil). Yaldaboath, who is also the embodiment of jealousy, is angry that his son has greater authority than he, so he engenders Death and sets it to rule over the sixth heaven. But he becomes ashamed when he perceives the great light and finally realizes Pistis/Sophia's immense power.

At this juncture another androgynous being appears, Eros, who introduces sexuality to the cosmos. Two trees, a fig and a pomegranate (the Tree of Life and the Tree of Knowledge) spring up on earth, followed by all the other vegetation as Sabaoth creates Paradise. Sophia, on her part, makes the stars of heaven and six more eternal realms are formed: ruled by archangels, these are better than the heavens of Chaos ruled by the cloned authorities of Yaldabaoth.

Zoe is instructed to fashion human life on earth, so she creates an immortal being in the likeness of her mother, calling her Eve. To counter this development the authorities of Chaos now cast their semen on the earth and fashion a man, Adam, but he has no spirit, so they abandon him. Eve, however, breathes life into him and commands him to come alive. The authorities are now deeply concerned because they have become aware that Eve is identical to the force which first appeared to Yaldabaoth in the light. They plan, therefore, to impregnate Eve, defiling her immortality, so that she can no longer return to the light. They will then make Adam sleep and give him the impression that Eve has been formed from his rib. But Eve is not to be outdone. She makes a mortal likeness of herself, leaves it beside Adam and merges her true self forever with the Tree of Knowledge.

Recognizing the power of Pistis/Sophia, the authorities become distraught, but when they recover their senses they are deluded into the belief that the mortal replica is actually the immortal Eve, so they impregnate her through the agency of Adam. As Adam and Eve mate the authorities watch with satisfaction, fondly imagining that the offspring are their own likeness, lacking in knowledge and thus ready to serve with blind obedience. But they come to realize the truth and know that real danger still lies in the immortal Eve should she impart her knowledge to the pair. They instruct Adam and Eve to eat the fruit of any of the trees in Paradise except that of the Tree of Knowledge. The couple are told that if they consume its fruit they will die.

Adam and Eve are persuaded to eat of the Tree of Knowledge by 'the wisest of creatures', the instructor, and thus they gain knowledge and, with it, a sober awareness of their own mortality. Too late the

authorities discover that Adam has become like themselves, understanding the difference between light and darkness. All that they can
do is impotently to curse the instructor, the woman, the man, their
offspring and the land itself. They are, however, further alarmed that
in his new state of awareness Adam may eat the fruit of the Tree of
Life, become immortal and denounce them. So they throw the pair
out of Paradise and set their terrifying guardians, the *cherubim*, around
the Tree of Life.

Sophia is enraged when she discovers what the authorities have
done and she chases them from the heavens of Chaos, hurling them to
earth, where they can exist only as demons. But still their powers
continue as they create a retinue of spirits to lead mankind into evil
ways.

The epic creation myth ends with a series of homilies on the future
course of the errant human race as it steers towards the final
apocalypse.

OWIOT AND CHINIGCHINICH

CULTURE OF ORIGIN: native American – Californian (Acagchemem mountain
  tribes) [San Juan Capistrano, California]
PROVENANCE: recorded from an oral tradition in an extract titled *Chinigchinich; A Historical Account of the Origin, Customs, and Traditions of the Indians
  at the Missionary Establishment of St Juan Capistrano, Alta California, called the
  Acagchemem Nation* by G. Boscana. *Life in California* A. Robinson. New
  York, 1846. See also *Nocuma and Owiot*, page 58.

In the beginning there exist two sibling beings, a brother, Heaven,
living above, and a sister, Earth, living below. This pair engender
matter, producing earth and sand, followed by rocks and stones,
trees, grass and herbs. When these things are made they create all the
animals and, finally, they fashion a supreme being, the father of the
human tribe, whose name is Owiot (Dominator).

After a time Owiot becomes old and infirm and his spirit children
decide to kill him because he is too aged to rule properly. They give
him poison and he staggers down to the seashore where his mother,
Earth, mixes him an antidote in a shell and sets it in the sun to brew.
The spirit, Coyote, picks up the aroma and upsets the potion so that
Owiot dies, whereupon his children build a great funeral pyre,
placing his corpse on top. At the last moment Coyote jumps on,
claiming that he wants to die too. This turns out to be a ruse: Coyote
tears out a piece of Owiot's flesh, eats it and runs away.

The celestial children are now faced with finding food instead of the
clay which they have eaten traditionally. As they debate, another

spirit appears, naming himself Chinigchinich and announcing that he is greater than Owiot. He tells the children that he intends to create mankind to do the spirits' bidding while the spirits, for their part, will provide a bountiful natural world. So Chingchinich creates the native American race from the clay of a lake.

THE CREATION OF THE WORLD BY PAN GU (P'AN KU)

CULTURE OF ORIGIN: Chinese Daoist (Taoist)

PROVENANCE: recorded in various texts and art from an oral tradition which may be derived from a foreign source and probably originates at a comparatively late date. The earliest version of the myth is alleged to have come from the Daoist writer Ko Hung in the fourth century AD; he may have adapted a south-east Asian story. The first definitive copy, however, is contained in the eleventh-century Wai Zhi records.

The myth is unusual in that none of the expected Chinese mythological personalities are present. Pan Gu himself is depicted as a dwarfish man wearing either a leaf skirt or a bearskin. The story is part of the staple fare of Chinese creation mythology and it is coloured by the fact that, at the time of its composition, the Chinese had an impressive grasp of cosmogony and astronomy. They were aware of the approximate size of the earth, that it is round, and that it is tilted – a phenomenon explained in the Shan Hai Zhing (Book of Mountains and Rivers) written in about the third century BC.

It should be noted that the anglicized equivalents of Chinese characters vary considerably in transliteration. The official Chinese Pinyin system is applied here and is followed, where appropriate, in brackets, by the more generally encountered Wade-Giles system.

Pan Gu is the mythical embodiment of the universe. He engenders himself within a cosmic egg floating in the formless dark void of chaos. Over a period of 18,000 years, Pan Gu grows within his dark cocoon at a rate of six feet a day, chiselling out the structure of the universe as his frame expands until, one day, he smashes the eggshell and light floods in, dividing heaven and earth. To keep these two primordial elements apart, Pan Gu pushes the heaven with his head and the earth with his feet.

His task of cosmic creation complete, Pan Gu has grown old and is close to death, but his body is destined to fashion the very matrix of the universe. His head becomes the mountains, his teeth and bones are rocks, his eyes are the sun and moon. From his breath are created the winds and in his beard shine the stars. His flesh is the soil, his blood the waters of the earth and his limbs the four quarters. From his hair grows the greenery nourished by the rain of his sweat. Finally from the lice which run over his body he engenders the human race and with that he completes his task.

Pan Gu now realizes that he needs a suitable mortal carrier for his spirit, so he searches until he finds a hermit of great virtue, who is both unsullied and hermaphrodite. Each day the hermit climbs to the mountain peaks to breathe in the strength of the sun and moon. Pan Gu waits until the hermit takes a deep breath and swiftly enters his body in the form of a ray of light. His spirit lives within the hermit for twelve years and then emerges as a child who takes the name Yuan-Shih T'ien Wang (see also *The Battle of Mu*, page 189).

According to the *Shan Hai Zhing* text (see above), the demon Kung Kung attempts to destroy the world by shifting the mountain of Bu Zhou Shan (part of a range in north-western China). He does no more serious damage than to dislodge the sky, but his endeavour accounts for the fact that the pole star does not rest directly overhead in the night sky.

NOTE: in separate mythology, the creation of mankind is left to the goddess Nu Gua.

PEMBA

CULTURE OF ORIGIN: Bambara (Mali, West Africa)
PROVENANCE: recorded from oral tradition

Pemba, the creator being, is present before there is anything other than the great emptiness, the *fu*. Turning himself into the seed of a white acacia, he descends to the earth and grows into a great tree. From the wood Pemba engenders humankind, first the souls and then the bodies. In the first instance the primal woman bears a tail and a snout and, in this form, she gives birth to all the forebears of the animals in the world.

The next deity to descend to earth is Faro, the god of sweet water. He comes after a long drought when most of the living things of the earth perish and he promises to fill the lakes and rivers if the people of the earth will remember that water is a sacred thing and must be revered always. Faro does all that he can to help the human race, including giving the boon of fertility to women but working against him is the evil spirit of the hot dry wind from the desert, Teliko. Faro knows that Teliko possesses a fatal weakness in that he is vulnerable if he crosses a river, so Faro waits until Teliko is caught off guard and when this eventually happens, uses the current to hurl him against a rock.

Freed from the evil of his rival, Faro now proceeds to create order and discipline in the living world. He fixes the length of days, the points of the compass and creates seven heavens above the earth, the first of which is the heaven of clouds and the second the heaven of the clear sky above. The third heaven is black and the final resting place of the soul. In the fourth and fifth Faro keeps his ledgers and pronounces judgement against wrongdoers. The sixth heaven is where all the secret things are kept and the seventh is where Faro lives and drags the sun up each morning on a rope.

THE CREATION OF THE PICKAXE

CULTURE OF ORIGIN: Mesopotamian – Sumerian
PROVENANCE: the earliest inscribed version of the myth dates from about 2000 BC, shortly after the collapse of the Third Dynasty at Ur, but it undoubtedly originates in an earlier oral tradition. The names of the deities appear on inscriptions dating from about 3500 BC.

The myth opens with an introductory passage describing the creation of the cosmos. To assist humankind in its labours, Enlil, god of the air, creates a pickaxe of gold and lapis lazuli, and a basket. He introduces the concept of labour in the fields and he directs power into the objects, passing them to the Anunnaki, the children and courtiers of An, the god of heaven. The Anunnaki in turn give the pickaxe and basket to the 'black-headed people' (i.e. the mortal race) and the value of the pickaxe is described in glowing terms.

PURUSA-SUKTA
(Hymn of Man)

CULTURE OF ORIGIN: Vedic and Brahmanic Hindu [India]
PROVENANCE: the *Rg Veda* collection of 1028 hymns (Vedas) composed in Sanskrit circa 1200 BC and based on an oral tradition which was in circulation among the Aryan immigrants to the subcontinent circa 1700–700 BC. Used as hymns of praise at the time of religious sacrifice, the Vedas provide less of a narrative than various comments on the mythology and it is from later works, including the Brahmanas (900–700 BC) and the Upanisads (circa 700 BC) that cosmogony is dealt with in more detail. In these the primeval being of the Vedas, Purusa, becomes Prajapati.

Purusa-Sukta is one of the later hymns of the *Rg Veda* and follows an ancient notion of dismemberment leading to the creation of life (see also *Isis and Osiris*, page 235).

The myth identifies a gigantic creator being, Purusa, with a thousand heads, a thousand eyes and a thousand feet. He is the immortal ruler, past, present and future, who pervades all matter. From him is engendered the active female principle of creation, Viraj, and paradoxically he is born by her. The great gods (it is not clear how they arise) engender Rudra, the god of sacred rites; Agni, the god of fire who fashions the semen of Purusa; and Vac, the goddess of speech. As he commits incest with his daughter, some of Purusa's semen falls upon the womb of the earth, the *yoni*, and becomes the Angirases, a class of beings who act as mediators between gods and men.

Through primordial sacrifice the creator being becomes the victim. The gods, the demi-gods and the sages dismember him and anoint him before spreading him upon the sacred grass and consigning him to the funeral pyre. From the fat of the sacrifice are created all living things, all inanimate things and all abstract things. From his mouth, arms, thighs and feet come the four *varnas* or classes of Vedic society.

The moon from his mind was born, and from his eyes the sun.
From his mouth came Indra and Agni,
From his breath was Vayu born.

As the gods and their attendants burn the being he becomes both the victim of sacrifice and the object of oblation. Thus is the first model laid down for ritual conduct.

The Brahmana texts elaborate further on the incest of Prajapati (Purusa) with his daughter Viraj (Rohini), introducing the primordial 'lord of creatures' as a stag while she takes the form of a doe. The gods see what Prajapati has done and wish to punish him, but they are unable to find a champion to administer appropriate justice so they assemble all that is fearsome in the cosmos and from it create the malevolent storm god Rudra.

As the stag ejaculates, his semen becomes a lake and is surrounded by the protecting flames of the fire god, Agni. As the semen ignites, the first part of it becomes Aditya (probably here applied as an epithet of Surya, the sun god); the second part becomes Bhrgu, the 'Crack of Fire'; and the third part becomes the six lesser sun gods, the Adityas. The charred wood becomes the black cattle and the red earth becomes the tawny cattle.

In another of the Brahmanas, it is the offspring of Prajapati who commit incest with one another to bring about the birth of Rudra.

QUETZALCOATL AND THE CREATION OF MANKIND

CULTURE OF ORIGIN: Aztec – classical Mesoamerican [Mexico]
PROVENANCE: probably worshipped circa 750 AD until 1500 AD and known
from tradition in pre–Columbian codices and detail on stone carvings.

Represented as a feathered hybrid, Quetzalcoatl (feathered serpent) is
a manifestation of the sun god Tezcatlipoca (smoking mirror) and
presides over the second of the five world ages represented by the sun
Ehecatl. Quetzalcoatl engenders mankind from drops of his own
blood, but he discovers that the people he has formed have nothing to
eat. So he turns himself into an ant and makes his way into the side of
a mountain to steal a single grain of maize which the ants have hidden.
From this seed, the crops which feed humanity are grown.

QUETZALCOATL AND TEZCATLIPOCA

CULTURE OF ORIGIN: Aztec (classical Mesoamerican) [Mexico]
PROVENANCE: probably worshipped circa 750 AD until 1500 AD and known
from traditions in pre–Columbian codices and detail on stone carvings.
The mythology of Quetzalcoatl is known primarily from the six-tiered
step–pyramid at Teotihuacan and from the vast pyramidal structure of
Cholula on the plain of Puebla.

Quetzalcoatl (feathered serpent), the ruler of the second of the five
world ages and creator god of the Aztecs, engages another aspect of
the sun god, the black Tezcatlipoca (smoking mirror), in a titanic
struggle which results in the creation and destruction of four of the
five world ages and their ruling suns which have existed since the
beginning of time. But the pair also work in concert to restore the
shattered universe and to initiate the fifth and present sun, Ollin.

The two deities pass through the toad–like body of the monstrous
creator goddess, Tlaltecuhtli, and split it into two halves to form
heaven and earth (see also *Enuma Eliš*, page 42). Tlaltecuhtli
swallows the sun each evening and vomits it up in the dawn of the
new day.

Quetzalcoatl descends into the underworld of Mictlan to obtain
from its rulers the bones and ashes of all the previous generations of
mankind. He intends to use these remains to create the inhabitants of
the fifth world, but he inadvertently drops the bones and smashes
them. When they are re-assembled, their haphazard nature accounts
for the differing statures of people. He also re-incarnates himself as an

avatar, Mixcoatl-Camaxtli, the so-called Red Tezcatlipoca who creates the boon of fire for mankind.

RANGINUI AND PAPATUANUKU

CULTURE OF ORIGIN: Polynesian Maori
PROVENANCE: recorded in recent times from oral traditions, including *The Ancient History of the Maoris, Mythology and Traditions* J. White 6 vols. Wellington, 1887.

Contrary to some popular opinion, the large wooden totems of Maori culture are not representations of Papatuanuku and other deities, but depictions of ancestors. The presence of the earth goddess is signified by small, inconspicuous carved stones or pieces of wood. The myth of a sky god and an earth mother, at first in eternal embrace until they are separated to create the space between heaven and earth, and thus provide room for living creatures to breathe and grow, is a universal one. Parallels are to be found in the Greek myth of Ouranos and Gaia (see *The Birth of the Gods of Olympus*, page 94), and in the Egyptian account of Geb and Nut (see *The Sun God of Heliopolis*, page 47).

In the darkness of chaos before the creation of the cosmos exist two primordial and self-created beings, Te Po, the personification of night, and Te Kore, the empty void. In the cosmic night they engender the prime parents of the Polynesian pantheon, Ranginui (father of the sky) and Papatuanuku (mother of the earth). A separate Polynesian tradition accounts the pair as being engendered from the androgynous being Vatea (Atea).

Ranginui is the sky father from whom comes the light, while Papatuanuku evolves to become the apotheosis of *papa*, the earth. The pair begin a period of sexual intercourse, intended to last for eternity, during which the pantheon of deities is conceived. Their children, however, find that the space between the two bodies, earth and sky, is becoming increasingly congested and decide to attempt to separate their parents. All their efforts seem destined to failure. One of the children, Tumatauenga, the god of war, elects to slaughter Ranginui and Papatuanuku, thus solving the problem, but his siblings disagree and he is relegated to responsibility for mankind (*tangata*). In response Tumatauenga gives the human (Maori) race his lust for warfare and violence.

It is left to Tanemahuta, the god of forests and subsequently of light, to offer a more pragmatic solution. He uses the great trees to lift Ranginui off Papatuanuku and to support the sky for ever more, even though the sky god complains bitterly about his forcible separation from his consort. Light spreads over the earth and all the creatures, once concealed between the bodies of the prime parents, begin to grow and multiply.

THE SWAHILI CREATION (1)

CULTURE OF ORIGIN: Swahili [Kenya, East Africa]
PROVENANCE: recorded from oral tradition. The myth has clearly originated
   as a local tribal tradition, but is typical of many which have been
   adulterated severely under Christian missionary influence.

One day the creator god decides that light is needed in the dark void.
When he has engendered the light he takes the brightest part of it in
the palm of his hand and from it he squeezes the souls of angels and
humankind alike. Now the god creates the sky as a roof which he
spreads beneath the light. Curtains are drawn across it at night with
tiny holes in them through which the light shines as stars.

   The creator sits, invisible, on a throne beneath which is a heavenly
tree on whose leaves are inscribed the names of every living person.
When a leaf falls, the person dies. God also possesses an emerald tablet
on which the divine law is written by an angel who inscribes the tablet
with white ink. All of mankind's activities, good and bad, are entered
on to the tablet and are examined when the angel of death comes and a
leaf falls.

THE SWAHILI CREATION (2)

CULTURE OF ORIGIN: Swahili [Kenya, East Africa]
PROVENANCE: recorded from oral tradition, from a different part of the same
   tribal area as the previous entry. The original form of the myth has been
   lost. It shares themes common to many other creation accounts, but in its
   present state it has been subject to heavy Christian influence.

The creator god lives in the dark and empty void filled only by the
primeval waters until, one day, he decides to bring light into the
world which he fashions into all the beautiful colours of the rainbow.
Having created light he takes some of it and engenders the souls of
humankind – first the souls of shamans, holy men, transparent and
luminous angels, prophets, and finally the souls of ordinary people.

   The god now builds the seven fundamental structures of the world.
First he makes the canopy, Arishi, which stretches over the Kurusi
throne upon which he rests. He makes a giant quill reaching between
earth and sky which will write the destiny of mankind day and night
for all eternity. He fashions the trumpet which will announce the end
of the world and the day of judgement. Finally he builds the paradise
garden to which the souls of the righteous will pass, and the hell fire in
which the wicked will be punished. Beneath the throne grows a
mighty cedar tree on whose leaves the names of every soul is written.
When a future human being (for mankind has not yet been created) is

destined to die, the angel of death will read the name and descend to earth to collect the soul. The leaf bearing the name will then fall from the tree.

The time has come for the god to fashion the earth itself from the primeval waters. He makes the sun which rises and travels across the water each day. The heat of its rays begins to evaporate the water, creating clouds and exposing the dry land. First the continents are revealed and then the smaller and smaller islands. The land rests on the back of a huge bull which stands upon the back of a fish swimming eternally in the ocean.

Greenery springs up and forests are formed. As the sun descends to the western horizon the god lights the night sky with little lamps and commands a cockerel to stand in the heavens and to crow when it is time for the sun to emerge once more. He makes all the animals and finally he creates humankind, instilling into each mortal frame one of the souls he has fashioned from the primordial light.

TANEMAHUTA

CULTURE OF ORIGIN: Polynesian – Maori
PROVENANCE: recorded in recent times from oral traditions including *The Ancient History of the Maoris, Mythology and Traditions* J. White 6 vols. Wellington 1887.

Spellings of the name of the principal character in Polynesian mythology vary. His Maori name is usually shortened to Tane but, in Hawaii, it becomes modified to Kane.

Tanemahuta is born of the prime parents Ranginui (heaven) and Papatuanuku (earth). One of his brothers, Tumatauenga, suggests that the only way of separating heaven and earth to create space is to slaughter the prime parents, but Tanemahuta proposes the more pragmatic course of merely forcing them apart. This he does using the great trees as props and so he becomes the god of light. He searches for a wife but because, with the exception of his mother, all the gods of creation are male, his quest is in vain. So Tanemahuta creates a woman out of the red earth and breathes life into her; she becomes Hine-Ahu-One (maiden formed of the earth). They have a child called Hine-Ata-Uira (daughter of the sparkling dawn) who descends into the underworld where she takes the new name of Hine-Nui-Te-Po (great woman of the night), the goddess of death with eyes like jade, seaweed hair and the teeth of a shark.

In a separate myth, it is Hine-Nui-Te-Po who becomes the consort of Tanemahuta and it is to her dark kingdom that he descends at dusk at the close of each day.

TANGAROA AND THE CREATION OF THE WORLD

CULTURE OF ORIGIN: Polynesian – Maori

PROVENANCE: recorded in recent times from oral traditions including *The Ancient History of the Maoris, Mythology and Traditions* J. White 6 vols. Wellington 1887.

Contrary to some popular opinion, the large wooden totems of Maori culture are not representations of deities but depictions of ancestors. The presence of the gods is signified by small, inconspicuous carved stones or pieces of wood.

The names given to any one deity vary in their spelling throughout Polynesia, so that while the Maori tradition knows him as Tangaroa, in Tonga he becomes Tangaloa, in Samoa, Tagaloa and in Tahiti, Ta'aroa. The name alters more obviously in Hawaii and becomes Kanaloa. Tangaroa is a creator god whose task of fashioning the world and mankind varies according to different cultural origins.

Vatea, the moon god, marries the earth goddess, Papatuanuku, who swells so much with the waters trapped inside her body that she bursts. She liberates two sons, Tangaroa, the god of the ocean, and his brother, Rongomatane, the god of agriculture (who may be one and the same as the god Maui) as the first of five siblings. Tangaroa becomes responsible for the oceans and the creatures which swim in them. So vast is his stature that he only breathes twice a day, which is why the tide ebbs and flows. Tangaroa then sets about the task of creating land from the ocean. In Hawaiian mythology Kanaloa takes the form of a seabird flying over the primeval waters which lays an egg that floats upon the surface and then breaks open; from its two halves the earth and sky are created. When he has created dry land, Tangaroa engenders Tanemahuta, the god of light and forests, whose consort is Hine-Ahu-One, so that there can be night and day.

Tanemahuta is also, in parallel mythology, described as the offspring of Ranginui and Papatuanuku. In Tahitian tradition he has a daughter, Hina, the moon goddess, who lives in one of its dark spots, a grove of trees that she once carried from earth in a canoe and planted. A separate Tahitian tradition tells that Ta'aroa lives in and fashions the world from inside the gigantic shell of a mussel which rests in the primeval waters. In all versions of the Tangaroa myth the living creatures of the earth, including mankind, emerge from inside his vast body.

The myth of creation in the Marquesas varies in that Tanaoa is a primordial being who lives in the perpetual darkness of night until he engenders the supreme being, Atea (in the Hervey Islands, Atea is born of the primordial mother Vari-Ma-Te-Takere inside a giant coconut which is the cosmos). Atea is perceived as 'space' and through him emerges the female light of dawn, Atanua. She and Atea marry and from their union comes the first man, Tu-Mea, although in the new and bustling cosmos Atea is consigned to the darkness and silence of the depths of the ocean.

TECCIZTECATL AND NANAHUATL

CULTURE OF ORIGIN: Aztec (classical Mesoamerican) [Mexico]
PROVENANCE: probably worshipped circa 750 AD until 1500 AD and known from tradition in pre-Columbian codices and detail on stone carvings.

On the fifth day of the creation of the fifth, and present, world age, the gods sit in assembly to elect a new sun god. Tecciztecatl, the son of the rain god Tlaloc, and Nanahuatl, the son of the sun god Quetzalcoatl, are considered to be the main contenders, but the two youths are of contrasting character. Tecciztecatl possesses great wealth but is of cowardly disposition, while Nanahuatl, though impoverished and sickly, shows great courage. According to different traditions both either cremate themselves or are thrown into a sacrificial fire by their respective fathers as a sacrifice for the benefit of mankind. The heart of Nanahuatl, representing courage and light, ascends to become the new sun, Atl, while that of Tecciztecatl becomes the moon.

The creator goddess Cihuacoatl-Quilaztli employs a magical vessel in which she grinds the bone fragments obtained from previous world ages of mankind into a powder. The gods then collectively commit self-sacrifice, allowing their blood to drip into the vessel and from the resulting mix the human race of the fifth sun is formed.

TIKI AND HINE

CULTURE OF ORIGIN: Polynesian (including Maori and others)
PROVENANCE: recorded in recent times from oral traditions including *The Ancient History of the Maoris, Mythology and Traditions* J. White 6 vols. Wellington 1887.

The myth of the first man and woman on earth has, to an extent, been Christianized in Polynesian tradition, but it is still possible to discern original strands. The names vary throughout the Polynesian islands but the underlying mythological theme remains constant.

In Maori tradition, Tiki, the first mortal man, who is also a demi-god, is created by the god Tumatauenga. He lives a solitary existence until he discovers a woman swimming in a lake. She is Hine, the first woman, who seduces Tiki with her feminine charms and, after a lustful courtship, becomes his wife.

The Hawaiian myth of 'Adam and Eve' is focused on Kane as the first mortal. Like Tiki, he wanders the earth in solitude until he asks the earth mother Papatuanuku for someone to keep him company. She responds by engendering first the great trees, then the other plants, and populating the forest with birds of brilliant plumage. Kane is still lonely, however, and he persists in his request for a companion in his own image. Papatuanuku tells him to fashion a likeness of himself from the mud, but to omit sculpting any genitals on to the model. He must then lie down beside the form and embrace it. Kane does as he has been instructed and the clay figure comes to life in his arms.

In Samoan tradition Tuli, the bird-like son of the god of the ocean, Tagaloa, alights upon a rock in the primeval ocean, the only existing dry land, where two grubs appear in the grass. These grow into a man and a woman, though at first they are without spirit. Tagaloa then orders the rocks to be split so as to form more islands and into the mortal forms he injects Heart, Will, Thought and finally Spirit. They become alive and produce four children, two boys and two girls.

TONACATECUHTLI AND TONACACIHUATL

CULTURE OF ORIGIN: Aztec (classical Mesoamerican) [Mexico]
PROVENANCE: probably worshipped circa 750 AD until 1500 AD and known from myths in pre-Columbian codices and detail on stone carvings. The tradition of the four deities supporting heaven is narrated in the codices *Borgia* and *Vaticanus B*. The previous world ages are represented on the Stone of the Four Suns in the Yale Peabody Museum.

In the primordial void, the being Tonacatecuhtli (Lord of our Flesh) engenders himself and combines with the female principle Tonacacihuatl. Between them they fashion the thirteenth heaven in which they reside for all eternity and then they proceed to fashion the rest of the Aztec pantheon (in a separate mythological account Tonacatecuhtli rules the sixth of the thirteen heavens). They begin by creating the sun god Tezcatlipoca, who brings light into the cosmos, and from him all other deities stem. It is he who rules the first period of the world.

Three world ages each lasting for 2028 heavenly years (a celestial year being fifty-two terrestrial years) are represented by the sun deities Ocelotl, Ehecatl and Quiahuitl, and are presided over respectively by the gods Tezcatlipoca, Quetzalcoatl and Tlaloc. The first age is populated by a race of giants and ends when a new race of huge and ferocious jaguars devours them. The second ends in a destruction caused by hurricanes when all the inhabitants are turned into monkeys

The third ends with a great fiery rain in which the population is transformed into dogs, turkeys and butterflies.

The fourth world age is represented by the sun deity Atl and is presided over by the god Chalchiuhtlicue. It ends with a cataclysmic destruction caused by a deluge during which all the human population is turned into fish. Tonacatecuhtli drives four great channels through the centre of the earth to drain away the flood waters and his four sons, aided by four unnamed beings, raise the sky which has collapsed; they prop it up on great trees created by Tezcatlipoca and Quetzalcoatl at the four cardinal points. Alternatively the heaven is supported by deities, including the ruler of the twelfth of the thirteen heavens, Tlahuizcalpantecuhtli (lord of the dawn), in the east; the ruler of the ninth heaven, Ehecatl-Quetzalcoatl, in the west; the ruler of the sixth heaven, Mictlantecuhtli, in the south; and Chalchiuhtlicue in the north.

The new fifth world age represented by the sun god Ollin and destined to end in a cataclysmic earthquake is presided over by the creator god Tonatiuh (soaring eagle).

TRIVIKRAMA
(The Three Steps of Višnu)

CULTURE OF ORIGIN: Vedic, Brahmanic and Puranic Hindu [India]
PROVENANCE: the *Rg Veda* collection of 1028 hymns (Vedas) composed in Sanskrit circa 1200 BC and based on an oral tradition which was in circulation among the Aryan immigrants to the subcontinent circa 1700–700 BC. The Vedas were used as hymns of praise at the time of religious sacrifice. The myth of Vamana is elaborated in the later *Satapatha Brahmana*, composed circa 900–700 BC and in the *Vayu Purana* (circa 350 AD).

Ten major incarnations, or *avataras*, of Višnu are conventionally understood and each of these is explained by its own myth. In making three giant strides Višnu is seen to be separating the realms of the cosmos by propping them apart. While the first two separate earth and sky the third step is regarded as symbolic of Višnu himself, the embodiment of 'all creatures'.

Višnu appears in his fifth incarnation as Vamana, a dwarf, symbolizing the puny state of mankind set against the vastness of the cosmos. He has taken this guise in order to trick Bali, the demonic son of the sun god Virocana, whose tyrannical dominion over the world has become a serious threat. To restore equilibrium Vamana requests of Bali a plot of land on which he may meditate. The area of ground is to be a modest one, three paces wide.

Bali is deceived and grants the dwarf's request, upon which Višnu returns to his full stature. With his first stride he demarcates and separates the earth and with his second the heaven. The third step separates the living world of creatures. An alternative tradition suggests that Višnu resists taking a third step which would claim the underworld and, instead, binds Bali with ropes, sending him and his kind to be its rulers.

VARI-MA-TE-TAKERE

CULTURE OF ORIGIN: Polynesian – Cook Islands and Hervey Islands
PROVENANCE: recorded in recent times from oral traditions

Vari-Ma-Te-Takere (woman in the very beginning) is the primordial female being who lives in the cramped space at the very bottom of the world coconut or egg which rests in the land of Te-Enua-Te-Ki (the land of eternal silence) in the depths of the primeval ocean. So restricted is her living space that she is obliged to sit with her knees touching her chin.

Vari-Ma-Te-Takere engenders six children from her own body, three of whom she plucks from her left side and three from her right. The first of these offspring is Avatea (Vatea), the first man on earth, who is also perceived as a moon god. The primordial mother plucks him from her left side and when he grows he divides vertically into a hybrid being; his left side is fish-like but his right side is human. Although he is born in the bottom of the world coconut Avatea ascends and finds a place at the opening of the upper world where he is given the earth to live upon, a place called 'Under the Bright Moon'.

The second child, taken from the right side, is Tinirau, the younger brother of Avatea, who becomes the god responsible for fish. His home is immediately beneath that of Avatea, on the sacred island of Motu-Tapu, where he looks after all the different kinds of fish in great ponds. Like his older brother he develops in the form of a fish-man, his left side being in the form of a sprat.

The mother goddess's third child, plucked from her left side, is Tango, who lives in Enua-Kura, the land of the red parrot feather, immediately below that of Tinirau. The fourth, Tumuteanaoa (echo) comes from the right and lives in the land of hollow grey rocks, Te-Parai-Tea.

Vari-Ma-Te-Takere's fifth child, coming from the left of her body, is Raka (trouble), who makes his home in the deep ocean. His mother also gives him a birthday gift of a great bag containing the winds, which become his foster-children. Each of these is provided with a hole at the edge of the horizon through which it may blow. In spite of his name, Raka is also imbued with knowledge of things which help mankind and which he passes on to the people of the earth.

The sixth and last child, born from the right side, is Tu-Metua (stick-by-parent). He elects to stay with his mother in her confined space at the bottom of the world coconut where he lives, like her, in perpetual silence.

According to the Cook Island tradition, the second of the six offspring is the earth mother Papatuanuku, who becomes the consort of her brother Avatea.

ZULU CREATION – THE GREAT ONE

CULTURE OF ORIGIN: Zulu [Natal, South Africa]
PROVENANCE: oral tradition recorded by Wilhelm Bleek, Zululand, 1856.
    In some versions of the story the lizard is replaced by a hare, but the implication is that the chameleon is a wise and steady creature, while the lizard and the hare are reckless and unpredictable.

In the beginning, before there is anything, the Great One emerges from the dark void beneath the earth, bringing with him the sun and the moon which he places in the sky. He directs that the sun shall appear by day and the moon by night, each travelling their appointed paths.

When he has done this he creates the black Bantu people and provides them with all their needs – cattle, goats, sheep and dogs. He also engenders all the white people of the earth and all the wild animals which will populate it. Now he calls upon the services of Unwaba, the chameleon, and Intulo, the lizard. He sends Unwaba to the chief of the Bantu people with a message that the people on the earth will never die permanently, but will come back just as the moon does. Intulo is armed with a similar message, to make doubly sure that it gets through.

The two messengers set off but, while the chameleon treads his path slowly and carefully, the lizard scuttles along at great speed. Intulo thus reaches the people of the earth first. On the way, however, he has become confused about the message he is supposed to deliver and it is passed on in a significantly different form – everybody is destined to die forever! Meanwhile Unwaba the chameleon plods along, munching leaves as he goes. He eventually delivers the correct message, but it is too late. Once the word of the Great One has been uttered, even in error, it can never be rescinded so, as people and animals grow old, they begin to die.

Meanwhile the Great One directs that the white people will live near the sea and the black people will inhabit the hinterland. He begins to put people together in pairs – white man with white woman, Bantu man with Bantu woman – so that the different races of people begin to develop and prosper. He also directs that, while the black races will breed and tend domestic animals and will go hunting dressed in skins and armed with spears, the white people will wear clothes and go armed with guns.

Now the Great One emerges from his subterranean kingdom and rises up out of the reeds fringing the water. Through the seed of the Bantu forefathers he creates all the major tribes of Africa, including Zulu, Swazi, Tsonga, Xhosa and Basuto. He also creates all the minor tribal clans. He gives mankind the gift of water to drink and fire with which to cook. Women, he directs, will cultivate the soil, plant millet seed, fetch firewood, grind corn and cook, while men will cut down the forest trees, build homes and fashion tools for the women to use.

When a man wishes to take a wife he will pay her father the bride price in cattle and if he dies his younger brothers shall take his wives as their own to protect them from adulteration by other tribes. A man shall become wise in the breeding of cattle so that he may hand fine beasts over to his sons when he reaches the end of life.

MISCELLANEOUS

POLYNESIAN (MAORI): the primordial being Io, a deity to whom many epithets are given, lives alone in the immensity of the cosmos which stretches dark and empty above the primeval waters. He resides in the twelfth and highest heaven, Te-Toi-o-nga-Rangi. Through his own thoughts and the power of his word he fashions light, which interrupts the darkness to become the first day. He separates the earth and sky by raising up the latter, creates dry land from the waters and engenders the sun, the moon and the stars.

PAPUA NEW GUINEA: a turtle swims alone in the primeval waters before the land has been created. She becomes tired and begins to mound up the sand from the bed of the ocean until it breaks through the surface. When she has created enough land she lays eggs in a hole on the beach, two of which hatch to become the first people, Kerema-Apo and Ivi-Apo. The third and fourth eggs to hatch become coconut palms and the remaining eggs from the clutch give rise to all the other animals and plants which inhabit the earth.

PAPUA NEW GUINEA: the primordial mother goddess possesses fertility, but has no vagina. She meets with a male deity named Siambuka to whom she is attracted and explains her problem. In response he takes a splinter of bamboo and uses it to make an incision between her legs, after which he thrusts his penis into the wound and the goddess becomes pregnant with the living creatures of the earth.

PAPUA NEW GUINEA: the primordial being, Timbehes, lives alone in the dark world. She decides that she wants to bear children, but since she has no husband she is at a loss to know how to proceed. She takes a banana and inserts it into her vagina to make herself pregnant and she bears a son, Bangar. Using more bananas she engenders a family of offspring including a daughter, Sisianlik, but still she is not satisfied. She instructs Bangar and Sisianlik to lie together so that she may enjoy grandchildren and so the human race is begun.

HAWAIIAN: With his snout, Kamapua'a, the great cosmic boar of creation, pushes up vast mounds of the sand from the ocean floor to fashion dry land. He also digs wells for fresh water. With his war club he defends gods and mankind alike from their enemies and he falls in love with Pele, the goddess of fire. At first she spurns him, but when he threatens to shovel mud over all her fires and extinguish them, she aquiesces and they marry.

4

Myths of Birth

This section includes a disparate collection of myths which generally feature the birth of a god or demi-god, or of a mortal being the creation of whom is directly influenced by a god.

The curse of infertility particularly troubled the rulers of ancient kingdoms. For them, as is still often the case, the absence of a son and heir had serious and far-reaching implications for the succession of the dynastic line. Thus, in the Mesopotamian legend of Etana of Kiš, the preoccupation of the king involves a desperate search for the boon of fertility through the device of a magical plant. Just as there is imagined to be an elusive elixir of immortality, so a similar secret which will bring fertility is always tantalizingly just out of reach.

In many cases a mother goddess or fertility deity is closely involved in the tales of birth and in an interesting number of cases, from cultures as far removed as those of ancient Greece and modern central Africa, one finds that the birth of a deity does not occur by familiar natural means. Thus the goddess Athena springs, fully armed, from the forehead of Zeus, while the divine super-hero of Nkundo myth, Lianja, emerges in like manner from his mother's thigh. In such instances the normal processes of birth, infancy and adolescence are bypassed so that the newly born character is mature and ready to carry out his or her duties 'at once'. The birth process also tends to be cathartic and violent.

The implication is that deities cannot be born by the same process as that which allows a mortal child into the world. Were such beings to be delivered by normal means it would perhaps dilute their numinous character. Gods and goddesses are, nonetheless, perceived to procreate by sexual means, although very often the impregnation, like the birth, is marked by violence. There exist many cases in myth of goddesses whose pregnancy begins when they are raped by other deities or by demons. This violence does not occur throughout all cultures, however, and, at the opposite end of the spectrum, goddesses may be impregnated through something as unworldly and meta-physical as the consciousness of other deities. There is strong illustration of the latter theme in Hindu mythology.

In some instances the birth of a child presages the demise of an older deity, often the father and, perversely, it may be fiercely resisted by the senior god who believes his position is about to be usurped.

In any event gods and goddesses, it seems, have to be born by some means or other.

THE BIRTH OF ADONIS

CULTURE OF ORIGIN: classical Greek, but subsequently adopted into Roman culture

PROVENANCE: modelled on a Syrian oral tradition, the myth has provided rich subject material for several Greek authors. It closely parallels the much older Phrygian myth of *Attis and Kybele*, suggesting, in its later theme, a common source perhaps in the Mesopotamian tradition of the dying-and-rising god Dumuzi. Hesiod and Apolloduros both mention Adonis in passing. Adonis is the son, according to differing versions, of Phoenix and Alphesiboea (Hesiod); Kinyras and Metharme (Apolloduros); or Theias and Smyrna, who is also called Myrrha.

Through the agency of a nurse, Hippolyta, the goddess Aphrodite tricks Theias, son of the Babylonian king Belos, into committing incest with his daughter, Smyrna. Implicit in the myth is the sugges-tion that Smyrna develops a craving for illicit sexual encounter as a punishment for impiety towards Aphrodite. Alternative versions suggest that Smyrna, discovering the truth of her passion, tries to hang herself or that Theias is enraged when he realizes whom he has slept with and tries to stab Smyrna to death. Regardless of these variations, the gods rescue Smyrna by transforming her into a myrrh tree, which subsequently splits open to release her son, Adonis. When Aphrodite sees the child she is so struck by his beauty that she gives him into the foster care of the queen of the underworld, Persephone, who then refuses to return him. A compromise is reached whereby Adonis is destined to spend one third of each year with Persephone and the remaining two thirds with Aphrodite. The life of Adonis is, alas, cursed to an even greater extent because as a youth he is fatally gored by a wild boar and the river Adonis (now disappeared) flows red with his blood each year on the anniversary of his death. See also *Attis and Kybele*, page 224, and *Persephone and Demeter*, page 241.

THE BIRTH OF APOLLO AT DELOS

CULTURE OF ORIGIN: classical Greek, but subsequently adopted into Roman culture

PROVENANCE: recorded from oral traditions by the epic Greek poet Hesiod in the *Theogony* and the *Hymn to Apollo* during the eighth century BC.

Apollo is generally regarded as Zeus's favourite son, and the site of his temple at Delos is still visited.

The mother goddess Leto, daughter of the Titans Koeos and Phoebe, has been impregnated by Zeus and is carrying the unborn god Phoebus Apollo. She wanders all over Greece and the nearby islands of the Mediterranean and Aegean seeking a suitable birthplace, but she is constantly harassed by Hera, the wife of Zeus, who is jealous that Leto is to bear his most illustrious son. Thus Leto is rejected in one place after another out of fear of Hera's wrath and only on the impoverished and rocky island of Delos is she made welcome. She warns the inhabitants that Hera will offer them no favours, that their agriculture will never be prosperous and that if they build the temple to Apollo the pilgrims who will come from all over the world to offer sacrifice will have to be tended. Leto swears an oath, however, that the island of Delos will receive honour and renown above all others.

Leto is in labour for nine days and nights, surrounded by the other Olympian goddesses, with exception of Hera who remains, unforgiving, in Zeus's court. The messenger goddess Iris is sent to fetch Eileithyia, the goddess of birth, who is also a daughter of Zeus and Hera. Iris's instructions are to draw Eileithyia out of Hera's presence and to tempt her, with a massive golden necklace, to assist in Leto's labour.

When the birth goddess arrives on Delos, the final stages of labour commence and at the foot of a palm tree Leto gives birth to Apollo and his sister Artemis. Apollo is fed, from his first breath, on nectar and ambrosia and he takes from Zeus the divine symbols of the lyre and bow. As he grows to manhood he wanders far and wide and shrines are dedicated everywhere in his honour, but nowhere is his presence felt as strongly as in the great temple on Delos; the island becomes rich with the offerings of the pilgrims who come to honour Leto and her offspring.

THE BIRTH OF BAGISHT

CULTURE OF ORIGIN: Prasun Kafir [Hindukush]
PROVENANCE: oral traditions recorded chiefly by M. Elphinstone (1839); G. Morgenstierne (1951); G.S. Robertson (1896).

The myth focuses on the ambivalent relationship, which often exists in primitive societies, between gods and demons.

The fertility goddess Disani is engaged in milking her cows in a water meadow when a demon sneaks up on her and rapes her. When the infant she carries turns in her belly so that he is facing up the valley towards the sacred lakes of the gods, Disani's labour begins and she delivers a child imbued with great strength. It is Bagist, the god of the waters, and straightaway she places him in his domain of the river, having given him a blue tunic to wear.

COMPERT CON CULAINN
(the Birth of Cu Chulainn)

CULTURE OF ORIGIN: Celtic – Irish

PROVENANCE: recorded from oral traditions possibly as early as the eighth century AD by the chief bard of Ireland, Snechan Torpeist, in the *Book of Druimm Snechtai*. This is lost and no early copies have survived prior to the eleventh century. A more or less complete version is contained in *Leabhar ne h-Uidhre; Book of the Dun Cow*, compiled in the eleventh century by the Christian monk Mael Muire Mac Ceilechai [Royal Irish Academy].

The myth is known in two distinct versions, both of which are considered to have been corrupted by the Christian writers but which, in essence, tell the story of the birth of Ulster's most famous hero. Cu Chulainn is born to a mortal mother but with the ambivalent pedigree of a father from the otherworld, the god Lugh, and a mortal stepfather. He thus takes on the aspect of a demi-god in Irish mythology. Under modern convention the tale is classified as part of the Ulaid (Ulster), or Craobh Ruadh (Red Branch), Cycle of myths which, from a historical viewpoint, relate an ongoing conflict between the Ulaid clan(s) who lived in the Armagh region of what is now the Ulster province and others who were based further south in Connacht (Connaught).

In the oldest version of the myth the chieftains of Ulster and their king, Conchobhar Mac Nessa, have gathered at the royal seat of Emain Macha as a great flock of birds devastates the crops in the surrounding countryside. Deichtire, the daughter of a Druid, Cathbad (in some interpretations the sister of Conchobhar) is with the king as his charioteer. The birds start to fly overhead but, towards evening, three break away from the main flock and head for Bruig na Boinde.

During the night it snows heavily and the Ulstermen have to seek shelter at a small house. A drunken evening develops in the outside barn during which the host informs the king and his retinue that his wife is in labour. Deichtire goes to help in the midwifery and, as the housewife gives birth to a son, a mare belonging to the Ulstermen foals simultaneously with two colts. These are given to the newborn child as a gift and Deichtire nurses him.

The Ulstermen take the child and the colts back to Emain Macha. Some years later the youth falls ill and dies, and now Deichtire dreams that a stranger, Lugh, has impregnated her and that she is to bear a son of her own for whom the colts are destined. The boy is to be called Setanta. A rumour spreads, however, that Conchobhar has impregnated Deichtire during a bout of drinking and, to avoid scandal, he betroths her to Sualtaim Mac Roth.

Deichtire (in a clearly corrupted ending) kills the unborn child, sleeps with Sualtaim and bears him a son. In the conclusion of the more recent version she is carried off into the otherworld by the flock of birds on the eve of her wedding to Sualtaim. She is impregnated by the god Lugh and returns to Emain Macha with a baby boy, Setanta, who is then assumed to be the son of Sualtaim.

NOTE: the name Cu Chulainn, in either event, is an adoption from another episode in which Setanta kills the hound of Culann, the smith to Conchobhar, and agrees to guard Culann's house until another animal can be trained. Thus he takes on the title Cu Chulainn (the Hound of Culann).

THE BIRTH OF DIONYSOS

CULTURE OF ORIGIN: classical Greek, but subsequently adopted into Roman culture.

PROVENANCE: recorded from an oral tradition by Hesiod in the *Theogony* and in two separate *Hymns to Dionysos*. In Roman tradition the story is modified to accommodate the god Bacchus.

The daughter of Cadmos, Semele, is seduced by Zeus and she conceives a son. Because the sight of Zeus in his true form and at close quarters is too awful for a mortal to withstand, the leader of the gods always courts Semele in disguise. She begs him to reveal himself and he relents, but as he does so, in her sixth month of pregnancy, the lightning which flashes about his person strikes her down and she dies. Zeus wrenches the unborn foetus from her womb and implants it into his thigh, where it completes its gestation and is thus named Dionysos or 'twice born'.

Zeus's consort Hera is, as always, bitterly jealous of her husband's philandering and in order to circumvent her wrath, Zeus gives the child into the foster care of King Athamas of Thebes and his wife Ino, instructing them to dress Dionysos as a girl. Hera discovers the ruse, sending the foster parents mad, and Zeus now places the child in the care of the nymphs of Nysa, who disguise him as a kid until he grows to manhood. Even now Dionysos is not safe from Hera and she causes *him* to go mad, living as a demented vagrant until his sanity is restored by the Phrygian mother goddess Kybele.

ETANA OF KIŠ

CULTURE OF ORIGIN: Mesopotamian – Old Babylonian and Assyrian
PROVENANCE: the Old Babylonian version was discovered at two sites, Susa in Elam [modern Iran] and Tell Harmal [Iraq]. There is also a Middle Assyrian rendering known from Aššur during the second millennium BC. The version generally followed by modern scholars is that discovered in the royal library of Aššurbanipal at Nineveh, though this late text omits some sections of the story.

The length of the original myth is unknown, but in its existing form it appears to be incomplete in the sense that it is without a conclusive ending. Its authorship is thought attributable to Lu-Nanna, a scribe and advisor of Šulgi of Ur, who reigned over the Sumerian city state in southern Mesopotamia between 2150 and 2103 BC. It may well have stemmed from a much older orally transmitted tale local to Kiš, though the tutelary gods of the city play little or no part in the narrative. The only deity who takes an active role is Šamaš, the Babylonian-Akkadian sun god, who derives from Utu in the Sumerian pantheon. Ištar, listed as the tutelary goddess of Kiš, appears only indirectly.

The purist may argue that the story of Etana constitutes less of a myth than a legend, but it is so closely linked with the gods and man's quest for life that it must properly be included here. Etana was a one-time king of the city of Kiš and he is attested in the Sumerian King List. Of dubious historical authenticity, he is said to have lived during the heroic age of Sumer shortly after the flood, though any entries for this period are impossible to verify.

The myth opens with an explanation of the foundation of the city of Kiš by the great gods and their search for a potential ruler. There is then a significant gap in the text which resumes on a second tablet with an obscure and rambling dialogue between an eagle and a serpent. The pair live close by the royal throne and appear to be in competition with each other. Eventually the rivals swear by Šamaš a sacred oath of allegiance and set out, with good intentions, to live in harmony with each other. The trust is broken when the eagle transgresses by eating the serpent's brood. Šamaš, angered by the eagle's behaviour, instructs the serpent to place a wild bull in a pit as a lure for the bird, which is duly trapped and punished by Šamaš for its impiety by having its wings clipped.

At this juncture Etana enters; he is described as a devout and pious monarch but one whose consort is childless and barren. He prays to the sun god for help to provide him with a son and heir.

You have eaten, O Šamaš, of the fattest parts of my sheep;
O earth, you have drunk the blood of my lambs.
I have honoured the gods and revered the departed spirits.
The sailtu's [priests] have used up my incense,

The departed spirits from many sacrifices have used up my lambs.
O Lord, from your mouth may the commandment go forth.
Give me the plant of birth!

Etana is told that he must find the eagle trapped in its pit because it alone can reveal the whereabouts of the magical plant. This task Etana carries out and he teaches the eagle to fly once more. The eagle searches in vain for the plant of birth and eventually it suggests to Etana that they fly to the heavens to visit the goddess of fertility, Ištar.

Come, my friend, let me carry you up to the sky.
Let us meet with Ištar, the mistress of birth . . .
. . . put your arms over my sides,
Put your hands over the quills of my wings.

There follows a drawn-out and dreamlike sequence in the narrative, the sense of which is obscure, and the myth ends as the eagle and Etana climb higher and higher into the sky, finally passing through the gates of heaven in anticipation of their audience with Ištar.

The Etana myth is virtually the only one which scholars are agreed is identifiable in Mesopotamian art. The scene of Etana ascending to the heavens on the back of the eagle is found engraved on to cylinder seals of the Akkadian period. See also *Ganymedes*, page 232.

THE BIRTH OF GANEŠA

CULTURE OF ORIGIN: Puranic Hindu [India]
PROVENANCE: the myth appears in the *Brhaddharma Purana* (1250 AD). It constitutes one of a group of stories which focus on the dissatisfaction of the creator deities, Šiva and Parvati, concerning the birth of their children. These progeny are usually engendered or conceived by the one without the involvement of the other. In this account Ganeša is produced by Parvati alone and it is worth noting that in other myths she employs him as a guardian keeping Šiva away from her bed. Ganeša is one of the best loved of all Hindu deities, not least because of his personal misfortune. There develops an implicit sexual rivalry between Šiva and his 'son' which results in the decapitation of the child; he is restored with the elephant head by which he is most familiar in iconography.

Šiva and Parvati are the source of all life but only in so much as they are the *causes* of progeny rather than physical parents. Thus, in practice, Šiva has no son and heir. When Parvati points out this omission Šiva retorts that an offspring would serve no purpose:

'Daughter of the mountain, I have no death, and so I have no use for a son.
Where there is no disease, what need is there of medicinal herbs?'

Parvati nonetheless yearns for a child of her own and she gently encourages Šiva, telling him that once he has played his part he may leave the upbringing of the child wholly to her and be free to practise his contemplative life undisturbed. Šiva is infuriated and goes off in a temper, but when he sees how unhappy he has made Parvati he begins to relent. He teases her by making a rag-doll son from the material of her dress and, miraculously, when she holds it to her breast it takes life as a little boy.

Parvati offers the infant to Šiva who takes it and inspects it for flaws. Then the god recalls that, in the moments of primal creation, it was he who swallowed the deadly poison *halahala* to save mankind from its effects (see *Gods, Demons and the Ambrosia of Immortality*, page 142). Siva perceives therefore that his son is doomed and with a stroke of his hand he decapitates the child as its head is turned towards the north.

Parvati is striken with grief and a contrite Šiva attempts unsuccessfully to fix the head back on to the corpse. A heavenly voice advises him to restore the torso with the head of another individual who is also facing north at the time. Šiva therefore summons his bull-god attendant, Nandin, instructing him to search for a suitable donor. Nandin sets out upon his quest and when he comes across the great elephant of the weather god Indra, which happens to be facing northwards, he begins to hack off its head with his sword. Indra is outraged at this violation and engages Nandin in a ferocious fight, mounting the elephant and using it as a charger. Nandin, however, beats off the attack and completes his task of removing the elephant's head before returning with it to Šiva.

Šiva is delighted and places the head of the elephant upon the corpse of his child, who at once revives and becomes not unattractive in his curiously hybrid state, with a round benign face and a pot belly. The other gods are astonished at what has taken place and they bring gifts for the elephant child. The sages, for their part, give him the name Ganeša meaning 'ruler of hosts'. Anxious to make reparation concerning Indra's vehicle, Šiva tells him to cast his now headless elephant into the ocean, whence it will be restored and gain immortality.

THE BIRTH OF GISH

CULTURE OF ORIGIN: Prasun Kafir [Hindukush]
PROVENANCE: oral traditions recorded chiefly by M. Elphinstone (1839); G. Morgenstierne (1951); G.S. Robertson (1896)

In common with many myths of Asian origin, the gods have lived as mortal heroes in a once-upon-a-time age. The god of war, Gish, was not born of woman but created by the breath of the supreme god Imra. Nonetheless he subsequently fell in battle. The myth also illustrates the close relationship between gods and demons.

A demoness named Utr becomes pregnant and carries her child for eighteen months. During this time she can hear it talking in her belly and it instructs her to plant a walnut seed. When the seed grows it becomes a mighty tree with eighteen branches and only then is the infant born. It is the war god, Gish, who emerges fully grown and with some violence in that he breaks forcibly out of his mother's body. He stitches her belly with a steel needle and then gives her a magical potion which not only heals her completely but also endows her with wisdom.

Gish takes his place in the pantheon and his mother collects nuts from the walnut tree with which to feed his warriors. Gish's spear has magical properties which can move mountains or generate sustenance with equal ease.

KALI, ŠIVA AND ADISAKTI

CULTURE OF ORIGIN: Puranic Hindu [India]
PROVENANCE: the story appears in the *Skanda Purana* (700–1150 AD) under the general heading of myths associated with Parvati, who is depicted here in two of her conflicting aspects – as the brilliant corn goddess Uma/Gauri and as the dark goddess of death Kali.

The myth centres on the complex and often jealous love/hate relationship between Šiva and Parvati in which, as often happens, their sons become key players. The importance of asceticism in Hindu faith is also underlined.

Šiva observes that his body, with its crescentic moon symbol, is pale against the dark skin of Parvati.

'Your lithe form, which gleams darkly against my whiteness, is as a black serpent wrapped around a white sandalwood tree. You are as the darkness of night touched by the pale light of the moon.'

Parvati takes the remark as an insult and she rounds on Šiva, pointing out that she has always accepted him as he is and does not constantly list his faults. She threatens to abandon her earthly body through asceticism since all it brings her is criticism. Šiva tries to pacify her by explaining that the remark was made only in jest, but when she threatens to leave he accuses her of the coldness and hardness of the Himalaya. Again Parvati's anger is aroused and as she rushes away, Viraka, who is both her son and Šiva's attendant, tries to stop her. She explains to him gently that she is going to practise asceticism in the mountains so that her skin will become golden in colour (as Gauri). She also points out that Šiva is a philanderer and that Viraka should make sure that there is no impropriety in the bedroom while she is away.

Parvati leaves Viraka behind but she takes Ganeša, his elephant-headed brother, to be a guardian on her travels. She meets with the mountain goddess Kasumamodini and requests that she also keeps an eye on Šiva's bedroom. And so, high in the Himalaya, the goddess begins her time of asceticism, watched over by Ganeša.

Meanwhile the demon Adi, whose father was once vanquished by Šiva, enters Šiva's house through deception (in the guise of a snake) and then takes the form of Uma, a beautiful aspect of Parvati, placing sharpened nails inside 'his' vagina with the intention of slaughtering Šiva. Šiva, however, is suspicious and, realizing that the apparition is not the true aspect of his wife, he places a lethal weapon over his penis. As their bizarre intercourse begins, Adi screams and dies.

Parvati hears of what has happened and, in her rage at Šiva's infidelity, she curses Viraka to death for his lack of diligence. A ferocious lion is formed from her breath. The god Brahma visits her and she cries to him that she wishes no more than to be 'one' with Šiva. Brahma grants her wish and, from her body, comes an androgynous being with a dark blue skin and three eyes – a combined form of Parvati and Šiva – Kali, the goddess of death. Now, as her other and newly acquired aspect, Gauri, with skin the colour of gold, Parvati returns to Šiva. She discovers from Viraka that Adi entered the house disguised as a serpent and that, once the apparition of Uma appeared, Šiva was never deceived and only had intercourse out of desire to slay the demon. He then instructed that no woman was to be allowed inside except his true love, Parvati.

The goddess realizes that jealousy has clouded her reasoning and she reveals her true identity to Viraka, telling him that, while she cannot lift her curse upon him, he will be reincarnated as the bull-god Nandin and will return to become the new guardian of Šiva's door.

KRŠNA AND BALARAMA

CULTURE OF ORIGIN: Puranic Hindu [India]

PROVENANCE: the myth appears in the Puranic text *Harivamsa*, composed in about 450 AD. Kršna, as an adult, is a significant though not central character of the *Mahabharata* epic written between 300 BC and 300 AD, but his childhood is not related until the later period of the Puranas. Kršna is considered to be the eighth incarnation or *avatar* of Višnu.

Kamsa, the brother of the mother goddess Devaki, is of the belief that her eighth child will bring about his death. His first instinct is to kill Devaki but her consort, Vasudeva, begs for her life and Kamsa moderates his threat on the condition that all of Devaki's offspring are handed over. Kamsa slaughters the first six children and Devaki is made an effective prisoner in her own house.

Visnu learns of Kamsa's retribution and decides to intervene. He recalls that the six embryos which have apparently perished were once the six demon sons of Kalanemi. They were cursed by their great-grandfather, Hiranykasipu, whom they once served as ascetics, but renounced when they obtained the boon of immortality from Brahma. They are not dead, but asleep in the underworld. Višnu decides that he will place incarnations of himself within the womb of Devaki as the seventh and ninth offspring, Balarama and Kršna. He arranges with the goddess of death, Kali, that the eighth child will in fact be an incarnation of herself and though Kamsa will dash her against a stone, he cannot kill death. He will thus be deceived into believing that he has destroyed the eighth offspring. Višnu arranges that the seventh embryo to be carried by Devaki will be transferred, in the seventh month of pregnancy, to the womb of the minor goddess of fortune, Rohini. She will foster Balarama, and Kamsa will believe that Devaki has miscarried. Kršna, the ninth offspring, will also be removed from Devaki's womb and placed in that of Yasoda, the consort of Kamsa's cowherd Nanda, thus providing double insurance against Kamsa.

When the eighth child is born, a baby girl, Kamsa arranges for it to be slaughtered and the goddess rises from its corpse to heaven. There, as Kali, she utters sentence upon Kamsa. She will smash his body and drink his blood. He realizes that he has met with his own death.

THE BIRTH OF MAUI

CULTURE OF ORIGIN: Polynesian – Maori
PROVENANCE: recorded in recent times from oral traditions including *The Ancient History of the Maoris, Mythology and Traditions* J. White 6 vols. Wellington 1887.

Maui may be perceived as a Maori super-hero along the lines of the Mesopotamian Gilgameš.

Makea-Tutara is the god of the underworld whose consort is Taranga. They have several children of whom the fifth is born prematurely while Taranga is walking on the seashore. The child is still-born and in her sorrow Taranga wraps it in a shroud of her own hair and commits it to the sea. The body of the infant is taken to a place of

safety by the sea sprites, the Ponaturi, but a storm wrenches it loose
and it is cast back upon a shore where it is discovered by one of the
dead ancestors, Tama-Rangi. This spirit being restores the infant to
life, fostering him and teaching him the history of the Maori people.
Maui grows into a young man and then leaves his ancestor so that he
may seek out his earthly mother.

Maui finds Taranga in the village meeting house in the company of
his brothers. Unobserved, he takes his place with them and it is not
until he reminds his mother of the moment, long past, when she
threw him into the sea that she recognizes him. She is overjoyed to
find her youngest son alive, but the older siblings become jealous of
the attention he is receiving.

That night Maui sleeps in his mother's bed but, as the dawn breaks,
he finds the room empty. He goes in search of Taranga and discovers
her as she is about to enter the underworld to visit Makea-Tutara.
Taking the form of a wood pigeon he follows her beneath the ground,
where he finds his mother resting beneath a tree in the company of the
lord of the underworld. Makea-Tutara, delighted to meet his son,
dedicates him as a demi-god though he is unable to provide Maui with
complete immortality. Maui thus returns to the upper world, imbued
with special powers of magic but irrevocably mortal.

ENLIL, NINLIL AND THE BIRTH OF NANNA

CULTURE OF ORIGIN: Mesopotamian – Sumerian
PROVENANCE: the earliest inscribed version of the myth dates from about
2000 BC, shortly after the collapse of the Third Dynasty at Ur, but it
undoubtedly originates in an earlier oral tradition. The name Nanna
appears on inscriptions dating from about 3500 BC.

After an introductory passage extolling the virtues of the city of
Nippur, Ninlil, the goddess of the air and of grain, is instructed by her
mother, Ninsebargunnu, the barley goddess, on how to attract the
god Enlil in marriage.

At the pure river, O maid, at the pure river wash thyself . . .

Ninlil dutifully goes to the Euphrates and while she bathes she is
impregnated by Enlil, impersonating the waters of the sacred river, so
that she conceives the moon god Nanna. Enlil now leaves Nippur and
heads towards the netherworld, followed by Ninlil. In an enigmatic
section Enlil instructs the gatekeeper of the netherworld not to reveal
his whereabouts to Ninlil, but then Enlil himself assumes the role of

the keeper and, in this disguise, he carries out his own wishes, refusing to tell Ninlil where she can find him! She, however, reminds the man she believes to be the gatekeeper that although Enlil is his master she is also his queen.

Still disguised, Enlil impregnates Ninlil again and she conceives a second offspring, Meslamtaea, the aggressive aspect of the underworld god Nergal. For a third time, Enlil assumes a disguise as the 'man of river of the netherworld' and this time he fathers the netherworld god Ninazu on Ninlil. Finally Enlil begets a third underworld deity on Ninlil whose name, in the known version of the myth, is unintelligible. The story ends with a eulogy to Enlil as a fount of great abundance.

NSONGO AND LIANJA

CULTURE OF ORIGIN: Nkundo [Zaire, central Africa]
PROVENANCE: recorded from oral traditions.

The myth provides an illustration of the effects of Christian missionary influence on local traditions. There is little doubt that Lianja was once regarded as a god by people living in the Congo Basin, but today he has been relegated to the role of a super-hero in local folklore. The myth underscores the belief in reincarnation, since the spirit of the dead father enters the womb of the mother as the son is due to be born. Lianja I and his grandson Lianja II are destined to be born on the day their fathers die.

Queen Mbombe is heavily pregnant and she hears the child in her belly calling to her, 'The King is dead, long live the King!' The unborn infant commands that his mother prepare a suitable way for him to come into the world, since the time is now right. Mbombe replies that there is only one way for her son to be born, but the child argues that he is no ordinary commoner and therefore the manner of his birth must be dramatically different.

As he speaks, Mbombe's thigh begins to swell and bursts open. From the wound leaps a fully armed and handsome youth who immediately springs, like a bird, on to the roof of the house to survey his kingdom. At the same time his twin sister Nsongo emerges and flies upwards with him. She is destined to become his consort and together they fly down to the central square of the town, where once their father beat the sacred drum. There Lianja pronounces himself chief of the Nkundo people and introduces his sister with whom he will live as man and wife. The elders bow down, revering the miracle which has taken place.

After many years Lianja comes close to death and, as his spirit prepares to leave him, history repeats itself. At the moment of death the wife of his son, Likanda, gives birth to Lianja II.

THE BIRTH OF THE GODS OF OLYMPUS

CULTURE OF ORIGIN: classical Greek, but subsequently adopted into Roman culture

PROVENANCE: recorded by Hesiod, the epic Greek poet, during the eighth century BC in the *Theogony*.

The myth essentially relates a complex genealogy of the primordial beings and deities who arise in the beginnings of the Greek world. Most of them produce offspring with whom they then form incestuous relationships because of the general lack of available partners!

It should be noted that other accounts of the origins of the Greek pantheon offer slight variations in that, for example, Zeus may be accounted as the father of minor deities who in the *Theogony* are fathered by Ouranos or Pontos. Note also that some authors use Romanized spellings of names when e.g. Ouranos becomes Uranus and Kronos becomes Cronus.

In the beginning there exists only Chaos until the earth, Gaia, comes into being. From her all the races of immortal beings are destined to arise. Out of Chaos next emerges Erebos, the personification of the infernal shades, and Nyx, the night, his sister. Erebos and Nyx form an incestuous liaison and from their union come Aether, the god of light, and Hemera, the goddess of the day. Elsewhere in the *Theogony* account Nyx is also the mother of Thanatos (death), Somnus (sleep), Momos (blame), Nemesis (revenge) and the Hesperides (nymphs of the setting sun), who live in the west and guard the golden apples. Gaia then bears the Moirai (fates) – Clotho (the spinner who generates the thread of man's life), Lachesis (who assigns the destiny of man by casting lots) and Atropos (she who cannot be turned from the inevitability of death).

Gaia also engenders from within herself Ouranos (heaven), the hills, and Pontos (the raging sea) and with both of these latter offspring she enjoys an incestuous relationship.

> *And Earth first bare starry Heaven, equal to herself, to cover her on every side, and to be an ever-sure abiding place for the blessed gods.*

Through Ouranos, Gaia bears six pairs of children. Her sons are the Titans, the race from whom the Olympian pantheon is descended. These deities include Okeanos (god of the primal sea) and Tethys (goddess of the life in the seas); Koeos and Phoebe; Hyperion (primordial light) and Thea; Kreos and Eurybe, or Themis (law); Iapetos and Klymene, also known as Asia; Kronos and Rhea. Mnemosyne (memory) may also be accounted as one of the daughters of Ouranos and Gaia.

Next Ouranos fathers the Cyclopes (orb-eyed) and finally the Hecatoncheires. The Cyclopes, a trio of one-eyed storm deities, include Brontes (Thunder), Steropes (Lightning) and Arges (Thunderbolt), characterized by their great strength and manual dexterity. The monstrous Hecatoncheires – Cottus, Briareos and Gyes – each possess fifty heads and a hundred arms.

Ouranos imprisons all his offspring within the body of Gaia, where they live in terror of his power. Gaia is, however, determined to see them liberated and so she fashions from flint a great jagged sickle with which to castrate Ouranos.

> *And when each was born Ouranos hid them away in a secret place of Gaia and would not suffer them to come up into the light and he rejoiced in his evil. But Gaia, in distress, groaned and conceived a crafty and evil plan.*

Kronos, the youngest of the Titans, hates his father for the hardship Ouranos has inflicted on his children and so he agrees to carry out the task, slashing off Ouranos's manhood and hurling it into the sea, where its semen creates the goddess Aphrodite. But the drops of blood which fall on the earth give rise to still more frightful children, the Erinyes followed by the Gigantes and the Meliads. The Erinyes – Alecto, Tisiphone and Megaera – are depicted as fearsome goddesses, the guardians of civil order and the punishers of crime. They bear wings and snakelocks and live in the deepest part of the underworld, where they torture the guilty with whips until they go mad. Tradition has it that Gaia gives birth through her own wishes to the Gigantes, the giants, in order to avenge and liberate the imprisoned Titans. The Gigantes possess great strength and are of terrifying appearance with bushy beards and legs formed from the bodies of huge snakes. The Meliads are the nymphs of the ash trees, from which the warlike third age of people on earth is said to have sprung.

Gaia also forms a liaison with Pontos and through him she bears Nereus, a minor sea god whose wife is Doris and who fathers the Nereides, the spirits of the sea who attend on Poseidon. Through Nereus and Doris fifty daughters are born, the best known of whom is probably Amphitrite, and they in turn produce successive generations of minor deities.

Kronos forms a incestuous marriage with his sister Rhea and through him she bears the great Olympian gods, including Hestia, Demeter, Hera, Hades, Poseidon and Zeus. Hyperion and Thea become the parents of Helios (sun) and the goddesses Eos (dawn) and Selene (moon). Iapetos fathers the heroes Atlas and Prometheus, Menoetius and Epimethius. These deities, and others, are destined to control all from the heights of Olympus, the heavenly realm, to the depths of Tartaros, which lies beneath the underworld and in which they imprison their adversaries. The immediate children of Ouranos are to be regarded as the old order of Titan gods.

Zeus, as the head of the new and more youthful order of deities, is depicted as the father of the Olympian pantheon. Both Hesiod and Homer leave little doubt that he is a philanderer to a degree which at times appears excessive, since he manages to seduce and father offspring with almost all the goddesses who are the grandchildren of Ouranos. In this trait of womanizing he compares with Othin in Norse (Icelandic) mythology.

THE BIRTH OF SIN

CULTURE OF ORIGIN: native American – Haida [British Columbia and Queen Charlotte Islands]
PROVENANCE: recorded from oral traditions. Principal sources include *Haida Texts and Myths* J.R. Swanton. Bulletin 29, Bureau of American Ethnology. Washington, 1905.
   A strongly animistic thread runs through the myth, in which spirits are perceived to inhabit the bodies of birds.

Digging on the beach, the daughter of a Haida chief hears a cry coming from a cockle shell. She opens it and finds a baby inside which she takes home, fostering it with great care. One day the child seems to be imitating the drawing of a bowstring, so she hammers out a little bow and arrows from the metal of a copper bracelet and the child becomes an accomplished hunter, bringing the woman small trophies each day.

The woman marries a carpenter (arguably the spirit being Master Carpenter) who builds the family a fine house. One day he takes the boy, whose name is Sin, down to the ocean and makes him sit facing out over the Pacific. All the time that he stays in this position the weather remains fine and the seas calm and the father can go fishing in safety. One day, however, Sin accompanies his father and when they reach the fishing ground Sin instructs his father to utter a magical formula. The fishing line is tugged violently and the boat is hauled three times round a small island until they reel in a huge halibut.

Later Sin obtains a cloak made of wren feathers and he flies away from his mother to hover over the ocean like a bank of clouds. He then substitutes a cloak of jay feathers and hovers over the waves in shining splendour. The next cloak is of woodpecker feathers and when he wears this the sea is bathed in the colour of fire. It is time for Sin to bid a permanent farewell to his foster mother. He tells her that he will return no more, but that if his father sees his face in the sky, as it was when he used to stare out over the ocean, the weather will remain fair.

The woman understands at last that she has fostered the great spirit of the sky. Her mortal husband also goes away and she is left alone, but not without supernatural power of her own. When she sits on the shore and loosens her cloak the winds and storms arise; the more she loosens the garment the greater the tempest. She is Fine Weather Woman and when the weather bodes ill she tosses a handful of feathers towards her son as an offering. They fall as flakes of snow.

THE BIRTH OF UHLAKANYANA

CULTURE OF ORIGIN: Zulu [Natal, South Africa]
PROVENANCE: oral tradition recorded by Wilhelm Bleek, Zululand, 1856.

This mythological hero of the Zulu tribe is well known to other clans in southern Africa, though sometimes by different names – thus he is Mpfundlwa, the hare, to the Tsonga people in the Transvaal region. The message of the story is that Uhlakanyana, like many other dwarfs, has been imbued with the cunning and wisdom of his ancestors, which enables him to cheat his fellow man and always to have food in his belly. He therefore fulfils the ideal dream of most tribal people whose best hope, in reality, is to be able to eke out a meagre subsistence.

While still in his mother's womb, Uhlakanyana tells her that the time has come for him to be born into the world. Immediately she goes into labour and he falls to the earth, a small, dwarfish child. Grasping his father's sacred spear he severs his own umbilical cord and walks off to where the village elders are about to partake of a freshly slaughtered beast. Without asking their permission Uhlakanyana takes a piece of flesh and eats it. He generously offers to deliver the rest of the carcass around the village but, having deceived the elders with his good intentions, he secretly eats all the meat.

Uhlakanyana leaves the village in search of adventure and meets up with a fellow traveller, a hare. Once again his powers of deception are put to use. He lulls the hare into a sense of well-being, but then devours it. Next he meets a cannibal and pretends to befriend him also, but traps him in the hut they build together and promptly eats all the cannibal's cattle while the hut and its hapless prisoner are struck down by lightning.

THE BIRTH OF ZEUS

CULTURE OF ORIGIN: classical Greek, but subsequently adopted into Roman culture
PROVENANCE: recorded from oral traditions by the epic Greek poet Hesiod in the eighth century BC

The Titan siblings Kronos and Rhea, offspring of Ouranos (heaven) and Gaia (earth), form an incestuous liaison and Rhea bears several children including the hearth goddess Hestia, the mother goddess Demeter, Hera the future consort of Zeus, and Hades the god of death.

As each infant deity is born, Kronos swallows them because he has been told that it is his destiny to be vanquished by his own son. Rhea becomes pregnant again and is due to give birth to Zeus, the future leader of the Olympian deities. So distraught is she by Kronos's treatment of her other children that she calls upon her parents, Ouranos and Gaia, for help in devising a scheme whereby Zeus's birth can be concealed from Kronos and he can be punished for his treatment of his father (see *The Birth of the Gods of Olympus*, page 94).

When she is due to give birth, Rhea is sent to the safety of Lyctus in Crete and when Zeus is born he is given to Gaia, his grandmother, to raise. Gaia hides the infant Zeus in a remote cave on Mount Aegeum and to Kronos she gives a bundle of swaddling clothes concealing a heavy stone which he immediately swallows, believing it to be his son.

Zeus grows into a mighty warrior and eventually Kronos vomits up the stone he has erroneously swallowed. Zeus sets it as a marker at Pytho, near Parnassus, and proceeds to liberate the Cyclopes, who have been imprisoned by Ouranos since the day of their birth. In return, Zeus is presented with their elements of thunder, lightning and thunderbolts, which become his symbolic weapons and give him the pseudonym of the 'earth shaker'. The scene is thus set for the great cosmic battle between the old Titan gods and the younger generation of Olympian deities.

MISCELLANEOUS

CELTIC (WELSH): Math, a sovereign ruler of Wales, is under a spell which means that he may only live if his feet are resting in the lap of a virgin. The goddess Arianrhod, in the guise of his niece Goewin the sister of Gwydion, seeks to be his footholder, but she is obliged to undergo a test of her virginity by stepping over Math's magical sceptre. As she does so she gives birth to two offspring, Dylan and Llew, said to have been fathered incestuously by either Gwydion or his brother Gilfaethwy, who have taken Goewin by force at the time of the battle between Gwydion and Pryderi (see *Pryderi*, page 193). Arianrhod (Goewin) is shamed before the royal court and her ignominy is compounded when Gwydion takes the prematurely born Llew and raises him as his own child. In revenge the goddess beneath the mortal frame places a curse upon Llew that he shall benefit from neither title, nor arms, nor wife.

5

Myths of Childhood

This small section of myths needs little explanation other than to point out the near-universal concept of the storytellers that the children of deities grow up very fast. They are fully developed gods in miniature!

One of the most dramatic illustrations is that of the Hindu god Kršna, into whose mouth his mother looks when he is a child. Inside she perceives the whole world. Less startling are the adventures of the Greek god Hermes who, within hours of his birth, is performing the feats of a grown man. These are myths with little substance but a good deal of entertainment value.

(BALA)KRSNA SLAYS THE DEMON GODDESS PUTANA

CULTURE OF ORIGIN: Puranic Hindu [India]
PROVENANCE: the story appears in the *Bhagavata Purana*, composed circa 950 AD.

In Hindu culture there is much emphasis on that fact that not all is what it seems through the normal senses. In this myth a perceived infant is, in reality, the mighty and immortal god Kršna, while a beautiful woman provides the masquerade for a powerful and hideous demon. The myth also exemplifies another recurrent theme – that of the ambivalent nature of the primeval ocean, which is a fount of nourishing milk, yet also of deadly poison.

The demon king Kamsa instructs the demoness Putana (putrid) to go out into the world infecting and killing children through disease. One day she visits the village of Bala-Kršna's foster parents, Nanda and

Yasoda, where she takes the form of an attractive woman, finely dressed with full breasts and flowers in her hair. The local peasants who catch sight of her find the vision so beautiful that they assume her to be Laksmi, the consort of Višnu. Putana then finds the infant Kršna who is pretending to be asleep.

> *His true energy was concealed, like a fire covered with ashes. His eyes were closed but [he] the soul of all that moves knew her to be the demon who slays children. She cradled the infinite one upon her lap as one might pick up a deadly serpent believing it to be a piece of rope.*

Kršna's foster mother is less perceptive than her baby son and she stands immobile, imagining that she is observing a kind and motherly woman. The demon, however, offers a breast smeared with deadly poison to the infant. Bala-Kršna sucks with such force upon her nipple that he begins to draw the very life from her body. She screams out for him to release her, but without avail; the earth shakes as her agony increases and finally she falls lifeless. As she dies, Putana reverts to her true and hideous form and Yasoda and Rohini (the foster mother of Balarama) hastily remove Kršna, performing protective rites over him before putting him back to bed.

The villagers dismember the corpse and burn it, but in the act of giving milk to Kršna it has been purified. Putana's soul therefore ascends to heaven, the reward of all mothers.

THE BOYHOOD OF HERAKLES

CULTURE OF ORIGIN: classical Greek, but subsequently adopted into Roman culture

PROVENANCE: accounts of Herakles's exploits are drawn from a number of Greek authors and many are undoubtedly recorded from earlier oral traditions. Hesiod refers to him briefly in the *Theogony* and his marriage to Megara is recorded in *Herakles Furens* by Euripides. Much is included in the Homeric epic the *Iliad* and the events presaging his deification are described chiefly by Sophocles in the *Trachiniae*. Herakles 'officially' begins life as a mortal man and therefore may correctly be a personality of legend rather than myth, but his true father, as with many Greek heroes, is the god Zeus. The role of Herakles in Greek tradition is also inextricably bound up with the gods and his subsequent deification makes it appropriate to treat his story as myth.

NOTE: in the Roman tradition Herakles becomes Hercules, Zeus is Jupiter and Hera is Juno. See also *The Labours of Herakles*, page 183.

Herakles's mortal parents are Amphitryton, the grandson of Perseus, and Alkmene. A woman renowned for her chastity, Alkmene refuses to consummate the marriage until Amphitryton has avenged the death of her brothers at the hands of one Pterelaus. While Amphitryton is away, however, Zeus disguises himself as Alkmene's husband, convinces her further by giving her a gold cup belonging to Pterelaus and gains access to her bed, where they beget Herakles. Hera, the wife of Zeus, develops a strong jealousy towards Alkmene and orders the birth goddess Eileithyia to delay the arrival of Herakles in order to thwart a prophecy of Zeus that the next child to be born amongst Perseus's descendants shall rule Mycenae. The birth of Herakles's cousin Eurystheus is brought forward and he thus becomes the rightful heir to the throne.

Herakles is born at Thebes, but it is necessary for Hera to suckle Zeus's hated offspring in order that he may achieve proper immortality. The resources of the wily Hermes are called upon to place the child at her breast while she is asleep and, too late, she awakens to push the infant away. (It is the milk spurting from her nipples that creates the stars of the 'Milky Way'.)

At ten months the infant Herakles is again subject to Hera's vindictiveness when she introduces two serpents to the nursery. His twin brother Iphikles begins to scream, but Herakles calmly strangles the snakes. As he grows up he slays his tutor, Linos, in a fit of temper and Amphitryton sends him out of harm's way to become a herdsman. He is taught the arts of warfare by Amphitryton, the mortal Polydeukes's twin brother Kastor, and the archer Eurytos; in time he grows to a massive strength and stature. Among his early achievements he kills a ferocious lion at the age of eighteen. On his way back to Thebes he confronts the Minyan king, Erginus, who has laid siege to the city, and defeats him, in reward for which the Theban ruler Kreon gives Herakles the hand of his daughter Megara.

The story of Herakles and Megara has a tragic ending, though it varies according to different authors. In Euripedes's account, Thebes is attacked by one Lycus while Herakles is absent. Lycus is about to slay Megara and her children when Herakles returns and kills him. But then, in a fit of insanity perhaps orchestrated by Hera, Herakles slaughters his family by his own hand. Realizing what he has done he tries to commit suicide, but is instead persuaded by the hero Theseus to exile himself to Athens.

THE BABYHOOD OF HERMES

CULTURE OF ORIGIN: classical Greek, but subsequently adopted into Roman culture

PROVENANCE: recorded from oral traditions by the epic Greek poet Hesiod in the *Homeric Hymns* during the eighth century BC.

Hermes, the messenger of the gods, is portrayed as a complex, Machiavellian character full of trickery and sexual vigour. The stories surrounding his babyhood explain how he gains the attributes which, in later life, may be used to the benefit or the detriment of the Olympian gods. Thus his services are called upon for such tasks as the liberation of Ares, god of war, from a barrel; he organizes a truce between Priam, King of Troy, and Achilles; and he is the only deity who can safely negotiate the path between Olympus and the underworld kingdom of Hades.

Maia, a nymph, has been seduced by Zeus in a remote cave in the Arcadian mountains and she gives birth to a son whom she calls Hermes. From the beginning he displays extraordinary powers. He is born at sunrise but by midday he is playing the lyre and by nightfall he has stolen the cattle of Apollo.

For then she bare a son, of many shifts, blandly cunning, a robber, a cattle drive, a bringer of dreams, a watcher by night, a thief at the gates, one who was soon to show forth wonderful deeds among the deathless gods.

Hermes first wanders out of his mother's cave where, to his delight, he finds a tortoise browsing on the grass. He considers that, while it is alive, it will guard against witchcraft, but dead it will better serve as a fine musical instrument, a lyre.

The tortoise thus meets an untimely end (Hesiod does not relate the details) and Hermes removes its flesh, boring holes in the shell. He stretches lengths of reed between the holes and covers the shell with cow hide, fitting seven sheep-gut strings and tuning them before trying the instrument and singing snatches of popular song.

As dusk gathers, Hermes becomes bored with his newly fashioned plaything, tossing it back into his cradle. He runs off into the mountain pastures of Thessaly, where the god Apollo grazes the heavenly cattle, and he cuts out fifty prime beasts from the herd. Cunningly, he makes them walk backwards so that they appear to be moving towards the meadow rather than away from it, and he disguises his own footprints with sandals made of tamarisk and myrtle twigs.

Hermes's thieving is witnessed by an old man tilling his vineyard, but the infant god warns him to keep silence about what he may have heard and seen. Hermes hurries on through the night, driving the cattle before him until he reaches the meadows beside the river Alphaeus at Pylos, where he feeds and waters the cows and drives them into the byre for the night.

Once more Hermes is bored and seeks a new challenge, this time the art of making fire. He makes a fire board and stick from a laurel branch and, rubbing them together, applies the sparks to a pile of dried wood. Next, the precocious infant drags two of the stolen cattle to the fire and breaks their necks. He spreads the hides on the ground and proceeds to roast the flesh, dividing it on a flat stone into twelve portions which he offers up in sacrifice to the twelve great gods. He is tempted to eat some of the meat but remembers, just in time, that he is a god and therefore may not partake of mortal fare. He hides what is left of the carcasses in the byre, scatters the ashes of the fire, covering them with sand, and finally throws his sandals into the river. At dawn, all traces of his nocturnal games obliterated, he wends his innocent way home, slips in through the keyhole, and settles himself into his cradle with his lyre!

Maia is not unaware of Hermes's escapade and she threatens him with punishment from his father, but the infant god responds shrewdly. Why spend the rest of their lives in a lonely cave? Why not go out and obtain the riches and the good life with which the rest of the gods indulge themselves?

> If my father will not give it me, I will seek – and I am able – to be a prince of thieves. And if Leto's most glorious son [Apollo] shall seek me out, I think another and a greater loss will befall him.

Hermes thus sets out upon a career of infant crime. Meanwhile Apollo has discovered the theft of his cattle and he too comes upon the old man tending his vineyard. The countryman relates how he has seen a baby driving the beasts backwards and he directs Apollo towards the place where their tracks are visible. Guessing that Hermes is responsible, and in a fine temper, Apollo visits Maia's cave. When Hermes hears his approach, he pretends to be asleep, all the while clutching his lyre beneath the covers. Apollo discovers a vast hoard of stolen gold, silver and other finery and threatens to throw Hermes into the depths of Tartaros (the abyss beneath the underworld kingdom of Hades) unless he owns up to the theft of the cows. Hermes, however, answers innocently that he does not know what Apollo is talking about since he has neither seen nor heard of any stolen cattle.

Unable to settle the argument Apollo and Hermes seek the arbitration of their father, Zeus, on Mount Olympus. Apollo accuses Hermes of thieving and trickery and Hermes accuses Apollo of threats and intimidation. Hermes protests, truthfully, that he has neither stolen the cows nor taken them home. Zeus, seeing through the deceit, is thoroughly amused and sends the pair on their way, telling Hermes that he must, without further protest, lead Apollo to his cattle.

Hermes is obliged to obey but then he begins to play upon his lyre and to sing. He also makes, in Apollo's presence, a set of reed pipes (the Pipes of Pan) and so enchanted is Apollo by the sound of these instruments that he begs them for himself. Ever mindful of striking a bargain, Hermes agrees to barter, but on the condition that he may become the herdsman of Apollo's cattle. This Apollo accepts and in token of their new friendship he gives Hermes the gold serpent-entwined staff, the *kerykeion* (caduceus), which is to become his magical symbol and which will protect him from danger. Hermes makes one further request – to learn the art of soothsaying – but Apollo refuses, since he alone has been taught and entrusted with the art by Zeus. Apollo does, however, make a concession by pointing Hermes towards the Thriae of Parnassus, three virgin sisters who are teachers of divination.

Finally Zeus himself ordains that Hermes shall become lord over birds of omen, shepherds, their flocks and predators, and that he shall be the messenger of the gods.

KRŠNA'S MOUTH

CULTURE OF ORIGIN: Puranic Hindu [India]
PROVENANCE: the story appears in the *Bhagavata Purana*, written circa 950
  AD, but is based loosely on a myth from an earlier cultural period
  contained in the *Mahabharata* (300 BC to 300 AD)

Rama and Kršna are playing in the mud, occasionally returning to their mothers' breasts for comfort and reassurance. Kršna, in particular, gets up to all sorts of boyish pranks with the cattle of the village and other objects of amusement. Sometimes his behaviour is more reprehensible, when he steals from neighbours or when he pees on their clean floors!

One day some of Kršna's playmates report to Yasoda, his foster mother, that he has been eating dirt and Yasoda scolds him severely. Kršna, however, asserts that the other boys are lying. Yasoda commands this infant incarnation of Višnu to open his mouth. Inside she perceives, not dirt, but the whole universe – the heavens, the earth and all its features – and she becomes deeply confused, wondering if she is under some strange delusion or if she is indeed witnessing the power of a god. As soon as Yasoda understands the true nature of the vision before her, Višnu removes all trace of the experience from her memory, but still she understands that Višnu, in one of his multitude of aspects, has been made incarnate as her son.

THE BIRTH OF PRINCE NINIGI

CULTURE OF ORIGIN: Japanese Shinto
PROVENANCE: recorded in various texts and art from oral traditions.

Prince Ninigi, whose parents are Taka-Mi-Musubi and Ame-No-Oshi-Ho-Mimi, is by tradition (prior to 1945 when the association was dropped), the ancestral deity of the imperial Japanese dynasty, who were all considered to be of divine origin. He is the grandson of the sun goddess Amaterasu, and her heir apparent; he is also the god of the rice harvest.

Ninigi's birth is heralded when Amaterasu ordains the descent to earth of the apotheosis of the rising sun, the god Kushi-Dama-Nigi-Haya-Hi. Before his own descent Amaterasu gives Prince Ninigi jewels and the sword of Susano-Wo, the storm god. On his journey through the heavenly clouds he is accompanied by his sister, the goddess of dancers, Ame-No-Uzume, whose realm is the floating bridge of heaven, and he is guarded by a cohort of warrior deities, including the Raijin gods of the storms, led by Take-Mika-Dzuchi. He alights on the top of Mount Takachihiat, the point where eight earthly roads lead away in every direction. There he is confronted by the fearsome deity who guards all pathways, including the floating bridge. Through the intercession of Ame-No-Uzume, the guardian god takes Ninigi and shows him all the kingdoms of earth, in reward for which service Ninigi gives him the hand of Ame-No-Uzume in marriage. Prince Ninigi, for his part, takes as his consort the princess Ko-No-Hana (Sengen), the goddess of flowers and daughter of the mountain god Oho-Yama. She is the goddess of the sacred Mount Fuji and she also guards the elixir of eternal life. Prince Ninigi meets her on the seashore and asks Oho-Yama for her hand, but the mountain god tries to persuade him to choose Ko-No-Hana's older sister, Iha-Naga, who is stronger than the delicate princess of blossoms. Ninigi is determined, however, to wed the beautiful woman of his choice. He lives happily with Ko-No-Hana for several years and she bears him three sons, but his increasing feelings of jealousy undermine the marriage and ultimately she commits suicide by self-immolation.

6

Myths of Apocalypse, Fire and Flood

Apocalyptic visions of the end of the world are an integral part of many mythologies, irrespective of time, place and the degree of sophistication demonstrated by the society which spawns them. Much as we need tidy explanations of origins for that which is familiar around us, so we also need to visualize the mechanism for its eventual collapse. We seem resigned to the notion that 'all good things must end'. The Aztecs went further and perceived at least four worlds in existence previous to the present one, each of which ended in a great catastrophe. In Buddhism there is a similar notion of world ages which, albeit conducted over a vast time span, are finite and terminable. Perhaps the most significant apocalyptic traditions are those of Christianity, which convinced itself that the day of judgement would come, and the Nordic religions, which followed a similar train of thought in their idea of Ragnarok. In both cases the demise of the old is anticipated to herald the birth of a new and better universe. In Hindu myth there emerges the final incarnation of the god Višnu as Kalkin who will rid the earth of the destructive age of Kali and make it a better place for humankind.

The concept of the end of the world usually reflects the particular preoccupations of the society which generates the myth. Thus the Christian book of Revelation and the Osirian *Book of the Dead* from ancient Egypt depict a dreadful colossus who will toss souls into the scales and weigh them to evaluate their suitability for a life after death, an eschatological concept. On the other hand, for the Nordic races, among whom ice and perennial darkness were the overwhelming fear, the end was seen as a day when the phantom wolf, Fenrir, would be unleashed from his chains to chase and swallow the sun, presaging a time of freezing darkness.

Fire is frequently perceived to be a final cleansing agent, often preceding flood. Out of the ashes of the old, purified and washed will arise the new and better world.

One has to ponder on why so many cultures envisage a great flood or deluge having taken place sometime during their early history. The notion of the underground primeval waters which will rise again to engulf a sinful and errant humankind is universal. Perhaps it can be accounted for most simply by the fact that many parts of the world at one time or another experienced great inundations either through the flooding of river valleys, or tidal waves, or encroachment by the sea.

THE RIVER OF BOANN

CULTURE OF ORIGIN: Celtic – Irish
PROVENANCE: recorded from oral traditions under the general heading of the Mythological Cycle

A sacred well on the hill of Sidhe Nechtan (Carbery, County Kildare) is forbidden to all except the water god, Nechtan, and his cup-bearers. His consort, Boann the river goddess, ignores the taboo and marches around the well in an anti–clockwise circle. In response to her violation the waters flood out and as she flees eastwards trying to escape them they engulf her, forming the course of the river Boyne.

THE EYE OF RE

CULTURE OF ORIGIN: Egypt
PROVENANCE: from the *Book of the Divine Cow*, of which a lengthy extract is inscribed on the walls of a room adjacent to the burial chamber in the tomb of Seti I (Valley of the Kings).

Though described as the 'Eye of Re', this entity operates independently to the extent that it can become personified by another deity. In this case it is transmuted into Hathor, the cow goddess, normally a benign and maternal figure. Hathor is, however, linked with the vengeful and destructive goddess of war, Sakhmet. She is described on occasions as 'mistress of the house of Sakhmet' and both goddesses are listed as daughters of Re. Under Re's influence, as his Eye, Hathor becomes imbued with the personality of her dark sister.

The sun god Re heads the pantheon of gods ruling over all Egypt and he discovers that the human race is plotting to overthrow him. He reminisces to the primeval force, Nu, about how the human race was engendered from his tears and asks for her opinion before he annihilates them for their impiety. Nu responds that the 'Eye of Re', the symbol of power and justice in the heavens, will carry out an appropriate and terrifying sentence.

Having driven much of mankind into the desert wastes and slaughtered them without respite, Hathor takes a day off to regain her strength before a further bout of terrorism. Re, however, has a change of heart and becomes concerned that the destruction of mankind may rebound unfavourably on the godly hierarchy. Unfortunately Hathor is by now mad with bloodlust and eager to run amok on the following day. Re is thus obliged to organize an urgent rescue plan for the progeny of his tears and he instructs one of his attendants to run at top speed to Aswan, where he is to collect a large quantity of red ochre. Slaves are then commanded to mix the ochre with barley and to ferment a large quantity of beer. The resultant blood-red brew, a quantity of no less than seven thousand jars, is tipped out over the place where Re anticipates that Hathor will recommence her slaughter. His gamble pays off and when Hathor arrives, at daybreak, she drinks the brew believing it to be human blood. She becomes hopelessly drunk and, in her inebriated state, forgets her violent mission to finish off what is left of the human race.

GENESIS
(The Flood)

Culture of origin: Judaic/Christian
Provenance: the *Vetus Testamentum*.
   This account of the flood parallels many others in the ancient Near East, some of them perhaps considerably more than five thousand years old in their oral origins. All stem from the notion of a cathartic act by the gods to remove the old order of mankind and to replace it with a new and improved society. A similar sentiment is recognizable in Nordic (Icelandic) mythology when, at Ragnarok (the day of doom), the sea engulfs the land and cleanses it. See also *Atrahasis*, page 36, and *The Epic of Gilgameš*, page 179.

The creator god perceives that the human race has become dissolute and evil and he regrets having engendered mankind. He decides therefore to destroy that which he has created. Only one man, Noah, who has three sons, Šem, Ham and Japeth, is looked upon with favour as a just and honourable being.

God warns Noah that within seven days he intends to destroy the life on earth; he instructs Noah to build a ship (an ark) in which he can protect his wife and family from the elements and look after pairs of every living creature. When the rains come they are unceasing for forty days and nights and the waters cover every quarter of the earth so that the land is inundated and all life perishes, except that which sails in the ship of Noah. For 150 days even the mountain tops are covered with water and then the creator god relents and sends a breeze to abate the seas. They recede until the tops of the highest mountains become visible and the ship comes to rest on the summit of Mount Ararat.

After forty days Noah releases a raven and a dove to seek out any evidence that the waters have receded from the land. The dove returns and Noah keeps it in the ship for another seven days before sending it out again. This time it returns with an olive leaf in its beak and Noah takes the sprig of greenery as a sign that he can open the ship and release the creatures charged to his safekeeping.

The creator god instructs Noah to disembark from the ark with his family, whereupon Noah builds an altar on the dry ground and sacrifices representative species from all the creatures he has brought with him. In response the god makes a covenant that he will never again inflict such a draconian punishment upon mankind and, as a token, he sets a rainbow in the heavens to appear each time the clouds gather and the rains fall.

NOTE: in common with many of the Old Testament characters, Noah seems to have lived a long and happy life (950 years).

GRIMNISMAL
(Lay of Grimnir)

CULTURE OF ORIGIN: Teutonic – Nordic and Germanic (Icelandic)
PROVENANCE: the *Codex Regius* No. 2365, composed by an unknown hand circa tenth century AD. The manuscript lay hidden until it was rediscovered by Brynjolfur Sveinsson, bishop to the Icelandic community, circa 1643, and preserved on the instructions of Frederic III. It is housed in the Royal Library of Denmark [Copenhagen]. A derivative version is contained in the *Codex Arnamagnaeanus* No. 544 (*Hauksbok*) [Copenhagen University] and the narrative is also paraphrased in part by Snorri Sturluson (1178-1241) in the *Prose Edda*.

Grimnismal begins with a short prose narrative but, as with the other Eddic lays which set out the ancient mythology of northern Europe, the main part of the myth is written in simple measure as poetry designed to be recited. It appears to be composed as a didactic instruction in mythological lore and takes the form of a monologue delivered by Othin. He talks mainly to one of two sons of a king, Hrauthung, but initially he addresses one of the king's grandsons. The use of a traveller's costume in which Othin disguises himself so that he may gain knowledge of the world, incognito, is a persistent theme in Nordic/Icelandic myth.

Two brothers, Agnar and Geirroeth, are caught at sea in a storm. Having reached the haven of an island they stay for the winter. In the spring Geirroeth pushes his brother out to sea in a small rudderless boat and abandons him to the waves, while he becomes ruler of his father's kingdom.

Othin and his consort Frigg argue about the meanness and cruelty with which Geirroeth may be treating his subjects while Agnar is obliged to live with an ogress in a cave. The two deities make a wager with each other about whether Geirroeth is guilty. Othin disguises himself as a traveller, Grimnir, who wears a long blue cloak. He sets out to visit Geirroeth's palace where the king proceeds to torture him by chaining him between two fires for eight nights. The king's ten-year-old son, also named Agnar, takes pity on the stranger and brings him a drink of beer. At this juncture the narrative changes to a poetic style.

Speaking to the young Agnar, the disguised Othin first complains of the heat of the fire which has singed his cloak, but he praises the boy for his compassion. Then Othin begins to weave his story. He tells of the various homes of the gods. In Thruthheim (land of strength) Thor, the thunder god, lives in his timbered hall awaiting Ragnarok, the doom of the gods. On the plains lives Ull, the god of justice. Of Othin's three halls the first, Valaskjalf, is thatched with silver; the second is Sokkvabekk (the sunken hall) where he rests with his consort Frigg, drinking all day long from cups of gold; the third is Valholl (hall of the slain), the place to which mortal heroes are carried each day by the Valkyrie warrior maidens.

Othin continues with his tale, accounting for still more heavenly abodes. The sixth is Thrymheim (noise home), residence of the giant Thjatsi and his daughter Skathi, the consort of the god Njorth. Seventh is Breithablik (the far shining), where Balder, the good but ill-fated son of Othin, lives. Heimdall, the guardian god, lives in the eighth hall, Himinbjorg (heavenly mountain), while the ninth, Folk-vang (battlefield), is where Frigg collects her share of the noble slain.

The tenth hall is known as Glitnir (shining), built of silver and gold and owned by the god Forseti who is regarded as a good arbiter of disputes. The eleventh, Noatun (harbour), is the home of Njorth, god of the sea, who lives alone separated from his giantess wife Skathi.

Othin next lists several homes of minor deities and tells of his two ravens, Hugin and Munin, which soar each day over the earth. He then tells of the great river, Thund, which flows around the ramparts of Valholl and of the gate of the fortress, the Gate of the Battle Slain. Valholl contains 540 rooms through which, on the day of doom, eight hundred warriors will march to face the adversaries of the gods, including the phantom wolf, Fenrir.

Othin tells of the goat, Heithrun, and the stag, Eikthyrnir, which feed off the leaves of the world ash tree, Yggdrasil, and of how drops from the antlers of the deer fill the world's rivers. Coming towards the end of his monologue, the god explains about the world tree, whose roots spread in three directions: to the land of the giants, to the underworld of Hel and to Mithgarth, the land of mortal men. An eagle rests in its branches, the serpent Nithhogg gnaws at its roots and a squirrel named Ratatosk races between the two delivering messages. The tree is sick from the predations of the animals and the serpent.

The Yggdrasil doth wrong endure,
more than to men is known:
its foliage the stag consumes,
its trunk decays,
and Nithhogg gnaws its roots below.

In the beginning the earth was formed from the primordial being Ymir. His blood became the sea, his hair the trees, his bones the hills and his skull the sky. From his eyelashes the gods fashioned Mithgarth and from his brows came the clouds.

Finally Othin recites the list of his pseudonyms and Geirroeth begins to understand the true and awesome identity of his supposed victim. By this time the drunken Geirroeth has condemned himself through his own indifference and callousness and Othin, still hanging from his fiery chains, hands out the sentence.

Soon shall thou drink in Othin's hall,
as mortal life shall from thee flee.
Thy fate the norns have uttered:
now Othin thou shalt know;
come hither if thou canst.

The king, realizing at last the true identity of the traveller he has tortured, takes a step to release him, but he is very drunk and his sword drops from his hands to pierce him as he falls. Othin disappears and Agnar reigns in Geirroeth's place.

NOTE: for a more comprehensive account of Nordic cosmogony see *Voluspa*, page 122.

GUAN YIN AND THE LO YANG PROPHECY

CULTURE OF ORIGIN: Chinese Daoist (Taoist)

PROVENANCE: recorded in various texts and art from an oral tradition brought to China through Buddhist influence sometime between AD 384 and 417, but established more clearly during the Tang dynasty (AD 618–906). Guan Yin (Kuan Yin) is the Daoist form of the Buddhist god Avalokitesvara. Transition from god to goddess and the adoption of the name Guan Yin probably began circa AD 600 and was complete by AD 1100. Tradition identifies Guan Yin as a mortal princess, Maio Shan, whose apotheosis transformed her into a goddess with both fertility connotations and a merciful guardian image invoked when danger threatens (see also *Maio Shan*, page 238).

It should be noted that the anglicized equivalents of Chinese characters vary considerably in transliteration. The official Chinese Pinyin system is applied here, followed, where appropriate, in brackets, by the more generally encountered Wade-Giles system.

One autumn morning a ferry boat is crossing the dangerously swollen and windswept Lo Yang River which runs through the Chinese province of Fukien. The river, notorious for its drownings, has thus far proved impossible to span with a bridge, but when the waves threaten to swamp the small ship a figure dressed in white appears in the bows. It is Guan Yin, the goddess of mercy, who stretches out her arms to calm the wind and waves.

One of the passengers on the ferry is a pregnant woman called Fong Tsai. Guan Yin approaches the woman and tells her that she will give birth to a son who will one day design and build a bridge to cross the river. Fong Tsai names her son Tsai Xiang (Ts'ai Hsiang) and each year, as he grows into a successful young man, his mother reminds him of Guan Yin's oracular message. Eventually Tsai Xiang rises to the post of Chief Minister in the Emperor's government but, although he governs well, he is constantly refused permission to leave the capital to visit Fukien province. In consequence he has been unable to tackle the project of a bridge across the Lo Yang River.

One day, using honey smeared on the leaves of a plantain tree, he writes the message, 'Tsai Xiang, return home to fulfil your duty!' Then he waits while ants eat the characters out of the leaves. The Emperor walks by and reads the words aloud, whereupon Tsai Xiang claims that an imperial edict has been given. Tsai Xiang thus gains reluctant imperial permission to return to Fukien for two months as a magistrate.

At first all attempts to construct foundations for the bridge are washed away by the current, but Tsai Xiang sends a courier to the Dragon King, Ao Guang (Ao Kuang), requesting that he should reduce the water level for three days. To this Ao Guang agrees, sending his reply written on the palm of the courier's hand. The waters duly recede, leaving the river bed dry, but after the first day only a third of the task is complete and the army of workmen, having no food left, threaten to stop work. Tsai Xiang now prays to Guan Yin for money to buy provisions and she appears once more in the bows of a boat, calling that any man who can throw gold or silver into her lap may possess her. The boat soon fills with money! The goddess places the bullion at the feet of Tsai Xiang, who thus proceeds to complete the construction work on the bridge over the infamous Lo Yang.

THE HUICHOL ARK OF THE DELUGE

CULTURE OF ORIGIN: native American – Huichol [Sierra Madre, north-east of the Rio Grande]

PROVENANCE: recorded from oral traditions. The myth was related to Carl Lumholtz at the turn of the century and recorded in the Memoirs of the American Museum of Natural History 1900-1907. It has clearly been subject to a level of Christian influence, but retains a considerable amount of original concept.

A man is felling trees to prepare the land for planting, but each day he discovers that the trees have grown again. On the fifth day he decides to find out what is going on, so he stays out all night. He sees, rising from the ground in the clearing, an old woman with a stick which she directs towards the four points of the compass, first south, then north, west and east; finally she points it up and down. All the trees which were felled the previous day immediately stand up again.

The man approaches the old woman and complains about what she is doing. She replies that she wishes to talk with him. Her name is Tako'tsi Nakawe and she warns him that in five days a great flood will arise, accompanied by a sharp and bitter wind. She tells him to make a box from the wood of a fig tree, as long and as wide as himself, and to make a well-fitting cover. He is to take into the ark with him five grains of each colour of corn, some fire and five squash stems to burn. He is also to take with him a black bitch.

The man does as he is instructed and by the fifth day all the necessary things are prepared. He climbs into the ark and Tako'tsi Nakawe fits the lid, carefully sealing the cracks. Then she sits atop the vessel with a macaw and a parrot on her shoulders. When the inundation comes the ark drifts for a year to the south, then for a year to the north, a year to the west and a year to the east. During the next year the waters begin to subside and the ark comes to rest on the top of a mountain, Toapu'li [Santa Catarina]. At first when the man emerges from the ark all the land is inundated, but the parrot and the macaw begin to excavate river valleys with their beaks and the water runs off. The birds create five oceans and, as the land dries, the earth mother Tate' Yuliana'ka plants grasses and trees.

Tako'tsi Nakawe becomes the wind and the man returns to the task of clearing his field by day while at night he lives in a cave with the black bitch. She stays at home while he labours. Every evening, however, he finds corn cakes prepared for him and after five days his curiosity prompts him to hide in the bushes and watch. The bitch takes off her skin and hangs it up. She transforms into a young woman who grinds the corn. The man steals up, grabs the skin and hurls it into the fire. At first the woman whines like a dog, but he bathes her with water mixed with ground corn and she remains in human form. They produce a large family which consititutes the beginnings of the human race. They plant corn and live happily.

MATSYA AND THE FLOOD

CULTURE OF ORIGIN: Brahmanic and Puranic Hindu [India]
PROVENANCE: the story appears, with minor variation, in the *Satapatha Brahmana* (900–700 BC) and in the *Matsya Purana* (introduced circa 250–500 AD).

Ten major incarnations, or *avataras*, of Višnu are conventionally understood and each of these is explained by its own myth. Matsya, the fish, is the first of them. In each myth Višnu is perceived, to a greater or lesser extent, as a benign deity anxious to help rather than hinder mankind. There is, however, a subtle distinction between earlier and later interpretations of the story of Matsya. In the Brahmanic version he saves the god Manu from the flood while in the Puranic account he becomes part of the doomsday apparatus against which Manu is directed to save not just himself, but all life on earth.

One of the primordial creator gods, Manu, an offspring of the sun god Surya, is washing his hands when a small fish warns him of a great impending deluge and promises to rescue him from the disaster. At first, looking at the size of the minnow (which is in reality an incarnation of Višnu), Manu is scornful, but the fish points out that if the god will care for him it will grow much bigger and stronger. Steadily the fish, Matsya, grows. It instructs Manu to build an ark into which he must enter when the flood arrives.

The time of the deluge comes and when Manu does as he has been instructed Matsya swims to the ark, dragging it through the waters to the refuge of a mountain top. Matsya tells Manu to secure the ark to a tree trunk but advises that, as the waters recede, he must allow the craft to float down with them. Thus Manu, of all living things, survives.

In the later Puranic myth Manu puts the minnow first into the River Ganges and then into the ocean, both of which it outgrows. Manu becomes frightened of its powers, believing that it is some awful demon, but then realizing that it can be none other than an incarnation of Višnu.

'Who art thou? A lord of demons? Are you Vasudeva [an aspect of Višnu]? Who else can be like this? Who else can be equal to twenty thousand leagues?'

Višnu compliments Manu on recognizing him correctly and tells him to assemble all creatures into an ark which the gods have built. He predicts a fearful apocalypse. For a hundred years drought will pervade the earth, after which Agni and his fires will engulf the universe, incinerating all to ashes. The seven clouds of doom, the sweat of the fire god, will assemble to inundate and purify the earth, and in the new order Višnu will proclaim to Manu the sacred *Vedas*, the hymns in praise of creation.

NU GUA (NU KUA) AND THE HOLE IN THE SKY

CULTURE OF ORIGIN: Chinese Daoist (Taoist)
PROVENANCE: the myth is recorded in various texts and art from oral traditions, though the precise origins of Nu Gua are uncertain. She probably arose as an ancient creatrix or fertility goddess, but in later times became a goddess of marriage. One tradition identifies the creation of Nu Gua, whose role is to engender humankind, as being the last act of Pan Gu (the primordial being of Daoist mythology). A separate source places her as the daughter of the water god Shui Zhing-Tzu and dates her birth to 2953 BC. According to other traditions Nu Gua is either the consort or the sister of the emperor Fu Xi (Fu–Hsi), the first of the mythical rulers of China. His existence has no historical foundation and his reign allegedly spanned 115 years from the thirtieth century BC. The explanation of the tilting of the earth's axis is beautifully depicted in the *Shan Hai Zhing* (Book of Mountains and Rivers), composed in about the third century BC.
Nu Gua is a goddess possessed of great beauty, her face framed by black hair, although her torso is fashioned from the bodies of two intertwined serpents. When she is identified as the daughter of Shui Zhing-Tzu, her lower body is depicted as that of a water snail.
It should be noted that the anglicized equivalents of Chinese characters vary considerably in transliteration. The official Chinese Pinyin system is applied here, followed, where appropriate, in brackets, by the more generally encountered Wade–Giles system.
The myth of the Hole in the Sky is set in a time shortly after the creation of the cosmos by Pan Gu (P'an Ku) and may be seen as a Chinese version of the deluge accounts known the world over.

Heaven and earth have moved apart and Nu Gua begins to engender men and women from river mud which she fashions into human form and into which she breathes life. One day, when she has become tired of the slow and laborious process of moulding lumps of clay, she discovers a length of rope lying in the river mud. She finds that by twirling the rope she can create people, in large numbers and much faster, from the drops of muddy water which are shaken off. Those which arise from this process are, however, poor and weak, while the much smaller band which she continues to fashion from clay become the strong, the wise and the wealthy of human society.

When the emperor Fu Xi dies, Nu Gua takes his place as the Empress Nu-Huang in the reign of the element Wood. She has created enough people to populate the world, but realizes that it is a difficult and dangerous place for them to survive in. She therefore assembles all the heroes she has made from clay, arms them with weapons and sends them out to subdue the earth, making it hospitable for its weaker inhabitants. Two of the warriors, Kung Kung and Zhang Xu, attempt to overthrow her authority by applying the element Metal to Wood but she counters their strategy by applying the element Fire to melt the Metal and then Water to put out the Fire. The two warriors turn upon each other and Kung Kung (also perceived as the god of water) is defeated. He escapes to the west where he takes revenge by using his body to set off an avalanche on the Imperfect Mountain, which drags down the pillars supporting the heavens in the north-west quarter.

As the sky collapses downwards, a great hole appears, the earth is tilted off its axis, the sun is obliterated and rain starts to cascade through to the distress of Nu Gua, who sees the devastation which mankind has brought upon the earth.

According to separate traditions, Zhang Xu is made emperor, Kung Kung is captured and executed, and Nu Kua repairs the sky by building a palace whose roof supports it. She then fills the gap with five differently coloured rocks which equate with the Five Elements (Wood, Fire, Earth, Metal and Water). Another source narrates that she first slaughters a turtle, planting its feet in the four quadrants so that everyone will know the points of the compass, and then she blocks the hole in the sky temporarily with the corpse of a dragon while she sets about searching for a boulder which will seal the gap permanently. Just as the dragon's body begins to sag under the weight of water, Nu Gua finds a stone of suitable colour and shape and pushes it into place, sealing the sky for ever more.

THE REVELATION OF JOHN

CULTURE OF ORIGIN: Christian
PROVENANCE: the *New Testament*.

This extract from the Book of the Revelation of John the Divine (19.11) strongly parallels the Hindu account of *Visnu and Kalkin* in prophesying the coming of a righteous and avenging deity who, as the word of God, will ride through a sea of blood to cleanse and purify and so herald in a new order by defeating the anti-Christ which is identified as 'the beast'. The words are those found in the King James version of the Bible.

And I saw heaven opened, and behold a white horse; and he that sat upon him was called Faithful and True, and in righteousness he doth judge and make war. His eyes were as a flame of fire, and on his head were many crowns; and he had a name written that no man knew, but he himself. And he was clothed in a vesture dipped in blood: and his name is called the Word of God. And the armies which were in heaven followed him upon white horses, clothed in fine linen, white and clean. And out of his mouth goeth a sharp sword, that with it he should smite the nations: and he shall rule them with a rod of iron: and he treadeth the winepress of the fierceness and wrath of Almighty God. And he hath on his vesture and on his thigh a name written, King of Kings and Lord of Lords.

And I saw an angel standing in the sun; and he cried with a loud voice, saying to all the fowls that fly in the midst of heaven, come and gather yourselves together unto the supper of the Great God. That ye may eat the flesh of kings, and the flesh of captains, and the flesh of mighty men, and the flesh of horses and of them that sit on them, and the flesh of all men, both free and bond, both small and great. And I saw the beast, and the kings of the earth, and their armies, gathered together to make war against him that sat on the horse, and against his army. And the beast was taken and with him the false prophet that wrought miracles before him, with which he deceived them that had received the mark of the beast, and them that worshipped his image. These both were cast alive into a lake of fire burning with brimstone. And the remnant were slain with the sword of him that sat upon the horse, which sword proceeded out of his mouth; and all the fowls were filled with their flesh.

VAFPRUONISMAL
(Lay of Vafthruthnir)

CULTURE OF ORIGIN: Teutonic – Nordic and Germanic (Icelandic)

PROVENANCE: the *Codex Regius* No. 2365, composed by an unknown hand circa 870 AD. The manuscript lay hidden until it was rediscovered by Brynjolfur Sveinsson, bishop to the Icelandic community, circa 1643, and preserved on the instructions of Frederic III. It is housed in the Royal Library of Denmark [Copenhagen]. A derivative version is contained in the *Codex Arnamagnaeanus* No. 544 (*Hauksbok*) [Copenhagen University] and the narrative is also paraphrased by Snorri Sturluson (1178-1241) in the *Prose Edda*.

As with the other Eddic lays which set out the ancient mythology of northern Europe, the *Vafpruonismal* is written in simple measure as poetry designed to be recited. The myth is composed as a didactic dialogue between the god Othin and the *etin* (giant) Vafthruthnir in the style of a series of questions and answers covering the essentials of Nordic cosmogony.

Othin and his consort Frigg are talking together. Othin wishes to pit his esoteric knowledge against that of Vafthruthnir, whose wisdom is renowned, but Frigg is apprehensive about the proposed visit since the giants represent the permanent adversaries of the gods of Asgarth.

When Othin comes to the giant's home and offers his challenge of wits, Vafthruthnir at first adopts a hostile attitude, but Othin dispels the mood with modesty, sits down and so the talk begins. It is the giant who first tests Othin's mettle with simple questions about Nordic cosmogony. He asks the names of the horses which bring day and night, of the sea which runs between the land of the gods and that of the giants, and of the final battlefield of the gods. These Othin answers easily. Now it is the turn of the god to set his own questions.

Othin begins with equally basic tests about the origin of the cosmos. Where did the heavens and earth come from? Vafthruthnir replies that the earth was made from the flesh of the primordial being Ymir, the hills from his bones, the sky from his skull and from his blood came the salty sea. Othin requires to know the origin of the moon and sun, day and night. Again the giant answers correctly, giving the right names and genealogies.

For his next series of questions Othin demands to know the origin of the race of giants. Vafthruthnir gives the correct names and explains that out of the cold rivers of the far north came drops of venom which congealed into Aurgelmir, the progenitor of the race. From Aurgelmir's armpits grew the first man and a woman who, through him, conceived a six-headed child.

Othin's questions become more difficult. He asks the nature of the invisible wind which blows across the sea. It is the 'corpse swallower', replies Vafthruthnir, that sits at heaven's end in the shape of an eagle beating its huge feathers.

Now Othin begins to direct the questioning towards the serious issue of the end of the world, Ragnarok, the day of doom. He asks from whence came Njorth among the gods. Vafthruthnir explains that he is from the rival and older race of Vanir gods, sent as a hostage to the Aesir gods of Asgarth after the first great battle between the two races. Othin then asks where mortal heroes take on immortality? In Othin's home, where they drink wine in eternity, comes the reply.

What then is the fate of the gods, Othin's twelfth question begins. The giant explains that he knows of nine worlds beneath heaven to which the dead are doomed on the terrible day, but that not all will perish. Some will survive in a new and better order. The sun will be swallowed by the phantom wolf, Fenrir, but a daughter orb will replace it. The giant tells of three wise women, the Norns, who spin the thread of fate.

Othin demands to know who among the gods will survive to rule the new order when the great cleansing fire of Surt (the fire god who lives in the realm of Muspell in the south) is extinguished. It will be Vithar and Vali, Othin's surviving sons, while offspring of Thor, Mothi and Magni, will inherit their father's magical hammer, Mjolnir. At whose hands will Othin be slain? The wolf, Fenrir, will swallow him, but his death will be avenged by Vithar. Now Othin asks the one question that will reveal his identity to Vafthruthnir, a question that none but he can answer.

'I have wandered, and much afield,
in strength with gods have I fought:
what did Othin whisper in his ear of his son,
ere Balder was stretched on the bale?'

Vafthruthnir replies wistfully:

'No mortal man knows what thou said'st
in the days of yore to thy son:
with idle tongue have I flaunted my lore
and spoken of days of doom.
Alas with Othin my knowledge I matched:
but of all thou art wisest born.'

NOTE: for a more comprehensive account of Nordic cosmogony, see *Voluspa*, page 122.

VARAHA SAVES THE EARTH

CULTURE OF ORIGIN: Brahmanic and Puranic Hindu [India]
PROVENANCE: the basis of the myth of Varaha, the incarnation of Višnu as a boar, first appears fleetingly in the *Taittiriya Samhita* and the *Satapatha Brahmana* (900–700 BC) but it is not properly developed until it emerges in the *Višnu Purana* (circa 450 AD) and the *Kalika Purana* (circa 1350 AD). Ten major incarnations, or *avataras*, of Višnu are conventionally understood and each of these is explained by its own myth.

In Hindu tradition the boar is a sacrificial animal which, though part of the Brahmanic mythology, is not associated directly with Višnu until the later Puranic texts. The cosmic boar, its substance fashioned out of the sacred Vedas, dwells at the interface between cosmos and chaos but it also symbolizes the interface between earth and water. In this particular incarnation, associated closely with Brahma, Višnu 'creates' the earth after discovering it resting in the primordial waters.

The early brahmanic myths describe how the primordial being, Prajapati (in this instance an epithet of Višnu), moves over the primeval water and, when he perceives the germ of the earth, becomes the cosmic boar, Emusa, which seizes it and raises it up. He then becomes Visvakarman and spreads the earth out, calling it Prthivi.

In the *Visnu Purana*, Višnu takes the form of the boar, the Vedic sacrifice, so as to preserve the universe. He raises the earth from the depths upon his tusk and the water pours from his body while the earth floats over the surface of the ocean. Varaha then piles up the mountains and divides the earth into seven continents.

In the *Kalika Purana*, which is a Saevite text, Višnu is confronted by Šiva, who tells him that he should abandon his incarnation as a boar. He implies that Višnu has impregnated Prthivi (the Earth) while she is menstruating and that she will bear a demonic being which will, in time, wreak destruction upon the gods. Višnu appears to agree but, when Šiva has gone away, he retains the body of the boar and recommences his love-making with Prthivi, who bears him three brahmin sons. Still his lust is not assuaged and he continues to have intercourse with the earth until the combined effect of his exertions and the playful romping of Prthivi's sons causes her to be shattered. Višnu is aware of the destruction he is wreaking, yet he is unable to quench his desire for Prthivi and abandon his body as Šiva advised.

Afraid for the consequences, the gods approach the creator god of earth, Narayana, and explain the catastrophe being caused by the sport of Varaha and his children, who have now destroyed the mountains and stirred up the primeval waters causing a flood.

Šiva returns as a terrifying eight-legged beast, the *sarabha*, and confronts Varaha and his offspring. A great battle ensues and the inundation of the earth becomes total so that almost all life is drowned. Brahma now approaches Višnu, who is still in his boar incarnation, and points out the destruction he has wrought. Višnu is contrite and, determined to save the sacred Vedas and the ancient sages from destruction, he takes the form of a fish and places them upon his back before transferring them to a boat.

Still Višnu is unable voluntarily to abandon his *avatar* as Varaha; he therefore begs Šiva to kill him in order that the universe may be spared. Šiva, in his *sarabha* form, obliges, also slaying the sons of Varaha, and all four become the sacrifice through which the earth is saved from final dissolution.

VIŠNU AND KALKIN

CULTURE OF ORIGIN: Puranic Hindu [India]
PROVENANCE: the story appears in the *Višnu Purana*, written circa 450 AD, and constitutes one of the few futuristic myths in Hinduism.

Kalkin is the final incarnation or *avatar* of the god Višnu, the only one who is yet to appear at the end of the present age of mankind, the age of the goddess Kali. He will herald in the new Krta Age. Kalkin is thus envisaged as the avenging sword of righteousness who will cleanse the world of the evil symbolized by Kali. Some authorities consider that the idea of a messianic coming in Hinduism first took shape at the time of the Scythian and Parthian invasions of India in the third and fourth centuries AD. There are strong parallels to be drawn with the prophetic Christian myth to be found in the Book of Revelation 19,11. Kalkin is also the counterpart of the Buddhist salvationist *manusibuddha* (future human Buddha) Maitreya.

The kings of the Age of Kali are corrupt and power-hungry to the extent that ordinary people will become greatly impoverished and seek refuge in the remote mountain valleys, where they will eke out an existence foraging for honey, roots and wild vegetables. The population will wear ragged clothes, it will become too large for the sparsity of the land to support and it will face great physical hardship from the elements. Since the longest that anyone will live is twenty-three years, the entire race is faced with destruction.

The Vedas and other sacred texts will become scattered and, when all seems lost, a messiah will come riding upon a white horse, to punish evil and reward good. He will be a part of the creator god Brahma. This champion of a new order, the tenth incarnation of the god Višnu, will be named Kalkin, 'the Fulfiller' and he will be born in the house of the chief brahmin of the village of Sambala. He will destroy all invaders of India and everything that is evil to herald in the new and flawless Age of Krta.

VOLUSPA

CULTURE OF ORIGIN: Teutonic – Nordic and Germanic (Icelandic)

PROVENANCE: the *Codex Regius* No. 2365, composed by an unknown hand circa 870 AD. The manuscript lay hidden until it was rediscovered by Brynjolfur Sveinsson, bishop to the Icelandic community, circa 1643, and preserved on the instructions of Frederic III. It is housed in the Royal Library of Denmark [Copenhagen]. A derivative version is contained in the *Codex Arnamagnaeanus* No. 544 (*Hauksbok*) [Copenhagen University] and the narrative is also paraphrased by Snorri Sturluson (1178-1241) in the *Prose Edda*.

As with the other Eddic lays which set out the ancient mythology of northern Europe, the *Voluspa* (prophecy of the seeress) is written in simple measure as poetry designed to be recited. It is the first of the lays incorporated in the *Codex Regius*.

The creator god, Othin, summons the seeress from her endless sleep deep within the earth to foretell the fate of the world to the Aesir gods assembled in the great Hall of Valholl in Asgarth. The seeress begins by reminding her audience of the world's beginnings:

Hear me, ye hallowed beings all
ye high and low of Heimdall's children:
Thou knowest, father, that I well set forth
the destinies of the world.
I remember the kin of giants,
long ago they gave me life.
Nine worlds I know, the glorious realms
of the tree in the ground below.

The seeress tells of the time when the primordial beings Ymir and Buri were alone in Chaos and neither heaven nor earth had yet come to exist. (NOTE: from elsewhere in Icelandic literature we know that Ymir was formed from the mists of the void and Buri emerged from blocks of salty ice on which the cosmic cow Audhumla fed. Buri created for himself a son, Bor, who engendered the first trio of the Aesir gods, Othin, Vili and Ve.) The seeress reminds that the sons of Bor lifted up the Middle World, Mithgarth, which was to become the world of men. The sun shone for the first time on the virgin soil and green things began to grow.

In the new cosmos, the gods assembled and gave names to that which they had created. On the Shining Plain of Asgarth they built their temples, made tools, fashioned gold and generally lived through an age of innocence. The euphoria ended with the coming of the Fates, the three Norns of destiny: Urth, the past, Verthandi, the present and Skuld, the future.

The seeress speaks of the world ash tree, Yggdrasil, which is also the tree of knowledge whose roots are watered by the Well of Fate and beneath which sit the Norns who spin the Thread of Fate. The seeress tells of the first great war between the Aesir gods of Asgarth and the older Vanir gods. Gullveig, a primordial witch, is, for some obscure reason, speared and burnt in Othin's hall. Three times she is burnt, and three times she is reborn. The war ends in disaster for the Aesir and their fortress is partly demolished.

The spear of Othin o'er the host hath sped:
and great battle commenced in the world;
the breastwork of Asgarth was trampled down,
when Vanir strode the field of battle.

From the race of giants, who represent brute force and ignorance, comes a builder who offers to restore Valholl to the Aesir gods with walls strong enough to withstand any future attack. His price is to be the sun, the moon and the goddess of love and prosperity, Freyja. But when the work is completed Othin breaks his sacred oath and although Freyja is saved from her fate by Thor, the thunder god, who sends the giant fleeing, Othin's breach of contract plunges the godly race into a new and bitter conflict with the giants. It is this which will ultimately bring about their end.

The seeress explains that the horn of the guardian god, Heimdall, the instrument which will summon the gods to their doom, Ragnarok, is hidden beneath the Yggdrasil tree. It is to this holy ash that she travels to commune with Othin, who has given his right eye to the god of wisdom, Mimir, in exchange for knowledge of the world's, and his own, destiny. Othin reveals that the Valkyries, the warrior maidens, are ready at his command to go out and collect slain mortal heroes and bring them to Valholl in preparation for the final onslaught. The seeress is told of the approaching death of Balder, the 'Shining One', Othin's dearest son, whose slaughter with a magic dart of mistletoe hurled by the blind god Hoder is to herald the beginning of Ragnarok (see *The Death of Baldr*, page 227).

In a dramatic vision of the future, the seeress warns of the day when the cataclysm will be loosed and the old order will come to an end. In the dark forests, the forces of evil are waiting. The dragon, Nithogg, gathers strength by feeding off human corpses; the Hall of Hel, its walls dripping poison and writhing with serpents, stands ready. The phantom wolf, Fenrir, awaits his time to chase and swallow the sun.

In the forests of the east sat the old one,
where Fenrir spawned his brood;
from amongst them, worse than they all,
the wolf shall engulf the sun.

He feeds on the flesh of the battle slain,
their blood stains the seats of the gods:
through summers thence the sun shall grow dim,
and the weather shall carry its woe.

The sun grows dim and a cockerel crows to awaken the giants to final combat. At last the wolf breaks loose from his chains to run amok, dissolution and the breakdown of law and order presage the end, and man betrays man. The world tree, Yggdrasil, quivers in fateful anticipation.

The huge worm of Mithgarth, the serpent which lies in the seas encircling the earth, lashes his tail, turning the ocean into a tempest. The Naglfar, the ship of the dead, sets sail steered by the mischievous, Machiavellian character of Loki, half-god, half-giant, whose loyalties to Asgarth have always been suspect. Surt, the spirit of fire, comes from the south to cleanse the world with his consuming flames.

The gods go out from Valholl to join the final battle against the forces of ignorance, cold and darkness. Othin challenges the phantom wolf who is even then chasing the sun, and the god Freyr takes on Surt. Both heroes are slain and, as predicted, it is Vithar, Othin's son, who is left to avenge his father's death. As the battle of Ragnarok rages, the flames of purification rise and the sea wells up to flood the world. Darkness spreads in the apocalypse.

But from the ashes a new world arises ruled by another less corrupt generation of gods.

Through the grass shall the golden figures come,
and the far-famed ones will be found again,
as they were in olden days . . .

I see a hall brighter than the sun,
roofed with red gold, it is Gimle's hight.
There, blameless, will the gods be enthroned,
forever in their ease and joy.

So ends the prophecy of the seeress. It is not clear who Gimle is, but this could be yet another of Othin's many pseudonyms.

NOTE: the *Hauksbok* version includes a codicil which seems to presage the coming of the Christian god, but this is not found in the *Codex Regius* version and is probably an adulteration.

VOLUSPA HIN SKAMMA
(The Short Prophecy of the Seeress)

CULTURE OF ORIGIN: Teutonic – Nordic and Germanic (Icelandic)
PROVENANCE: the *Codex Regius* No. 2365. The manuscript lay hidden until it was rediscovered by Brynjolfur Sveinsson, bishop to the Icelandic community, circa 1643, and preserved on the instructions of Frederic III. It is housed in the Royal Library of Denmark [Copenhagen]. *Voluspa hin Skamma* is thought to be a late composition, possibly written in the twelfth century, but based on older Eddic compositions, including the *Voluspa*. The work is very brief.

The myth opens in a time after the death of Balder when the Aesir gods of Asgarth number only eleven. The god Vali has taken revenge for his brother's death and slaughtered the blind god Hoder who hurled the magic and lethal mistletoe projectile.

There follow some disjointed snatches of the genealogy of the Aesir and giant races. The poem explains that all witches are spawned from the giant Vitholf, and all warlocks from Vilmeith. Soothsayers are the progeny of Svarthofthi and the giants stem from the primordial being

Ymir. The birth of the god Heimdall is noted, born of nine giant sisters whose names are listed.

More significantly the poem accounts the mating of the half-god, half-giant Loki, first with the giantess Angrbotha to conceive the terrible wolf Fenrir, and then with Svathilfari to engender the magic eight-legged steed of Othin, Sleipnir. The poem tells of how Loki once found a half-burnt woman's heart and ate it, upon which he became pregnant and bore the race of ogres. The day of doom is prophesied and the myth ends with an arguably Christian addition identifying a new and mighty god whose name cannot be uttered.

NOTE: for a more comprehensive account of Nordic cosmogony, see *Voluspa*, page 122.

MISCELLANEOUS

POLYNESIAN: the children of the sky god Ranginui and the earth mother Papatuanuku fall out with one another and begin to fight. In particular the storm god Tawhiri-Matea takes an aggressive stance against his brothers, Tane-Mahuta, Tangaroa and Ua-Roa, the god of rain. Tawhiri-Matea and Ua-Roa, in their anger, instigate a deluge which inundates the entire earth so that the whole of Papatuanuku's body is submerged. She, however, is determined to quell her fighting children and restore herself. So she rises up, little by little, until parts of her form are clear of the ocean. Thus she fashions the Polynesian Islands.

7

Myths of Confrontation

Humankind requires that the perennial conflict between good and evil, light and dark, is reflected in its mythological store, though sometimes the distinction between the rights and wrongs of opposing forces is vaguely drawn or even ambivalent. In Hindu mythology, for example, the two sides may merge with and even replace one another, each taking on the character-istics of the opposing protagonists.

Gods may also be seen to be the harbingers of their own misfortunes against demons or other adversaries. Thus in Nordic mythology, Loki, the hybrid progeny of the gods and their arch-enemies, the giants, is courted by the gods when they have need of his cunning, but is otherwise spurned and generally given a hard time by the rest of the pantheon, with the result that he harbours a grudge against them. This animosity eventually resolves itself in the day of doom, Ragnarok, when Loki's demonic offspring rise up to defeat the pantheon of gods and bring about the end of the world.

Confrontation may not necessarily mean battling armies pitting them-selves one against the other through force of arms. Sometimes, as in the tale of the Norse gods Othin and Thor (see *Habarzljoo*, p. 144), the match is one of wits and adroitness of speech.

Early confrontation sagas tend to be conducted between the spirits of animals, hence such tales as that of Beaver and Porcupine in North American Haida tradition. Next, in terms of cultural evolution, come battles between gods and the forces of nature, be they monstrous beasts or tempests and storms. Only in later times, as more sophisticated concepts develop, does the conflict turn into one between gods and gods or gods and demons. Some-times an actual historical event, such as the battle of Mu which took place between old and new orders in Chinese history, is rewritten, taking on the mythical proportions of a conflict between celestial forces.

The story of St George and the Dragon, although not included in this volume since it falls into the category of legend, is perhaps the best known of all confrontation adventures and it is puzzling why so many cultures have resorted to a wholly fantastic, fire-breathing, lizard-like creature as the chief adversary in such tales. The snake or serpent provides more understandable subject matter since it combines the ability of endless regeneration (by sloughing its skin) and the appearance of great wisdom (its unblinking and penetrating stare) with a more lethal talent.

Often, though by no means invariably, the heroes of confrontation sagas are seen to live in the sky or at least on mountain tops while the villains of the piece live in dark places beneath the earth. The stories inevitably provide a mix of vicarious entertainment – heroes and villains battling it out in the style of a good Western – beneath which runs a more profound message, bearing on the conduct and fate of each and every person.

The stories also reflect the preoccupations and lifestyles of the audience. Thus confrontation in nomadic hunting societies tends to take place between hunter and spirits of the hunted beasts; those in areas which experience severe climatic conditions are between heroes and the forces of tempest, heat or cold; those of herders tend to be composed within the framework of such incidents as great cattle-rustling expeditions, for example the Celtic *Tain bo Fraoch*; while the sophisticated battles of the Greeks are conducted by huge and apocalyptic forces battling between Mount Olympus and the depths of the underworld. Often as in both Greek and Nordic mythology, there has been some divisive event in the heavens which has left rival factions of gods seeking supremacy. Hence there exist in Greek tradition the gods of Olympus and their arch-rivals the Titans, over whom the Olympian gods eventually secure victory.

There is an element in most confrontation myths of the trials and tribulations which beset humankind. Thus in the Celtic tale of Noinden Ulad, the goddess Macha completes a running race while in the final stages of labour. There is also an underlying morality message in most confrontation myths so that the tyrant or evil-doer is eventually vanquished. The Greek myth of Atlantis typifies this position, but there are more subtle messages to be found. Thus in the myth of Ariadne, Theseus and the Minotaur the hero, who becomes increasingly cavalier after slaughtering the monster, faces tragedy when his father Aegeos commits suicide: this may be interpreted as fate taking a hand against complacency.

ANZU

CULTURE OF ORIGIN: Mesopotamian – Old Babylonian and neo-Babylonian
PROVENANCE: known from two sources, the earlier of which consists only of a small part of the account and dates from early in the second millennium BC. The later and more complete version dates from the first millennium and copies have been found at a number of sites, the most significant being the royal library of Aššurbanipal at Nineveh. In each version the principal characters vary.

The myth is a confrontation epic, the focus of which is possession of the Tablet of Destinies. It is a battle between a god, Ninurta, the main heroic character, representing good and righteousness, and a demonic lion-headed eagle, Anzu. Ninurta is the god of thunderstorms and of the plough; his cult centres included the Sumerian city state of Nippur but, more importantly, the Assyrian fortress city of Kalakh (Biblical Calah), built by Šalmaneser I and reaching its zenith under Aššur-nasir-apli in 884 BC. The temple of Ninurta was adorned with wall carvings depicting a cosmic battle which may represent the Anzu epic.

After a short eulogy to Ninurta, the scene is set with the birth of Anzu. Ellil, god of the air, decrees that Anzu will henceforth serve the gods as a protective beast and that he will safeguard the Tablet of Destinies. But Anzu has another purpose in mind:

'I shall take the Tablet of Destinies to myself
And control the orders for all the gods.
I shall possess the throne and be master of rites.
I shall rule every one of the Igigi [the pantheon of younger sky
gods headed by Ellil].'

While Ellil is bathing, Anzu seizes the Tablet of Destinies and flies off to the mountains. Chaos ensues and Anu, the god of heaven, convenes a crisis meeting to discover if there is a hero among the gods who will challenge Anzu. They call upon Šara, a minor god of war, identified in some texts as the son of Ištar and as the tutelary deity of the city of Umma, but Šara declines the challenge. The god of wisdom, Ea, then proposes that he shall search among the ranks of all the gods to find one who will be able to conquer Anzu. The plan being agreed, Ea calls upon Belet-Ili, the Babylonian mother goddess, to persuade her favourite son, Ninurta, that he must champion the cause of the sky gods. She thus exhorts Ninurta to join battle:

'Make a path, fix the hour,
Let light dawn for the gods whom I created.
Master your devastating battle force,
Make your evil winds flash as they march over him.
Capture soaring Anzu
And inundate the earth, which I created – destroy his abode,
Let terror thunder over him,
Let fear of your battle force shake in him
Make the whirlwind rise up against him.'

Battle is joined upon a mountainside and darkness falls as the opposing forces of good and evil confront each other. Although Ninurta hurls all his strength against Anzu, he cannot destroy the demon who holds the Tablet of Destinies and he is forced to send his attendant Šarur back to Ea reporting failure.

Ea exhorts Ninurta to redouble his efforts, battle commences anew and finally good triumphs over evil:

He [Ninurta] caused an arrow to pass through pinion and wing,
A dart passed through heart and lungs.
He slew the mountains, inundated their proud pastures;
Ninurta slew the mountains, inundated their proud pastures,
Inundated the broad earth in his fury,
Inundated the midst of the mountains, slew the wicked Anzu.

Thus the Tablet of Destinies is restored to its rightful ownership by Ninurta and the epic ends with a further generous hymn in praise of the triumphant warrior.

Ninurta originates as a Sumerian deity and in earlier literature he confronts the demon Kur. In these texts Šarur is identified as a weapon which becomes personalized and which develops its own intelligence as the chief adversary, in the hands of Ninurta, of the forces of evil.

ATLANTIS

CULTURE OF ORIGIN: classical Greek, but subsequently adopted into Roman culture

PROVENANCE: recorded from an oral tradition, supposedly arising in Egypt, by the Greek writer Plato in *Timaeus and Critias*

Atlantis is an island lying in the Atlantic Ocean to the west of the Pillars of Herakles; it is ruled over by King Evenor and his consort Leucippe. They have a daughter, Clito, who is seduced by the sea god Poseidon. Poseidon builds a fortifed house for her on a mountain in the centre of the island and there she bears him five pairs of twin sons, the first-born being the giant Atlas. To accommodate the sons, the island is divided up into ten provinces, each son ruling his own region with Atlas taking the domain at the summit of the mountain. Atlantis acquires great wealth and prestige and rich cities are built with the proceeds of trade and commerce.

The descendants of the ten offspring rule peacably for many generations, but they become steadily more ambitious and tyrannical until they attempt world conquest. A great battle is fought between the Atlantaeans and the Athenians in about 9000 BC, the outcome of which is defeat for the forces of Atlantis. The island and all its inhabitants become engulfed by the sea as Poseidon takes final retribution against the arrogance of his descendants.

BEAVER AND PORCUPINE

CULTURE OF ORIGIN: native American – Haida [British Columbia and Queen
Charlotte Islands]
PROVENANCE: recorded from oral traditions. Principal sources include *Haida
Texts and Myths* J.R. Swanton. Bulletin 29, Bureau of American Ethno-
logy. Washington, 1905.

Beaver has laid in a proper store of food while Porcupine has been
lazy, so while Beaver is out one day Porcupine comes along and steals
his larder. When Beaver demands to know if Porcupine is the culprit,
Porcupine protests his innocence because it is impossible for spirit
beings to steal one from another. Beaver is less than impressed by this
excuse and goes to bite Porcupine, but he fights back and Beaver is
forced to retreat, his face stuck with Porcupine's quills. The Beaver
People rise up to avenge Beaver's affront, but Porcupine merely hurls
insults at them until they demolish his house, drag him off to an
uninhabited island and abandon him.

There is nothing on the island suitable for Porcupine to eat and he is
faced with starvation. When he thinks all is lost, however, he hears a
voice whispering to him to call on North-wind for help. A little
sceptically, he sings a song to North-wind, upon which the weather
turns so cold that the water freezes over. When the ice is thick enough
the Porcupine People set out in search of their lost relative. Eventually
they find him, but he is so feeble that he has to be carried home. They
consider Beaver's reason for abandoning him a poor excuse and
declare war. Unfortunately for the Porcupine People they lose the
battle with ignominy but, not to be outdone, they carry Beaver to the
top of a tree and abandon *him*! They have not, however, considered
Beaver's gastronomic prowess. He merely eats the tree and goes
home!

FLED BRICREND
(Bricriu's Feast)

CULTURE OF ORIGIN: Celtic – Irish
PROVENANCE: recorded from oral traditions, possibly as early as the eighth
century AD, by the chief bard of Ireland, Snechan Torpeist, in the *Book of
Druimm Snechtai*. This is now lost and no early copies have survived prior
to the eleventh century. The complete version is contained in *Leabhar ne h-
Uidhre; Book of the Dun Cow*, compiled in the eleventh century by the
Christian monk Mael Muire Mac Ceilechai [Royal Irish Academy]. Under
modern convention it is classified as part of the Ulaid (Ulster) or Craobh
Ruadh (Red Branch) Cycle of myth which, from a historical viewpoint,
relates an ongoing conflict between the Ulaid clan(s) who lived in the

Armagh region of what is now Ulster and others who were based further south in Connacht (Connaught).

Though the myth ostensibly appears to be a rambling saga of confrontation between three heroes, it also possesses hints of regenesis in the decapitation sequence. Bricriu is revealed as a Machiavellian rogue with a personality not unlike that of Loki in Nordic (Icelandic) mythology. Over all the myth is a vicarious and at times comical tale of adventure and bravery which would have appealed to the Celtic male spirit. It may be compared, in its decapitation episode, to the English legend of *Sir Gawain and the Green Knight*, since the churl (Cu Roi in disguise) possesses certain attributes which bear similarity to those of the Green Knight.

For a year Bricriu Nemthenga (Poison Tongue) has been preparing a feast in honour of Conchobhar, the King of Ulster, in a magnificent house which he has built especially for the occasion. He has also arranged for a private bower to be constructed overlooking the window of the royal bedchamber. When all is prepared, Bricriu sets out to greet Conchobhar and his Ulster chieftains at Emain Macha. Conchobhar is willing to take up the invitation to the feast, but his adjutant Fergus Mac Roth is wary, warning that Bricriu will set guest against guest. Bricriu promptly retorts that he will do exactly that, setting chief against chief, *unless* everyone attends the feast. When the reluctance continues Bricriu issues further dire intimidations until the Ulstermen agree to attend, but only after deciding on a plan to safeguard themselves against Bricriu's malicious ways. They elect to demand hostages from Bricriu and, with his consent to their condition, they set off for the feast.

Bricriu still ponders ways of winning the day. He approaches, separately, three of the great fighting heroes of Ulster – Loegure Buadach, Conall Cernach and Cu Chulainn. To each he offers the champion's portion of the feast without disclosing that he has made a similar offer to the others. Each champion assumes that the portion will rightly be his.

As Bricriu leaves the royal gathering he instructs, publicly, that the champion's portion is to go to the best warrior. The three champions are soon fighting with each other and it is left to Conchobhar and Fergus Mac Roth to separate the combatants on the understanding that the matter will be adjudicated by an 'independent', Ailill of Connacht, in the morning. Next, Bricriu attempts to incite the wives of the champions by playing on their vanities and telling each in turn that she who enters the house first shall be queen over the whole of Ulster. Thus, as with the men, he sets one against the other, but this time with a war of words. The heroes, for their part, tear away pieces of the house and even lift it from its foundations so that their wives can be the first to enter!

When the house is restored, good will returns for a while, but the women soon start to squabble again and the men all but return to open hostilities. Each challenges the other to feats of charioteering and, as they race over the province, each is confronted by an ogre. This terrifying giant defeats Loegure and Conall but is worsted by Cu Chulainn, upon which Bricriu offers him the champion's portion. The decision is promptly rejected by Loegure and Conall and again the dispute is referred to Ailill in Connacht for arbitration.

As Queen Medb watches the approach of the three heroes she is fearful for the welfare of herself and Ailill, since she feels that the two losers will inevitably take their revenge on the arbitrator. She greets the three and offers each a sumptuous guest house in which to rest. Ailill is reluctant to offer judgement straight away and requests a three-day adjournment. Medb now takes the deceitful role, offering each champion in turn the champion's portion but, while Loegure and Conall agree, Cu Chulainn sees through the ploy and accuses her of mocking him like a fool.

On the following morning Ailill and Medb set the contestants more feats of strength and bravery, including wheel-throwing, confrontation with giants, spectres and other dangers. In each test it is Cu Chulainn who wins through: the others either lose or withdraw from the challenge. The burden of arbitration is now passed to Cu Roi, the King of Munster and son of Dare. His binding judgement is rendered and he promises Cu Chulainn the championship of Ulster.

There awaits an ultimate test in which the three heroes are challenged by a hideous churl to mutual decapitation. The churl offers each man the chance to cut off his head and then allow him to retaliate. Three times the churl picks up his head and replaces it, but while Loegure and Conall flee when it is their turn to be the victim, thus failing to keep the pledge, Cu Chulainn is willing to go through with the ordeal. When the axe blade is poised to fall on his neck it miraculously turns away and the churl reveals himself to be none other than Cu Roi, who has kept his promise to Cu Chulainn of gaining the champion's portion.

CAIN AND ABEL

CULTURE OF ORIGIN: Judaic/Christian
PROVENANCE: the *Vetus Testamentum*.

The story of the fatal conflict between Cain and his brother Abel is not, in the pure sense, a myth, since it does not directly involve godly personalities. It does, however, parallel other traditional conflict sagas so closely that it should be included here. Like many such accounts, it is concerned with the confrontation between light and dark, good and evil, prosperity and dearth that humankind has recognized from the beginning of recorded history and beyond.

The first-born son of Adam and Eve, the ancestral forebears of the human race, is Cain, who becomes a farmer, tilling, sowing and harvesting the land. Eve's second son is Abel, who becomes a herdsman, keeping and breeding flocks of sheep. In due course of time the two brothers bring sacrificial offerings, the product of their respective labours, to the altar of their god. For reasons which are never explained, the god appears to accept the oblation of Abel (lambs and fat) but not that of Cain (harvest fruits). Cain is deeply offended:

> The Lord said unto Cain, Why are thou wroth? And why is thy countenance fallen? If thou doest well, shalt thou not be accepted? And if thou doest not well sin lieth at the door. And unto thee shall be his desire, and thou shalt rule over him.

An argument develops between Cain and Abel, as a result of which Cain slaughters his brother. God demands to know where Abel has gone and when Cain protest innocence of the matter, saying, 'Am I my brother's keeper?', he is cursed for ever. The land which has received the blood of his brother will become barren under Cain's hand and he will become a vagrant against whom the hands of other men are set. Nevertheless God also sets a mark upon Cain which determines that any who lays hand upon him shall suffer sevenfold. Thus Cain leaves the land of his birthright and sets about the procreation of future generations:

> And Cain went out from the presence of the Lord and dwelt in the land of Nod, on the east of Eden. And Cain knew his wife; and she conceived and bare Enoch.

See also *Emeš and Enten*, page 135.

EME'MQUT AND YA'CHINA'UT

CULTURE OF ORIGIN: Siberian – Koryak

PROVENANCE: from an oral tradition amongst the Koryak reindeer hunters living on the Kamchatka Peninsula of south-eastern Siberia. The myth was related by a shamanka named Ty'kken in a hunting camp on the Tapolovka River. Modern authorship is that of the Swedish ethnologist Waldemar Jochelson, who recorded the tale during the Jesup North Pacific Survey of 1900, sponsored by the American Society for Natural History [Memoirs of the American Museum of Natural History, 10, 1905].

When he awakens one morning while on a hunting trip deep in the forest, Eme'mqut, the son of the creator being Tenanto'mwan, discovers that his brother Qeskina'qu (Big Light) has gone missing. Eme'mqut goes home and his father immediately asks him where Qeskina'qu has gone. Eme'mqut sets out again to search for his brother, but his quest is in vain until one night, exhausted from his journeying, he is lying on the top of a hill staring at Ya'china'ut, the moon. She descends and asks what Eme'mqut is thinking about, to which he replies that he is pondering over his brother who has been lost.

Ya'china'ut suggests that, if Eme'mqut will offer suitable compensation, she will reveal where Qeskina'qu has gone. Eme'mqut demands to know what kind of compensation the moon has in mind.

'I do not require payment,' she says.

'So what am I supposed to do?' he asks.

'Marry me!'

In an effort to provide her with a token of his sincerity about the proposed arrangement Eme'mqut embraces Ya'china'ut fervently, but she says that such a gesture really means very little and that Eme'mqut will abandon her once she has revealed that which he needs to know. So Eme'mqut puts his hand down the front of her trousers and fondles her private parts, saying that things are now just the same as if he had married her.

At this Ya'china'ut is pacified and she reveals to Eme'mqut that his brother has been slaughtered by the evil *kalau* spirits of the under-world. They have flayed him and used his skin as they would use the hide of a reindeer. Eme'mqut returns home and reports the news to his father, who decides he must go to his son's rescue.

Tenanto'mwan arrives at the underground house of the *kalau*, located on an island. He discovers the skin of his son, retrieves it and goes out, passing by an iron barrel. When he looks inside the barrel he finds one of the daughters of the *kalau* hiding there, so he takes the barrel and the hostage home. He sends for Ya'china'ut and asks her if she will restore Qeskina'qu to life. The moon spirit takes the skin, beating it on the ice of the river, and as she does so the body begins to reappear, first the fingers and toes, then the arms and legs, and finally the whole torso until she restores the living brother. As reward for her services Eme'mqut marries Ya'china'ut and Qeskina'qu marries the captive daughter of the *kalau*.

EMEŠ AND ENTEN

CULTURE OF ORIGIN: Mesopotamian – Sumerian

PROVENANCE: the earliest inscribed version of the myth dates from about 2000 BC, shortly after the collapse of the Third Dynasty at Ur, but it undoubtedly originates in an earlier oral tradition. The names of the deities appear on inscriptions dating from about 3500 BC.

Enlil, the god of the air, decides that he must engender trees and crops to bring prosperity to the land. To oversee these living things he creates two gods: Enten, who will look after cows, calves, goats, sheep and lambs, and Emeš, who will take responsibility for the woods and fields and their produce. At first all seems to run smoothly but then a jealous dispute breaks out between Enten and Emeš over who shall lay claim to the title of 'farmer god'. The two claimants go to Nippur to seek the arbitration of Enlil. Enten states his case:

'O father Enlil, knowledge hast thou given me
so that I might bring the water of abundance;
farm I made to touch with farm, high I heaped the granaries;
like Asnan, the kindly maid, I caused strength to appear.'

Enlil's judgement is made in favour of Enten and he berates Emeš for comparing himself to the true 'farmer god'. Emeš accepts the arbitration with good grace and presents Enten with peace offerings so that the two rivals settle to a harmonious relationship.

ENMERKAR AND THE LORD OF ARATTA

CULTURE OF ORIGIN: Mesopotamian – Sumerian
PROVENANCE: the earliest inscribed version of the myth dates from about 2000 BC, shortly after the collapse of the Third Dynasty at Ur, but it undoubtedly originates in an earlier oral tradition. The names of the deities appear on inscriptions dating from about 3500 BC. The acknowledged translation is that of S.N. Kramer, made in 1952 [University of Pennsylvania].
   Though Enmerkar is recorded as being one of the early kings of Sumer, the following story constitutes more of a myth than a legend and it exemplifies the constant tide of petty squabbles which flared up between the disparate city states constituting the loose Sumerian federation.

The scene is set with an introduction focusing on the greatness of Erech, the city of the fertility goddess Inana, compared with neighbouring Aratta. Enmerkar, whose father is Utu the sun god, wishes to turn Aratta into a vassal state so, before the shrine of Inana, he vows to coerce the people of Aratta into supplying gold, lapis lazuli, carnelian and other precious materials in order to build new and splendid temples. Inana instructs him to send a messenger across the mountains to the Lord of Aratta with a warning that his kingdom will be destroyed unless he complies. The messenger is to repeat, as a salutary caveat, the 'Spell of Enki', which relates how the god of wisdom ended mankind's golden age.

The Lord of Aratta refuses to comply and even when, to his consternation, he is told that the matter has the endorsement of Inana, he sends an answer that he prefers to stand and fight. He does, however, offer the proviso that if Enmerkar will send Aratta a quantity of grain, Aratta will submit.

Enmerkar performs rites before Nidaba, the goddess of wisdom, and in response to her counsel he sends grain to, and receives carnelian from, Aratta. When Enmerkar returns his messenger to Aratta armed only with the sceptre of command, the Lord of Aratta appears to be ready to capitulate, but instead issues a fresh challenge to Enmerkar, demanding a single combat contest between champions representing the two cities.

Enmerkar accepts the challenge, but he also demands gold and other valuables for his patroness Inana and threatens wholesale destruction of Aratta unless more carnelian is sent with which to decorate Inana's temple.

The myth ends with an observation that Aratta is totally destroyed by flood but then restored by Inana, to whom the inhabitants submit large quantities of gold, silver and lapis lazuli.

ERRA AND IŠUM

CULTURE OF ORIGIN: Mesopotamian – Akkadian

PROVENANCE: copies of the text, inscribed on to five tablets and comprising about 750 lines, have been found at a number of different sites and the author is identified as Kabti-ilani-Marduk, whose family name first appears in the records in about 765 BC. The sites include Babylon, Ur, Aššur and Nineveh and the material dates, at the earliest, from the eighth century BC. The written narrative is almost certain to incorporate much older oral traditions. This is revealed in the opening lines which take the form typical of a tale transmitted by word-of-mouth.

Extracts were popular as monumental inscriptions and were also often inscribed on to talismanic amulets. The wording shows considerable variance, suggesting that differences in the story content persisted at local level, even though the written version became fairly standardized.

It is difficult to categorize this myth, which is more of a rhetorical poem than a saga. The characters make declamatory speeches and some authors suggest, though there is nothing to confirm or deny the argument, that the composition may have formed the basis of a ritualized drama. The personalities include Erra, the Babylonian god of war and plague (also referred to as Nergal, who is a major underworld and fertility god), Išum, his attendant and god of fire who is also brother of the sun god Šamaš, and Marduk, the Babylonian national god. The epic is set at a time when Babylon is faced with armed aggression and it focuses on the awesome and highly unpredictable nature of Erra, whose temper is being directed against Babylonia. Her defence lies in an aged and decrepit Marduk whose potency leaves something to be desired and it is left to the statesmanship of Išum, acting as a shield between Erra's anger and suffering humanity, to defuse the situation.

After a preface outlining the theme, the concept is introduced that Erra is preparing for war. Erra, speaking in the third person, is undecided whether to wage war or not. With some hesitation, he orders his generals, the Sebitti, the seven great warrior gods fathered by Anu, home until such time as they are called to arms. This section is followed by a flashback to the time when Anu named and decreed the destinies of the seven Sebitti. Meanwhile the Sebitti chide Erra for his hesitation:

They said to Erra, 'Rise! Stand up!
Why do you stay at home like a weak old man?
How can you stay there like a lisping child?
Are we to eat women's bread,
as one who has never marched on to the battlefield?
Are we to be fearful and nervous
as if we had no experience of war?'

This plea to Erra has the desired result and he turns to Išum, telling him to open up a path and release his cohorts to wage war. Išum, however, urges restraint:

'Lord Erra, why have you planned evil for the gods?
You have plotted to overthrow countries and to destroy
their people, but will you not turn back?'

Erra points out that he is the great war god, afraid of nothing, yet the people of Babylon no longer fear him because of the influence of Marduk, who has now neglected his responsibility. He goes to meet Marduk and chides him for his lack of purpose and slovenly appearance. There follows an exchange of words between the two in which Marduk querulously threatens the stability of the world if he is obliged to rise up and fight. He reminds Erra that he created a great flood during which he sent all the craftsmen of the world to the bottom of the Apsu, instructing them never to return. Erra, for his part, warns that until Marduk rectifies matters, he himself will take control of the heaven and the earth.

In Tablet II, Erra displays his anger at Marduk's impiety in plotting to destroy the land and the people, and in sending all the craftsmen of the world away. The goddess Ištar tries to intervene, but Išum explains that Erra is too angry to be placated and there follows another long rhetorical outburst from Erra in which he outlines to Išum the havoc he will cause if Marduk does not capitulate:

'I shall devastate cities and make of them a wilderness.
I shall destroy mountains and fell their cattle.
I shall stir up oceans and destroy their produce.
I shall dig out reed thickets and graves and I shall
burn them like Gerra.'

Tablet III continues in the same vein and, as Erra momentarily exhausts his spleen, Išum again urges restraint. Erra's mood becomes one of indignation that Išum is adopting an appeasing attitude while Marduk's behaviour is swaggering and irresponsible. Išum, however, continues with his diplomacy, pointing out to Erra that, as war god, he wields immense power and that it is impossible for warfare to take place without his consent. Why, therefore, he asks, does Erra believe that the gods despise him? Tablet IV suggests that Erra has been equally guilty of acting like an aggressive braggart who is influencing the people of Babylon to take up arms:

He who is ignorant of weapons is unsheathing his dagger,
He who is ignorant of bows is stringing his bow,
He who is ignorant of battle is making war,
He who is ignorant of wings is flying like a bird.

Išum makes the terse observation that Erra is the decoy and the people of Babylon are the birds whom Erra has ensnared. He prophesies a grim fate for the city should Erra pursue his murderous intent.

At this juncture Marduk, also in the third person, speaks, a senile caricature who rambles about past events without any coherent thrust to his argument. It is not clear whether the poet intends Marduk to be seen wholly thus or whether the point of his oratory is merely difficult to follow.

The text returns to the debate between Erra and Išum, the latter redoubling his diplomatic efforts with the war god. Erra is persuaded to leave Babylon unscathed and channel his anger and energy into battles elsewhere. Tablet V begins with Erra proclaiming his bellicose nature, but Išum again takes the role of the diplomat:

'Warrior, be still and listen to my words!
What if you were to rest now, and we would serve you?
We know that nobody can stand up against you in your day of wrath!'

Išum's patience and counsel pays off as Erra is persuaded to relent and the epic ends in curious fashion as the scribe identifies himself and explains that he has learned the composition in a dream. Erra, now in the first person, appears to endorse it.

'Let this song endure forever, let it last for eternity!
Let all countries listen to it and praise my valour!
Let settled people see and magnify my name!'

TAIN BO FRAOCH
(The Cattle Raid of Froech)

CULTURE OF ORIGIN: Celtic – Irish

PROVENANCE: recorded from oral traditions, possibly as early as the eighth century AD, by the chief bard of Ireland, Snechan Torpeist, in the *Book of Druimm Snechtai*. This is now lost and no copies have survived prior to the eleventh century. The complete version is contained in the *Leabhar Laighnech: Book of Leinster*, compiled circa 1160 by Aed Mac Crimtheinn [Dublin Institute for Advanced Studies].

After the *Tain bo Cuailgne* (see page 175), *Tain bo Fraoch* is the second most popular of the Irish Celtic cattle-raid stories and, according to some authorities, the derivation of the English *Beowulf* saga. Under modern convention it is classified as part of the Ulaid (Ulster) or Craobh Ruadh (Red Branch) Cycle of myths which, from a historical viewpoint, relate an ongoing conflict between the Ulaid clan(s) who lived in the Armagh region of what is now Ulster and others who were based further south in Connacht (Connaught). The story serves, in part, as a cameo prelude or scene-setter for the great *Tain bo Cuailgne* saga, but it is also a love myth. It recounts the rocky path trodden by Fraoch to gain the hand of Findabair, the daughter of Ailill and Medb of Connacht, the price for which is Fraoch's support in the cattle raid against Ulster.

Findabair falls in love with Fraoch, son of Idath and one of the Tuatha de Danaan (people of the goddess Danu, the collective name for the Irish pantheon) who live in the realm of Side (the other world). When Fraoch hears of Findabair's infatuation he goes to the goddess Boann (Board) to obtain bridal gifts, including rich clothes, weapons, horses, hounds and slaves, and the company sets out for Cruachan, the stronghold of Ailill and Medb in Connacht. A huge crowd comes out to greet them, they are welcomed in the royal palace with apartments set aside for them and Ailill offers to prepare food. Medb, however, is reluctant. She settles down instead to play games of *fidchell* (chess) with her guests while musicians entertain them on harps and, though they play the game for three days, no food is provided. Medb is ashamed to discover that so much time has passed, agreeing with Ailill that it is time to eat, and a feast is laid out which lasts for three more days.

When Fraoch is asked the purpose of his visit he is evasive, but requests that the stay is extended for a week, to which Ailill agrees. Until now Fraoch has made no contact with Findabair but, one day at dawn, he goes to the river, where he meets her. She gives him a ring as a token of her love, but tells him she will not leave with him unless he pays a fair compensation to the people of Connacht. Not suspecting the dawn meeting, Ailill is wary that Findabair will elope with Fraoch, but Medb points out that such a liaison may be to Connacht's advantage in the forthcoming cattle raid against Ulster. Ailill therefore offers Findabair's hand, provided that Fraoch pays a price which will include, among other items, help in plundering cattle from the Ulster hero Cu Cuailgne. Fraoch refuses the terms, arguing that the price is excessive even by Medb's standards, and Ailill and Medb now plot to kill him, persuading him to swim in a river inhabited by a monster. When Ailill finds Findabair's ring in Fraoch's clothing he knows that his fears are justified and throws it into the river, where it is swallowed by a salmon. The monster attacks Fraoch, but Findabair saves his life by swimming out with a sword with which he decapitates the beast. Ailill and Medb admit that they were wrong to plot against Fraoch, but agree that Findabair must die for deceiving her father. They invite Fraoch to a feast offering him a ritual bath in a meat broth which heals his wounds and restores him to health.

Realizing that Findabair is to be punished, Fraoch instructs a lad to search for the salmon and to give it to Findabair to cook. When Ailill demands to see the ring he has given to Findabair and sentences her to death unless she can produce it, she, for her part, insists that she has been unjustly accused and she will not stay in Ailill's house if the ring is produced. The ring is discovered lying on the cooked salmon and, to exonerate Findabair from blame, Fraoch offers a gallant explanation of how he came by it. Honour is restored all round and it is agreed that, if Fraoch returns with his cattle for the raid against Ulster, Findabair will be his.

Fraoch, however, discovers that his own cattle (and his means of gaining Findabair) have been stolen. With his ally Conall Cernach he sets out on a trail which takes him to Europe and across the Alps and, eventually, he locates his animals in a place where he finds a woman from his own people. She assists Fraoch and Conall in their endeavour and the two heroes slaughter the cattle thieves before returning to Ireland, where Fraoch, as promised, goes to assist Ailill and Medb in the great cattle raid of Cuailgne.

GLOOSKAP (The Liar) AND MALSUM (The Wolf)

CULTURE OF ORIGIN: native American – Algonquin
PROVENANCE: oral traditions recorded in *Algonquin Legends of New England* C.G. Leland, Boston and New York 1885.

This myth is a typical confrontation narrative between the forces of light and darkness, with Glooskap standing·on the side of light and Malsum opposing him.

The protagonists are brothers, spirits whose mother has died in childbirth. From her corpse Glooskap, who is seen as benevolent though in a cunning manner (hence his nickname), creates the sun, the moon and all living things, while Malsum makes all the things which he believes will harm or hinder mankind. These include the mountains and hills, snakes and scorpions. The siblings each possess an 'Achilles heel' which each keeps secret from the other. Glooskap attempts to delude his brother by telling him that his fatal weakness is the touch of an owl's feather. Malsum responds by confiding that, for him, to be struck by a fern root would be a lethal blow.

Malsum fells an owl and, with one of its feathers, brushes the sleeping Glooskap, who appears to expire, only to revive again. Again Malsum tries to learn the secret of Glooskap's fatal weakness and is told that a blow from a pine root will do the trick. Once more he attempts to deliver the lethal strike and once more Glooskap revives and derides him.

Glooskap now chases his brother deep into the forest. He sits down by a stream and whispers the truth, that only a flowering rush can kill him. He knows as he utters the words that they will be overheard by Quah-beet, the Beaver, and that Quah-beet cannot resist gossip.

The Beaver runs off and relates what he has heard to Malsum, asking, in return, that Malsum gives him wings so that he may fly. Malsum roars with laughter and the Beaver, infuriated, goes back to Glooskap and confesses his crime. Glooskap decides he has had enough of his brother's treachery, digs up a fern root and promptly slays Malsum.

Malsum is not lost altogether, though. He returns as the spirit guardian of wolves, animals which constantly harry and threaten mankind.

GODS, DEMONS AND THE AMBROSIA OF IMMORTALITY

CULTURE OF ORIGIN: Vedic and Brahmanic Hindu [India]
PROVENANCE: the *Rg Veda* collection of 1028 hymns (Vedas), composed in Sanskrit circa 1200 BC and based on an oral tradition which was in circulation among the Aryan immigrants to the subcontinent circa 1700–700 BC. Used as hymns of praise at the time of religious sacrifice, the Vedas provide less of a narrative than various comments on the mythology and it is from later works, including the *Brahmanas* (900–700

BC) and the Vedic commentary of Sayana (circa 1350 AD), that a more coherent narrative emerges. The main source is the *Satapatha Brahmana*.

The myth accounts for the triumph of light over darkness and immortality over death, but in Vedic mythology confrontation is not so clear-cut as in other sagas. It is sometimes difficult to distinguish gods from demons. The schemes by which the gods triumph become modified during the period of Hindu classical writing so that while the Vedas describe a heroic conflict, the epic myths introduce more devious stratagems and the Puranas reveal even more elaborate deceptions. The epic myth described here is full of apparent paradoxes.

Out of the void of chaos, and through the power of Brahma, the primordial being Prajapati creates two classes of beings, the gods who enter the sky from his mouth and the evil demons who stem from his thigh (from his downward breath) and enter into the earth to become the apotheosis of the night. As he spawns them the gods appear to Prajapati as light and the demons as darkness.

Gods and demons alike are originally imbued with both truth and falsehood, but as they evolve the gods follow the path of truth and abandon deceit while the demons take the opposing position. Yet paradoxically the gods become poorer and weaker because they choose truth, while the demons become rich and powerful. The gods therefore elect to use deceit as a weapon against the demons. They make animal sacrifice, but cover their actions when they believe the demons are likely to discover them. By completing the sacrifice overtly they lay the foundations for triumph over their fraternal enemy.

The gods, assembled in the heavens on the golden mountain of Meru, wish to obtain the divine elixir, ambrosia. The god Narayana suggests to Brahma that gods and demons alike shall churn up the primeval ocean. The plan is agreed and it is further decided that Mount Mandara shall be uprooted by the serpent Ananta for use as a churning stick. Kurma, the tortoise incarnation of the god Višnu, agrees to hold the churning stick and the tip of the mountain is tied in place on his back. The king of the serpents, Vasuki, is employed as a rope wound around Mount Mandara.

As the gods hurl Vasuki back and forth, smoke and flame come from his mouth and there is a sound of thunder as the ocean starts to churn. Vast numbers of water creatures are crushed and the whole mountain becomes enveloped in flame; all its animals and birds are burned alive. The sap of the great trees and the juices of the herbs cascade from the stick-mountain and flow into the ocean. These juices, combined with liquid gold and water, are destined to form the ambrosia of immortality.

The gods complain to Brahma that they have been churning for a long time and that they are tired, but have thus far tasted no ambrosia.

All that has happened is that the sea has turned to milk and from it has come clarified butter. The god Narayana is instructed by Brahma to give them strength and they resume their task. But now from the ocean of milk a black poison, *halahala*, exudes. From it comes Jyestha, the goddess of misfortune, and its fumes threaten to poison the entire world until the god Šiva agrees to swallow the toxin in order to preserve the universe.

Finally the physician god, Dhanvantari, emerges from the milk, carrying a white bowl containing *amrta*, the ambrosia, but the demons see it and steal it for themselves. The situation is temporarily resolved when the goddess Mohini, a female incarnation of Višnu, seduces the demons into returning the ambrosia. Mohini offers the elixir to the gods to drink, upon which the demons become enraged and a great battle commences. Naharana enters the fray, followed by Nara, another manifestation of Višnu, with his divine bow. From the sky Višnu calls upon his discus, which he hurls, slaughtering demons by the thousand. The demons respond by hurling back mountains. Nara fires off volleys of arrows and eventually the demons retreat into the earth and the depths of the ocean. Mount Mandara is returned to its rightful place and Indra gives the ambrosia into the safe keeping of Visnu.

In a separate episode, related in the *Kathaka Samhita*, the demons keep the ambrosia, prior to battle, in the mouth of Susna, a drought demon ultimately slaughtered by Indra. When the demon warriors fall dead, Susna revives them by breathing the ambrosia into them. To combat Susna, Indra turns himself into a drop of honey which Susna eats. He then transmutes into a falcon and flies away with the precious ambrosia.

HARBARZLJOO
(Lay of Harbarth)

CULTURE OF ORIGIN: Teutonic – Nordic (Icelandic)

PROVENANCE: the *Codex Regius* No. 2365, composed by an unknown hand circa tenth century AD and probably Norwegian. The manuscript lay hidden until it was rediscovered by Brynjolfur Sveinsson, bishop to the Icelandic community, circa 1643, and preserved on the instructions of Frederic III. It is housed in the Royal Library of Denmark [Copenhagen]. The latter part is contained in the *Codex Arnamagnaeanus* No. 544 (*Hauksbok*) [Copenhagen University]. There seems to be no verse scheme to the composition, which makes it unusual among the Eddic literature.

The myth sets the two best known deities of the northern pantheon against each other in a traditional matching of prowess and accomplishment. Othin, the supreme god, perhaps representing nobility, is in verbal contest with the thunder god, Thor, who may epitomize the peasant stock. The victor of the exchange is always going to be Othin and the myth is perhaps a social comment on the strict and often confrontational class structure which once existed in Norway (though not in Iceland – hence the suggested origin of authorship).

Thor is returning home from a foreign troll-slaying trip and he reaches a river. He calls to the ferryman, who is on the opposite side, to fetch him across, boasting that he is carrying a basket of the finest food. The ferryman calls back with sombre, if spurious, information that the people back home are in mourning because Thor's mother, Fjorgyn the earth goddess, is dead. He adds a scathing observation that Thor looks too shabby a person for his mother's demise to cause much of a stir.

Thor ignores the gibe and demands to know the name of the ferry owner. The ferryman replies that his master's name is Hildolf (Battle-wolf). Thor then identifies himself with some bravado and the ferryman introduces himself more modestly as Harbarth (Hoar-beard) which, unknown to Thor, is one of the many pseudonyms of Othin. The two then banter with each other from opposite sides of the river, exchanging mild insults. The ferryman taunts Thor by telling him that since a huge giant called Hrungnir has been slain, nobody really bothers him. Not to be outdone Thor points out that it was he who slew the giant.

The ferryman turns the subject of discussion to his conquests with women:

'Outwitted them with guile did I,
with sisters seven I lay,
my fond desires through them I worked.
But what, in meantime, Thor, didst thou?'

Thor can only respond with a further catalogue of conquests on the battlefield:

'Slew I the mighty giant Thjatsi,
and the dreaded eyes of Alvaldi's son
I tossed to the cloudless sky.
These are the marks of my conquest,
which now the world may see.
But what didst thou, in meantime, Harbarth?'

The ferryman continues with his tales of prowess in the bedroom, though with increasing reliance on his skills in wit and smooth talk. Soon he is beginning to gain a verbal edge over the man on the opposite shore, mentioning casually that while Othin slays noble-men, Thor only manages to vanquish slaves. This is a barb which clearly pricks Thor's sensitivities, so the ferryman begins to lay on the taunts more thickly. He reminds Thor of an occasion when the thunder god and his companions had been obliged to shelter for the night in the glove of a ferocious giant:

'In terror thou didst never risk
a fart or sneeze,
lest Fjalar thee awoke.'

As the contest of words continues, it is the ferryman, by now quite obviously a disguised Othin, who wins the match with his sophisticated ironies and acid wit. Thor begins to look increasingly the stouthearted yeoman with too much brawn and too little brain. Othin emphasizes his own ability simultaneously to charm maidens and to slay noblemen, while Thor can only keep up his tedious recitation of giant-slaying for the good of mankind.

Thor becomes increasingly frustrated by his own gaucheness and his inability to match Othin's dexterity of tongue and the final insult comes when Othin refuses, contemptuously, to row across the water for his customer and tells Thor to walk the rest of the way home.

NOTE: for a more comprehensive account of Nordic cosmogony see *Voluspa*, page 122.

HORUS AND SETH

CULTURE OF ORIGIN: Egyptian
PROVENANCE: identified in fragmentary scenes from the Pyramid Texts inscribed during the Old Kingdom period (circa 2649–2152 BC), from Coffin Texts dating from the Middle Kingdom (circa 2040–1783 BC) and from later New Kingdom papyri (circa 1567–1085 BC). These include material contained in the Papyrus Chester Beatty I [Dublin] and the Papyrus of Nebseni. There is further evidence in the Temple of Horus at Edfu in Upper Egypt. The court proceedings are recorded on a papyrus dating from the XX Dynasty (1200–1085 BC).

The protracted and detailed account of this epic mythological conflict between the forces of abundance and desolation, light and darkness, is of great significance in respect of the legitimate succession of the Egyptian crown since, during his lifetime, each and every Pharaoh was considered to be the embodiment of the god Horus. The coronation of the new ruler was thus enshrined in, and sanctified by, mythical precedent.

Seth has murdered his brother Osiris (see also *Isis and Osiris*, page 235). Horus, the son of Isis and Osiris, has been brought up in great secrecy by his mother and he has pledged both to avenge his father's death and to take his rightful place on the Egyptian throne. Horus takes his case to the supreme court of law, the Broad Hall of Geb, presided over by the sun god of Heliopolis, Re, on the auspicious occasion when the god of wisdom, Thoth, is to present Re with the 'Sacred Eye' or the 'Eye of Re' (see page 108), the sacred symbol of justice.

The two protagonists gather support from the other gods in the pantheon, Seth receiving the powerful backing of Re since he is the elder claimant. No initial agreement is reached and an impasse develops which lasts for eighty years. Eventually the arbitration of the goddess Neith is sought and she adjudicates that Horus shall inherit the crown and that Seth shall be given the daughters of Re as compensation. Re finds the judgement unacceptable, so Horus and Seth are ordered back to court and the wrangling commences again.

Seth claims that his unequalled strength makes him the only contender suitable to defend Egypt from her enemies, including the demonic serpent god of the underworld, Apophis. Supporters of Horus argue that, as the son of Osiris, he has more legitimate claim to the throne than Seth, the brother.

Isis, the consort of the slain Osiris, predictably backs Horus and proves herself to be a clever barrister to the extent that Seth threatens to slaughter one god every day with his war club if Isis is permitted to continue attendance at the hearing. Re complies reluctantly and orders that the proceedings be continued on an island from which Isis is barred. She, however, disguises herself as an old hag and dupes the ferryman. Once across the water she changes her appearance to that of a beautiful young woman and, through a devious ploy in which she calls on Seth to defend herself and her son from injustice, she deceives him into championing her cause and thus, by implication, into an admission of guilt, since there is a direct parallel with the 'real' events taking place in the story.

Subsequent episodes of the dispute become bizarre. Isis has ambivalent sentiments about Seth with whom she has a strong blood bond and at one juncture, when he takes the guise of a hippopotamus, she spears him with a harpoon. However, she soon relents and removes the barb from his body. Horus, enraged at the sparing of Seth's life, decapitates his mother although her head is subsequently and inexplicably restored to her body. Seth gouges out Horus's eyes, but these are also restored, miraculously, by the goddess Hathor.

The dispute takes on new dimensions when Seth attempts to bugger Horus, but the potential victim catches Seth's semen in his hands and Isis, through another piece of trickery, turns the situation to Seth's disgrace and humiliation. In one version of events Seth's leg and testicles are ripped off by Horus and when the latter emerges triumphant, Seth is doomed to carry the victor forever on his shoulders.

In other texts Osiris is called upon to make judgement from the underworld. He votes in favour of his son and heir, issuing threats of dire retribution if his wishes are not met and the court is obliged to concede victory to Horus.

At Edfu, Seth's demise is more violent. In his hippopotamus guise he is attacked without mercy by Horus, who spears him no less than ten times in different parts of his body. The hippopotamus is finally dismembered and, on the advice of Isis, distributed among the other cities of the country. This ritual was enacted annually at Edfu in a religious drama which involved a model hippo and the eating of a hippo cake cut into ten slices.

HUITZILOPOCHTLI AND COYOLXAUHQUI

CULTURE OF ORIGIN: Aztec – classical Mesoamerican [Mexico]
PROVENANCE: probably worshipped circa 750 AD until 1500 AD and known from tradition in pre-Columbian codices and detail on stone carvings. Much of the iconographic description of Coatlicue is gained from a colossal headless statue and the primordial battle is depicted on the walls of the Great Temple at Tenochtitlan. The revenge of the sun god for the death of his mother signifies the triumph of light over darkness.

Coatlicue (she-with-the-serpent-skirt), the creator goddess of the earth and mankind, is the consort and female principle of Ometeotl, the primordial god who rules the highest of the thirteen heavens, Omeyocan, which lies above the sun, moon, wind and other elements. Coatlicue bears the moon goddess Coyolxauhqui (golden bells) and four hundred sons who become the stars of the southern sky, but she is then widowed when the world age ends. Later she conceives another great astral deity, the sun god Tezcatlipoca in his aspect as Huitzilopochtli (blue-humming-bird-on-the-left-foot). He is engendered in a mysterious manner when Coatlicue is impregnated by a ball of feathers as she sweeps the serpent mountain of Coatepec [near Tula] and so outraged at the apparent dishonour are her other children (who represent the forces of darkness) that they decapitate her. Huitzilopochtli, however, springs fully armed from his mother's womb, taking revenge for her death by slaughtering Coyolxauhqui and hurling her corpse from the top of a mountain. He engages his half-brothers in a primordial cosmic battle and vanquishes them also. The outcome of the battle is that night is banished for day.

A separate mythological source suggests that Coyolxauhqui sides with Huitzilopochtli in the epic struggle. She is fatally wounded and, in order to save her existence, the sun god decapitates her and hurls her head into the sky to become the orb of the moon.

ICTINIKE AND BUZZARD

CULTURE OF ORIGIN: native American – Sioux, including the Iowa and
   Omaha tribes [north of the Arkansas River to Lake Michigan and up the
   Missouri Valley]
PROVENANCE: recorded from an oral tradition.
   The subject of the myth was generally regarded as a trickster, though
the Omaha tribe apparently viewed him as a war god. It is a typical tale of
good winning through against evil. There is also a considerable focus on
animistic beliefs in which spirit beings inhabit the bodies of animals.

Ictinike meets Buzzard and requests a lift on his back. Buzzard
obliges, but flies over a hollow tree trunk into which he drops Ictinike
who becomes imprisoned until a hunting party passes by. Ictinike
happens to be wearing raccoon skins, so he pokes one of the tails out
and waves it about until some women see it. When they enlarge the
hole he jumps out and frightens them away. He lies on the ground
feigning death and waits. First Eagle, Rook and Magpie descend,
intending to eat him, but after a while Buzzard is lured down. Ictinike
leaps up and scalps him, which is why the American buzzard is bald!

ICTINIKE AND RABBIT

CULTURE OF ORIGIN: native American – Sioux, including the Iowa and
   Omaha tribes [north of the Arkansas River to Lake Michigan and up the
   Missouri Valley]
PROVENANCE: recorded from an oral tradition.
   The subject of the myth was generally regarded as a trickster, though
the Omaha tribe apparently viewed him as a war god. It is a typical tale of
good winning through against evil. As in the previous entry, there is also a
considerable focus on animistic beliefs in which spirit beings inhabit the
bodies of animals.

Ictinike, the son of the sun god, is thrown out of heaven for his
deceitful behaviour. One day he meets with Rabbit, who offers to
assist Ictinike in any way he can. On request Rabbit shoots down a
bird flying in the sky and Ictinike tells him to go and fetch the game
from where it is caught in a tree. At first Rabbit is reluctant, but
eventually he strips off his clothes and climbs the tree to a point where
he too becomes stuck. Ictinike is greatly amused, dons Rabbit's
clothes, sets off for the nearest village where he meets two beautiful
daughters of a chief and promptly marries the elder sister. The
younger girl marches off to the forest and sulks until she hears Rabbit
calling from the tree. She obliges by cutting the tree down, melting
the gum which has stuck to his fur and, having discovered they are

both victims of the same villain, taking him back to the village, where he causes some ribald amusement.

At this juncture an eagle flies overhead and Ictinike attempts to shoot it down. Rabbit, however, brings it to earth, upon which each of its feathers transforms into a new eagle. Each morning Ictinike fires an arrow at one, misses, and it is left to Rabbit to bring it down.

Time passes and the clothes which Ictinike stole from Rabbit become worn out. Rabbit, however, is generous enough to return the garments which Ictinike left behind when he stranded Rabbit up a tree. Rabbit now commands the tribe to beat their drums and Ictinike jumps up and down so that every bone in his body is shaken. Finally the drums beat so loudly, and he jumps so high, that he breaks his neck and Rabbit is avenged.

ILLUYANKA

CULTURE OF ORIGIN: Hattic or pre-Hittite – Anatolian
PROVENANCE: cuneiform text derived from an oral tradition and discovered on tablets at the site of Boghazkoy in Turkey. KUB xii. 66; KUB xvii. 5 and 6 translated by Albrecht Goetze (*Ancient Near Eastern Texts* ed. J.B. Pritchard).

The myth undoubtedly accompanied, and was recited during, the New Year *Purulli* festival and it celebrates the triumph of benevolent over destructive forces of nature in a mountainous region where storms bring life-giving rain. It is essentially a good–versus–evil myth and is typical of the 'slaying the dragon' stories which occur worldwide, although the reference to Hupasiya being forbidden to look out of his windows resists any explanation other than the ubiquitous notion that those who have been taken into the company of the gods may no longer maintain contact with the mortal world. The legend of St George and the Dragon offers strong comparison.

NOTE: the myth predates the introductions to the pantheon made under Hurrian domination of the region and where Hurrian titles are recognized they are included in brackets.

The storm god Taru (Tešub) confronts the dragon Illuyanka in a place called Kiskilussa. In their first encounter, Taru is vanquished. He demands assistance from all the other deities and, in particular, from his daughter Inara. To encourage the gods of Hatti to co-operate Inara prepares a feast and asks a mortal hero, Hupasiya, to help her in the task of tricking Illuyanka into submission. Hupasiya agrees, but on the condition that Inara will sleep with him.

Inara dresses Hupasiya in her clothes and leads him, thus disguised, to the dragon's lair where he entices Illuyanka out on the pretext of inviting him to the feast. The dragon and his children accept the invitation and become hopelessly drunk. In his inebriated state Illuyanka cannot return to his lair and Hupasiya trusses him up with ropes so that the storm god can slay him.

To honour her pledge to Hupasiya, Inara builds a cliff-top house in the land of Tarukka in which she instals the hero. There is one condition to his tenancy: while Inara is away he must not look out of the window because, should he do so, he will see his wife and children. For twenty days Hupasiya obeys, but then he looks out and sees his family. Inara is enraged and kills him while Taru sows the weeds of dereliction over the house. Inara returns to Kiskilussa where she becomes the consort of the king.

A later version of the myth tells how Illuyanka first steals the eyes and the heart of Taru. The storm god then marries the daughter of a poor man and she conceives a son. When the boy grows to manhood he, in turn, marries the daughter of Illuyanka. Taru asks that, when the son goes to his father-in-law's house, he brings back Taru's eyes and heart. This the son does and when the storm god is restored he goes to the sea to engage Illuyanka in battle once more. This time he slays both the dragon and his own son who has sided with his old adversary.

INDRA AND THE ASSAULT ON DITI

CULTURE OF ORIGIN: Epic Hindu [India]

PROVENANCE: the epic text known as the *Ramayana of Valmiki*. The *Ramayana* was written down sometime between 300 BC and 300 AD and essentially it narrates the abduction of the wife of Lord Rama by a foreign (Sri Lankan) deity and her subsequent restoration and fate. It also serves to introduce several of the more important deities in the Hindu pantheon within a dramatic context. In this episode the weather god Indra and his storm-god sons, the Maruts, are the key players in a drama involving abortion, fratricide and incest which illustrates the ongoing conflict between gods and demons. The victim of assault is Diti, the daughter of Daksa and mother of a race of demons.

Most of the sons of Diti, the demonic Daityas, have been slaughtered by the soldiers of the storm god Rudra at the time of the churning of the primeval ocean. Diti desires a son who will slay Indra and, in order to produce an offspring of suitable calibre, she practises severe asceticism. Her husband, Kasyapa, agrees to her wishes and impregnates her before going away to become an ascetic himself. While she is practising her asceticism Rudra supplies all her physical needs, but when she lies down to sleep she does so in an impure position, with her head facing north, which indicates to Rudra that Diti is pregnant. When the storm god sees this he enters her body, cutting the living embryo into seven pieces with his thunderbolt. The embryo cries out, causing Diti to awaken, but still Rudra continues to dissect it. Diti is overcome with grief and she begs that the seven portions should survive as celestial beings, the Maruts. Rudra, in a moment of magnanimity, accedes to her request and the differences between the two deities are reconciled.

INDRA AND VRTRA

CULTURE OF ORIGIN: Vedic and Brahmanic Hindu [India]
PROVENANCE: the *Rg Veda* collection of 1028 hymns (Vedas), composed in Sanskrit circa 1200 BC and based on an oral tradition which was in circulation among the Aryan immigrants to the subcontinent circa 1700 BC–700 BC. Used as hymns of praise at the time of religious sacrifice, the Vedas provide less of a narrative than various comments on the mythology and it is from later works, including the *Brahmanas* (900–700 BC) and the Vedic commentary of Sayana (circa 1350 AD), that a more coherent narrative emerges.
     The slaying of the demonic god Vrtra is one of the great heroic deeds of Hindu myth and it symbolizes the release of the vital rains which have been imprisoned by Vrtra. The story represents one of the many ubiquitous versions of the 'slaying the dragon' myth. The hero, in this instance, is Indra, the leader of the gods. The episode also represents the triumph of the Aryan peoples over their enemies and the establishment of order in the cosmos out of the corpse of Vrtra, who symbolizes chaos.

I sing of the heroic deeds of Indra
which he who controls the thunderbolt accomplished.
The dragon he slew and released from it the waters.
The bellies of the mountains he sliced open.
He slew the dragon which lay upon the mountain.
For him Tvastr made the roaring thunderbolt.
The waters flowed to the sea like lowing cattle.
Like a rampant bull he took the soma and drank from the three bowls.
Indra took up the thunderbolt weapon.
He hurled it and killed the first born of dragons.

The hymn goes on to explain that at the precise moment when the dragon is slain, struck by Indra's thunderbolt, the sun, the sky and the dawn come into being and Indra becomes invincible. The life waters of Vrtra's mother, the goddess Danu, depicted as imprisoned cattle, burst out and flow over him as she lies like a cow with her calf.

KODOYANPE AND COYOTE

CULTURE OF ORIGIN: native American – Chinook and Californian
PROVENANCE: recorded from oral traditions. Principal sources include *Chinook Texts* F. Boas, Bulletin 20, Bureau of American Ethnology, Washington 1895.

These separate tribes have subscribed to conflicting views about which of the protagonists is good and which is bad. The Chinook hero is Coyote, the spirit of the night, who emerges from his underground lair at dusk; that of the Californian tribes, including the Maidu, is Kodoyanpe, personifying the sun who travels from east to west each day.

Together Coyote and Kodoyanpe create the world and make it fit for mankind, whom they engender out of small pieces of carved wood. They then discover that the wooden dolls are useless for the purpose, so they make them into animals instead. At length Kodoyanpe gains the impression that Coyote is acting to thwart his good intentions and the two spirits fall out. Each resolves to dispose of the other, Kodoyanpe with the assistance of a general called Conqueror, and Coyote with a terrifying army of monsters. Eventually Coyote gains the upper hand and defeats Kodoyanpe. The latter, however, has secretly buried many of the wooden dolls which he once carved, and these now spring up to become the native American peoples.

LAHAR, AŠNAN AND THE CREATION OF CATTLE AND GRAIN

CULTURE OF ORIGIN: Mesopotamian – Sumerian
PROVENANCE: the earliest inscribed version of the myth dates from about 2000 BC, shortly after the collapse of the Third Dynasty at Ur, but it undoubtedly originates in an earlier oral tradition. The names of the deities appear on inscriptions dating from about 3500 BC. A strong comparison may be drawn with the Biblical myth of *Cain and Abel* (see page 133), although in the story of Lahar and Ašnan the dispute between siblings is settled without recourse to violence and murder.

The Anunnaki, the children and courtiers of An, the god of heaven, complain that they need proper food and clothes, so two deities, Lahar, the cattle god, and his sister, Ašnan, the goddess of grain, are engendered in the creation vessel of the gods. When, however, these two begin to provide the produce of the land, the Anunnaki are still at a loss because they are unable to make proper use of it. In consequence humankind is created and Lahar and Ašnan descend to the mortal realms to bestow their cultural benefits upon the mortal population.

Enlil, god of the air, and Enki, god of sweet water, provide Lahar with sheepfolds and with the plants and herbs needed to support grazing. For Ašnan they make horses, ploughs and yokes. The earth becomes abundant and prosperous until Lahar and Ašnan get drunk one day and quarrel over the farms and fields. Their bickering goes on until Enlil and Enki intervene and restore peace. See also *Emeš and Enten*, page 135.

LOKASENNA
(The Flyting of Loki)

CULTURE OF ORIGIN: Teutonic – Nordic (Icelandic)

PROVENANCE: the *Codex Regius* No. 2365. Probably composed during the later part of the tenth century AD, the manuscript lay hidden until it was rediscovered by Brynjolfur Sveinsson, bishop to the Icelandic community, circa 1643, and preserved on the instructions of Frederic III. It is housed in the Royal Library of Denmark [Copenhagen].

A *flyting* is a traditional form of defamatory dialogue which, in this instance, is directed by Loki at the other gods in the Nordic pantheon. The objective of the writer in slandering the gods through the convenient agency of a third party is unclear, but it certainly has the effect of showing the seamier side of heaven!

The myth opens at a feast which Othin, his consort Frigg and many of the other Aesir gods are attending. Thor is notably absent. The gods have been praising Fimafeng, one of the servants of the giant who is host for the occasion. For some obscure reason, however, Loki takes offence and slaughters Fimafeng, upon which the other gods drive Loki away into the woods. Loki returns, nonetheless, and asks the giant's other servant, Eldir, about the subject of current discussion within the hall. Eldir replies that the gods' talk is of weapons and glorious deeds, and that no one has a good word to say for Loki.

Loki decides to return to the feast and demands a drink but Bragi, the god of poetry, brusquely refuses to extend hospitality. At this Loki addresses Othin, reminding him of a pact that the two shall never drink one without the other and Othin grudgingly offers him a seat.

Once he has established himself, Loki renews his verbal assault, lashing out with his tongue at Bragi and accusing him of being an accomplished coward. Bragi starts to remonstrate, but the goddess Idunn, his consort and the keeper of the golden apples of immortality, urges him not to tangle with Loki. Now Loki directs his venom at her, telling her that she is mad since she has wed her brother's assassin.

The young goddess of agriculture, Gefjon, steps in, but she too comes under attack from Loki's tongue when he accuses her of being little more than a common prostitute. Even the supreme god Othin is not spared: Loki accuses him of bias when arbitrating the fate of men in battle. Othin's consort Frigg is also branded as being of easy virtue as Loki lists the men she has seduced.

The fertility goddess, Freyja, tells Loki he is insane, but he turns on her, accusing her also of unbridled lustings:

'Mind thee, Freyja, whore thou art,
thou hast been bent on ill;
in thy brother's bed the holy gods
caught thee when thou didst fart.'

The attacks are not over. The god Njorth is verbally abused and further accused of incest with his sister. For the war god, Tyr, Loki has nothing but spite. Tyr, in the process of chaining up the wolf, Fenrir, which Loki is said to have sired, has previously lost his hand. Loki, far from sympathetic, reveals that he has slept with Tyr's wife and given her a bastard son. The other gods sitting at the feast come in for similar abuse until Thor arrives. He threatens Loki with the hammer, Mjolnir, unless Loki holds his malicious tongue. Although Loki is reluctant to exclude Thor from his venom, he eventually accedes, knowing well the power of Mjolnir. Once again he leaves the feast.

At the end of the myth Loki hides behind a waterfall, but the irate gods chase after him, tie him up and hang a poisonous snake above his head so that the poison drips on him until he shakes like an earthquake.

NOTE: for a more comprehensive account of Nordic cosmogony see *Voluspa*, page 122.

MANDI AND THE FORTRESS OF THE GIANT

CULTURE OF ORIGIN: Prasun Kafir [Hindukush]
PROVENANCE: oral traditions recorded chiefly by M. Elphinstone (1839); G. Morgenstierne (1951); G.S. Robertson (1896)

A clan of giants, possessing great wealth and power, live in a castle in the sky above the upper valleys. Their presence is an evil threat to the peace and prosperity of the world and so the gods decide to wage war against them. Imra, the supreme deity; Mandi, his youthful and heroic adjutant; Zuzum, the god of winter cold; Wushum, the god of law; Gish, the war god; and the fertility goddess Disani all come together to hold council.

They advance upwards and reach the house of an old woman called Budeli, the sister of the giants, who is sitting by her fire. Mandi makes a fireplace with three stones and places upon it a pot of porridge which he shows the woman how to prepare and cook. In gratitude she offers him a gift of flour, but when he presents a hollow bone in which to place the flour she finds it impossible to fill it up. So, in compensation, Mandi questions her about the fortress and the old woman tells him that her seven brothers live there, possessed of great wealth and property. They have also captured the sun and the moon, pulled from the heavens to warm their fields. The old woman reveals how the secret ropes by which the fortress hangs from the sky may be rendered visible.

Three times Mandi forgets the secrets that the giantess has told him and three times he has to return to her house while the other gods poke fun at his forgetfulness. At last the gods begin their attack but their arrows bounce off the castle, which is built of iron. They try another ploy by asking Disani to sow seed. The seed grows in a crop which is threshed and winnowed and the chaff is cast up into the sky where it sticks to the magic rope supporting the castle, thus rendering it visible.

Mara uses his magic arrows to cut through the ropes; the castle falls, but then immediately rises again. The gods hurl themselves against it in renewed attack, but it remains impregnable.

Disani now tries a ploy of her own. She lowers her trousers and invites Mandi to inspect her thighs. At the sight of her white flesh his ardour is aroused and in a frenzied state of sexual excitement he smashes down the castle door. Invincible, he slays all seven giants, dragging them outside for burial. The threat to the world vanquished, Mandi now acts as the progenitor of the human race by assuaging his lust for Disani.

MARSYAS AND THE FLUTE OF ATHENA

CULTURE OF ORIGIN: classical Greek, but subsequently adopted into Roman culture

PROVENANCE: recorded from oral traditions

The war goddess Athena sculpts a deer bone and makes for herself the first double-piped flute (a different instrument from the syrinx or 'Pipes of Pan'). So comical does she look while blowing it that, having seen her reflection in a river, she throws it away. It is rescued by one Marsyas, whose brother Babys already plays a single flute. Marsyas discovers such marvellous music in Athena's discarded toy that the two brothers challenge Apollo to make lovelier sounds with his lyre. The winner will be permitted to inflict whatever punishment he choses on the loser.

Babys plays so badly on his single pipe that Apollo takes pity on him and eliminates him from the challenge, leaving Marsyas as the serious rival. The first contest results in a tie, but then Marsyas is challenged to play his flute upside down and he loses, so Apollo binds him to a pine tree and beats him to death. The god then feels remorseful, however, and he turns Marsyas into a stream. See also *Midas and the Ass's Ears*, page 6.

ARIADNE, THESEUS AND THE MINOTAUR

CULTURE OF ORIGIN: classical Greek, but subsequently adopted into Roman culture

PROVENANCE: recorded briefly by the epic Greek poet Hesiod in the *Theogony* and in *Catalogues of Women*, and by Apolloduros and Diodoros. Theseus is accounted in the *Life* by Plutarch. Homer mentions the death of Ariadne and the shade of Minos in the *Odyssey*. Ariadne's association with Daedalos is referred to in the *Iliad*.

When Minos claims the Cretan throne following the death of his father, Asterios, the legitimacy of his succession is contested, so he prays to the sea god Poseidon to send a bull from the ocean as a sign of heavenly endorsement. Minos, however, fails to honour a pledge to sacrifice the animal and, to punish him, Poseidon inflicts a sexual infatuation for the beast upon Minos's consort, Pasiphae, one of the daughters of Helios. She goes to grotesque lengths in her lust, calling upon the help of the artisan Daedalos to construct a wooden cow with which she can disguise herself in order to perform intercourse with the animal. She thus becomes pregnant and gives birth to the hybrid monster which she names Asterios, but which becomes better known as the Minotauros (the bull of Minos). To contain the creature the services of Daedalos are called upon once more to construct a vast and complex labyrinth from which escape is almost impossible.

Held responsible for the death of Minos's son, Androgeos, at an athletics meeting in Athens, the Athenians become burdened with payment of a tribute to Minos, consisting of seven youths and seven maidens delivered into his hands annually (or in alternative tradition once every nine years), to be cast as prey to the Minotaur in its labyrinthine palace.

Minos pledges, however, that if the Minotaur is slain, the victims may return home, so when the third tribute is due the Athenian hero, Theseus, includes himself with the young men and women. His intention is to conquer the beast.

Theseus's father, Aegeos, provides his son with two sets of sails for the galley carrying its tragic human cargo, one set black and one white. The ship is to depart rigged with black and if Theseus is slain the black sails must remain. If, however, he is victorious, the white set must be rigged.

Ariadne, the daughter of Minos and Pasiphae, falls in love with Theseus and to assist him in escaping from the labyrinth she calls again on the advice of Daedalos. On his suggestion she gives Theseus a ball of thread which he will unravel as he goes and which will permit him to retrace his footsteps to the exit. Theseus confronts the Minotaur, slays it and flees, escaping Minos's wrath with Ariadne and the potential sacrifice. Daedalos's complicity comes to light and Minos imprisons him, with his son Icaros, in the labyrinth, where they remain until Daedalos manufactures the wax wings with which they can both escape.

When Theseus puts into port on the island of Naxos he abandons Ariadne while she is sleeping and sails away. It is never clear why Theseus leaves her, but the god Dionysos falls in love with her and she becomes his bride. Her ultimate fate is confused, some traditions suggesting that she gains the boon of immortality while others indicate that she is slain by the goddess Artemis on the island of Dia (Naxos) at Dionysos's bidding.

There is also a suggestion that the goddess Aphrodite is involved in securing Theseus's victory over the Minotaur because of a long-standing antagonism between herself and Poseidon and, on his way home, Theseus is said to have dedicated a statue in her temple on the island of Delos.

The myth ends in tragedy because Theseus forgets to hoist the white sails of victory. When Aegeos sees the vessel decked in black he assumes the worst and commits suicide by throwing himself from the cliffs by the Acropolis where he has kept vigil for his son's return.

NOTE: the name of the Aegean Sea is derived from King Aegeos.

NINURTA AND KUR

CULTURE OF ORIGIN: Mesopotamian – Sumerian

PROVENANCE: the earliest inscribed version of the myth dates from about 2000 BC, shortly after the collapse of the Third Dynasty at Ur, but it undoubtedly originates in an earlier oral tradition. The names of the deities appear on inscriptions dating from about 3500 BC.

The tale of Ninurta and Kur is typical of the 'slaying the dragon' stories which emerge in widely separated cultures around the world and which include the George and the Dragon myth and those involving the Greek heroes Herakles and Perseus. The incident reflects the age-old conflict between forces of good and evil, light and dark. The myth also touches on the 'Achilles' heel' of Mesopotamia – the progressive poisoning of the land by salt-laden water carried down from the mountains to the flood plain by the Tigris and Euphrates Rivers. Salt contamination, exacerbated by the building of dykes which effectively trapped it in salt pans, caused many of the Sumerian cities to be abandoned during antiquity.

The background to the main story, of which there are several versions, explains that shortly after the separation of heaven and earth, the goddess Ereškigal is forcibly abducted to the netherworld realm of the serpent-like demon Kur. In the first version, which forms the preface to the myth of *The Epic of Gilgameš* (see page 179), and in which Ninurta does not feature, Enki sets out in his boat bound for the netherworld to attack Kur and avenge the rape of Ereškigal. Kur retaliates by hurling stones of various shapes and sizes and attempting to swamp Enki's craft with the waters of the primeval sea.

In the main version Ninurta, the god of thunderstorms and the plough, is addressed by his weapon Šarur, the hypostasis of a spirit being, which believes that Kur must be destroyed by Ninurta. The god sets out to do battle with Kur, but is overwhelmed and flees. Once again Šarur urges him forward and Ninurta attacks with all the weapons at his disposal. This time Kur is vanquished, but a blight overtakes the land because the primeval sea flood upwards and poisons the earth with its salt so that no fresh water can reach the fields.

When the waters of the sacred River Tigris do not rise to flush away the salt, the gods of the land become desperate and Ninurta piles up a mound of stones over the corpse of Kur to create a great retaining wall across the land. The primeval waters are held in check and Ninurta causes the Tigris to flood, flushing the earth once more with fresh water.

Ninurta visits his mother Ninhursağa and tells her that the mound of stones he has heaped up shall be named *hursag* (mountain) and dedicated to her as queen of the mountain. He blesses the mountain and it becomes fruitful, though the stones, which have resisted him in his task, he curses.

See also *Anzu*, page 128.

THE BATTLE OF THE OLYMPIAN GODS AND THE GIANTS

CULTURE OF ORIGIN: classical Greek, but subsequently adopted into Roman culture

PROVENANCE: recorded from oral traditions by the epic Greek poet Hesiod in the *Theogony* during the eighth century BC. Also recorded in the poems of Homer.

In the beginning, amongst the offspring of Ouranos (heaven) and Gaia (earth), are born the huge and monstrous Hecatoncheires – Cottus, Briareos and Gyes – each of whom possesses fifty heads and a hundred arms. Ouranos imprisons them, with the rest of his offspring, within the body of Gaia and all live in terror of his power. These offspring are the Titans, the youngest and most influential of whom is Kronos. Eventually Zeus releases most of the children of Ouranos from their imprisonment and the stage is set for a great cosmic war of attrition between the old order of Titan gods, headed by Kronos, and the younger pantheon of Olympian deities, descended from the Titans, whose leader is Zeus.

> *The Titan gods and as many as sprang from Kronos had long been fighting together in stubborn war with heart-grieving toil, the lordly Titans from high Othrys, but the gods, givers of good, whom rich-haired Rhea bare in union with Kronos, from Olympus.*

The war is waged for many years with neither side gaining significant advantage. Zeus, however, succeeds in releasing the Hecatoncheires from their incarceration and their terrible might added to his forces is destined to tip the balance. Battle is waged with renewed ferocity, the Hecatoncheires hurling huge boulders at the Titan warriors. The earth and the sea shake and heave to the sounds of war and even the limits of Olympus and Tartaros (the heights and depths of the earth) are affected by the ferocity of charge and countercharge. Thus far in the course of events Zeus has held back, but now he advances from Olympus with terrifying might, hurling his thunderbolts and wielding the fire of lightning. The sea boils, the earth catches fire and the flashes of light are blinding in their intensity. It is as if heaven and earth themselves are being smashed together, accompanied by earthquakes, dust storms, thunder and lightning. The Hecatoncheires rain three hundred boulders on the opposing forces of the Titans and drive them down beneath the underworld and into the depths of Tartaros, a place feared even by the gods of Olympus. It is so deep that it will take a heavy anvil ten days to reach the bottom. Here the Hecatoncheires bind the forces of Ouranos in chains and, surrounded by eternal night and by walls of bronze fashioned by Poseidon, the defeated Titans are condemned to be incarcerated and guarded for eternity by Cottus, Briareos and Gyes.

Above this awful place, the home of the children of dark night so vast that if a man fell from its gates it would take him a year to reach the floor, stands the giant Atlas, who has been condemned, for his part in the war against the Olympian gods, to bear the heavens upon his shoulders (see also Šu supporting Nut in *The Sun God of Heliopolis*, page 47).

PARVATI (DURGA) AND MAHISA

CULTURE OF ORIGIN: Puranic Hindu [India]

PROVENANCE: the stories appear in the *Skanda Purana* (700–1150 AD) and a late inclusion in the *Markandeya Purana* (introduced circa 550 AD). The mother goddess Devi is known to have been worshipped from prehistoric times, but her admission to the Hindu pantheon, usually with the epithet Parvati, took place at a comparatively late date. The myths which collectively make up the story reproduced here are usually prefaced with an account of the birth of Parvati, the *sakti* or female persona of the god Šiva, in her terrible form of Durga, and of the buffalo demon, Mahisa. Points of particular interest include the powers of asceticism and the way in which the goddess Durga is created through the collective consciousness of the other deities.

According to the *Skanda Purana* the mother of the race of demons, Diti, is anxious about her children's defeat in the great primordial battle with the gods, and instructs her daughter to go and practise asceticism. The daughter takes upon herself the guise of a buffalo and builds four fires between which she sits; above her head is the fifth fire, the sun. While she is in this state of self-denial the sage Suparsva tells her that she will bear a son, Mahisa, who will have the head of a buffalo and the body of a man and who will challenge the great warrior god Indra.

The sage's premonition comes true and Mahisa grows to be a mighty champion among the demons, who counsel him on winning their kingdoms and rights back from the gods. Thus commences another war, which lasts for a hundred years. In the first onslaught the gods suffer a massive defeat with many of their leaders being brought down. The creator god Brahma consults with the gods Šambhu (an epithet for Šiva) and Kršna and demands that they protect what is left of the pantheon. Šiva, with Višnu and the company of gods, summons up great anger and from the collective rage of the deities is generated Durga, a terrible goddess, the *sakti* of Šiva who is 'more dangerous than all the gods and demons' and who will provide an effective challenge to Mahisa. (In another version, Durga already exists and the gods merely load their weapons upon her in order to challenge and vanquish the buffalo demon.)

The gods attempt to find a haven with the goddess Gauri (another epithet of Parvati) and describe to her the power which the demons have assembled – their elephants, horses and attendants – and how

Mahisa is draining even the ocean of its riches. Gauri tells them that the key to overcoming the demons is to be found in the power of asceticism and that she will draw Mahisa into a trap herself. When the deities have left she turns herself into a seductress, leaving four guardian youths to protect her sacred mountain while she practises asceticism.

Mahisa meanwhile roams far and wide with his demon army, leaving a trail of destruction until he reaches the sacred mountain of Gauri. He hears of the beautiful ascetic and gains entry to her retreat disguised as an old man. He is told that the maiden is practising asceticism to propitiate her beloved and he now announces his true identity. Not knowing who she is, he laughs at the maiden's efforts in love. She, however, replies that it will take a mightier man than he to win her and Mahisa flies into a rage, hurling the mountain peaks with his horns.

The gods go to stand before Durga, the terrible goddess of their own creation, giving her their weapons. Riding upon her lion the goddess goes to confront Mahisa and, according to the *Markandeya Purana*, he fights until his army is destroyed. He stands alone against the soldiers of Durga and she throws her noose around him, binding him tightly. As their fight progresses he transforms into a lion, she decapitates him, he becomes human in form, she attacks him with bow and arrows, he becomes an elephant, she cuts off his trunk, he reverts to his buffalo form and hurls more mountains at her. Finally she mounts him, using her own superior strength to destroy him with her sword.

PERSEUS AND THE DEATH OF MEDUSA

CULTURE OF ORIGIN: classical Greek, but subsequently adopted into Roman culture

PROVENANCE: recorded from oral traditions by the epic Greek poet Hesiod in the *Theogony* and in the *Shield of Herakles*

Medusa is the one mortal among three Gorgon sisters; the two immortals are Stheno and Euryale. The daughters of Keto and Phorkys, these women live in the far west, in the same vicinity as the Hesperides sisters who guard the golden apples of immortality (Hesiod describes the Gorgons as being Hesperides). The Gorgons are of monstrous appearance, with golden wings, a scaly neck, boar's tusks and snakelocks; so terrifying are they that anyone who looks at them is turned instantly to stone. Only the sea god Poseidon can withstand the sight, since he has slept with Medusa and fathered her children – a giant named Chrysaor and the winged horse Pegasos, both of which are born when Medusa is decapitated by the hero Perseus.

During a roisterous feast Perseus, the son of Zeus and the mortal princess Danae, is challenged by a tyrannical local ruler, Polydektes, to bring back the head of Medusa. Unless Perseus surmounts this challenge, the forfeit will be the rape of Danae by Polydektes.

Perseus calls upon the assistance of Athena, the goddess of war, and Hermes, the messenger god. The two deities send him to counsel three old women, the Graeae, also daughters of Keto and Phorkys. At first the Graeae are reluctant to help, but when Perseus steals the single eye which they share between them they are obliged to reveal to him that he needs three objects in order to overcome Medusa: a pair of winged sandals, a helmet belonging to Hades which will render him invisible, and a bag in which to place the head. These things he is to obtain from the Nymphs to whom the Graeae direct him.

Accompanied by Athena, and armed with a sword made from a very strong steel, adamantine, provided by Hermes, Perseus sets out in search of Medusa, leaving his mother in the care of Polydektes.

Perseus locates the terrifying Gorgons asleep and rises into the air on his winged sandals. While Athena holds her shield before him so that he can see only a reflection, he decapitates Medusa and thrusts her head into his bag. Although the immortal sisters attempt to follow him, they are foiled because the magical helmet of Hades has rendered Perseus invisible.

While he is travelling home Perseus comes across Andromeda, who is about to be sacrificed to a monster; rescuing her from her fate, he falls in love and marries her. Taking Andromeda with him and carrying his lethal cargo he returns to Polydektes who, he discovers, has tried to force himself upon Danae. Infuriated, Perseus takes revenge by lifting the Medusa's head from its bag, thus turning Polydektes to stone. Perseus returns the sandals and helmet to the Nymphs and gives the fearsome head to Athena, who sets it on to the boss of her shield.

PROMETHEUS
(Foresight)

CULTURE OF ORIGIN: classical Greek, but subsequently adopted into Roman culture

PROVENANCE: recorded from oral traditions by the epic Greek poet Hesiod in the *Theogony* in the eighth century BC. Separate traditions of Prometheus are narrated in the *Iliad* of Homer. Essentially the mythology surrounding Prometheus is one of confrontation with Zeus, who regards him as an equal in wit and therefore a potential source of challenge.

In the *Theogony* Prometheus is one of the sons of the Titan Iapetos and his sister Klymene (other traditions identify his mother as Asia). Prometheus's brothers include Epimethius, Atlas and Menoetius (see *Epimethius (hindsight) and Pandora*, page 210). In one episode Zeus becomes jealous of Prometheus and binds him with chains to a rock in the Caucasus, driving a lance through the victim's stomach and employing an eagle, generally assumed to be one of the monstrous offspring of the demonic nymph Echidna, to torture him each day by tearing at his liver. The suffering is perpetuated because, being an immortal, Prometheus recovers each night so that by morning his liver is fully restored. His suffering is ended by the heroic god Herakles (Hercules), who slays the eagle and releases Prometheus from his chains while journeying to collect the Golden Apples of the Hesperides (see the *Labours of Herakles*, page 183).

In a further confrontation, on an occasion when the gods are assembled at Mecone, Prometheus cuts up an ox and divides it into two unequal shares. One contains the flesh and innards deceptively wrapped in the hide on which is placed the stomach (making the choicest meat appear to be the offal), the other contains only the bones disguised attractively with fat. Prometheus offers Zeus the choice of portions and the god selects what appears to be the best (the suggestion in the *Theogony* is that Zeus knows he is being deceived). Bitter at Prometheus's powers of trickery which he has also taught to mortal man, Zeus witholds the boon of fire from the human race, but Prometheus, not to be outdone, steals the fire in a fennel stalk from the crippled blacksmith god, Hephaestos, and gives it to mankind. Out of spite for this impertinence, Zeus burdens the world with the first mortal woman, Pandora, and her troubles.

Prometheus is generally depicted as a benefactor and ally of humanity and he is also credited, though not in the *Theogony*, with having created mankind out of lumps of clay.

QUETZALCOATL

CULTURE OF ORIGIN: Aztec – classical Mesoamerican [Mexico]
PROVENANCE: probably worshipped circa 750 AD until 1500 AD and known from tradition in the Florentine and other pre-Columbian codices and detail on stone carvings.

Quetzalcoatl and Tezcatlipoca were considered to have engaged in a titanic struggle resulting in the creation and destruction of four world ages prior to the current one. They also bore responsibility for restoring the shattered universe and initiating the fifth and present sun.

Quetzalcoatl and the Toltec inhabitants of the city of Tula become very lazy and neglectful until three gods – Uitzilopochtli, Tezcatlipoca and Toltecatl – arrive, announcing that the city will be destroyed.

Tezcatlipoca transforms himself into a little old man with very white hair and, in this guise, he visits the home of Quetzalcoatl, demanding a meeting. The servants try to send him away, saying that Quetzalcoatl is sick and the visit will upset him. Tezcatlipoca persists and the servants agree to consult with their master. They warn Quetzalcoatl that this is probably a trap, but he replies that he has been waiting for Tezcatlipoca to arrive for a long time.

When Tezcatlipoca, still appearing as a little old man, gains his audience with Quetzalcoatl he asks after the health of his rival; when he learns that Quetzalcoatl feels very tired he appears to commiserate, saying that he too is weary. He offers him a spiked potion of *pulque*, telling Quetzalcoatl that the drink will revive him, but will also make him think about his own impending death. At first Quetzalcoatl refuses, but then he takes a small sip, then a larger sip; finally he drinks deeply.

Quetzalcoatl announces that the pain and weariness have gone away, but he promptly falls into a drunken stupor from which he emerges feeling very sad. He also knows that Tezcatlipoca has tricked him out of his sense of neglect by inflaming his heart and making him consider his own fate.

In his sad frame of mind Quetzalcoatl decides to leave the city. He has all his possessions burned, including his gold palace, his mansion of sea shells and other valuables. He sees himself in a mirror and concedes that he is now an old man and no longer fit to rule. His tears fall as hailstones as he walks away.

In a separate tradition explaining the disappearance of Quetzalcoatl, Tezcatlipoca descends from heaven on a rope made of cobwebs and transforms himself into an ocelot. In this guise he plays a ball game (*tlachco*) with Quetzalcoatl and drives him away from Tula.

QUIKINNAQ'U AND THE WAR WITH THE CHUKCHEE

CULTURE OF ORIGIN: Siberian – Koryak

PROVENANCE: from an oral tradition amongst the Koryak reindeer hunters living on the Kamchatka Peninsula of south-eastern Siberia. The myth was related by a shamanka named Ty'kken in a hunting camp on the Tapolovka River. Modern authorship is that of the Swedish ethnologist

Waldemar Jochelson, who recorded the tale during the Jesup North Pacific Survey of 1900, sponsored by the American Society for Natural History [Memoirs of the American Museum of Natural History, 10, 1905].

The myth underlines the constant rivalry between the neighbouring tribes of Koryak and Chukchee, both of whom inhabit the Kamchatka Peninsula.

Quikinnaq'u (Big Raven) and Eme'mqut live by themselves in a deserted village surrounded by many empty houses. Quikinnaq'u tells Eme'mqut that the places have been empty for as long as anyone can remember.

One day Eme'mqut goes away hunting and the creator spirit Tenanto'mwan arrives at the village with Mai'nica'ican (Great Cold). Having agreed to sit at the fire in one of the empty houses and ease their wounds, they take off their coats and warm themselves.

When Eme'mqut returns from his hunting trip he peers in through the window and sees the two figures, noticing that they are covered in arrow wounds. He enquires how they obtained such scars and Tenanto'mwan replies that they are the result of an illness. Eme'mqut retorts that the visitors are telling lies and that the wounds are clearly from arrows. Tenanto'mwan then relates the account of how once there were many Koryak people living in the village, but that they were killed off during raids by the neighbouring Chukchee. The attackers, though inflicting serious wounds, had been unable to kill Tenanto'mwan and Mai'nica'ican.

Everyone goes off to bed except Eme'mqut, who puts on his snow shoes and travels up river to the Chukchee camp. He turns himself into a fog and looks into one of the tents where there are people warming themselves and sharpening axes while they relate tales of old battles with the Koryak. Eme'mqut waits until all the Chukchee have gone to bed; when they are asleep he takes an axe and decapitates one of them. He goes home with his trophy and impales it on a pole which he plants outside his front door. The Koryak people are now worried that the Chukchee will mount a reprisal raid.

Their fears are justified, for the father of the murdered man discovers his corpse and vows to kill all the Koryak. Eme'mqut prepares for confrontation and Quikinnaq'u offers him a suit of iron armour. Eme'mqut, however, refuses and springs up on to the roof of the house armed only with his spear. From there he slides down the house post and disappears underground. As the Chukchee advance he spears them one by one from below and then emerges victorious.

Once more Eme'mqut climbs to the rooftop, where he announces to the assembled Koryak clan that the Chukchee warriors are vanquished and everyone is free to go to the enemy camp and slay the women and children.

TENANTO'MWAN AND THE KALAU

CULTURE OF ORIGIN: Siberian – Koryak

PROVENANCE: from an oral tradition amongst the Koryak reindeer hunters living on the Kamchatka Peninsula of south-eastern Siberia. The myth was related by a shamanka named Kucanin in a hunting camp on the Chaubuga River. Modern authorship is that of the Swedish ethnologist Waldemar Jochelson, who recorded the tale during the Jesup North Pacific Survey of 1900, sponsored by the American Society for Natural History [Memoirs of the American Museum of Natural History, 10, 1905].

Eme'mqut, one of the sons of Tenanto'mwan, the creator being, is ill and the creator believes that the evil influence of the underworld spirits, the *kalau*, is to blame. Tenanto'mwan therefore dons his cloak of raven feathers, transforming himself into a bird, and he flies off to the *kalau* camp to investigate. When he arrives he overhears a plot to attack and destroy his home, so he flies back to his own camp again and prepares to receive his conniving guests.

When the *kalau* arrive, Tenanto'mwan welcomes them with apparent courtesy and offers them seats on the beam which runs across the fireplace of the hut. He then instructs Eme'mqut to build a big fire in the hearth to warm the visitors, but when it is going well he closes the smoke hole in the roof. The *kalau* begin to roast and they plead to be released from the trap. Tenanto'mwan suggests, however, that since the *kalau* are partial to human flesh and since they are all cooking nicely, they might pass the time by eating one of their number!

At this juncture the *kalau* concede defeat and ask for some special stones which they will use to cast a curative spell. They also promise never to bother the creator again. Tenanto'mwan delivers their requirement and they weave their magic. Eme'mqut at once begins to recover from his sickness and the *kalau* depart.

NOINDEN ULAD AND EMUIN MACHAE
(The Labour Pains of the Ulaid and the Twins of Macha)

CULTURE OF ORIGIN: Celtic (Irish)

PROVENANCE: recorded from oral traditions possibly as early as the eighth century AD by the chief bard of Ireland, Snechan Torpeist, in the *Book of Druimm Snechtai*. This is now lost and no copies have survived prior to the eleventh century. The complete version is contained in the *Leabhar Laighnech: Book of Leinster*, compiled circa 1160 by Aed Mac Crimtheinn [Dublin Institute for Advanced Studies].

Under modern convention the myth is classified as part of the Ulaid (Ulster) or Craobh Ruadh (Red Branch) Cycle of myths, though the nature of the characters suggests that the link may be a doubtful one. From a historical viewpoint the Ulster Cycle relates an ongoing conflict between the Ulaid clan(s) who lived in the Armagh region of what is now Ulster and others who were based further south in Connacht (Connaught). The story has affinities with the great *Tain bo Cuailgne* saga (see page 175) in that it explains why Cu Chulainn comes to be alone in his defence of Ulster against the raiders from Connacht.

The myth recounts how the pregnant horse goddess, Macha, races against the horses of the king to meet a wager laid by her mortal husband and at the end of the course gives birth to twins. It thus also explains the origin of the place name Emain Macha (Twins of Macha), the sacred seat of the kings of Ulster [the mound of Navan to the west of Armagh].

Cruinniuc Mac Agnomain of Ulaid is a widower who lives alone with his sons until a strange and beautiful woman arrives at his stronghold, becoming his wife and bringing him great prosperity.

The Ulaid hold a fair which includes a horse-racing contest and, at the end of the day, Cruinniuc states that while no horses can beat those of the king which have swept the field, his wife is able to do so. This news is imparted to the king, who holds Cruinniuc captive with his life at stake.

Cruinniuc's mysterious wife is heavily pregnant and she requests that the trial be postponed until she has given birth. Her request is denied and when she prophesies doom on the Ulaid, the king demands to know her name. She tells him she is Macha, whereupon she races against the king's horses.

At the end of the course, when she has won the race, she gives birth to twins, a brother and sister, the Emain Macha. As she delivers the babies she screams that any man within earshot will suffer her birth pangs for five days and four nights. It is this curse, laid upon the men and women of Ulster for nine generations, which renders them impotent in their struggle against the men of Connacht. The only people to be spared the curse are Cu Chulainn, his women and his children.

ULLIKUMI

CULTURE OF ORIGIN: Hittite – Anatolian
PROVENANCE: cuneiform text derived from an oral tradition and discovered on tablets at the site of Boghazkoy in Turkey, translated by Albrecht Goetze (*Ancient Near Eastern Texts* ed. J.B. Pritchard).

The story of Ullikumi is essentially a good–versus–evil myth and is typical of stories occurring worldwide in which a hero battles with and defeats a demonic adversary. The Hattic kingdom was a mountainous one and, in many cultures which have their history in such regions, myths have circulated that the world was once made uninhabitable by demons in the form of mountains which were subsequently brought under control and reduced in stature.

NOTE: this myth probably predates the Hurrian introductions to the pantheon, although the names incorporated here are the later adoptions.

Kumarbi, the king of the gods, who has been dethroned by the storm god Tešub, is determined to create a demonic champion who will restore his rule over Hatti. He goes to the sea where he visits the mother of rocks, repeatedly raping her before sending his messenger, Imbaluri, to inform the sea that he, Kumarbi, is destined to be restored as king of the gods. Sea replies that her kingdom trembles in fear because of Kumarbi's threats and when he goes to visit her she offers him a feast by way of appeasement.

Kumarbi instructs his vizier, Mukisanu, to tell the waters that they must attend the mother of rocks as she gives birth. The mother goddess produces a son, a creature made of crystalline diorite, whom Kumarbi names Ullikumi, predicting that he will ascend to the kingship of heaven and vanquish Tešub. The messenger Imbaluri now goes to the minor Irsirra gods, ordering them to hide Ullikumi until he grows up, since the great gods will otherwise seek him out and destroy him. Ullikumi is to be placed on the shoulder of a giant named Ubelluri, from where he will grow at tremendous speed.

The god of the air, Ellil, is aware of what is taking place but is powerless to intervene and after fifteen days Ullikumi has grown so vast that the sun god catches sight of him rearing from the sea. The sun god goes down into the surface for a closer inspection and then returns to the sky for a crisis meeting with Tešub. They join each other for a feast and Tešub leaves with his brother Tašmisu to confront Ullikumi. When they see the creature's dimensions they become afraid and retreat until the goddess Ištar berates them for their cowardice.

The sea tells Ištar that Ullikumi must be brought down while he is deaf and blind and has no will in his heart, otherwise he will become invincible. Ištar relates this to Tešub and the information persuades him to attack the demon with the help of Tǎsmisu. The outcome of the combat is indecisive and, although many of the other gods join the fray, Ullikumi remains undefeated. He is now nine thousand leagues in stature, so tall that he blocks off the heavens from the earth, and he makes Hebat, the patron goddess of Hatti, abandon her temple. So concerned is Hebat that she calls all the thousand gods into assembly, warning them that she believes Ullikumi may have slain the storm god. Tasmisu reports that Tešub has gone to the netherworld, where he may have to stay for a required number of years. Hebat falls fainting.

The gods go before the great god Ea in the Abzu to learn their fate in the tablets of destiny. Ea warns Ellil that Kumarbi has created a monstrous being to rival Tešub and then causes Ullikumi to be partially disabled by crippling his feet with the copper knife used to separate heaven from earth. To the end Ullikumi boasts that he is invincible, but the storm god vanquishes him and peace is restored on earth.

VIŠNU BECOMES THE BUDDHA

CULTURE OF ORIGIN: Puranic Hindu [India]
PROVENANCE: the story appears in the *Visnu Purana*, composed circa 450 AD, and is possessed of a logic based on fighting fire with fire. Višnu does not become the Buddha as a palliative to Buddhism (or Jainism), about which there has been and still is fanatical antagonism among many Hindu devotees, but in order to make use of a foreign doctrine. Buddhism is perceived as an evil armament with which Višnu may fight more effectively against the demonic forces which threaten Hinduism. The myth underlines a fundamental of Hindu thinking – that gods and demons are distinguishable less by the conventional Western typecasting of 'heroes' and 'villains' and more according to the doctrinal paths they follow.

When, after a conflict which has lasted a hundred years, the gods are defeated by the demons, they retire to the shores of the primeval sea to practise asceticism and to propitiate the creator god Višnu. Višnu appears to them in his aspect of Hari, mounted on his Garuda bird and carrying all his weapons. The gods entreat Višnu to save them, pointing out that the demons are rendered invulnerable because they too follow the Vedic laws and practise asceticism.

Višnu uses his powers of illusion to change his appearance and he tells the Hindu gods to have no fear. Posing as a naked Jain ascetic, Višnu approaches the demons on the banks of the Narmada River and begins to argue the case that there is a better doctrine open to them than that of following the path of the Vedas. As the demons' conversion proceeds, Višnu's form changes to that of the Buddha and he continues to draw their loyalties away from the triple path of the Vedas until they are set wholly on the wrong course.

Seeing their enemy thus weakened, the Hindu gods prepare once more for battle and on this occasion are victorious.

8

Epic Myths

Each culture seems to be prompted to produce at least one great literary offering to acount either for some mythological event of outstanding importance, or for the biography of a godly hero. This outpouring is usually of sufficient substance to be classed as an epic.

Such epic tales, recited round camp fires, may have taken hours rather than minutes to relate and their preservation demanded extraordinary powers of memory. Some, though by no means all, of the epics of oral tradition were perhaps not constructed as complete sagas but first remembered and related as separate episodes which have only been assembled in their familiar epic form during the subsequent literary period. Nonetheless the storytellers would spend the greater part of their lives specifically training successors in the art of memorizing and reciting material which was sometimes of great length. Thus they passed on vital literary traditions in a father-to-son fashion of inheritance.

Arguably one of the finest of all epic tales is that of Gilgameš, the Mesopotamian hero whose initial quest for glory and adventure is transcended by one which takes him in search of the elixir of immortality. The Gilgameš epic probably originates as a series of loosely connected stories subsequently assembled by scribes into the present format of twelve chapters.

Epic myths involve adventure and often reach their climaxes with some all-consuming conflict between good and evil. Thus they might equally be incorporated into the section of confrontation myths. The opposing forces may be those of nature, typified by the Canaanite story of Baal and Anat, or they may be historical antagonists. The climax of the Hindu *Ramayana* epic occurs when Rama and the monkey king Hanuman clash with the evil tyrant who has abducted Rama's wife, Sita, but the underlying message is of conflict between India and her traditional arch-enemy Sri Lanka. Likewise the battle on which the Celtic myth of Tain bo Cuailgne is based – that of the famous cattle raid to secure the Brown Bull of Cuailgne – actually describes the long-standing historical enmity between the Irish kingdoms of Connaught and Ulster.

It is not possible in this volume to do justice to the epic myths, many of which are composed in brilliant and moving style. The *Ramayana*, for example, occupies a whole literary volume in its own right. The best that can be offered here is a blunt précis which skates the surface: the reader should seek out a good translation of the original work to enjoy it in its full splendour.

BAAL AND ANAT

CULTURE OF ORIGIN: Canaanite – Ugaritic
PROVENANCE: this is the largest and most significant saga in the cycle of Baal myths discovered at the site of the Canaanite capital, Ugarit [Ras Šamra]. See also *Baal and Mot*, page 225.

The story opens on a world dominated by the increasing power of the demonic sea and river deities known as the tyrannies, for whom great palaces are being constructed. Baal, the fertility god, in sombre mood, asks whether he is about to be deprived of his limited area of rule and points out that he has not even a palace of his own. Emissaries of Sea and River arrive at the palace of the creator god, Il (also referred to as Tor-Il), and they enter the Assembly of Gods, demanding control over that which is ruled by Baal:

'Give up O Gods, him whom thou protect
He whom the multitudes protect.
Give up Baal and his followers
Dagan's son, so that I may inherit his province!'

Il replies that Baal is already the servant of Sea but this comment enrages Baal, who strikes out at the messengers with his knife. He is restrained by the goddesses Anat and Astarte, who remonstrate that he must not attack the emissaries in this manner.

Baal decides to take the fight to Sea and River directly. He marches away and, using the magic weapons Ktr and Hss, fashioned for the battle, he slays the sea and river tyrannies. The weapons proclaim Baal's power.

'Did I not tell thee, O Prince Baal,
Nor declare, O Rider of the Clouds?
Lo, thine enemies, O Baal,
Lo, thine enemies wilt thou smite.

Lo thou wilt vanquish thy foes
Thou wilt take thine eternal kingdom
Thine everlasting sovereignty!'

Baal is rebuked by Astarte, one of his named consorts, for the demise of Sea and River. Nonetheless Baal is the conqueror and takes on the mantle of kingship, indulging himself in a lavish victory feast.

The focus of attention moves to the goddess Anat, the sister of Baal and goddess of fertility and war, the so-called Lady of the Mountain. She is discovered engaged in ferocious combat.

Much she fights and looks, battles and views
Anat gluts her liver with laughter
Her heart is filled with joy
Anat's liver exults
For knees she plunges in the blood of soldiery
Thighs in the gore of troops.

Anat washes and adorns herself in her finest apparel because she has received an invitation to visit Baal in his mountain sanctuary of Šapan, where he is to reveal a secret. As she approaches, however, she is greeted not by Baal, but by two of his attendant deities, Gupan and Ugar, and she is at once afraid that the conqueror of Sea and River has met with some new adversity. The attendants assure her that all is well, instruct her to make a suitable offering of food and drink to the earth and, having done so, to hasten to join Baal.

Baal notes the approach of his sister and sends women to escort her and others to prepare her bath. Meanwhile he orders a feast in her honour, killing a fatted calf. Baal has invited Anat to Šapan not to share a secret, but to help him to obtain a palace for himself so that he can live up to the image of kingship. To achieve this she is to plead Baal's case before Il. Anat therefore sets off for Il's mystical abode at the course of the Two Rivers.

Lo, Baal has no house like the gods
Nor a court like the sons of Ašerah.

Il seems to agree with Anat's request and the emissaries of Ašerah, the primeval mother goddess of Canaan and creatrix of the gods, the so-called Lady Ašerah of the Sea, are despatched to Ktr and Hss, the divine craftsmen, with Baal's request. Ašerah has an ambivalent attitude to Baal. She supports him at times, as in this instance, but at others she will side against him.

Ktr and Hss visit Il to obtain more detailed instructions in a passage of the text which is very fragmentary. There follows an obscure section which is in part repetitive and it is by no means certain that the sequence in which the tablets are currently arranged is the correct one.

The reader is reminded of Anat's gory exploits and her visit to Baal. Ktr and Hss make fabulous gifts in silver and gold with which firstly to gain Ašerah's good will so that she will intercede with Il and secondly to obtain the go-ahead from the creator god himself. A good deal of entreating goes on and eventually, as Baal retreats to his mountain sanctuary to await the outcome, Ašerah mounts her donkey and sets off for the abode of Il, where she begs him to grant Baal's request. Il is pleased to see her and drops any formality, inviting her to sit down, eat and drink her fill. Ašerah now presents her request and the creator god adopts a gently mocking attitude.

'Am I both to act as a lackey of Ašerah
And am I to act as the holder of a trowel!
If the handmaids of Ašerah will make the bricks
A house shall be built for Baal like the gods
Yea a court like the sons of Ašerah.'

At last the housebuilding is started with cedarwood, silver and gold, and Anat rushes off to give Baal the good news. Ktr and Hss now wish to instal a window in the palace; at first Baal is reluctant, but he arranges a great housewarming feast and, in benevolent mood, agrees to the casement.

The tone of the text now changes and Baal's great adversary, Mot, the god of natural adversity, enters the saga. Mot issues a challenge to Baal, who has refused to pay him due respect and Mot threatens that he alone has the power to rule over the gods. In reply Baal sends his attendants, Gupan and Ugar, to the underworld with a message of challenge, a scathing piece of cynicism suggesting ironically that Baal shall be Mot's slave for ever. Gupan and Ugar return and the god himself descends the path to the underworld where, for reasons that are not wholly clear, he has intercourse with a cow.

In a passage of text which is lost Baal apparently loses his life; the narrative is rejoined as he lies prostrate and dead upon the earth. Il is unconsolable, roaming the mountains in his grief, and Anat sets out to find Baal's corpse with the help of the sun goddess. When she discovers the body she lifts it and carries it back to his palace in Šapan where she performs the proper rituals over it and makes the correct sacrifices.

A successor is named from among the sons of Ašerah, Attar the Terrible, who takes Baal's place. He seems, however, an incompetent and poor substitute whose 'feet do not reach the footstool nor his head reach its top'. Anat now goes in search of Mot to plead for the restoration of Baal and, when Mot admits to the killing, she slaughters him.

With a sword she cleaves him

With a pitchfork she winnows him
With fire she burns him
With millstones she grinds him
In the fields she plants him
So that the birds do not eat his flesh
Nor anyone destroy his portion.

Il dreams that Baal is alive and he instructs Anat to go and find his risen form with the help, once again, of the sun goddess. Baal returns to the land of the living and the natural world, devastated since his demise, becomes green and fertile again. Baal himself seeks out Mot and this time vanquishes him. For seven years Mot is subdued, but at the end of that period he protests to Baal about his misfortunes. Again they fight a terrible battle until the sun goddess intervenes, warning Mot that, unless he desists from this wasteful rivalry, Il will get to hear of it and be dangerously displeased.

There follows a piece of text which may or may not be in correct sequential order with the rest of the myth. Baal eulogizes over Anat and then mates with a cow. After the animal has given birth, Anat goes to the mountain of Šapan and greets Baal with the news that he has sired a bull calf. In another disjointed but graphically written passage Baal indulges in passionate sex with Anat herself.

The known text of the myth becomes so badly broken up at this stage that it is difficult to gain any real sense of meaning or intent about the end of the saga.

TAIN BO CUAILGNE
(The Cattle Raid of Cuailgne)

CULTURE OF ORIGIN: Celtic – Irish

PROVENANCE: recorded from oral traditions possibly as early as the eighth century AD by the chief bard of Ireland, Snechan Torpeist, in the *Book of Druimm Snechtai*. This is now lost and no copies have survived prior to the eleventh century. Incomplete versions are contained in *Leabhar ne h-Uidhre; Book of the Dun Cow*, compiled in the eleventh century by the Christian monk Mael Muire Mac Ceilechai [Royal Irish Academy], and in *Leabhar Laighnech: Book of Leinster*, compiled in the twelfth century by Aed Mac Crimtheinn [Dublin Institute for Advanced Studies]. Further material is found in the *Yellow Book of Lecan* compiled circa 1391 AD [Trinity College, Dublin].

The best known of the epic Irish Celtic sagas, this myth narrates the attempt by Medb, the goddess queen of Connacht, to capture the Brown Bull of Cuailgne. Under modern convention the myth is classified as part of the Ulaid (Ulster) or Craobh Ruadh (Red Branch) Cycle of myths which, from a historical viewpoint, relate an ongoing conflict between the

Ulaid clan(s) who lived in the Armagh region of what is now Ulster and others who were based further south in Connacht (Connaught). The saga is divisible into four distinct 'chapters': the mustering of forces; the march; the boyhood of the Ulster hero, Cu Chulainn, who carries on a more or less lone defence of Ulster at a time when his countrymen are afflicted with a debilitating sickness; and the final confrontation.

The riches of Medb and her husband Ailill match one another in all respects but cattle. Ailill possesses a magnificent white horned bull, Finnbhenach, of which Medb is increasingly jealous, her irritation exacerbated by the knowledge that the animal was calved from her own stock. In a previous incarnation it was the swineherd of Ochall of Connacht who, as a bull, had considered it undignified to be owned by a woman and had thus migrated forcibly to Ailill's herd.

Having tried to persuade Ailill to return the animal, Medb approaches Fergus Mac Roth to enquire where she may obtain a superior beast and he tells her of the existence in Ulaid (Ulster) of Donn Cuailgne, the Brown Bull of Cuailgne. In a previous incarnation this beast was Nar Thuathcaech, the swineherd of Bodb Dearg (Bodb the Red), a son of Dagda. The two swineherds had been arch rivals.

Medb authorizes Fergus to purchase the Brown Bull of Cuailgne in exchange for cattle, land and even Medb's personal favours to its owner. If the barter fails Fergus is to obtain the bull by whatever means he deems fit. At first the owner agrees to the sale, but during the evening his servants overhear a derogatory conversation among Fergus's men to the effect that the deal has been generous only by Ulster standards and had the bull not been gained so easily it would have been taken anyway. In the morning the exchange is called off!

Medb complains to Ailill that she has suffered an intolerable affront and so Connacht prepares to march against Ulaid and to capture the Brown Bull by force of arms. Such is the strength of feeling that provincial kings from as far distant as Munster and Leinster become embroiled on the side of Connacht. The combined forces are led by Fergus Mac Roth, himself a dissident refugee from Ulster, having been driven out at the time of the slaughter of his son Naoise (see *Oidhe Cloinne Uisneach*, page 200).

Medb decides, irrationally, to reject a force of three thousand men from northern Leinster on the grounds that they will outshine her own forces. When Ailill questions the sense of this plan, pointing out that either sending the force home, or keeping it in Connacht, is likely to prove dangerous, Medb's proposal is to slaughter the Leinster men. Fergus protests that if Medb kills one part of the army she will have to kill all of it, since the Leinster men and their king are now his personal allies. An acceptable solution is offered by Ailill, who suggests dispersing the Leinster troops throughout the Connacht forces so that their talents will be evenly distributed. The army now marches on Cuailgne and the opposing forces of King Conchobhar of Ulaid.

The men of Connacht cross an expanse of bog where they slay a herd of deer before encamping for the night by the Shannon River. One of their bards envisages a brutal and destructive conflict in which a man of terrifying strength and resource will single-handedly spear-head the opposition. This prophecy spreads disquiet amongst the troops. Fergus sends a salutary warning ahead, hoping that conflict may be averted, but there is no response from the forces of Ulaid who are, unbeknown to Medb and Ailill, suffering under a debilitating curse laid by the horse goddess Macha (see *Noinden Ulad and Emuin Machae*, page 167).

The lone Ulster champion not inflicted with sickness, Cu Chulainn, sets out for the river crossing where he anticipates the army of Connacht will invade Ulster and he leaves a challenge carved on a cattle spancel-ring. Meanwhile Fergus, his loyalties stretched, adopts delaying tactics, hoping to give his fellow Ulstermen time to muster a reasonable defence force. When Medb challenges him, Fergus explains that he is taking a circuitous route to avoid Cu Chulainn. The spancel-ring is discovered, and on it Cu Chulainn's warning to the Connacht army to come no further unless one among them, other than Fergus (bound by an oath of friendship to Cu Chulainn), can fashion a similar hoop single-handedly. The druids advise that, unless the challenge can be met, Fergus must lead his army no further.

On Ailill's instruction, Fergus takes the army on another detour and camps in heavy snow near Tara. Cu Chulainn moves to flank him and, at another ford, throws down an audible challenge. A pair of chariots break away to attack him. He decapitates the enemy, impaling their heads on a forked tree-trunk, and reports filter back to Fergus that a vast enemy force awaits the men of Connacht. When, however, Fergus inspects the tree with its bloody trophies, he finds it has been hurled into the river by one of great might who has posted another challenge, warning the men of Connacht not to cross unless they can match that feat of strength.

Fergus now reveals to Ailill and Medb the identity of Cu Chulainn, the 'Hound of Culann', and recounts his story. At the age of seventeen he was a warrior unparalleled in strength, intellect and bravery. The son of Dechtire, daughter of Cathbad, he came to Emain Macha at the age of five, voluntarily and unaccompanied, to study the use of arms. The other 150 trainees at Emain Macha had set upon him on his arrival and been thwarted. Such was his prowess that the king, Conchobhar Mac Nessa, set him as leader and guardian of the rest. By eight he was fully versed in the arts of war and his prowess had grown sufficiently during his childhood that while many chose to challenge him none succeeded. He now possessed certain physical attributes in that, before a conflict, his hair stood on end and seemed to catch fire and, while one eye almost receded into his head, the other expanded and rolled in its socket.

Cu Chulainn's cousin, Conall Cearnach, takes up the story of how he came by his name. On the way to a feast hosted by Culann, the royal smith, Conchobhar and his retinue witnessed Cu Chulainn competing single-handedly against the 150 other boys and invited him to join the party. Left outside, playing with stick and ball and temporarily forgotten by the king, Cu Chulainn was attacked by Culann's hound, but he smashed it against a pillar before ramming the ball down its throat.

Since the smith was now without a guard dog the youth offered, by way of compensation, to train another and to guard the smith's house himself in the interim. The druids thus named him Cu Chulainn, the 'Hound of Culann'.

As the Connacht army moves forward they are obstructed by a massive felled oak which, under the rules of combat, they are obliged to jump in their chariots. Many fall in the attempt while others, for several days following, are picked off one by one by Cu Chulainn; his victims include Orlam and Maine, two of the sons of Ailill.

Sensing the closing battle, the Brown Bull becomes restless and breaks loose from his stall, running amok until Ailill and Medb believe him trapped, but followed by fifty heifers he stampedes through the Connacht camp, wreaking havoc.

It is decided that a single warrior must be found who has the bravery and stamina to oppose Cu Chulainn but he splits the first challenger neatly in half and the second, after a fight with spears, he quarters. Although the Connacht forces succeed in recapturing the Brown Bull, the attempts at killing Cu Chulainn in single combat fail until Medb is obliged to consider suing for peace. First, though, she has several further attempts to defeat the Ulster hero, including the dispatch of six brothers against him (counted as one since they were from the same womb), luring him into an ambush and finally sending no less than a hundred men against him at the ford. This trickery produces only fatal consequences for the Connacht warriors and all the while the rest of the Ulster force is ailing under the curse of Macha.

The climax of the campaign is reached in Cu Chulainn's own stronghold, the Plain of Muirthemne [between Dundalk and Boyne], where the entire forces of Medb and Ailill are instructed to march as a man and crush him. The battle continues from autumn until spring, when Cu Chulainn's father, the god Lugh, comes to his aid from the other world to restore him bodily and to allow him to sleep in safety for three days and nights. Thus fortified with magical protection, and in monstrous form, the Ulster hero proceeds to slaughter or maim a large part of the invading force. Still Medb will not concede defeat and, finally, she sends against Cu Chulainn the renowned warrior Ferdia, son of Daman the Firbolg, who has been a close friend of the Ulster hero since childhood. Ferdia is deeply reluctant, but finally engages Cu Chulainn. After four days of unrelenting combat Ferdia is slain and Cu Chulainn falls exhausted. He is assumed dead and the forces of Medb and Ailill pour across the ford in triumph, pausing only to bury Ferdia and to set up a standing stone in memoriam.

Cu Chulainn is only temporarily indisposed and, furthermore, the Ulstermen have recovered from their sickness. The Ulster king, Conchobhar Mac Nessa, raises his own army, determined to rout the invading force, and Fergus Mac Roth, realizing the strength of the opposition, again urges Ailill and Medb to sue for peace. The Connacht rulers will have none of it, battle commences once more, but now Medb and Ailill are forced to retreat, taking with them the Brown Bull which is still in their possession.

It is the turn of the two bulls to fight, Donn Cuailgne against Finnbhenach, and they battle for a day and a night. In the end, the Brown Bull of Cuailgne emerges victorious but mortally wounded, carrying the dismembered parts of his old rival hanging from his horns. As he attempts to return home to Ulster bits of the White Bull's carcass fall off in various places along the way and, finally, on the Plain of Muirthemne, Donn Cuailgne himself falls dead, so ending the saga.

THE EPIC OF GILGAMEŠ

CULTURE OF ORIGIN: Mesopotamian – Akkadian, based on Sumerian and other oral traditions

PROVENANCE: uncertain and confused since the source material is perhaps woven from many separate tales which arose around camp fires in pre-literate Sumer, probably in the city state of Uruk, where Gilgameš is reputed to have reigned as a mortal ruler. A profusion of copies has been discovered in sites that are widely separated, although these copies are often fragmentary. No complete version of the work has ever been brought to light.

The Akkadian version generally accepted as 'standard' dates from the seventh century BC and was found in the royal library of Aššurbanipal at Nineveh. It consists of twelve tablets and, in origin, is largely ascribed to Sin-leqe-unnini, a priest who lived during the Kassite period in the middle of the second millennium BC. His composition was copied repeatedly over many centuries thereafter as a narrative consisting of eleven tablets. Tablet XII was almost certainly added as an afterthought some time during the seventh or eighth centuries BC. For a long time the purpose of its inclusion was a mystery, but it is now known to constitute the final chapter of a separate Sumerian story involving Gilgameš.

Some early Old Babylonian versions written in Akkadian deviate from the so-called standard composition in the omission of the prologue. They may also not have included the flood account. This features a man blessed with immortality but seemingly synonymous with the central character of the *Atrahasis* myth (see page 36).

The popularity of the *Epic* was such that copying parts of it was a favoured task for schoolchildren and fragments often display immaturity in writing skills.

The Sumerian tales of Gilgameš, some of which are known from original Sumerian language sources, were not slavishly followed. They were adapted or modified to suit new cultural needs and vogues. In some instances significant episodes have not been incorporated, while in others new exploits seem to have been dreamed up. The more copies that are discovered, the more confusing the authentic tale becomes, because each copy is accountably different. Perhaps the saga evolved chronologically, or perhaps it was varied by different folk traditions in different regions of the land.

The *Epic of Gilgameš* is arguably the greatest and most profound of all the ancient Near Eastern sagas and has been worked skilfully into a story centring on the perennial quest of the hero, Gilgameš, first for fame and fortune and then for the secret of immortality. The narrative might properly be described as a legend, yet Gilgameš came to be regarded as a god and most of his exploits brought him into contact with immortal beings of one genre or another. It was also perhaps never a religious work in that there is no evidence it was recited as part of a ritual. It may always have been a saga recited for vicarious entertainment, yet it is of such major significance in the theosophy of the Mesopotamian cultures that it deserves to be included here.

Tablet I opens with the prologue introducing a traveller who describes the city of Uruk and, in particular, a box in which are to be found the tablets accounting the *Epic of Gilgameš* proper. These tell of a great legendary warrior:

A hero born of Uruk, a goring wild bull.
He marches at the front as leader,
He goes behind, the support of his brothers,
A strong net, the protection of his men,
The raging flood wave, which can destroy even a stone wall.
Son of Lugalbanda, Gilgameš, perfect in strength,
Son of the lofty cow, the wild cow Ninsun.

This places Gilgameš in history as the son of the shepherd king Lugalbanda, who is known from the Sumerian King List in the period after the flood. His mother is Ninsun, the cow goddess, described as the consort of Lugalbanda and, in later times, as the tutelary goddess of the famous King Gudea of Lagaš. Gilgameš is described as being two thirds divine and one third mortal man. Throughout the *Epic* he is portrayed, at a superficial level, as the 'Superman' of the ancient world, beloved of the sun god Šamaš, a rumbustuous tyrant, at times almost Rabelaisian, a great warrior and a notorious philanderer who left neither son with father nor daughter with husband.

In order to temper Gilgameš's energies, the mother goddess Aruru is persuaded to create a wild man as his companion. With a lump of clay she engenders Enkidu:

His body is shaggy with hair,
He is furnished with tresses like a woman,
His locks grow luxuriant like grain.
He knows neither people nor country;
He is dressed as cattle are.
With gazelles he eats vegetation,
With cattle he quenches his thirst at the watering place.

There follows a passage which seems to be purely Akkadian in origin (there are no known Sumerian equivalents) in which Enkidu is seduced by the harlot Šamhat to tame him out of his wild ways and to make the cattle with which he has grown up forsake him. She stays with him for six days and seven nights, after which his body is washed clean and his legs can no longer keep pace with the wild animals. In this partially subdued state he is taken to Uruk to meet with Gilgameš for the first time. Gilgameš has dreamed of Enkidu as a great bolt of lightning sent from the god Anu and as someone he will come to love as a friend and equal.

Tablet II introduces the first major confrontation episode, that between Gilgameš, Enkidu and a terrifying beast, Humbaba, who guards the great pine forests of Lebanon in the west. In the original Sumerian tale, this malevolent character is one Huwawa, who lives in the Zagros Mountains to the east of Mesopotamia.

Humbaba, whose shout is the flood-weapon,
Whose utterance is Fire and whose breath is Death,
Can hear for up to sixty leagues throughout the [extent] of his forest . . .
Who, even among the gods, can face him?

Tablets III and IV take Gilgameš and Enkidu to the pine forest, though first they visit Gilgameš's mother Ninsun, who complains to Šamaš that he is putting Gilgameš's life at stake in order to rid the land of the dreadful creature. At fifty leagues they reach the edge of the pine forest and Gilgameš is struck with fear, but in Tablet V he prays to Šamaš for strength and, thus fortified, he takes on the monster.

They stirred up the ground with the heels of their feet,

Sirar and Lebanon were split apart at their gyrations,
White clouds grew dark,
Death descended over them like a fog . . .
Thirteen winds rose up at him and Humbaba's face grew dark.
He could not advance, he could not retreat.
Thus the weapons of Gilgameš succeeded against Humbaba.

Tablet VI narrates Gilgameš's ill-fated meeting with the goddess Ištar. Having returned triumphant from his battle with Humbaba, he washes and puts on his royal regalia; she attempts to seduce him but, in contemplative mood, he rejects her. She has, he claims, destroyed lives and happiness amongst too many of her suitors.

> *'And what of me? You will love me and you will treat me as you treated them.'*

Ištar is enraged at what she sees as this humiliation and she goes to her father, Anu, demanding the services of the Bull of Heaven which she intends to set against Gilgameš to strike him down for his impudence. Eventually Anu gives in to her pleas and the bull brings terror and death to the land of Uruk. Gilgameš and Enkidu challenge and slay it but, in doing so, they anger Anu and the seal is set on tragedy. In Enkidu's portentous dream, with which Tablet VII begins, the gods decree that Enkidu must die, though Gilgameš is fated to live on.

Tablet VIII provides a moving narrative throughout which Gilgameš mourns the impending loss and the death of his friend and ally:

'I must weep for Enkidu my friend,
Mourn him bitterly like a wailing woman.
As for the axe at my side, spur to my arm,
The sword in my belt, the shield for my chest,
My festive clothes, my manly sash:
cruel fate has risen up and taken them from me.'

In Tablet IX Gilgameš roams the country as a wild man, distraught in his grief and, at this juncture, the tone of the *Epic* changes. He has become preoccupied with thoughts of mortality and with fear of his own death.

> *'Shall I die too? Am I not like Enkidu?'*

Gilgameš's restless wandering takes him, in the text of Tablet X, to the holy mountain of Maṣu from which Šamaš rises each morning. He asks its guardian beasts to direct him to Ut-napištim, the one mortal being who has gained the boon of eternal life, but they are reluctant to help him so he travels on, by night, through the mountain paths. Eventually, thin and haggard, he comes to the house of Siduri, the alewife who lives by the primal deeps, the Apsu. She tells him that Ut-napištim lives across the sea which no one, other than Šamaš, has ever crossed because the maelstrom drowns all who try. It is the boatman, Ur-sanabi, who at last reveals to Gilgameš the means of crossing the ocean.

Tablet XI relates Gilgameš's arrival at the home of Ut-napištim and Ut-napištim's story of the flood. It tells how the god Ellil changed him from sage to mortal man but then relented, touching his forehead and returning him to immortality. Gilgameš is distraught that the dream of eternal life is beyond his reach, but then Ut-napištim instructs him to sail back across the sea towards Uruk. During the voyage, at the bottom of the ocean, he will discover an elixir, a magical plant. Gilgameš locates the plant but, as he rests beside a pool, a snake slithers up and eats it, casting its skin in the first of an endless series of rejuvenations. Gilgameš weeps bitterly and returns to Uruk.

The XII and final tablet of the *Epic* is the late addition which, in its Akkadian form, seems to have little relevance to the whole. Briefly it describes how Gilgameš loses the *pukku* and *mikku* – probably a sacred drum and drumstick – into the earth and how Enkidu (alive and well again) tries to recover them but dies in the process. On the face of it, the story does not fit the rest of the *Epic*, although the scribes must have had some logical reason for incorporating it. It is dealt with, in its complete Sumerian form, under a separate heading (see *Gilgameš and the Halub Tree*, page 252).

THE LABOURS OF HERAKLES

CULTURE OF ORIGIN: classical Greek, but subsequently adopted into Roman culture

PROVENANCE: accounts of Herakles's exploits are drawn from a number of Greek authors and many are undoubtedly recorded from earlier oral traditions. Hesiod refers to the slaying of the Lernaean Hydra and of Geryones briefly in the *Theogony*. The account of the twelve labours is included most notably in *Herakles Furens* by Euripides, though Homer's *Iliad* makes passing references. A shortened version is described by Apollodorus who lists only ten tasks.

Herakles 'officially' begins life as a mortal man and therefore may technically be a personality of legend rather than myth, but his real father, as with many Greek heroes, is a god. The role of Herakles in Greek tradition is also inextricably bound up with the gods and his subsequent deification makes it appropriate to treat his story as myth. The labours are generally divided into two groups of six, the location of the first group being the Peloponnese and of the second Crete.

NOTE: in Roman tradition Herakles becomes Hercules.

Herakles is instructed to carry out twelve labours by his cousin Eurystheus who has managed to usurp the throne of Mycenae, over him, through the tactics of the goddess Hera (see the *Boyhood of Herakles*, page 100). By implication Herakles may come to Mycenae only if he enters a period of servitude to the weak and cowardly Eurystheus as expiation for murdering his wife and children in Thebes.

The first task is to slay one of the offspring of the demonic nymph Echidna, the *Lion of Nemea*, a ferocious beast which has been terrorizing the region during forays from a den located in a virtually impregnable cave. Having failed to slaughter it either with bow and arrows or with his club, Herakles resorts to blocking up one of the cave exits and strangling the trapped beast. The animal is resistant to steel so he flays it with one of its own claws and uses the skin to fashion a garment, the head becoming his helmet. When Herakles returns to Mycenae with the carcass Eurystheus is so terrified that he refuses him access to the citadel and all subsequent trophies have to be left outside the gates.

The second task is to defeat another monstrous offspring of Echidna, the *Hydra of Lernea*, conceived through her liaison with the god Typhon. The serpent-like, many-headed monster which emits venomous breath has been fostered by the goddess Hera, who anticipates it will provide a suitable ordeal for Herakles. When the hero confronts the Hydra he tries first to kill it with flaming arrows, but then employs his nephew Iolaus to help him cut off its heads. As fast as the heads are severed they grow again, but Herakles thwarts this by setting fire to a neighbouring grove and using the burning branches to cauterize the severed stumps.

For his third enforced labour Herakles is required to capture the savage *Boar of Erymanthos*. On his way to the creature's mountain lair he is distracted temporarily when a herd of centaurs engage him in a battle, but eventually he locates the boar, luring it out and driving it through deep snow until it is exhausted. Then he slings it across his shoulders and carries it back to Eurystheus, who is so alarmed when he sees Herakles returning that he hides himself inside a large amphora (vase).

The fourth task is to capture the *Hind of Keryneia*, a beast of great size which decimates crops in the region. The animal has gilded horns and is sacred to the goddess Artemis, which means that it must not be harmed. Its flight is very fast and Herakles is obliged to chase after it for a year until it tires and rests on the slopes of Mount Artemisium. Before Herakles can capture the hind it flees again, swimming across the River Ladon in Arcadia. Here Herakles wounds it with an arrow and sets off to lead it back to Mycenae. On the way he is confronted by Artemis and Apollo, who wish to take the animal from him until they learn of the task he must fulfil. When he explains the position they allow him to continue his journey.

Eurystheus now sets Herakles the ordeal of destroying the *Birds of Stymphalos*. These creatures live in the safety of a forest but prey on the surrounding area and cause terror amongst the inhabitants. To drive them from the trees Herakles relies on castanets, the loud noise of which startles the birds. They fly into the open countryside where the hero dispatches them with his bow and arrows.

For his sixth and final labour in the Peloponnese, Herakles is required to cleanse the *Stables of Augeias*, King of Elis and the son of the god Helios. Augeias owns an impressive herd of horses which once belonged to Helios, but through neglect he has allowed their stables to become thoroughly fouled. This means that the fields have not been manured and the crops start to fail. Herakles demands, and is promised, a reward for his menial services, but when the task is complete, Augeias reneges on the deal and the hero is obliged to wage war against him. When the battle is won, and Herakles has returned to Mycenae, Eurystheus refuses to recognize the task among the labours since money has been involved.

The action now moves to Crete, where the seventh labour is to take place. This is the capture of the *Bull of Minos*. Various traditions suggest that this animal emerged from the sea under the aegis of the god Poseidon in retaliation for certain impieties by King Minos; or that Minos's wife developed an unhealthy passion for it; or that Zeus had disguised himself as the bull in order to effect the abduction of Europa. In any event Herakles travels to Crete, where he asks Minos's co-operation to secure the beast. Minos declines to become directly involved, but gives Herakles permission to attempt the capture alone. When Herakles is successful he hands the bull over to Eurystheus, who wishes to dedicate it to Hera. The goddess, however, frees the bull out of continuing spite for Herakles and it roams the land until eventually it reaches Attica, where it creates terror on the Plain of Marathon. According to tradition, it is killed by Theseus, who is envious of Herakles's reputation as a slayer of monsters.

NOTE: the Bull of Minos is altogether distinct from the Minotaur slain by Theseus in the labyrinth of the royal palace at Knossos (see *Ariadne, Theseus and the Minotaur*, page 157).

The eighth labour involves the theft of the *Mares of Diomedes*. Four ferocious beasts – Deinus, Lampon, Podargus and Xanthus – are chained with iron shackles in the stables of the King of Thrace, where they feed off human flesh. Herakles releases the horses and leads them away, but he is attacked by Diomedes's soldiers. Giving the mares into the care of Abderus, one of the sons of Hermes, Herakles slaughters Diomedes and feeds his carcass to the mares. Though he defeats Diomedes's soldiers, his ally Abderus is killed in the battle and, in his memory, Herakles founds the city of Abdera before returning to Mycenae. Eurystheus is at a loss to know what to do with his latest acquisitions, so he dedicates them to Hera and releases them on Mount Olympus, where they succumb to predators more ferocious than themselves.

The next task is not actually undertaken at the instruction of Eurystheus but of his daughter, Admete, who demands the *Girdle of Hippolyta*, Queen of the Amazon women. The girdle is a symbol of male authority which Hippolyta is obliged to wear by the god of war, Ares. Thus, when Herakles arrives, she is willing to relinquish it. Hera, however, seeing that the task has become too easy, intervenes and provokes enmity between Herakles and the Amazons. Hippolyta is slain in the ensuing clash and Herakles returns to his tormentor having completed the ninth of his labours.

The rustling of the *Cattle of Geryon* constitutes Herakles's tenth task. Belonging to the three-headed giant son of Chrysaor and Callirrhoe, they graze on the island of Erythia across the Mediterranean in the west where they are tended by a herdsman, Eurytion, and a guard dog named Orthrus, born of the liaison between Echidna and Typhon. First, Herakles journeys across the Libyan desert where he is so overcome by heat that he threatens to shoot down the sun god Helios with his arrows. Helios entreats him not to do so and Herakles relents in exchange for the cup of the sun in which he can traverse the sea. He then threatens Okeanos for inflicting a storm upon him, but the tempest subsides and when he lands on the island, Herakles dispatches both Eurytion and Orthrus with his massive club. Geryon has, by now, learned of Herakles's arrival and advances to challenge him, but the hero slays the giant with casual ease. The herd presents more of a problem. So vast is it that Herakles is obliged to drive the cattle back to Mycenae in batches.

NOTE: it was on his journey in the western Mediterranean, and to commemorate his safe passage, that Herakles constructed the two columns (Gibraltar and Ceuta) which became known as the 'Pillars of Herakles'.

The final labours represent the most severe tests of Herakles's stamina and resolve. He is ordered to journey to the kingdom of Hades to obtain the *Capture of Kerberos*, the fifty-headed hound, born of Echidna and Typhon, which guards the gates of the underworld and dines off raw flesh. Herakles is led down the path to the underworld by Hermes, having been initiated into the Eleusinian Mysteries, held in honour of the goddess Demeter. The shades of the dead scatter before him, with exception of Medusa and Meleager, whom he threatens with his sword until Hermes points out that they are beyond death. When he reaches the palace of Hades, the underworld god grants permission to remove Kerberos with the proviso that Herakles captures the hound without resorting to the use of weapons. The hero overcomes his quarry by grasping its neck and thus returns with it to Eurystheus, who is so horrified by the achievement that he hides in his amphora again until Herakles has returned the animal to Hades.

The twelfth labour of Herakles involves the gathering of the *Golden Apples of the Hesperides*. These were a wedding present from Gaia to Hera on the occasion of her marriage to Zeus. She planted them near Mount Atlas to be tended by the Hesperides nymphs, but the daughters of Atlas used to pilfer the apples so she guarded them with a monstrous hundred-headed serpent, the offspring of Keto and Phorkys. To discover the whereabouts of the garden of the Hesperides, Herakles is obliged to capture the sea god Nereus and wring the information from him. Travelling via Libya, Egypt and Arabia, he reaches the Caucasus Mountains, where he frees Prometheus from his incarceration (see *Prometheus*, page 163). Prometheus tells him that only Atlas can obtain the apples so Herakles offers to take the weight of the sky on his own shoulders while the giant carries out the theft. Atlas returns with the prize only to inform Herakles that he intends to return to Eurystheus with the apples himself, leaving Herakles to bear the burden of the sky. Herakles appears to concede the point, but asks Atlas to take the weight briefly while he places a pad on his shoulders. When Atlas agrees, Herakles seizes the apples and returns to Eurystheus, his labours completed.

CATH MAGH TUIREADH
(The First and Second Battles of Moytura)

CULTURE OF ORIGIN: Celtic – Irish

PROVENANCE: recorded from oral traditions in an indefinite number of manuscripts, now lost, collectively known as the *Leabhar Gabhala* (the Book of Invasions). Much of the material survives in the *Leabhar Laighnech: Book of Leinster*, compiled circa 1160 by Aed Mac Crimtheinn [Dublin Institute for Advanced Studies]. It is also included in the work of the seventeenth-century Irish historian, Michael O'Cleirigh (published 1643), the source which is generally referred to.

The *Leabhar Gabhala* includes, under modern convention, the so-called Mythological Cycle of stories which involve, by and large, the deities of the Side, the Tuatha de Danaan (people of the goddess Dana) who overcame the ancient inhabitants of Ireland, the Firbolg and the Fomorii, and whose activities took place largely in the valley of the Boyne. The first Battle of Magh Tuireadh involves the conquest of the Firbolg and the second results in the defeat of the Fomorii.

The First Battle of Magh Tuireadh, involving the Firbolg (thought to mean 'bagmen' because they were obliged to carry bags of earth from the valleys to the hills during their enslavement to the Fomorii), is placed in the south of County Mayo, on the west coast near Cong. The Firbolg came to Ireland in the wake, or as descendants, of a tribe known as the Nemedians, who were decimated by the more powerful Fomorii and whose remnant had fled to Thrace in Greece. In time, however, the Firbolg evolved out of slavery and became prosperous landowners.

At the period of mythical history in which the first of the battles is set, the leader of the Firbolg, the King of the Great Plain, is Eochaidh Mac Erc, whose wife is Tailtu, daughter of the ruler of the Land of the Dead [in whose honour the Tailltinn games were celebrated until modern times]. A new wave of invaders arrive in Ireland, the Tuatha de Danaan. These are a race of gods who come from the north equipped with magical powers. They belong to the otherworld, the Side, and they bring with them four magical objects: the Lia Fail (Stone of Destiny) at Temuir, the Hill of Tara, in County Meath, which is to become the touchstone of the High Kings of Ireland and which screams under the foot of a rightful king; magical weapons including the spear of Lugh, the father of Cu Chulainn; the sword of the war god, Nuadu; and the huge cauldron of the supreme god, Dagda.

Animosity between the Firbolg and the invaders heightens until a full-scale battle breaks out at Magh Tuireadh. During the conflict Nuadu (Roman: Nodens) loses his arm, but the overall outcome is defeat for the Firbolg. Thus the Tuatha de Danaan come to rule all of Ireland with exception of the western province of Connacht.

The mutilated Nuadu is replaced by a tyrannical overlord, Bres Mac Elatha, whose parentage is reflected in ambiguous loyalties. His mother is Eriu, one of the aspects of the fertility goddess, the so-called Sovereignty of Ireland who comes from the Tuatha de Danaan. By tradition she weds a mortal husband, the Fomorian king, Elatha.

Under the rule of Bres there is an uneasy peace, but the Tuatha de Danaan are subjected increasingly to raids by the Fomorii who have begun to reassert themselves. These beings are the demonic deities of Irish myth, misshapen creatures who have already fought with the Nemedians. Fearing Bres's true motives, the Tuatha de Danaan depose him in favour of Nuadu, for whom the physician god, Dian Cecht, has made a perfect silver prosthesis to replace his severed limb and who thus becomes known as Nuada argatlam (Nuadu of the silver arm). The banished Bres and his mother seek reprisal by raising a Fomorian army to which Bres recruits the terrible one-eyed god of death, Balor, whose home is on Tory Island. By repute his eye is so huge that four men are required to lift the lid and its gaze is so evil that men are destroyed as soon as it is cast upon them.

An ancient prophecy warns that Balor can only suffer death at the hands of his own grandson so, to avoid risk, he incarcerates his only daughter, Ethnea (Ethlinn), in a distant cave. Here she grows into a beautiful woman guarded by twelve chaperones. She remains in her prison until a local hero, Cian, the son of Dian Cecht, helped by a druidess, Birog, discovers her and sleeps with her. She then becomes pregnant with triplets. Cian also impregnates her twelve attendants. When Balor discovers what has taken place he has all the children thrown into a whirlpool. One, Lugh, manages to escape to be reared by Manannan Mac Lir, the sea god, and he grows into a great spear-wielding warrior, one of his subsequent epithets being Lugh lamfhada (Lugh of the long arm). He also becomes the god of arts and crafts.

Nuada argatlam abdicates the throne of Ireland in favour of Lugh and presses him to engage the Fomorii. Thus begins the second Battle of Magh Tuireadh, fought between the Tuatha de Danaan and the Fomorii. At its climax the dreadful Balor marches forward and four of his attendants heave open his eyelid. All within its gaze are destroyed, but Lugh, who has stood back in anticipation, races forward as soon as the lid droops again, hurling a magic stone (*tathlum*) from his sling with such force that it smashes the huge eye to the back of Balor's brain, killing him and destroying twenty-eight Fomorian warriors in the process. Thus the Fomorii are defeated once and for all and the Tuatha de Danaan rule in Ireland until the arrival of the Celts.

THE BATTLE OF MU
(The Battle of Ten Thousand Spirits)

CULTURE OF ORIGIN: Chinese Daoist (Taoist)

PROVENANCE: recorded many centuries after the actual historical event in various texts and art from oral traditions. The factual provenance includes the offical Shi Zhi records and the writings of Su-Ma Zhien, who lived during the second and first centuries BC. The Battle of Mu took place in 1122 BC between old and new orders in Chinese history, the Shang and Zhou (Chou) dynasties, but it subsequently took on mythical proportions in which the mortal conflict was mirrored by a celestial battle fought between opposing forces of immortal beings. It is used in an exemplary fashion to explain how many deities of the old order became redundant and new names and personalities arrived. The celestial conflict, known as the Battle of Ten Thousand Spirits, is narrated in Daoist religious texts including the *Book on the Making of Immortals* and in the *Catalogue of Spirits and Immortals*.

It should be noted that the anglicized equivalents of Chinese characters vary considerably in transliteration. The official Chinese Pinyin system is applied here, followed, where appropriate, in brackets, by the more generally encountered Wade–Giles system.

The mythical overlords are Zhou Wang (Chou Wang) (1154–1121 BC) of the Shang Dynasty, the god of sodomy, who is cast as the evil tyrant of the old order, and Wu Wang (the so-called Military King known in his earthly existence as Fa, 1169–1116 BC), who becomes the first ruler of the incoming radical Zhou (Chou) Dynasty. The actual foundation of the dynasty in Daoist mythology is attributed to his father, Xi Beh (Hsi Peh), who became deified under the name Wen Wang.

The protagonists on the side of Wu Wang include Zhiang Tzu-Ya (Chiang Lu-Shang in mortal life), a heroic general who has previously changed allegiance from Zhou Wang to Wen Wang and who gains the reputation for raising those he has slaughtered in battle to the status of gods. It is through his power of ordaining apotheosis that many of the new deities emerge. The heroes of the new dynasty also include Li No-Cha, a fabulous warrior said to be sixty feet tall with eight arms wielding weapons of gold and with three heads each bearing three eyes. His voice causes the earth to shake and his breath is blue smoke. He possesses a magic golden bracelet with which, as a youth, he antagonized the Dragon King by killing one of his messengers. He also fights using another magical weapon, the so-called Wind-Fire machine.

Two of Zhou Wang's warriors, the spirit of the star Tiao Ko (Feng-Shui in mortal life), and his general, spirit of the star Sang-Men (Zhang Kuei Fang in mortal life), engage Li No-Cha in mortal combat, but are defeated by his golden bracelet. During the engagement, however, Li No-Cha hears his name uttered three times. In Daoist tradition this is a portent that the *hun* (the conscious soul which may or may not reach the heavenly paradise), and the *po* (the life force of the mortal body) are destined to separate. Li No-Cha, however, has changed himself into a lotus during the course of the fight and therefore considers himself immune from such a fate.

Zhiang Tzu-Ya is nevertheless worried that his champion may be about to die, so he requests an audience with Wu Wang, asking his emperor for permission to travel to the holy mountain of Kun Lun [allegedly somewhere in the Hindu Kush], the home of the Queen of the West, Xi Wang Mu (Hsi Wang Mu). On Kun Lun he meets first with one of the triad of supreme deities in the Daoist pantheon, Yuan-Shih Tien-Kun, and then with the guardian deity who controls the lifespan of mortals, Nan Zhi Xien-Weng (Nan Chi Hsien Weng), the so-called Old Man of the South Pole. As an insurance against mishap Nan Zhi Xien-Weng instructs Zhiang Tzu-Ya to build a shrine in which to display the list of Promotions to Immortality.

On his way home, Zhiang Tzu-Ya is accosted by an old ally who has given allegiance to the opposing forces, Shen Kung-Pao, who tries to persuade him likewise to change sides in the conflict and to hand over the Promotions to Immortality. Yuan-Shih has warned Zhiang Tzu-Ya against responding to anyone who speaks to him by name on the journey and Shen Kung-Pao now challenges Zhiang Tzu-Ya to a test of magic. If Shen Kung-Pao wins, Zhiang Tzu-Ya's forfeit will be to destroy the Promotions. Shen Kung-Pao claims to be able to cut off his own head and cause it to float in space. When he succeeds, Zhiang Tzu-Ya knows he has lost the bet, but Nan Zhi Xien-Weng intervenes and sends Shen Kung-Pao away with a severe reprimand.

As the battle progresses one of Zhou Wang's generals, Zhao Kung-Ming, is slain and his three immortal sisters, the Keng San Ku-Niang (the Three Lavatory Ladies) of Zhou Wang's celestial court, are determined to avenge his death. They use the Golden Bushel of Troubled Origins (their lavatory bucket) as a projectile until it is rendered impotent by Li No-Cha and his Wind-Fire weapon. Their diminished might is then taken on by Lao Tzu, a sage and keeper of the imperial records at the court of Wu Wang. One of the Lavatory Ladies, Zhiung Xaio, attempts to stab the sage with her golden scissors, but he waves the weapon away and all three are vanquished. When peace is restored, however, Zhiang Tzu-Ya elevates them to become midwife goddesses.

Wen Wang, the founder of the new dynasty, is fatally wounded by the god of thunder, clouds and rain, Lei Ku (Wen-Zhung Dai-Shih in mortal life), one of the senior ministers of Zhou Wang, who has three eyes, one of which emits a deathly ray, and who rides upon a black unicorn that travels at the speed of light. Wen Wang is restored with an elixir administered by another of his lieutenants, Jan-Deng Dao-Pen who has, for his part in the battle, slain Dou Mu, the mother of the pole star. In addition, he has incapacitated Tai Sui, the god of astrology (Yin Zhiao in mortal life) and son of Zhou Wang. (He is also reported, in separate mythology, to have fought for the opposing side.)

Facing defeat himself, Lei Ku starts to retreat towards the mountain Yen Shan but he is confronted by various of Wu Wang's generals. The first of them, Chih Zhing-Tzu, renders Lei Ku's unicorn impotent by flashing his magic Yin-Yang mirror at it. His ally, Lei Zhen-Tzu, then splits it in half with his staff. A third general, Yun Zhung-Tzu, bars the way of the fleeing Lei Ku and hurls magic bolts of lightning with which the victim is incinerated. It is in the ensuing peace that Zhiang Tzu-Ya gives Lei Ku his new role in the pantheon as the storm god.

Finally Wu Wang, the son of Wen Wang, advances his forces upon Lei Ku and defeats them, thus ending the old dynasty and clearing the way for the new.

THE SON OF MUNJEM MALIK

CULTURE OF ORIGIN: Prasun Kafir – Nuristan [central Hindukush]
PROVENANCE: oral traditions recorded chiefly by M. Elphinstone (1839); G. Morgenstierne (1951); G.S. Robertson (1896).

There are strong social elements in this myth reflecting a strongly chauvinistic society in which all women are viewed as second-class citizens and often of evil or demonic disposition. It underlines the pitfalls of polygamy but also the importance of family loyalty. It further reflects a primitive shamanistic belief in animism or shape-changing.

Munjem Malik, the earth god and one-time rival of the supreme deity Imra, possesses two wives (probably demonesses) neither of whom he cares for very much. One day he meets and falls in love with a very beautiful black-haired girl, whom he marries. When the girl becomes pregnant the god gives her a bell which she is to ring if she gives birth while he is absent. The other wives torment the girl to such an extent that she rings the bell in desperation. Munjem Malik surges up through the floor of the house and angrily tells her not to ring again until she has proper cause.

When the girl goes into labour the other jealous wives silence the bell and through their demonic powers deliver two babies, a boy and a girl, without the young mother's knowledge. She thus accepts that she is infertile and Munjem Malik cuts off her nose in punishment. Meanwhile the demonesses hurl the two infants into the bull shed, hoping to destroy them, but the children sit unharmed on the horns of the cattle and happily suck their thumbs. Now the demonesses place them in a box, intending to abandon them to their fate on the waters of the river, but the river goddess, Lunang, decrees that they shall not drift down the valley to the entrance of the underworld and mortal death; rather they shall be carried to Imra's sacred lake high in the mountain meadows.

Imra accepts the infants, but his wife, also a demoness, sends them to her mother on a false errand designed to end in their murder. By chance the fatal letter of instruction to Imra's mother-in-law is intercepted by a man, Amawal-ra, who alters it from a death warrant to a missal of honour. The boy, whose name is also Munjem Malik, now understands the plot against him and his sister. He manages to rescue his mother's nose from a shelf and he also takes a bird which is sitting beside it. As he and his sister run away another bird alerts the old woman and she chases after them. So the boy takes one of the legs of the bird he holds and breaks it, whereupon the demoness begins to limp. The boy crushes the bird and the old woman and her daughter die because the spirits of both are contained in the creature.

The boy returns to Imra for a while but then becomes an itinerant blacksmith, travelling until he reaches his mother's house. He takes some buttermilk from her, but when she recognizes him as her son he chastises her for neglecting him as a baby. Then he relents, understanding what has taken place, and he replaces the nose on her face. He transforms himself back into an infant and sits upon her lap, whereupon her breasts fill and flow with milk. The boy grows into manhood endowed with supernatural strength and sets out to slay his father, whom he clubs with such force that the elder Munjem Malik is rammed into the earth with only his head, still alive, protruding while the valley floor grows over his corpse. There at Arte, in the upper Parun valley of Nuristan, the earth god remains.

PRYDERI

CULTURE OF ORIGIN: Celtic – Welsh
PROVENANCE: recorded from oral traditions and linked thematically in the epic saga, the *Mabinogion*

Rhiannon, the daughter of the underworld god Hefaidd Hen, is betrothed to Pwyll, the Lord of Dyfed, who has fallen in love with her one day as she rides by on a white horse. One of the guests at the engagement feast, however, is Gwawl, also a member of the otherworld forces. Gwawl becomes enamoured of Rhiannon and when he craves a boon from Pwyll he is magnanimously granted anything that he desires. Gwawl requests both the feast and the bride-to-be and Pwyll is honour bound to agree. Rhiannon has little desire to be married to Gwawl and she reveals to Pwyll the secret by which his rival in love may be vanquished. At the new wedding feast Pwyll arrives in disguise and produces a bag which he asks to be filled with food. The bag has magical properties which means that it can never be filled unless, according to Pwyll, one of noble birth climbs in and presses down the contents with his feet. Gwawl duly obliges and is trapped in the bag which Pwyll's henchmen proceed to beat with clubs until Gwawl begs for mercy and agrees to relinquish his claims upon Rhiannon, who becomes the consort of Pwyll.

Rhiannon bears a son, Pryderi, who is abducted from his cradle by a monstrous claw, presumably sent from the otherworld at the behest of the thwarted Gwawl. The midwives, anxious that no blame should fall upon themselves, smear Rhiannon's face with blood to make it appear that she has devoured her child and, in penance, she is forced into a life of menial servitude: she stands at the horse block offering to take guests into the castle on her back. Pryderi remains missing until May-eve when he is discovered in a stable by Teirnyon Turf Liant, who is keeping vigil over a mare in foal. The claw also attempts to snatch the newborn foal but is repelled by Teirnyon, who takes the infant Pryderi and raises him as his own. As the boy grows Teirnyon observes in him a strong resemblance to Pwyll and feels obliged to return the child to his rightful parents, thus releasing Rhiannon from her penance.

When Pryderi grows to manhood he falls in love with and marries Cigfa, the daughter of Gwyn Gohoyw, and on his father's death he inherits the title Lord of Dyfed. All this time the kinsmen of Gwawl have been bent on revenge and now the land falls under an enchantment through the powers of Gwawl's cousin, Llwyd ap Cil Coed. Pryderi, Rhiannon and her new husband Manawyddan go out hunting, but Pryderi becomes trapped in a castle of the otherworld chained to a golden vessel. Rhiannon is also captured when she follows him to the castle and both remain incarcerated until Manawyddan rescues them and defeats Llwyd's magic through his own great powers of cunning and craft.

Pryderi's end comes about during the war between the kingdoms of Gwynedd and Dyfed. The deeper causes of the conflict are to be found in an enmity between Gwydion, the son of Don the enchanter, his brother Gilfaethwy and their uncle, Math, the brothers having been virtually accused of raping Math's virgin footholder Goewin. The immediate spark, however, comes when Pryderi's pigs, the only domesticated pigs in all the Celtic realm, presented to him by the underworld god Arawn, are stolen. In order to obtain them Gwydion disguises himself and attends Pryderi's court. In exchange for the pigs he offers horses and dogs and all their trappings. But when the deal is struck and the pigs have been driven off towards Gwynedd, Pryderi discovers that the goods he has obtained through the barter are made out of mushrooms which promptly revert to their own form.

Pryderi chases after Gwydion, but is slain in the ensuing combat. Gwydion and Gilfaethwy are hounded mercilessly by Math and his kinsmen, who eventually catch the brothers and turn them first into stags, then into sows and finally into wolves for a period of three years.

RAMAYANA
(The Adventures of Rama)

CULTURE OF ORIGIN: Hindu Epic and Puranic [India]
PROVENANCE: the epic text known as the *Ramayana of Valmiki* and in later Puranic literature. The *Ramayana* was written down some time between

300 BC and 300 AD. Essentially it narrates the abduction of the wife of Lord Rama by a foreign (Šri Lankan) deity and her subsequent restoration and fate. It also serves to introduce several of the more important deities in the Hindu pantheon within a dramatic context.

At one level the epic is the story of a Hindu deity who confronts and overcomes a foreign demon king, but it is also a morality play. Rama is portrayed less as a god than as a mortal hero and it should be remembered that, at the time when the epic was written, it was considered avant garde to attribute to Rama the status even of an *avatar* of Višnu. In spite of Rama's apparently cavalier attitude towards his wife Sita, both remain constant to each other and both are revered for their steadfastness in marriage.

The cult of Rama is known from the eleventh century AD and the myth gained enormous popularity not only on the Indian subcontinent but throughout many parts of the Far East, including Thailand and Indonesia, particularly Java, where it was translated into the Javanese language in about 900 AD. The epic contains many subplots, but the essence is given here.

The god Rama (Pleasing), the seventh incarnation of the Hindu creator god Višnu, takes as his bride Sita (Furrow), who is an incarnation of the goddess Laksmi. In the epic, Rama is depicted as the King of Ayodhya and the son of Dasaratha and Kausalya. Sita depicts the perfect Hindu wife, a model of fidelity and subservience, but early in her marriage she is adbucted by Ravana, the king and chief deity of the demonic Raksas in Lanka [Šri Lanka]. Ravana is a skilled warrior, bearing the scars of many battles, and is also a magician capable of changing form at will. Having captured Sita he flies off through the skies in his chariot with her and imprisons her. Despite her incarceration she manages to remain inviolate and continues to keep total fidelity with Rama.

Rama obtains the support of the monkey god Hanuman, the son of Pavana, god of winds. He becomes Rama's faithful servant and musters an army of monkeys from the forests. He is then commanded by Rama to set out in search of Sita. At first he is unsuccessful, but eventually he learns where she is being held. Through an enormous leap, Hanuman crosses the sea between India and Šri Lanka and makes his way into Ravana's stronghold (in an alternative version he builds a bridge of stones across the passage). Constantly changing his appearance, Hanuman searches the city undetected. At first he is unable to locate Sita, but then he is informed that she is being held in a nearby forest.

Sita is eventually discovered and a battle takes place between the armies of Rama and Hanuman, and that of Ravana. Hanuman appears to vanquish Ravana and attempts to punish him for his crime, but in the process Hanuman himself is paralysed and captured and his tail is set on fire. Using his divine powers he makes his escape and uses his burning tail to set the whole of Lanka alight. Ravana now proposes a massive counterattack on the armies of the Indian gods, though he is urged to restraint by his younger brother, who eventually deserts him for the opposing camp.

Sita meanwhile remains imprisoned. Rama and Hanuman now besiege Lanka. The monkey army, shrieking and biting, rip up trees and rocks to use as missiles, while the demonic forces of Ravana respond with clubs, axes, bows and arrows. Hanuman flies twice to the Himalaya to obtain healing plants for his wounded monkey soldiers. Rama and his adversary come face to face and Ravana almost defeats the Indian hero by growing a multiplicity of heads which reappear as soon as they are decapitated. Rama, however, relies on the ultimate magic of his own weapon, his bow, and Ravana is slain. Eventually, when the siege is successful, Hanuman is commanded to go to Sita and to ask her to come back to Rama. Sita is returned to her rightful place beside Rama, and Hanuman, his task complete, returns with his monkey soldiers to the forest.

Rama, however, is deeply suspicious of Sita's fidelity during the period of imprisonment and begins to treat her very badly, finally rejecting her. Sita threatens to immolate herself through the inner power of her own purity and, for a while, Rama grudgingly takes her back. She becomes pregnant, but Rama's doubts return and he banishes her; she is in exile when she gives birth to twin sons.

Sita is deeply unhappy and longs for death. Finally her mother, the earth, takes pity on her and a golden throne rises from the ground upon which Sita takes her place. The throne descends into the earth forever and Rama, realizing his loss too late, is left to mourn his much abused wife for eternity.

RUDRA, ŠIVA AND THE DESTRUCTION OF THE CITY OF DEMONS

CULTURE OF ORIGIN: Epic Hindu [India]

PROVENANCE: the epic text known as the *Mahabharata*, written down some time between 300 BC and 300 AD, which essentially narrates the epic battle between the Pandava clan and their rival cousins the Kauravas. It also serves to introduce several of the more important deities within the Hindu pantheon in a dramatic context.

The myth, in which Šiva destroys the forces of the demons, underscores a deep-rooted Hindu concept that cosmic annihilation is threatened if and when disparate forces of nature are brought together. In this instance, three cities representing heaven, sky and earth finally fuse into one another with apocalyptic results.

Tarakaksa, Kamalaksa and Vidyunmalin, the sons of a conquered demon, Taraka, undertake severe asceticism and ask the creator god, Brahma, for the boon of immortality. He explains that this is impossible, but he accedes to their second request, that they should build three cities which will last for a thousand years and will then merge into one great city which Śiva, in his terrifying aspect of Rudra, will destroy to signify the death of the brothers.

The demons employ Viśvakarman, the architect of the gods (whose loyalties are ambivalent, comparable to those of Loki in Nordic myth), to build the three cities – one of gold belonging to Tarakaksa; one of silver belonging to Kamalaksa; and one of iron belonging to Vidyunmalin. These cities symbolize respectively the three states of the cosmos – heaven, sky and earth. In the city of gold, and through the power of asceticism, Tarakaksa's son creates a magical lake which is found to revive slain demon heroes. Realizing that they have inadvertently achieved the power of immortality, the inhabitants of the cities begin to oppress and violate the rest of the world with great intolerance and inhumanity.

The leader of the gods, Indra, with the Marut storm gods, attacks the three cities, but is unable to subdue them. Afraid of the power which has been unleashed, the gods assemble before Brahma and relate their concerns. Brahma explains that the cities can only be brought down by a single arrow fired from the bow of Śiva (in his aspect of Rudra). All then practise asceticism and proclaim the sacred Vedic texts; they can now go before Śiva. He welcomes them in a friendly fashion and Brahma relates how, long ago, he gave a boon to the rulers of the three cities which is now being used against humanity. Śiva agrees that the demons must be destroyed, but he cannot fulfil the task single-handedly. He proclaims that all the gods must unite in strength, imbued with special powers which Śiva will conjure for them. He will confer on them half of all his strength.

The gods argue that if they take half of Śiva's power they will not be able to bear it, but if he will take half of *their* combined powers he can use it more effectively. Śiva agrees and the gods thus prepare weapons of terrifying strength for him. His cosmic chariot is fashioned by Viśvakarman from the body of the earth, its axle is made from Mount Mandara, the constellations are its shafts. Viṣṇu, Soma and Agni combine to forge the awful arrow of nemesis. The horses which pull the chariot are Indra, the leader of the gods; Varuna, god of waters; Yama, ruler of the dead; and Kubera, god of riches. Then the weapons of Śiva himself are placed in the chariot, with the sacred Vedas, and the great god envelops himself with the flames of his own immutable energy.

Śiva calls for a charioteer and when no one steps forward the gods return to Brahma to appoint someone of sufficient calibre to carry out the task. It is Brahma himself who mounts the chariot and takes up the reins. Śiva, appearing as the bull, bellows out a great roar and drives away towards the three cities. When he draws his bowstring with the arrow aimed, so great is the vibration that the chariot begins to sink until Viṣṇu also takes the form of a bull and supports it. Just as Śiva is about to loose the all-destroying missile, the three cities merge into one. A thousand years have passed. Śiva releases the arrow and the demons are destroyed, hurled into the sunset of the western ocean as their city burns to the ground.

As the myth ends on an apocalyptic note, Śiva refrains from reducing the whole world to ashes . . . on this occasion. Doomsday is yet to come.

SUN HOU-TZU (SUN HOU-SHI)
(Journey to the West)

CULTURE OF ORIGIN: Chinese Daoist (Taoist) and Buddhist

PROVENANCE: recorded in various texts and art from oral traditions, the *Journey to the West* is probably no more than a piece of vicarious entertainment, though it contains notable tones of Buddhism and Daoism representing the finer aspects of human endeavour which prevail over those of a less worthy nature. Though much of the incidental material is clearly fictitious, the tale is based on the historical journey of the monk Xuan Kang (Hsuan Tsang), to India to bring back the religious texts of Buddhism during the Tang Dynasty (AD 618–906).

It should be noted that the anglicized equivalents of Chinese characters vary considerably in transliteration. The official Chinese Pinyin system is applied here, followed, where appropriate, in brackets, by the more generally encountered Wade-Giles system.

Sun Hou-Tzu (Sun Hou-Shi) is the Monkey King (also called Sun Wu-Kong), a title given to him by Yu Huang Shang Di, the Jade Emperor, when he was born from a stone on Hua Kuo Shan Mountain. Sun Hou-Tzu, however, soon becomes restless and overly conceited. He obtains a magic weapon from the Dragon King, Ao Guang, but misuses it and is reprimanded by the Jade Emperor, who gives him the job of Chief Groom to the Celestial Stables to keep him out of mischief. This does not occupy him for long and he returns to his mountain stronghold, where he causes more trouble and becomes even more inflated with self-esteem. He is given the task of protecting the Peaches of Immortality but, in a fit of pique when he is not invited to the Feast of the Peaches by the Queen of the Western Heaven, Xi Wang Mu (Hsi Wang Mu), he eats them.

Sun Hou-Tzu behaves so badly that the gods decide he must be punished. They catch him, after some initial difficulties, with a magic ring and the services of Tien Gou (T'ien Kou), the Celestial Hound. The Celestial Court passes the death sentence but, since the Monkey King has eaten the Peaches of Immortality, this is ineffective and, in some exasperation, the Buddha asks Sun Hou-Tzu what will satisfy him. He replies that he wishes to be nothing less than the Ruler of the Universe. The Buddha agrees that Sun Hou-Tzu can take this supreme position, but only if he can jump beyond the Buddha's reach. The Monkey King accepts the challenge and leaps off into space. He jumps so high that he reaches the very edge of the universe, where he writes his name to prove he has been there. When he returns the Buddha casually shows the signature written on the palm of his hand and the Monkey King is obliged to admit defeat.

The Buddha decides to put the miscreant's ingenuity to constructive use and orders him to guide the monk Xuan Kang (Hsuan Tsang), riding upon a White Horse, to India to obtain the Buddhist holy scriptures. The journey is a dangerous one and the pair meet many adversaries, including the Black Bear, a monstrous pig called Zhu Ba-jai and a giant, Sha Ho-Shang. Zhu Ba-jai was once an official in the court of the Jade Emperor, but was reincarnated as a pig having tried to seduce the emperor's daughter. He immediately ate his porcine parents and lived on Fu-Ling Mountain, where he attacked travellers with a rake. Sha Ho-Shang was a one-time minister who fell from grace when he dropped a crystal bowl. In punishment he was reincarnated as a cannibalistic ogre. All three are persuaded by the Boddhisattva or Buddha-designate Guan Yin (the benign guardian goddess, the Daoist version of the Buddhist Avalokitesvara and the apotheosis of the princess *Maio Shan*, see page 238), to better their ways and join the pilgrimage. At one stage in the journey the monk and the Monkey King are obliged to call upon the assistance of Guan Yin to get them out of danger when confronted by a particularly malevolent demon. They are met, on another occasion, by Daoist priests who force them into menial labour until the Monkey King slays three demons and the Daoist ruler elevates followers of Buddhism to a status equalling that of Daoists.

The two pilgrims reach the River of Motherhood and, being thirsty from their travels, drink the water. But they find themselves pregnant and have to swallow an 'antidote' from the Well of Miscarriage. Now they enter the Kingdom of Women, where Xuan Kang narrowly escapes not only seduction by the queen but also the trap of the Seven Spider Women!

As their journey continues the Monkey King is confronted by, and has to overcome, his *alter ego*; they cross a volcanic mountain; rescue religious treasures from an ogre; and are incarcerated by a demon posing as the Buddha which requires special intervention from the Jade Emperor to effect their release. On one occasion they sink into a mire of rotting fruit on Persimmon Mountain: at this point the pig comes into his own, clearing a way through with his snout. Several times the supernatural powers and sheer ingenuity of the Monkey King are called upon to rescue Xuan Kang and, once, the Buddha himself extricates the monk from a particularly difficult situation when he is captured by demons.

Fourteen years elapse on the journey, during which Xuan Kang and the Monkey King travel through nine kingdoms and cover many thousands of miles before they obtain the sacred texts of Buddhism. They go back to China with 5,048 volumes and present these to the emperor, Tai Kung.

OIDHE CLOINNE UISNEACH
(The Exile of the Sons of Usnagh)

CULTURE OF ORIGIN: Celtic – Irish

PROVENANCE: recorded from oral traditions, possibly as early as the eighth century AD, by the chief bard of Ireland, Snechan Torpeist, in the *Book of Druimm Snechtai*. This is now lost and no copies have survived prior to the eleventh century. The complete version is contained in the *Leabhar Laighnech: Book of Leinster*, compiled circa 1160 by Aed Mac Crimtheinn [Dublin Institute for Advanced Studies]. Under modern convention it is classified as part of the Ulaid (Ulster) or Craobh Ruadh (Red Branch) Cycle of myths which, from a historical viewpoint, relate an ongoing conflict between the Ulaid clan(s) who lived in the Armagh region of what is now Ulster and others who were based further south in Connacht (Connaught).

The myth clearly originates in, and describes, a time when the Ulster monarchy was in a state of active decline. It sets out to provide an explanation of the political demise of Ulster and to identify why so many of the Ulaid champions (with exception of Cu Chulainn, who does not feature in this myth) were in exile in Connacht at the time of the great *Tain bo Cuailgne* cattle raid. (The myth is identified in some translations as the *Story of Deirdre*.)

Fedilmid Mac Dall, bard to the Ulster king, Conchobhar Mac Nessa, is entertaining the Ulaid chieftains to an evening of drinking. Somewhere in the house, Fedilmid's pregnant wife screams and Sencha Mac Ailella, the chief judge and bard of Ulster, commands her to be brought in to the hall so that she can be questioned about the terrible cry.

The wife turns to the high druid, Cathbad, explaining to him that she does not know the nature of the scream which came from her womb. Cathbad, however, prophesies that she carries a child who will grow into a woman of exceptional beauty, tall and fair-haired, with grey green eyes.

*'Parthian-red lips will frame those flawless teeth
High queens will envy her her matchless, faultless form.'*

Yet this woman, Cathbad predicts, will also be the cause of great destruction amongst the people of Ulster. He utters the name of the child – Deirdre – and warns that, through her, the great heroes of the Craobh Ruadh – the three sons of Uisneach (Usna), Naoise, Ainle and Ardan – will be exiled and slaughtered. The youthful warriors demand the death of the infant, but Conchobhar insists that he will take her away and foster her.

As predicted by Cathbad, Deirdre matures into an extraordinarily beautiful woman whom Conchobhar keeps jealously hidden from the rest of his court. Only a nurse named Lebarcham is allowed contact.

Deirdre becomes infatuated by the description of the eldest of the Uisneach brothers, Naoise, and while he is singing from the ramparts of Emain Macha, she slips out of her imprisonment to meet with him. She declares her ardour, but when he reminds her of Cathbad's prophecy she seizes him by the ears and demands that he takes her away. He begins to sing and the prophecy begins to take effect as the men of Ulaid rise up against one another in combat. Ainle and Ardan restrain Naoise but, when they discover what has happened, all three decide to leave the province, taking Deirdre with them.

They flee from Conchobhar and for many years travel from stronghold to stronghold, finding temporary protection amongst kings and chieftains. Finally they leave Ireland to seek protection with the king of Alba (Scotland) whom they serve as mercenaries. Always Conchobhar pursues them.

Out of fear that the dire prophecy of Cathbad will persist, the Uisneach brothers keep Deirdre hidden away, but the king's steward catches sight of her and reports to the king that he has found a woman worthy of his majesty. The king instructs his steward to woo her on his behalf, but she reveals the plot to Naoise and once again the four are obliged to flee, this time to a remote island. The chieftains of the Ulaid approach Conchobhar, urging him to let the refugees return in safety and he appears to agree to a reconciliation, sending Fergus Mac Roth as an ambassador to invite the brothers home. Fergus gives them his solemn pledge of safety but he is tricked into remaining behind while the brothers travel to Emain Macha with Deirdre, protected only by Fergus's son, Fiacha. When the party arrives, Eogan Mac Durthacht, one of Conchobhar's henchmen, attacks Naoise with his spear, breaking his back. Fiacha flings himself across Naoise and Eogan's spear is thrust through the bodies, killing both men. Now the younger brothers are hunted down and slain while Deirdre is bound and taken to Conchobhar.

When Fergus and his allies, including Dubthach and Cormac, hear of the killings they set out on a mission of revenge, slaying many of Conchobhar's men. But in the end three thousand rebels are forced to leave Ulaid for the comparative safety of Connacht.

For Deirdre there is no comfort. She remains with Conchobhar against her will, mourning the death of Naoise. When a year has passed Conchobhar asks her whom she hates the most and she replies that, after Conchobhar himself, it is Eogan Mac Durthacht. To punish her further he orders her to spend a second year with Eogan.

The myth comes to its tragic conclusion as the distraught Deirdre, accompanying Conchobhar and Eogan to a fair, commits suicide by smashing her skull to fragments against a boulder. In later, often romanticized, variants Naoise and his brothers are guarded on their ill-fated return to Emain Macha by Buinne and Iollan, the other sons of Fergus Mac Roth. After Deirdre kills herself she is buried across a lake from Naoise and from the graves grow pine trees whose branches intertwine.

9

Myths of Love

This small section confirms that deities, like the rest of us, fall in love and occasionally suffer the pangs of heartache. It is necessary, however, to realize that the social norms of the societies which gave birth to such stories are often very different to our own. Myths of passion among Nordic gods and goddesses thus tend not to be gentle affairs with the flavour of nineteenth-century romances but full-blooded and often seemingly crude seductions. Elsewhere in the volume one discovers that when the Kafir goddess Disani wishes to capture the heart of a male deity she is less inclined to flutter her eyelashes than to pull down her trousers!

By and large, though, myths of love follow the familiar pattern of human emotions the whole world over. Valiant gods become thoroughly shy when faced with the ordeal of approaching their hearts' desires and resort to sending coy messages through intermediaries. Thus in Norse myth, the otherwise rumbustuous fertility god Freyr dispatches his friend and confidant Skirnir to woo the giantess Gerth on his behalf. Goddesses, in the main, play on the weaknesses of their male counterparts in love with very human techniques, fobbing off the ardent suitors until all seems lost, then finally capitulating to the delights of seduction.

The myth tellers are not averse to incorporating immorality in their stories and gods frequently seduce other men's wives, using magical powers to delude the cuckolded husband. Nor do they shrink from prurience.

In certain traditions, particularly that described through Celtic myth, an underlying concept which needs to be clearly understood is that the goddess whose hand is sought in wedlock also represents the sovereignty of the land. She is the apotheosis of the 'national earth' which must, once taken, be secured and impregnated. The notion of the goddess and the earth being indistinguishable, incidentally, may well constitute the underlying theme of the celebrated *Canticus Canticorum* or *Song of Songs* in Judaic and Christian traditions.

APHRODITE AND ANCHISES

CULTURE OF ORIGIN: classical Greek, but subsequently adopted into Roman culture

PROVENANCE: recorded from oral traditions by the epic Greek poet Hesiod in the *Theogony* and the *Homeric Hymn to Aphrodite* during the eighth century BC. The incident is referred to by Homer in the *Iliad*.

Aphrodite has been depicted in mythology as one of the major deities of the Olympian pantheon, born from the foam of the ocean after her father Okeanos was castrated by Kronos and his genitals were hurled into the sea. Other accounts describe her as a daughter of Zeus. In any context she probably derives from the Phoenician model of Aštoreth, the goddess of love. She bears strongly sexual connotations and is often portrayed naked. This myth, however, is a tender and gentle love story accounting for the birth of the kind of demi-god super-hero of whom legendary tales abound.

NOTE: the son born to Aphrodite, Aeneas, is the central character in the epic saga *Aeneid* by the Roman writer Virgil. Aphrodite becomes the goddess Venus.

Though Aphrodite, the goddess of sexual love, is the object of lustful attention among the gods of Olympus, in particular Apollo and Poseidon, she swears an oath to remain a virgin. She is not, however, beyond manipulating the desires of others in any way that pleases her. Thus she directs Zeus himself on to a path of philandering, away from the jealous eye of his wife, Hera. Zeus, for his part, is determined that Aphrodite's charms shall not be wasted and that she shall find fulfilment with a mortal man; he therefore causes her to fall in love with Anchises, a Trojan shepherd tending his flock on the slopes of Mount Ida in Crete. So besotted is Aphrodite with the sight of this man that she goes immediately to her temple at Paphos in Cyprus where, behind closed doors and with the assistance of the three Gratiae (Graces), she bathes and perfumes herself, dressing in her most beguiling clothes.

Followed by a retinue of wild beasts she hastens to Ida and enters the humble home of Anchises, whom she finds playing upon a lyre. Anchises sees before him a beautiful woman whom he believes must be one of the immortals and he too falls in love at first sight.

Aphrodite denies that she is a goddess, naming as her father Otreus, King of Phrygia. She explains that Hermes has carried her off from a group of mortal maidens playing together and has told her that she is to be the wife of Anchises. She adds that if Anchises sends a messenger to her parents saying that she is safe and well, he will be rewarded with a fine dowry.

Anchises is persuaded of Aphrodite's mortal nature and so he leads her to the bridal chamber, where she takes off her fine jewels and her garments to stand naked before him. Thus the mortal Anchises weds the immortal goddess of love. But in the morning when he is awakened by her imperious command he realizes that his first instinct was correct. She who stands over him is no less than a radiant goddess and he is deeply afraid, since he knows that a mortal who lies with an immortal is surely doomed. Aphrodite, however, calms his fears. The gods, she tells him, hold him dear and through him she is to bear a glorious son, Aeneas, destined to become the father of a great dynasty of kings who will rule the city of Troy. She cites examples of Trojans, including Ganymedes and Tithonos, who have been favoured with immortality by the gods, but she tells Anchises that she does not wish to inflict such a life upon him even though he will, in time, become old and disfigured and she will be ridiculed by the other immortals.

Aphrodite foretells that when her son is born he will be brought up by the nymphs of the mountain forests, who rank with neither mortals nor immortals; after five years she will bring the boy to meet his father. Before she departs, though, she utters one warning to the shepherd: he must tell no living person what has taken place or he will die. There is no account of Anchises incurring Aphrodite's wrath for disobedience, so it is to be assumed that he kept her secret.

APHRODITE AND ARES

CULTURE OF ORIGIN: classical Greek, but subsequently adopted into Roman culture

PROVENANCE: recorded by the epic Greek poet Homer in the *Odyssey*. In Roman mythology Ares becomes Mars and Aphrodite is Venus.

Aphrodite, the goddess of sexual love and consort of the lame blacksmith god Hephaestos, enjoys an assignation in her husband's bed with the god of war, Ares, who has seduced her with flattery and gifts. But the sun god, Helios, happens to witness the event and reveals the lovers' secret to Hephaestos. Deeply embittered at his wife's infidelity Hephaestos plots revenge, forging strong chains with which to bind the lovers. He festoons the bedchamber with a net of these chains, some of them so fine that they are almost invisible, and pretends that he is about to leave for a visit to Lemnos.

Ares, believing Hephaestos to be out of the way, hastens back to Aphrodite and urges her to resume their lovemaking, with the result that both become entangled in the trap. Hephaestos, acting on Helios's information, returns home to confront the situation and, complaining of the unfairness of his disfigurement, he calls on Zeus to adminster justice for the affront to his marriage. The great gods assemble before Hephaestos's house, finding amusement in the snare he has set for the lovers, and some of them express the sentiment that they would be more than happy to replace Ares in his imprisonment, chained up in bed with Aphrodite.

Only Poseidon, god of the sea, urges that the pair be released, promising that he personally will punish Ares and that if he is unable to do so the gods may bind him in chains. Freed, Aphrodite flees to her sanctuary at Paphos in Cyprus and Ares makes his way to Thrace. Homer does not make it clear whether Ares is subsequently chastised for his dalliance.

ARIADNE AND DIONYSOS

CULTURE OF ORIGIN: classical Greek, but subsequently adopted into Roman culture

PROVENANCE: recorded briefly by the epic Greek poet Hesiod in the *Theogony* and by Homer in the *Odyssey*. The 'giving' of Ariadne by Theseus to Dionysos formed the basis of the rites in the Attic festival of Anthesteria, when the wife of the mortal king was offered as wife to the god Dionysos. This is a Greek version of the Sacred Marriage practised extensively in the ancient Near East.

Ariadne, the daughter of King Minos of Crete, helps the Athenian hero Theseus to escape from the labyrinth at Knossos, where he has slain the terrible Minotaur. Theseus elopes with Ariadne by sailing away to the island of Naxos but while she is sleeping he abandons her and returns to the kingdom of his father, Aegeos (see *Ariadne, Theseus and the Minotaur*, page 157).

The distraught Ariadne is discovered in her plight by the god Dionysos, who falls in love with her. According to the brief account given by Hesiod in his *Theogony*, Dionysos weds her and endows her with the gift of immortality. This account is endorsed by Homer:

> *And golden-haired Dionysos made brown-haired Ariadne, the daughter of Minos, his buxom wife: and the son of Kronos made her deathless and unaging for him.*

Alternative mythology suggests that Ariadne is shot dead by the goddess Artemis who has discovered her sleeping in the Dionysos sanctuary on Naxos before she has had the opportunity to be wedded to the god.

CANTICUS CANTICORUM
(Song of Songs)

CULTURE OF ORIGIN: Judaic/Christian
PROVENANCE: the *Vetus Testamentum*.

This account of a passionate love affair has been the subject of intense controversy within the Christian Church. The crux of debate is whether the dialogue represents an allegory describing the pure and celestial love between God and the holy city of Jerusalem or whether it describes the physical intercourse taking place during a much older ritual, the Sacred Marriage, first recorded in Mesopotamia more than a thousand years before the birth of Judaism.

The Judaean King Solomon is identified by name, but the dominant persona remains female. Notwithstanding the fact that she is described as being black, and therefore could be a North African queen (there are also hints that she is a woman of the Shulamite tribe), in a strongly patriarchal society like that of Biblical Syrio-Palestine such a female figure is less likely to have been mortal and therefore may represent the mother goddess. If the myth relates the progress of the Sacred Marriage then it includes many references to the seasonal absence 'asleep' of the dying-and-rising god and of his awakening in the spring (see also *Inana's Descent into the Underworld and the Death of Dumuzi*, page 233).

The narrative, as it is known today, is disjointed and is thought to have originated from several smaller fragments of tradition which the writer has edited together in an arbitrary, and not always successful or contiguous, fashion.

The woman of the story sings Solomon's praises. The love of King Solomon is unparalleled, his kisses are better than wine, he is the object of desire among young virgins, and he is much sought after. The woman compares his vigour with that of the horses which pull the chariots of the Pharaoh and offers tantalizing visions of the lovemaking which is to come. She pictures her lover lying beside her deep in the forest or in the leafy bower of the Sacred Marriage garden, his left hand under her head and his right hand embracing her, and she orders that he shall not be disturbed in his sleeping. She dreams of the moment when her lover awakes!

Behold he cometh leaping upon the mountains, skipping upon the hills. My beloved is like a roe or a young hart; behold he standeth behind our wall, he looketh forth at the windows showing himself through the lattice. My beloved spake and said unto me, Rise up my love, my fair one, and come away. For, lo, the winter is past, the rain is over and gone. The flowers appear on the earth; the time of the singing of birds is come, and the voice of the turtle is heard in our land; the fig tree putteth forth her green figs, and the vines with the tender grape give a good smell. Arise my love, my fair one, and come away.

The woman desires to see her lover's face appearing from the secret places of the earth as the spring unfolds and she reminisces about the long period of his absence when, as night is falling, she has wandered the streets of the city, demanding of the nightwatchman if he has seen her lost consort. When, at last, she has found him, she has taken him to her mother's house and watched over him.

Now it is the turn of the king to extol the virtues and beauty of the woman. As he slowly awakens he knows her and he paints a vivid and alluring picture. She in her turn provides new glimpses of the intimacy that is unfolding between them.

> My beloved put his hand by the hole of the door, and my bowels were moved for him. I rose up to open to my beloved; and my hands dropped with myrrh, and my fingers with sweet-smelling myrrh, upon the handles of the lock.

Yet the woman's lover is destined to stay only for a while. As winter approaches he departs again and is gone from her. Once more she calls upon the nightwatchman and searches vainly. In her anguish and her loss she is debased and abused. She calls upon the women of the city for help:

> I charge you, O daughters of Jerusalem, if ye find my beloved, that ye tell him that I am sick of love.

Once more the woman dreams of her husband's return and of how they will go together into the green places of the earth to renew their love and intercourse as the next season unfolds and the earth becomes fertile and germinates once more.

DRYMSKVIOA
(Lay of Thrym)

CULTURE OF ORIGIN: Teutonic – Nordic and Germanic (Icelandic)

PROVENANCE: the *Codex Regius* No. 2365. The manuscript lay hidden until it was rediscovered by Brynjolfur Sveinsson, bishop to the Icelandic community, circa 1643, and preserved on the instructions of Frederic III. It is housed in the Royal Library of Denmark [Copenhagen]. *Drymskvioa* is now thought to be a late composition, possibly from the pen of Snorri Sturluson circa 1220 AD, and the *Prose Edda* indeed makes no mention of the myth. It is one of the best loved of the Icelandic stories with an appeal to the most modern audience.

The thunder god, Thor, awakes to find that his hammer, Mjolnir, has gone missing. In a rage he tells his friend Loki of the theft and the pair go off to find the goddess Freyja, to beg the loan of her feather cloak. Loki dons the magic garment and flies to the land of the giants in search of the missing weapon. He discovers their chief, Thrym, sitting on top of a mountain, plaiting golden leads for his hounds.

Loki accuses the giant of stealing Thor's hammer and Thrym readily confesses that it is he who now holds Mjolnir. He intends to use it as a bargaining counter which he will exchange for the hand of Freyja (a fertility goddess whom the giants regularly lust after). Loki now flies back to Thor's palace and explains the situation, whereupon the two friends set off again to visit the goddess.

Freyja is, predictably, none too pleased with their news:

Enraged was Freyja, frothing with ire;
the gleaming halls trembled at her wrath,
the Brisings' jewel burst from her:
'Most foolish after men thou mayst call me,
if I follow thee to the giants domain.'

The gods therefore gather in counsel to decide how best to proceed and Heimdall comes up with a crafty plan. Thor shall be dressed in Freyja's clothes and presented to the giant.

'Let the keys of a wife hang from him,
let woman's weeds be worn.
Have him decked in bridal ornament,
a shawl upon his head, as becomes a bride.'

Thor is not wholly impressed by the plan, but the wise Loki persuades him of the advantages of recovering Mjolnir: otherwise the giants will soon be hammering on the doors of Asgarth, the gods' realm. So the gods deck out Thor in Freyja's most becoming outfit and he and Loki set off.

Thrym is thoroughly excited by the imminent arrival of the person he thinks is Freyja and orders a lavish feast, including an ox, eight salmon and a large quantity of beer. When everyone sits down to eat he is, however, immediately suspicious about the copious appetite of his intended, but Loki, dressed as a maid-in-waiting, points out that so eager has Freyja been to get to her lover that she has starved herself for eight nights. Now the giant lifts the lady's veil and recoils in astonishment. Loki again soothes him with the assurance that Freyja's eyes are only bloodshot because she has stayed awake for eight nights.

An elderly sister of the giant enters and begs a small bridal gift of some gold rings, but Thrym interrupts by uttering the words the two heroes most wish to hear:

'Bring the hammer that the bride may receive it;

on her lap lay down the sacred Mjolnir.'

The hammer is a generally recognized symbol of fertility, which explains why it is offered as a wedding gift. So it returns to Thor's hands, after which he is invincible. He slays Thrym at a stroke and proceeds to dispatch all the giant kin. He even finishes off the aged sister who has begged the bridal gifts and thus ends the tale.

NOTE: for a more comprehensive account of Nordic cosmogony, see *Voluspa*, page 122.

ENDYMION AND SELENE

CULTURE OF ORIGIN: classical Greek, but subsequently adopted into Roman culture

PROVENANCE: recorded briefly by the epic Greek poet Hesiod in the *Catalogues of Women* and in the *Great Eoiae*

Endymion is the son of Aethlios and Kalyce, though some traditions identify his father as Zeus. He is depicted as a youthful shepherd of great beauty with whom the moon goddess Selene becomes infatuated. She seduces him into sleeping with her and, in token of their love, she arranges that Zeus will grant him a single wish. Endymion wins the boon of eternal youth through everlasting sleep, 'to be the keeper of death for his own self when he is ready to die'. Selene gives birth to a son, the hero Naxos. According to the text of the *Great Eoiae*, Zeus eventually transports Endymion into heaven, where first he falls in love with the goddess Hera in the guise of a cloud and subsequently, being still a mortal, plunges down into Hades.

EPIMETHEUS (Hindsight) AND PANDORA

CULTURE OF ORIGIN: classical Greek, but subsequently adopted into Roman culture

PROVENANCE: recorded from oral traditions by the epic Greek poet Hesiod in the *Theogony* and the *Works and Days* during the eighth century BC.

The tone of the myth is strongly misogynistic, but it also offers a moral lesson: while suggesting that womankind is essentially an evil burden on the male of the species, it advocates that the only acceptable state for men and women is within wedlock! The myth offers striking similarities to the story of Adam and Eve and their banishment, through Eve's weakness, from a trouble-free paradise in the Biblical Garden of Eden (see *Genesis*, page 45).

Zeus, angry that Prometheus has stolen fire from the blacksmith god Hephaestos and given it to the human race, decides to punish mankind.

He orders Hephaestos to fashion the first mortal woman, Pandora, who will be made in the image of a goddess, but who will bring trouble to men on earth and be instrumental in outwitting Prometheus.

> *Forthwith he [Zeus] made an evil thing for men as the price of fire; for the limping god [Hephaestos] formed of earth the likeness of a shy maiden as the son of Kronos willed.*

Pandora is endowed with great beauty so that she will become irresistible to men and each of the gods presents her with a special quality: one gives her grace, another dexterity, another intelligence. Hephaestos, however, provides her with the talent for lying and deceit. She is clothed provocatively by the goddess Athena and a crown, fashioned by Hephaestos, is placed upon her head. Thus attired, she is destined to 'live among mortal men to their great trouble'.

Among the four offspring of Iapetos, Prometheus has a brother, the gullible Epimetheus. Having tricked Zeus on at least two occasions (see *Prometheus*, page 163), Prometheus is wary of retaliation from the leader of the gods and so, as a precaution, he forbids Epimetheus to accept any gifts from Zeus. His warning is to no avail, because when Zeus offers the hand of the fair Pandora Epimetheus is unable to resist her beauty and he takes her as his wife.

Almost as soon as she has arrived in her new home Pandora discovers a large urn, another dubious present from Zeus, which she is told not to open. Eventually, however, overcome by curiosity, she lifts the lid and in doing so she releases all the troubles into the world. Hope, which lies at the very bottom of the pot, is trapped when Pandora replaces the lid.

TOCHMARC ETAINE
(The Wooing of Etain)

CULTURE OF ORIGIN: Celtic – Irish

PROVENANCE: recorded from oral traditions, possibly as early as the eighth century AD, by the chief bard of Ireland, Snechan Torpeist, in the *Book of Druimm Snechtai*. This is now lost and no early copies have survived prior to the eleventh century. The complete text is preserved in the *Yellow Book of Lecan*, compiled circa 1391 AD [Trinity College, Dublin], and there is an incomplete version contained in *Leabhar ne h-Uidhre; Book of the Dun Cow*, compiled in the eleventh century by the Christian monk Mael Muire Mac Ceilechai [Royal Irish Academy].

The myth falls into three episodes covering several generations, each more or less independent of the others, but linked through the personalities of Etain and Midir the Proud, one of the more important sons of Dagda. There exists in the saga a recurrent theme of the passions of kings to possess supernatural women, who may perhaps be seen to epitomize the land or Sovereignty of Ireland.

The goddess Boann (Eithne) is persuaded to desert her husband, Elcmar of Bruig na Boinde, for the god Dagda (Echu Ollathir), king of the Tuatha de Danaan (people of the goddess Danu). Dagda sends Elcmar on an errand from which he intends to be back before nightfall but Dagda's magic powers make a journey which seems like a day in fact last for nine months. During Elcmar's absence Boann bears Dagda a child, Oengus Mac Og (young son) and Dagda weaves his magic so that when Boann's rightful husband returns she forgets everything.

Oengus is fostered by Midir the Proud, whose home is the mound of Bri Leith and with whom Oengus stays for nine years. He becomes the natural leader among his fellow children and believes himself to be Midir's son and heir. A jealous rivalry develops, however, between Oengus and another foster child of Midir, Triath, the son of Febal, one of the Fir Bolg people enslaved by the Tuatha de Danaan. In a heated moment Triath reveals to Oengus that he is a foundling. Midir then tells a distressed Oengus that he is one of the Tuatha, the son of Dagda and Boann.

Midir takes Oengus back to his real father and Dagda acknowledges his son, but declares that the land which will be his is still ruled by Elcmar. He suggests to Oengus that he arms himself and approaches Elcmar during the Samhain festival when none of Elcmar's men will be carrying weapons. He is to demand of Elcmar that he be crowned king of Bruig na Boinde for a day and a night and that any dispute about the arrangement be adjudicated by Dagda. Furthermore, unless the request is granted, Elcmar will pay with his life. Once in power Oengus is advised not to return the kingdom, on the grounds that he asked for kingship of day and night, in other words for ever. In due course the argument is brought before Dagda for settlement and he adjudicates that, since Elcmar surrendered his lands in exchange for his life, Bruig na Boinde rightfully belongs to Oengus.

A year passes and Midir pays a visit while Oengus and Elcmar, from vantage points in their respective strongholds, are watching children at play. The children quarrel and Midir acts as peacemaker, but in doing so he loses an eye to a sprig of holly. Oengus calls on the healing powers of the physician god, Dian Cecht, who restores Midir's sight.

Midir is about to depart, but Oengus persuades him to stay for a year in exchange for gifts including the fairest woman in the land, whom Midir is allowed to select. He chooses Etain Echrade, the daughter of King Ailill of Connacht, but Ailill agrees to part with his daughter only if certain terms are met, including land improvement and a dowry of gold and silver. Dagda complies and Midir gains his bride, but when the year is up and Midir is leaving, Oengus warns him against the wrath and magic of Fuamnach, his first wife, who is under the protection of the Tuatha de Danaan.

Etain is shown her new kingdom, but Fuamnach turns her into a pool of water from which hatches a beautiful scarlet insect. It follows Midir wherever he goes and eventually he realizes it is Etain. Fuamach meanwhile conjures up a great wind, preventing the insect from alighting anywhere until it finds refuge with Oengus. He becomes enamoured of Etain in her strange disguise and again Fuamnach blasts the insect away. It falls into a goblet of wine drunk by the wife of a warrior called Etar; she becomes pregnant and, in due course of time, gives birth to a restored Etain. Etar brings her up with fifty chieftains' daughters who become her maidservants. One day, when they are bathing in the river, a handsome young man rides up and recites a strange prophetic poem to Etain:

Because of her [Etain] the king will chase
the birds of Tethbae;
because of her he will drown his two horses
in the waters of Loch Da Airbrech.

Oengus fears that Fuamnach will discover Etain yet again and cause her further harm, so he seeks out Fuamnach and decapitates her.

In the second episode of the myth Etain goes from her husband, Echu Airem, to another man, Ailill, and back to her husband. Echu Airem is ruler of the five provinces of Ireland, but his subjects insist that they will pay no taxes to a king who has no queen. Echu Airem thus takes for his bride the virginal Etain, but Ailill, one of his brothers, also falls obsessively in love with her to the point of sickness. When Ailill is close to death Echu is called away, but instructs Etain to minister Ailill's funeral rites. Ailill begins to recover, admitting his passion in the process, and Etain agrees to meet with him secretly early in the morning. Three times he fails to awaken, missing the rendezvous, and each time another, who seems to be like Ailill, keeps the appointment. The stranger reveals himself to be Midir, the husband from whom she was parted in her previous existence and who has caused Ailill to fall in love with her, though not to dishonour her. Echu returns home believing that Etain has saved his brother's life.

In the final episode Midir and Echu Airem are the rival claimants for the hand of Etain. One day Echu finds Midir at his home wishing to play *fidchell* (a chess game). Midir loses the game and with it the stake of fifty horses. On the second day the game is renewed with a stake of fifty boars. Again Midir loses and continues to do so each day thereafter until he is obliged to fulfil some onerous tasks set by Echu Airem.

Finally Midir proposes a wager in which the prize will be to embrace and kiss Etain. This time Midir wins the game and Echu agrees that the wager will be settled a month hence. He surrounds his house with armed supporters, but Midir transforms Etain and himself into swans who fly up through the roof. The prophetic utterance of the second episode comes true as Echu orders the birds to be searched out by demolishing all the fortified houses in the land. Midir accuses Echu of unfair play but agrees to return Etain. He sends, however, fifty women of identical appearance from whom Echu is obliged to choose. Midir reveals to him that Etain was pregnant when he took her away and that the woman whom Echu has chosen is his own daughter. Echu is deeply distressed that he has slept with his daughter, who has now herself borne him a child. He cannot bear the presence of this little girl and has her taken away to be fostered by one Findlam and his wife. Time passes until she is abducted by a high king of Ireland, Eterscel, son of Iar, who makes her his queen; the saga ends when she bears him a son, Conare.

EUROPA AND ZEUS

CULTURE OF ORIGIN: classical Greek, but subsequently adopted into Roman culture
PROVENANCE: recorded by the epic Greek poet Hesiod in the *Theogony* and in *Catalogues of Women*

Europa is variously described as the daughter of Okeanos and Tethys (Hesiod); of Tityos, a giant son of Zeus and Elara; of Nilus, god of the Nile; or of Phoenix, one of the grandsons of Poseidon. She is discovered by Zeus picking flowers in a meadow (or by the coast at Sidon or Tyre) and he at once decides to seduce her. To impress her he transforms himself into a white bull who lies peacably at her feet and from whose mouth comes a crocus bloom. At first Europa is terrified, but when she is lulled into believing that the bull will do her no harm she is tempted to climb upon its back. At once it rears up, dashes to the sea and plunges in, still carrying her. The animal crosses the Mediterranean to Crete where, at Gortyna, Zeus resumes his proper form and sleeps with Europa, presenting her with three gifts – a bronze robot guardian called Talos, a hunting dog with formidable powers and a magical spear.

Europa's father, Agenor, sends his sons Kadmos, Phoenix and Kilix to search for their missing sister with instructions never to return unless they find her. Their mission fails and all three take exile abroad, Kadmos founding the city of Thebes.

Europa is forced to become the consort of the Cretan King Asterios and under his aegis she bears Zeus three sons – Minos, Rhadamanthys and Sarpedon. Her marriage to Asterios proves otherwise barren.

HERAKLES AND DEIANEIRA

CULTURE OF ORIGIN: classical Greek, but subsequently adopted into Roman culture

PROVENANCE: recorded by the Greek writer Sophocles in *Trachiniae* and in passing by some other tragic poets. The relationship between Herakles, Meleager and Deianeira is noted in Hesiod's *Catalogues of Women*.

In the account by Hesiod, Meleager, the heroic son of Oeneus of Kalydon and Althaea, is slain by Apollo during a battle with the demonic Kuretes (Korybantes) in defence of Kalydon. According to Homer and some other writers, however, Meleager's demise follows confrontation with a ferocious wild boar which is terrorizing the area. Meleager heads a combined force which eventually kills the animal, but a squabble arises over division of the carcass, during which Meleager slays his mother's brothers. Althaea curses him and he wastes away, leaving a sister, Deianeira, without material support.

In the underworld kingdom of Hades, the shade of Meleager is confronted by the hero Herakles, on his way to obtain the hound Kerberos as the object of one of his twelve labours (see page 183). Herakles is about to loose off an arrow at the ghost when Meleager describes the hapless fate of his sister and pleads with Herakles to marry her. Thus, on his return from Hades, the hero seeks out Deianeira, who is being courted by the river god Achelos. Achelos possesses the ability to change into whatever shape he chooses, but even so Herakles manages to vanquish him and take the hand of Deianeira. The couple live in Kalydon until the hero inadvertently slays Oeneus's cup-bearer, Eunomos, resulting in enforced exile for Herakles, his wife and their son Hyllos.

While they are crossing the River Evenos on their journey, the ferryman, a centaur named Nessos, attempts to rape Deianeira. Herakles shoots him through the heart, but as the ferryman lies dying he deceives Deianeira into believing that his blood will serve as a love potion should her husband's attentions ever stray. The blood is, in truth, a deadly poison.

Subsequently Herakles takes a mistress, Iole, and Deianeira decides to adminster what she thinks is the love elixir. She chooses an occasion on which Herakles is to consecrate a new altar to Zeus, when he wishes to wear a new cloak. She dips the garment in the poisonous blood of the centaur and when Herakles wears the cloak the poison burns and flays his skin.

Horrified, Deianeira kills herself and Herakles decides that his own life must end. He places Iole in the care of Hyllos and climbs to the summit of Mount Oeta, where he builds a funeral pyre and, having instructed his servant Philoctetes to set light to the wood, immolates himself upon it. He rises on a cloud to Mount Olympus, where his thorny relationship with his father's consort, Hera, is finally resolved and where he marries the goddess of youth, Hebe.

IO AND ZEUS

CULTURE OF ORIGIN: classical Greek, but subsequently adopted into Roman culture
PROVENANCE: recorded from earlier traditions by the epic Greek poet Hesiod under the title *Aegimius*, whose authorship he ascribes to the mythical Phrixus.

Various traditions explain the identity of Io. Hesiod places her as the daughter of the Corinthian King Peiren, but she is more generally regarded as the daughter of Leucane and Iasos, who is variously described as the son of Argos or of Triopas and a ruler of Argos (the Peloponnese). Invariably Io is identified as a priestess in the service of the consort of Zeus, the goddess Hera.

Zeus has become infatuated with Io and he causes her to dream that she must travel to the lake of Lernaea where she is to become his mistress. When she relates this premonition to her father, he consults with the oracles of Delphi and Dodona, both of which endorse the message of the dream. The princess Io thus begins a discreet liaison with the god, away from the eyes and ears of Hera. The supreme goddess, however, becomes suspicious and Zeus, to save Io from the jealous wrath of his consort, sends her first to Mycenae and then to the island of Euboea, where he changes her into a beautiful white heifer. He hotly denies that he has ever had intercourse with the animal but Hera, not to be fobbed off with excuses, demands the heifer for herself and promptly puts Io into the safekeeping of the many-eyed watchman Argos, who tethers her to an olive tree.

Zeus, determined to release his mistress from her fate, sends the messenger god, Hermes, to lull Argos to sleep with his pan pipes and to free the heifer. Hermes incapacitates the watchman and slays him before liberating the heifer but Hera sends biting horseflies to torment the animal. Io flees along the shores of what became known as the Ionian Gulf before crossing the Straits of Bosphorus to Egypt. There she returns to human form and delivers Zeus's son Epaphos. He is, however, seized and carried off by demonic spirits, the Corybantes, on the orders of the vindictive Hera. Zeus slaughters the demons with a thunderbolt, but Io is left searching for her lost child. She traces him to Byblos in Syria and brings him back to Egypt, where eventually he becomes king.

NOTE: according to one Greek tradition Io becomes syncretized with the Egyptian mother goddess Isis.

AISLINGE OENGUSSO
(The Dream of Oengus)

CULTURE OF ORIGIN: Celtic – Irish

PROVENANCE: recorded from oral traditions and linked thematically (though by artifice) to the *Tain bo Cuailgne* (see page 175), the story is perhaps not very old in terms of Irish mythology. It is mentioned in the *Leabhar Laighnech: Book of Leinster*, though the only complete version comes from the late *Egerton 1782* manuscript (dated provisionally to 1419 AD).

Modern convention places the *Dream of Oengus* in the so-called Mythological Cycle. The myth is also the derivation of Keats's *The Dream of Wandering Aengus*.

Oengus dreams of a beautiful girl who stands at the head of his bed and he is afflicted with a wasting love-sickness for a year during which the dream recurs nightly. He sends for Fergne, a physician of Cond, who correctly diagnoses the illness and Oengus's mother, Boann, is called. Fruitlessly Boann searches for the girl of Oengus's dreams for a year after which Oengus's father, Dagda, is summoned. Dagda is nonchalant, pointing out that his chances of success are no better, but Fergne proposes recruiting the assistance of Bodb, King of Mumu.

Bodb agrees to take up the search and a girl answering the description is eventually discovered at Loch bel Dracon. Oengus is taken to her and immediately recognizes the subject of his dream infatuation, but he is told that it is beyond the powers of Bodb to take her. She is Caer, the daughter of Ethal Anbuail of Connacht, in the land ruled by Ailill and Medb. Dagda goes to meet with them, but they too insist that they have no powers to hand the girl over. Next Ethal Anbuail is approached for the hand of his daughter but he refuses and, in consequence, Dagda and Ailill destroy his stronghold. Ethal Anbuail reveals that he cannot offer his daughter's hand because she possesses the magical power to change shape. One year she may be a bird, the next in human guise but during the festival of Samhain, Ethal reveals, she will be at Loch bel Dracon in the form of a swan. Ailill, Ethal and Dagda reconcile their differences and Oengus is told to visit the loch at the time of the next festival.

At the edge of the lake, Caer tells him that she will come to him but only if she may return to the water. At this he transforms himself into a swan and the pair live happily together.

NOTE: the link with the *Tain bo Cuailgne* comes with the suggestion that Oengus's relationship with Caer encourages him to contribute a contingent to the forces of the cattle raid.

THE MARRIAGE OF PSYCHE

CULTURE OF ORIGIN: classical Greek, but subsequently adopted into Roman culture
PROVENANCE: recorded from an oral tradition by Apuleios in *Metamorphosis*

Despite her outstanding beauty and notwithstanding the success of her sisters in finding husbands, Psyche remains unwed, her potential suitors intimidated by her striking appearance. Her father consults an oracle which tells him to dress her as a bride and lay her on a mountain summit where she will be ravished by a monster. She has been abandoned to her destiny when the wind carries her away and deposits her gently in the lawn of a magnificent palace where she discovers attendants to wait on her every need.

As night falls Psyche becomes aware of an unseen presence beside her. He reveals that he is the suitor for whom she is destined, but warns her never to look at his form unless she is to lose him for ever. Psyche remains, not unhappily, in the mysterious palace, but she becomes homesick and, realizing that her parents imagine her to be dead, she begs her unseen husband to let her visit her family. He agrees to her plea and the wind carries her back to the mountain top where she was first abandoned. Psyche's married sisters, although delighted to see her again, are also deeply jealous and they attempt to cast doubt in her mind by reminding her that she has never seen her husband. She is persuaded to take a lamp secretly to the bedchamber and to inspect her consort while he sleeps. When she does this she discovers no monster but rather a beautiful youth who is in fact Eros, the god of love. A drop of hot oil falls on his face and he awakes and flees from her, never to return.

Unprotected, Psyche is at the mercy of the goddess Aphrodite, who is envious of her beauty and who imprisons her in the palace, forcing her to carry out the most menial of tasks. She is ordered to go to the underworld of Hades to obtain some of the water of eternal youth from Persephone. On the return journey, and against instructions, curiosity makes her open the flask of liquid and she falls into a deep sleep.

The myth has a happy ending because Eros awakens Psyche with the tip of one of his arrows and, with the approval of Zeus, weds her to live in harmony ever after.

NOTE: this myth is the derivation of the romantic tale of the *Sleeping Beauty*.

SKIRNISMAL
(The Lay of Skirnir)

CULTURE OF ORIGIN: Teutonic – Nordic and Germanic (Icelandic)
PROVENANCE: the *Codex Regius* No. 2365, composed by an unknown hand circa tenth century AD. The manuscript lay hidden until it was rediscovered by Brynjolfur Sveinsson, bishop to the Icelandic community, circa 1643, and preserved on the instructions of Frederic III. It is housed in the Royal Library of Denmark [Copenhagen]. A limited section is contained in the *Codex Arnamagnaeanus* No. 544 (*Hauksbok*) [Copenhagen University] and the narrative is also paraphrased briefly by Snorri Sturluson (1178-1241) in the *Prose Edda*.
   The myth takes the form of a poetic dialogue. Its central character is Skirnir, the friend and ally of the god Freyr, who is sent to gain the favours of a giantess. Freyr is a member of the Vanir race of fertility gods and goddesses who are rivals of the Aesir gods headed by Othin. Here the writer abbreviates the name to 'Van'.

Skathi, the giantess stepmother of Freyr, commands Skirnir to find her stepson. Skirnir implies that when he does so he is likely to receive a sharp reprimand for his pains but he obeys nonetheless.

Skirnir discovers Freyr in a heavy-hearted mood and encourages the god to confide in him. Freyr reveals that in the hall of a giant called Gymir he has seen a beautiful maiden named Gerth with whom he has fallen hopelessly in love, but that the Aesir gods and the elves (whose opinion is respected) will have none of such a liaison. Freyr asks Skirnir to visit the giant's home on his behalf and beg the hand of the girl; to facilitate the journey, Freyr lends his horse to the messenger. It will carry Skirnir across barriers of mountain and flame.

Skirnir reaches the giant's domain, where he finds savage dogs standing guard. He speaks with a shepherd, asking him how best to approach the bower of the giantess maiden, but the shepherd, arguably Gerth's brother, offers no encouragement.

Gerth now enters into the dialogue, demanding of her handmaid to know what all the noise is outside, to which the handmaid replies that a strange horse and rider have arrived and that the young man wishes to talk with Gerth.

'Bid this bold youth come to my bower,

to greet me and to drink our ale;
though a foreigner he, I fear him not
my brother's slayer.

Art thou of the alf's or of Aesir come,
or art thou a wise Van?
Why farest thou through fiercest fire
to gaze upon our halls?'

When Skirnir is before her, he explains that he is none of the things she suggests, but that he has a gift of eleven apples from the god Freyr who requests her hand in love. Gerth is unimpressed. She refuses the apples and the proposal. Skirnir then offers the sacred ring which was taken from the finger of the god Balder when he was cremated. Gerth still offers no encouragement. Skirnir now resorts to intimidation, threatening her with his sword, but she replies contemptuously that her father will soon put Skirnir to death.

Skirnir's next threat is no less ominous. He threatens to bewitch the giantess with magic so that she shall become invisible. She will be doomed to sit atop a lonely hill and all men will become repulsive to her. When she recovers her appearance it will be that of a hag from whom even the Frost Giants will turn away and she will be fit only for the companionship of a three-headed monster to sate her lusts.

Improbably after such a barrage of threats, Gerth chooses to relent:

'Greetings hero, take to thy lips
this sparkling cup of mead;
ne'er thought that I should hither come,
in wedlock to a Van.'

Gerth agrees to meet with Freyr after nine nights at a trysting place called Barri. Skirnir returns to his friend who is impatient for answers. When Skirnir relates the outcome of proposal by proxy Freyr comments wistfully that even a single night is a long time when one is pining for love!

NOTE: for a more comprehensive account of Nordic cosmogony, see *Voluspa*, page 122.

TEZCATLIPOCA AS THE HUAXTEC

CULTURE OF ORIGIN: Aztec – classical Mesoamerican [Mexico]
PROVENANCE: probably worshipped circa 750 AD until 1500 AD and known from tradition in Florentine and other pre-Columbian codices and detail on stone carvings.

Tezcatlipoca is, by tradition, believed to have presided over the first of the five world ages in conjunction with the sun 4 Ocelotl. It is difficult to interpret the meaning, if any, behind the myth.

Tezcatlipoca disguises himself as a Huaxtec peasant and walks about naked, selling green peppers, with his penis dangling down. He goes to sit in the marketplace at the entrance to the royal palace where the daughter of Uemac lives. She is very beautiful and many Toltec lords covet her. Uemac refuses to give her to anyone, but when she sees Tezcatlipoca disguised as the Huaxtec peasant she becomes very excited at the sight of his penis. The vision makes her pregnant. It is as if Tezcatlipoca's member has entered her.

When Uemac discovers his daughter's condition he demands to know who is responsible and the women who chaperone her insist that it is the Huaxtec who sells green chillis. Uemac demands that the culprit be found and brought to book, so a worldwide search begins. Nobody can discover the whereabouts of the man, but eventually the Huaxtec presents himself at the palace. Uemac asks him where he comes from, but Tezcatlipoca evades answering. When asked why he is naked Tezcatlipoca merely replies that it is the way of the Huaxtecs! When Uemac demands to know what the Huaxtec is going to do about his daughter's condition, Tezcatlipoca replies 'Slay me!' Instead he is bathed and clothed and becomes Uemac's son-in-law.

The people are now angry because their ruler's daughter has married a peasant, so Uemac tells the Toltec warriors to take the Huaxtec off to war at Coatepec and conveniently abandon him. This they do, leaving him entrenched with all the dwarfs and cripples, and in due course of time they go home, relating how they have left the Huaxtec at the mercy of the enemy.

Tezcatlipoca, however, draws on his own supreme powers to rout and vanquish the enemy forces. When Uemac hears of his victory he is humbled and encourages the return of his now beloved son-in-law, whose triumph is then properly celebrated.

10

Myths of Death and Afterlife

One of the most persistent themes in the world's mythologies is that of death and resurrection. Since death is the ultimate and unknown factor facing all of humankind it is not surprising that stories frequently describe how godly heroes brush with death and emerge to enjoy a new vitality. Gods are perceived to be vulnerable to the experience of death, but they possess an innate ability to rise again. The Christian Passion story is certainly not new in this respect and may have been copied either from Greek or from ancient Near Eastern traditions, both of which offer very similar accounts. There is incontrovertible evidence that more or less identical themes to those central to the Christian story were known to audiences in the ancient Near East, at least two thousand years before the birth of Christ.

Often the demise of a god or goddess is taken as being an atonement which takes away the collective sins of the mortal world. Such is the case in the Christian dogma. This notion is, however, predated by the philosophy that out of the ashes of the old will spring the shoots of regenesis. In agricultural societies which experience a dead season of the year, be that period one of drought and heat, or of cold and darkness, the temporary demise of the natural world is explained by the death and rebirth of a fertility deity. Thus the ancient Sumerians recited the tale of the dying-and-rising god, Dumuzi, while the Phrygians told the tragic story of Attis which found its way into Greek and Roman traditions (in the Attis and Hilaria festivals). In certain instances, such as in the accounts of the deaths of Osiris and of Baal, there is strong emphasis on the dismemberment and scattering of the body, symbolizing the winnowing and sowing of seed at the beginning of the new agricultural season.

Often the dying-and-rising victim is male, reflecting the more unpredictable and whimsical aspects of the natural world. This is placed in stark contrast with the stoical and placid nature of the mother goddess, the consort of the seasonal god who mourns his loss while the natural world 'sleeps'. Sometimes the feckless god is absent altogether from the theme and it is part of the persona of the mother goddess herself which is found wanting. The most familiar example of this style of death-and-resurrection myth is that of Demeter and her daughter Persephone, who is obliged to spend a number of months each year in the underworld with the god Hades.

In more primitive societies one finds numerous examples of deities who are seen to be dead but who are raised to life again through magical means. This, however, probably reflects the real-life situation where an individual appears to be 'at death's door' only to make an astonishing recovery.

Sometimes, on the other hand, restoration after death is strictly beyond human experience and within the realm of the fantastic. Thus the popular Hindu god Ganeša, the son of Šiva, is decapitated as a child by his father, who seeks out the head of an elephant with which to restore him to substance and life.

ATTIS AND KYBELE

CULTURE OF ORIGIN: Phrygian [north-west Turkey], adopted into classical Greek and Rome through Minoan and Mycenaean culture

PROVENANCE: recorded from a Phrygian oral tradition by the Greek historian Pausanias and later by the Roman poet Ovid.

The vegetation god Attis and his hermaphrodite parent Agdistis are closely and fatally linked with the great Phrygian mother goddess Kybele and Attis is probably modelled on the Mesopotamian dying-and-rising god Dumuzi. The myth of Attis's death is the basis on which the Roman Attis festival took place from about 204 BC onwards. During the rites, the priests of Attis emulated the self-mutilation of the god, presenting their testicles to the altar of Kybele and burying them in the earth in a bizarre ritual of impregnation. The festival took place each year on 22 March, commencing with the Day of Blood and ending with the Hilaria orgy. There is some argument that the events of the Christian Good Friday and Easter are, in part, modelled on the Attis rites and the underlying message of the myth is that from death comes regenesis.

Zeus, enamoured of the goddess Kybele, accidently allows some of his semen to fall to the ground during a failed attempt at intercourse with her. From his seed grows the hermaphrodite Agdistis, who is then castrated either by a group of other gods, or specifically by Dionysos during a drunken bout. From the dismembered penis grows either an almond or a pomegranate tree from which Nana, the daughter of Sangarios, takes a fruit, placing it in her vagina. From it she conceives and gives birth to Attis, but immediately abandons him, leaving him to be fostered by a nanny goat – hence the name Attis, which means 'he goat'. A separate tradition places Kybele herself as Attis's mother.

Attis grows to be a handsome youth and is betrothed to the daughter of King Midas of Pessinus. Kybele, however, has become enamoured of Attis, and she and Agdistis argue over him to the point where, beneath 'a pine tree sacred to Kybele, the distraught Attis castrates himself and bleeds to death.

In another version describing the fate of Attis, he is gored to death by a wild boar, but in either event the wood violets grow from his blood. Agdistis is so grief-stricken that Zeus grants her wish that Attis's body will never decompose. See also *The Birth of Adonis*, page 82.

BAAL AND MOT

CULTURE OF ORIGIN: Canaanite
PROVENANCE: known from cuneiform tablets discovered at the site of Ugarit [Ras Šamra]. Authorship is ascribed to Elimelek, a student of the chief priest Atn-Prln during the reign of Niqmad at Ugarit.

The myth closely parallels the confrontation and fate episode in the longer and more complex saga of Baal and Anat (see page 172). It is a tale of confrontation, derived from the notion of good fighting evil, light against dark, which held such great popularity in Mesopotamian culture. Baal, the fertility and vegetation god, is in contest for the control of the natural world with the underworld god, Mot, representing death and desolation.

Mot issues a challenge to Baal, taunting the fertility god with the suggestion that, for all the latter's outward show of strength, Mot has the ability to crush and consume him and that, sooner or later, Baal will be drawn into the deathly embrace of the underworld. Baal's emissaries, Gupan and Ugar, go to Mot and return with his uncompromising message.

'Have you then forgotten, Baal, that I can surely transfix you
. . . for all that you smote Leviathan the slippery serpent
and made an end of the wriggling serpent,
the tyrant with seven heads
The heavens will burn up and droop helpless,
for I myself will crush you in pieces.'

Baal admits that he is in some awe of Mot's power. He knows that Mot has the ability to scorch the fertile earth and render it barren. He sends a reply to the effect that he is Mot's servant for all time. Mot is delighted and begins to brag that he will soon inherit Baal's kingdom.

The gods enjoy a great feast which Baal attends with his retinue of servants and his daughters Pidray (mist) and Tallay (showers) who are thought to have an obscure role in the fertility process. His third daughter Arsay has an equally obscure function in the underworld. Mot arrives and again threatens that he will bury Baal, his daughters and retinue in a hole in the earth. Baal is doomed to follow Mot's command. He mates with a young heifer in a pasture near the entrance of the underworld and dies. But the heifer becomes pregnant and gives birth to a bull calf, Baal's son.

Two travellers come to Il, the god of heaven, with a report that they have discovered Baal's lifeless body. Il is distraught, sitting on the ground, pouring the straw of mourning on his head and scourging himself.

He lifted up his voice and cried, 'Baal is dead.
What will become of the people of Dagan's son,
What of his multitudes?
After Baal I would go down into the earth.'

At this juncture Baal's sister Anat, the goddess of fertility and war, sets off in search of her brother's body. She finds him where he has fallen and, like Il, she mourns him and scourges herself. She demands the assistance of Šapaš, the sun god, to lift the dead hero and she takes him back to his mountain sanctuary of Saphon, where she affords him all the proper funeral rites and sacrifices.

Having laid Baal to rest, she turns towards the home of Il, where she falls at his feet and declares bitterly that the goddess Athirat, long envious of Baal, may rejoice and select one of her sons as his successor. Athirat proposes Attar the Terrible, although Il points out to her that he is a mere shadow of Baal in strength and ability. In practice Attar proves no match for the task and, having sampled life on the throne, he steps down.

Anat, however, cannot rest in her grief for Baal and she decides to seek out Mot. He brags to her that it was he, Mot, who had slain her brother.

'It was I who confronted mightiest Baal
I who made him like a lamb in my mouth
and he was carried away like a kid in the breach of my windpipe.'

Months pass and the earth grows desolate. Finally Anat has had enough. She visits Mot again and, on this occasion, she slaughters him, splitting, winnowing, burning, grinding and scattering him on the earth.

Il dreams that Baal has been restored and that the earth is once more fruitful but when he awakens he knows that the land is still parched and cracked under the summer heat of the sun. Anat sets forth again, this time to deliver to Šapaš, the sun god, an account of Il's short-lived hopes and his rapid return to despondency. Šapaš instructs her to pour a libation of wine and as this point part of the text is missing. When the narrative resumes Baal has been restored to life. With huge vigour he disposes of the sons of Athirat and Mot's henchmen and returns to his rightful throne.

After seven years the voice of Mot is heard to complain at his ill-treatment and he threatens that unless Baal hands over a suitable scapegoat he will destroy the earth. Baal answers contemptuously that if Mot is hungry he can eat one of his own retinue, but Mot is angered and the two adversaries enter into a great conflict. Šapaš urges restraint upon Mot, warning that if he continues Il will withdraw all support and break Mot's control of the underworld. With this ultimate threat Mot is subdued and he retreats.

THE DEATH OF BALDR

CULTURE OF ORIGIN: Teutonic – Nordic (Icelandic)

PROVENANCE: the *Prose Edda* (*Codex Wormianus*) composed by the Icelandic scholar Snorri Sturluson between 1178 and 1241 AD and dispatched in the seventeenth century by the historian Arngrimur Jonsson to a colleague in Denmark named Ole Worm.

The codex effectively constitutes a textbook, the first part of which is titled *Gylfaginning* (The Tricking of Gylfi) and represents an overview of Nordic mythology. The incident reported by Snorri, in which the god Balder is slain through the duplicity of Loki, is at variance in its details with the account rendered by the historian Saxo Grammaticus in his *Gesta Danorum*. Which of the contrasting assassination accounts is the more accurate in terms of tradition is unknown. In either event, it is clear that the slaying of Balder presages the end of everything at the day of doom, Ragnarok.

In the Snorri account the favourite son of Othin, Balder, has experienced strange dreams, including premonitions of his own end (see *Baldrs Draumar*, page 260). The gods are fearful of the danger that may threaten Balder and they ask the fertility goddess Frigg to demand of all living things on earth an oath of loyalty which will prevent harm from falling upon Othin's son. Once his life is protected by this magic the gods amuse themselves by hurling stones, darts and other missiles at Balder as target practice, knowing that he is invulnerable.

The god Loki, however, disguised as an old crone, approaches Frigg and discovers that one small, inconspicuous plant, the mistletoe, has failed to take the oath of allegiance since Frigg has thought it too puny to pose any threat. Loki, not a true member of the Asgarth pantheon, is full of spite for the deprecating way the other gods treat him, so he collects a sprig of mistletoe and places it in the hands of the blind god Hoder, persuading him to join in the sport. Guided by the hand of Loki, Hoder hurls the mistletoe and as he does so it transforms into a lethal projectile which pieces Balder through the heart. He falls dead.

Othin, wracked by grief, instructs the god Hermoth to ride to the kingdom of Hel on Othin's magic steed Sleipnir, with the request that Balder be released back into the world of the living gods. When Hel hears the request she is willing to comply on one condition, that every living thing shall shed tears of sorrow. If any creature fails to weep, Balder will remain forever incarcerated in the underworld. Hermoth returns to Othin with the fateful message and the supreme god commands all the world to weep for Balder. Each creature complies except for one, a giantess living deep in the forest. From her comes the reply:

> 'Neither living nor dead has Othin's son been use to me. Let Hel hold her victim for ever.'

The gods realize that the giantess is none other than Loki in another of his disguises. They catch the offender and tie him to a rock where a serpent endlessly drips poison on to his face from its fangs.

In the account of Saxo Grammaticus, Balder is portrayed as a lustful tyrant, a demi-god warrior who has 'sprung from celestial seed' and who is watched over by a team of Valkyrie maidens. He is killed by a rival who possesses a magic sword.

BLUE JAY AND IOI

CULTURE OF ORIGIN: native American – Chinook [Columbia River, northwestern USA]

PROVENANCE: recorded from oral traditions. Principal sources include *Chinook Texts* F. Boas. Bulletin 20, Bureau of American Ethnology. Washington 1895.

The character Blue Jay is typical of many found among hunting clans – an intercessor between gods and mortals who possesses supernatural powers and who occasionally runs the gauntlet of the spirit world. Sometimes the outcome is successful, sometimes not.

Blue Jay is asked by his sister, Ioi, to find a wife from among the dead to help with the housework; she suggests that the potential spouse should be elderly. Blue Jay agrees with part of the request, but marries the recently deceased daughter of a chieftain. When Ioi notices the girl's youth she tells Blue Jay that his partner is far too young to be dead and that he is to take her to the Land of Spirit People, where she will be revived.

When Blue Jay arrives in the Spirit People's village, they ask how long his bride has been dead. 'One day,' he replies, to which they retort that he must continue his journey to find the village where people who have been dead for a day are revived. When Blue Jay gets to the second village he tells the inhabitants that his wife has been dead for two days and, predictably, he is sent off again! By the time he reaches the fifth village and his wife has been dead five days, the Spirit People take pity on him and bring the girl back to life. They also make Blue Jay a chieftain.

Eventually Blue Jay tires of life among the Spirit People and takes his wife home. The old chieftain discovers that his daughter is not dead and is married to Blue Jay, so he sends a message demanding Blue Jay's hair in payment of the bride price. Receiving no reply, he marches angrily round to Blue Jay's house with the rest of the village, but Blue Jay turns himself into a bird and flies away, never to return to his wife. She pines away and eventually goes to the Land of Souls.

Meanwhile Ioi is abducted to Shadow Land by the Ghost People and after a year Blue Jay goes off to search for her. He locates her sitting amid a pile of bones which she tells him are those of her relatives who occasionally take human form, but who are instantly reduced to bones again if there is a loud noise.

Blue Jay goes fishing with Ioi's young brother-in-law and discovers, to his amusement, that every time he shouts the youth is reduced to a pile of bones. They catch nothing but sticks and leaves and Blue Jay resorts to amusing himself by playing tricks on his long-suffering sister and her ghost relatives. Eventually his mischief gets the better of him when there is a prairie fire. Ioi gives him five buckets of water and instructs him to douse the flames, but tells him that he is to ration the water with care. Inevitably Blue Jay disobeys her and when he has run out of water he tries to beat out the flames. He is so badly burned that he dies and becomes one of the Ghost People.

BRAHMA AND THE ADVENT OF DEATH

CULTURE OF ORIGIN: Epic Hindu [India]
PROVENANCE: the story appears in the *Mahabharata*, written circa 300 BC to 300 AD

Brahma, the creator god, has engendered all living things, which increase in age and number but do not die; the world is thus becoming exceedingly overcrowded. He finds difficulty in arriving at a solution which will allow him to eliminate some of his own creations and, in a rage, he breathes out a great fire which burns up most of the life on earth.

The creator god Šiva, lord of the Vedic sacrifice, who has the welfare of living things at heart, goes to discuss the matter with

Brahma and the latter offers him a boon. Šiva requests that Brahma show clemency to life on earth, but Brahma replies that he has engineered the destruction only in order to lessen the crush of living things. Šiva points out that the universe is largely reduced to ashes and all the creatures which have been made extinct by Brahma's fire will never return. It is perhaps worth exploring some other means of limiting populations in the future.

Šiva suggests that all life should be controlled by cycles of birth and death and, on hearing these words, Brahma suppresses his destroying fires. As he does so the goddess of death, Kali, emerges from his body, but when she learns of her future role as an instrument of destruction she is sorrowful.

'How can you, great god, have made a fragile woman such as I to carry such a dreadful burden, terrifying all that lives and breathes? I fear that I may break divine law; give me some task in keeping with that law.'

Brahma, however, is resolute in his intent and sends Kali away on her terrifying mission to destroy life. In an effort to avoid her grim task, for fifteen thousand million years Kali practises extreme asceticism by standing motionless first on one foot and then for an equal period of time upon the other; after this she goes to live a reclusive existence in the wilderness and then enters a period of fasting.

Again Brahma orders her to carry out her divine duties and again Kali respectfully refuses, until finally she is so afraid of the consequences of disobeying Brahma that she begins to destroy the life breath of creatures as their time on earth comes to an end. Her tears are the diseases which afflict mankind.

THE DEIFICATION OF DIN HAU (TIN HAU)

CULTURE OF ORIGIN: Chinese Daoist (Taoist)
PROVENANCE: recorded in various texts and art from oral traditions. The tradition of Din Hau is recorded on the walls of a sanctuary in Hangchow in 1228 AD and she was deified by the Mongol Emperor Kublai Khan in 1278. It was he who conferred the title 'Queen of Heaven'.

It should be noted that the anglicized equivalents of Chinese characters vary considerably in transliteration. The official Chinese Pinyin system is applied here, followed, where appropriate, in brackets, by the more generally encountered Wade-Giles system.

The Queen of Heaven, Din Hau (Tin Hau), originates as a mortal girl, the daughter of a minor official who was born on the island of Mei-Zhou in the Fukien province. She perfects herself and receives recurrent dreams of saving fishing boats from the waters close to her village until she dies at the age of twenty-eight. She ascends to heaven, where she becomes the consort of the Jade Emperor, Yu Huang Shang Di, and enjoys the ministrations of two grotesque figures, 'Thousand League Eyes' and 'Favouring Wind Ears'.

DISANI SLAYS HER SON

CULTURE OF ORIGIN: Prasun Kafir [Hindukush]
PROVENANCE: oral traditions recorded chiefly by M. Elphinstone (1839); G. Morgenstierne (1951); G.S. Robertson (1896).
   The myth underlines the concern in a primitive society about the unpredictability of nature, but also places the ritual of mourning in a mythological setting.

The fertility goddess Disani bears a son. When the boy grows to manhood he joins forces with the son of the god Diwog and together they plant various crops, including grapes, pomegranates and nuts, which effectively alter the balance of nature. They have done this, however, without obtaining the proper approval of the other gods, who become enraged and chase after them. When the son of Diwog conceals himself within a rock, his pursuers threaten him with death from thirst and starvation. The son of Disani, however, creates a water wheel beside the hiding place which the gods take as a further slight upon their authority.

   Disani sees the youth being chased and, unaware of his identity, she runs to cut off his flight and decapitates him. Horrified, she realizes that she has killed her own son and turns her wrath upon the other gods. They explain that the two youths had set out to change the order of nature and that their impiety had to be punished. To console Disani they instigate a requiem feast in which eighteen youths will dance and sing mournful songs.

ELEIO

CULTURE OF ORIGIN: Polynesian [Hawaii]
PROVENANCE: recorded in recent times from oral traditions

Eleio is a *kahuna*, a shaman with the powers to commune with the spirit world and, under certain circumstances, to bring the dead back to life. He sees a beautiful girl whom he follows to a sacred burial ground on a cliff top, but when she turns to confront him she tells him that she is a spirit and that he must tell her parents he has seen her and that she is happy in her new home.

When Eleio sees the mortal body of the girl lying in the burial chamber he returns to her parents' house, relates what he has seen and prepares a sacrificial meal. Then, accompanied by the girl's family, he returns to the burial ground and enters into a trance-like state in which he sees her spirit once more. Taking the leaves of a magical *kava* plant and applying them in the proper way he draws the spirit to him and pushes it into the lifeless corpse through the soles of the feet. At first it will only go in as far as the girl's knees, so he renews his efforts until the spirit re-enters all parts of the body and the girl is revived.

The family prepares a new sacrificial feast and invites Eleio to take the daughter as his wife.

See also *Hiku and Kawelu*, below.

GANYMEDES

CULTURE OF ORIGIN: classical Greek, but subsequently adopted into Roman culture
PROVENANCE: modelled on an oral tradition though with several variations

Ganymedes is a shepherd youth, the son of the king and queen, Tros and Callirhoe. He is guarding his father's flock on the slopes of Mount Ida near the city of Troy. The god Zeus sees him and immediately becomes infatuated with his beauty to the extent that he decides to abduct Ganymedes to Mount Olympus. According to some versions of the myth the boy is snatched, at Zeus's command, by an eagle. Alternatively Zeus himself takes the form of an eagle to carry out the mission.

In the realm of the gods Ganymedes replaces the goddess Hebe to serve as Zeus's cup-bearer and personal attendant. To compensate Tros for the loss of his son, Zeus provides the king with a stable of divine horses.

HIKU AND KAWELU

CULTURE OF ORIGIN: Polynesian [Hawaii]
PROVENANCE: recorded in recent times from oral traditions

Hiku, the son of the moon goddess Hina, journeys the world following the flight of his magic arrow until it lands at the feet of the beautiful Queen Kawelu. She picks it up and returns it to Hiku but, as she does so, she falls in love with the youthful stranger. Using her magic powers she keeps him in her palace, a virtual prisoner, until he manages to escape and fly away. Mourning his loss, the queen dies.

Hiku learns of the tragedy that has occurred and decides to visit the underworld in an attempt to bring Kawelu back. First he anoints himself with an oil that makes him smell of putrefaction and then he lowers himself, by means of a long Convolvulus stem, into the hole in the ground which leads to the underworld of the god Milu. Milu is deceived by the foul smell into thinking that Hiku is just another corpse. Eventually Hiku discovers the spirit of the dead queen, who has changed herself into a butterfly; he catches it in a coconut shell and ascends with it to the upper world.

Hiku takes the spirit back to the queen's palace where her body still rests and he cuts open the flesh of her big toe. Through the incision he pushes the spirit into her body and it slowly works its way up from the foot and into the legs. Kawelu is restored to life, though she remembers nothing of her experience in the underworld.

See also *Eleio*, page 231.

INANA'S DESCENT INTO THE UNDERWORLD AND THE DEATH OF DUMUZI

CULTURE OF ORIGIN: Mesopotamian – Sumerian, Old Babylonian and Assyrian

PROVENANCE: this complex and disturbing myth was, for many years, known only through small and largely disconnected fragments. The complete Sumerian version, as it is now recognized, results from at least twenty-eight different sources, comprising some 410 lines of text. It was only pieced together in its entirety in 1963. Prior to this a much shorter Akkadian version (140 lines) was known from both Old Babylonia and Assyria and dated, in the earliest instances, from about 1750 BC (Late Bronze Age). Much of the latter source material was discovered in the palace library of Aššurbanipal in Nineveh.

In the Sumerian story, two myths are effectively bound into a single epic tale, *Inana's Descent to the Underworld* and *The Death of Dumuzi*. In a separate Sumerian myth, that which relates the story of the Sacred Marriage, a celestial union is described which accounts for life on earth. In spite of this, the Mesopotamian summer and autumn bring annual drought and desolation. To explain the apparent reversal of genesis, the writers created a mythological antithesis.

With Dumuzi, the consort of the fertility goddess, periodically absent, the Sumerians were able to explain the annual demise of their natural world for six months under the savage heat of the Mesopotamian summer sun. The short Akkadian version, in which Inana becomes Ištar, does not properly explain this seasonal cycle of life and death.

Inana, the great goddess of fertility and war, descends into the nether world to confront and challenge the forces of evil. These powers are represented by the goddess Ereškigal, consort of the chthonic god Nergal and mistress of the underworld. In certain respects she may also be seen as the dark *alter ego* of Inana.

Inana dresses in all her finery and collects together the seven emblems of her power. As she descends the path to Ereškigal's realms, she is accompanied by her maid Ninšubur, to whom she gives certain instructions which are to be carried out if the venture fails. Ninšubur is to plead for the goddess's restoration before the great gods.

As Inana passes through the seven portals of the dead, the doorman of the underworld, Neti, opens each gate to her with a friendly welcome, but once she is within he strips her of her powers, one by one, until finally she is brought, naked and defenceless, before Ereškigal and the terrible judges of the underworld, the Anunnaki. In a bizarre parody of queenship, mirrored by the later Christian Passion story, Inana is placed on Ereškigal's throne.

When Inana had been subjugated, the garments that
had been removed were carried away.
Then her sister [Ereškigal] rose from her throne
and she [Inana] took her seat on her sister's throne.

The goddess of life is judged and condemned and life on earth withers and becomes barren. The Anunnaki fasten her with the gaze of death and she is hung, lifeless, from a stake. When three days and nights have passed, the maid Ninšubur sets off to carry out her mistress's instructions. She approaches, in turn, the gods Enlil, Nanna and Enki, but only Enki, the creator god, receives her with sympathy. He wills a pregnancy on Ereškigal and then sends two formless beings, Kalatur and Kugarra, ostensibly to minister to the underworld goddess. They are instructed to flatter Ereškigal until she promises them a reward for their services, the corpse of Inana.

[She will say to you] 'Who are you?
Who is echoing my cry of pain?
If you are divine I will promise you something
If you are mortal I will decree a good fate for you.'
Make her swear this by heaven and earth.
Should she offer you a river as a drink, do not accept,
Should she offer you a field of grain as a meal, do not accept,
but say to her: 'Give us the corpse which is hanging on that hook.'

Thus the two beings sprinkle the corpse with the food and water of life and Inana prepares to ascend to the upper world once more. The Anunnaki, however, insist that a substitute takes Inana's place in the underworld and the goddess is followed back to the world of the living by the *galla*, the demons who are to drag her back by force unless she complies. This forfeit agreed, Inana ascends back through the seven gates and at each she is returned one of her divine emblems.

Inana selects the victim wildly and in a moment of irritation because she chooses her consort in the Sacred Marriage, the demi-god Dumuzi. Realizing, however, the fearful implications for the safety of the natural world if she is prevented from enacting her holy coupling with Dumuzi, Inana relents and adopts a Solomonesque pragmatism: Dumuzi will, henceforth, reside in the underworld for half of each year, while his sister, Geštinana, will take his place for the other half.

ISIS AND OSIRIS (1)

CULTURE OF ORIGIN: Egyptian
PROVENANCE: the role of Isis and Osiris prior to his murder is recorded in Pyramid Texts dating from the Old Kingdom (circa 2649–2152 BC) and in Coffin Texts dating from the Middle Kingdom (circa 2040–1783 BC). There is also a good account on the Dynasty XVIII Amenmose stela [Louvre]. Accounts of the death of Osiris are more fragmentary, sometimes emerging in the New Kingdom funerary papyri collectively described as the *Book of the Dead*. There are further references on the Ikhernofret stela [Berlin]. The impregnation of Isis by the semen of her dead husband is best depicted in the Shrine of Sokar in the Temple of Seti I at Abydos.

Osiris may have begun his career as a tree spirit or as the spirit of the corn. By the time of the eighteenth dynasty at the beginning of the New Kingdom period (circa 1567–1085 BC), however, he had become a god almost equalling Re in importance, personifying the sun as its passes through the darkness of the underworld at night and becoming both god of the dead and the perennial victim of nature's curse. Thus he presides paradoxically over fertility and death.

The fate of Osiris is sealed through the murderous jealousy of his brother, Seth, the god of chaos and adversity who covets his brother's harvest. Seth is a complex character in Egyptian mythology, the god of chaotic forces who is both venerated and greatly feared. Tradition has it that he tore himself savagely from the womb of his mother, Nut, at his birth, reputed to have taken place in the Ombos-Naqada region of Upper Egypt.

Pyramid Texts refer to the slaying of Osiris near Abydos on the Nile at Nedyet. Isis is determined to bear a son who will avenge his father. In the years which follow she and her sister Nephthys hunt for Osiris's body until they discover it where it fell near Abydos. In the Plutarch myth (see *Isis and Osiris (2)*, below) Isis discovers a tamarisk tree with the coffin embedded deep in its trunk. She rescues it and flees deep into the mountains, where she can be safe from Seth. In this distant sanctuary, and in the form of a kite, she performs her magic over the dead body.

She made light with her feathers, wind she made with her wings.

She thus impregnates herself from Osiris's remains. The confrontation enters a new round when, in Plutarch's version, Seth discovers Osiris's body and, in a desperate attempt to destroy it, tears it into fourteen pieces. Thirteen he hurls out into the Nile and the last, the god's penis, he feeds to a crocodile so that the dead god may never be restored to father a child.

In the safety of the papyrus swamps at Khemnis in the Nile Delta, Isis gives birth to a son, Horus, the hawk god. At this stage of his life he is called Her-pa-khered (Horus the child). As he grows up he becomes Har-wer (Horus the elder) and is determined both to avenge his father's death and to take his rightful place on the Egyptian throne (see also *Horus and Seth*, page 146).

The myth of Osiris's death and subsequent fate underlines a peculiarly Egyptian philosophy which places him not as a dying-and-rising god in the Indo-Aryan (Mesopotamian) sense but as a triumphant ruler over the paradise kingdom of the dead, a destiny to which every Egyptian aspires. Osiris is depicted as a mummy with a green face and with only his hands free to hold the sceptre and flail of his authority.

ISIS AND OSIRIS (2)

CULTURE OF ORIGIN: Greek

PROVENANCE: compiled by the Greek historian Plutarch (circa 40–120 AD) but based on earlier Egyptian accounts, particularly that of the writer Manetho (fourth century AD) and adulterated with Greek philosophical traditions. In the view of the Egyptians the principal deities of the myth, Isis and Osiris, had once been a mortal king and queen who travelled the world teaching humanity how to cultivate the land. When they returned to Egypt they were transformed into immortals.

The sun god Helios (Re) discovers that his consort Rhea (Nut) has been unfaithful and has consorted with the god Kronos (Geb). He places a curse on her by which he intends to render her barren, decreeing that she shall bear a child 'in no month and no year'. Rhea, however, has also given her favours to the god Hermes (Thoth).

In a draughts game Hermes wins from the moon goddess the seventieth part of each day of the year. The Egyptian calendar was calculated not on the basis of the solar cycle, but on the rising of the star Sirius, which resulted in a year of 360 days. Out of the fractions of days earned in the game, Hermes makes up the remaining five days necessary to complete the solar year, knowing that these five days will remain outside the official calendar for the twelve-month period.

On each of the days which Hermes has thus provided to escape the curse of Helios, Rhea gives birth. Her first born son is Osiris, followed by Apollo (the elder Horus), Typhon (Seth), Isis and Nephthys. The siblings Osiris and Isis become an inseparable couple, a god and goddess intimately concerned with the fertility of the living world. As the eldest son, Osiris also inherits the right to govern Egypt.

Typhon, who hunts elephants and lions and lays waste the land, conspires with seventy-two others to destroy Osiris. He and his co-conspirators secretly measure Osiris's frame and build a beautifully crafted chest of exactly the same dimensions.

The gods indulge in a bout of drinking during which Typhon suggests a contest in which the winner, who will earn the chest as a prize, will be the person who fits into it exactly. All try and fail the test until Osiris steps inside and lies down. Typhon slams the lid shut and seals it with lead, turning the chest into a coffin in which Osiris is incarcerated alive. He tosses the chest into the Nile and, believing that he has seen the last of Osiris, usurps the throne of Egypt.

The chest floats down the Nile and out to sea, eventually coming to rest on the shores of Lebanon, where it is engulfed in the bole of a tamarisk tree which the local ruler subsequently cuts down to form a pillar for his palace. Isis follows the trail of the coffin and rescues it from Byblos but, one night, Typhon comes by, finds the chest and, determined that Osiris's demise shall be total, cuts the body into fourteen pieces. Thirteen he scatters throughout Egypt and the fourteenth, the penis, he throws to a crocodile.

Isis again follows the morbid trail, finding and burying each part of Osiris with proper ritual. Subsequently the places where, by tradition, the parts of the corpse land become sanctified with shrines and temples. His penis is never recovered.

Apollo enters a great battle with Typhon to win the crown of Egypt. When Typhon is vanquished he is led away in chains by Isis, but she later frees him, much to Apollo's annoyance. He tears the crown from his mother's head, but Hermes gives her a horned head-dress in its place. Typhon remains conquered and disgraced.

LLEW AND BLODEUWEDD

CULTURE OF ORIGIN: Celtic – Welsh

PROVENANCE: recorded from oral traditions and linked thematically in the epic saga, the *Mabinogion*. The myth bears strong resemblance, in certain respects, to the tragic story of the Norse god Balder, slain by the blind god Hoder when Balder's 'Achilles heel' is revealed. The Biblical parallel is that of Samson and Delilah.

The bastard son of the goddess Arianrhod, perhaps sired incestuously by Gwydion, the son of Don, is Llew Llaw Gyffes. He is taken to Arianrhod to be given a name and arms, but she curses him so that he will bear neither name nor weapons and will never marry a mortal woman. Gwydion responds with magical powers of his own. First he tricks Arianrhod into naming the boy Llew when he shows his dexterity with a sling shot (the name is a corruption of this aptitude). Next Gwydion raises a phantom army to storm Arianrhod's castle and thus enables Llew, disguised as a bard, to receive arms for the defence of the place. Lastly, with the help of his uncle Math, he creates a woman, Blodeuwedd, from the blossoms of flowers.

Although Blodeuwedd is presented to Llew as his bride she has no love for him and after a while she becomes infatuated with a hunter, Gronw Pebr, with whom she plots to murder Llew. Craftily she elicits from him information about the only means by which he may be slain – by a spear forged for just a year and thrust into him on a Sunday, neither inside nor outside and neither on foot nor on horse. The conclusion is that Llew is virtually invulnerable, but nonetheless Gronw Pebr forges the spear and Blodeuwedd persists in demanding that Llew show her the precise circumstances in which he will die. Llew builds a floating bath-house on the river-bank. Then, on a Sunday, he brings along a billy goat and balances himself with one foot on the bath and one on the goat! Gronw hurls the fatal spear but, just in time, Llew transmutes into an eagle, flying to safety until, through Gwydion's powers, he can be restored to his proper form.

MAIO SHAN

CULTURE OF ORIGIN: Chinese Daoist (Taoist)

PROVENANCE: recorded in various texts and art from an oral tradition brought to China through Buddist influence sometime between AD 384 and 417, but established more clearly during the Tang Dynasty (AD 618–906). Guan Yin (Kuan Yin) is the Daoist form of the Buddhist god Avalokitesvara. Transition from god to goddess and the adoption of the name Guan Yin probably began circa AD 600 and was complete by AD 1100. Tradition identifies Guan Yin as a mortal princess, Maio Shan, whose apotheosis transformed her into a goddess with both fertility connotations and a merciful guardian image invoked when danger threatens.

It should be noted that the anglicized equivalents of Chinese characters vary considerably in transliteration. The official Chinese Pinyin system is applied here, followed, where appropriate, in brackets, by the more generally encountered Wade-Giles system.

As the youngest of three royal sisters, Maio Shan becomes renowned for her intelligence, compassion and beauty. Sitting beneath a tree in the palace gardens one evening she grows drowsy at the sound of a cicada in the branches, but is instantly awakened when the insect is caught by a praying mantis. She climbs on to the seat to save the cicada, but loses her balance when the mantis turns to bite her; she falls and suffers a deep gash to her forehead. Over a period of time the scar heals, but it leaves a patch of red moles on her face.

According to one tradition, anxious to cure the ills of the world, Maio Shan prays to the Buddha for guidance and she is told of a magical white lotus which grows on the top of Mount Sumeru. If she can find it and bring it back her desire will be granted and she will ultimately become a Boddhisattva, a Buddha-designate whose essence is perfect knowledge.

With her maid, Yung Lien, Maio Shan sets off in search of the mountain and its bloom. On the journey the princess performs various acts of generosity and kindness to men and animals alike. After seventy days the supply of food the women carry is exhausted and the princess and her maid survive on a subsistence fare of berries scavenged along the way. Six months from the day they set out, they reach Mount Sumeru. It takes them three days to climb to the summit, where an image of the Buddha appears before them holding a water jug and a white lotus flower.

The Buddha explains that they must take the flower, in the jug, back to the palace and nurture it. Maio Shan must then devote herself to personal perfection through meditation. One day the flower will transform into a willow branch and on that day she will rise to heaven as a Boddhisattva. Maio Shan thus returns to her palace where she denies herself the comforts of the material life and obeys the Buddha's commands.

After two years, a boy, Shan Ying, thinks to play a trick on her by substituting the lotus blossom for a willow twig, but Maio Shan responds by telling everyone that she has dreamed of being assisted in her apotheosis by a child. She goes to sit by a lotus pool where one of the blossoms grows to cover the surface of the water. Maio Shan alights upon it and is transported gently to heaven, her task of self-perfection accomplished.

An alternative, and more violent, tradition has the Buddha direct Maio Shan to the island of Pu To, where she perfects herself over a period of nine years, finally committing suicide by self-strangulation and ascending to Yu Huang Shang Di (generally abbreviated to Yu-Di), the Jade Emperor, in the paradise of heaven.

After her deification Maio Shan becomes Guan Yin, the goddess of mercy.

PELE AND LOHIAU

CULTURE OF ORIGIN: Polynesian [Hawaii]
PROVENANCE: recorded in recent times from oral traditions.
The volcanic mountain of Kilauea in Hawaii is the subject of many local myths. This is one which loosely parallels other death and resurrection stories, including the Phrygian tale of Attis and Kybele (see page 224) and its Greek derivative, that of Adonis and Aphrodite.

The fire goddess Pele discovers a young man of great beauty and of royal blood with whom she falls in love. His name is Lohiau, Prince of Kaua'i, and she seduces him, though she avoids revealing to him her true identity. They marry, but after a while Pele leaves Lohaiu to return to her fire mountain home, promising him that, one day, she will come back.

Inconsolable in his loss, Lohiau starves himself to death. While his body lies in state, his spirit is captured by the female lizard demons Kilioa and Kalamainu, who incarcerate it in a cliff-top prison.

Pele's sister, Hiiaka, rescues the spirit of Lohiau, carrying it back to where his body rests. Lohiau is restored to life, but in the process he falls in love with Hiiaka. The pair escape to Hawaii, where the outraged and jealous Pele erupts from her mountain home, engulfing Lohiau in lava and promptly ending his brief second life.

The spirit of Lohiau quests over the ocean in search of Hiiaka, but meanwhile she has gone to the kingdom of the underworld god, Milu, to await him! Her father, Kane Hoalani, now intervenes by catching the spirit of Lohiau and returning it to the lava pillar at the foot of Mount Kilauea. He smashes away the lava covering and, once more, Lohiau is restored to life. Awakening, he finds Pele standing before him and in terror he begs her forgiveness. To his surprise she tells him that her love for him was in a previous existence and that he is now free to marry whomsoever he choses. With this she vanishes. Kane Hoalani offers Lohiau the use of a tiny magical seashell which will grow into a great boat and transport him wherever he needs to go. Lohiau thus sails away in search of Hiiaka and, by chance, comes ashore on the island of Oahu, where a song festival is in progress. Lohiau stands listening and is astonished to hear the voice of Hiiaka singing of her love for him. He responds by singing of his own infatuation and together they sail away into the sunset back to Kaua'i.

PERSEPHONE AND DEMETER

CULTURE OF ORIGIN: classical Greek, but subsequently adopted into Roman culture

PROVENANCE: recorded from oral traditions by the Greek epic poet Hesiod in the *Hymn to Demeter* during the eighth century BC.

The fateful story of Persephone and her mother Demeter forms the basis for the Eleusinian Mysteries, the annual Greek drama of death and rebirth in nature. The identity of Persephone is closely intertwined with that of Demeter and the two may perhaps been seen as aspects of each other. Persephone is also *kore* (the girl), the immature form of the corn goddess. In the Hesiod version the abduction of Persephone takes place on the Plain of Nysa, though other traditions set the episode at Enna in Sicily, in Crete near Knossos, by the River Kephissus at Eleusis, or in Arcadia at the foot of Mount Kyllene.

NOTE: Roman authors change the names of the main characters in the myth to Proserpina and Ceres.

Zeus seduces and impregnates the corn goddess, Demeter, the second daughter of Kronos and Rhea, and she bears a child, Persephone. One day, when Persephone has wandered away from her mother into the meadows on the Plain of Nysa, accompanied by the daughters of Okeanos, the Okeanides, she comes across a rare and beautiful flower (thought to be either a lily or a narcissus). So struck is she by this glorious bloom that she reaches down to pluck it from the ground. As she does so the earth yawns open and the god of the underworld, Hades, appears in his golden chariot. At the behest of Zeus he seizes Persephone and drags her screaming into the subterranean depths. The only persons to hear her cries for help are the gentle goddess Hecate, daughter of Persaeus and Asteria, and Helios, the son of Hyperion and Thea.

In great anguish Demeter searches vainly for her lost daughter. She roams far and wide for nine days and nights, carrying torches to guide her through the hours of darkness (see also *Telepinu*, page 244), until she meets Hecate, who has done no more than hear the voice of the abductor and thus can only offer faint clues. Demeter then seeks out Helios, who reveals the full account of the fate which has befallen her daughter.

> *'None other of the immortal gods is to blame, but only cloud-gathering Zeus, who gave her to Hades [Aidoneus], her father's brother, to be his wife.'*

Demeter is so deeply affronted by Zeus's conduct that she rejects the company of the Olympian gods and takes to wandering the fields of the earth in the guise of an old woman, without bathing or changing her clothes and without eating or drinking. She comes, fortuitously, to the home of Keleos, the ruler of the district of Eleusis, and seats herself by the Maiden Well until the daughters of Keleos come to draw water. Under the pseudonym Doso, Demeter offers her services as a wet nurse to Keleos's wife, Metaneira, but when she enters the palace her stature and radiance reveal her to be a noble lady and Metaneira offers her a cup of wine.

It is settled that Demeter will nurse Metaneira's son Demophon (in other traditions Triptolemos), but as the child grows, Demeter weaves her magic over him, keeping him from mortal food and bathing him in fire so that he becomes ever more like one of the immortals. When Metaneira discovers what is happening and protests, Demeter is angry and snatches the child from the flames, hurling him to the ground and telling Metaneira that now Demophon will age and die like other mortals. Demeter reveals herself in her true stature as a goddess, casting off her disguise and leaving the palace. Demophon, however, continues to grow like an immortal and, in gratitude, Keleos builds a temple in Demeter's honour.

During her time of wandering Demeter has neglected the earth and its fecundity, with the result that crops fail to grow, the ground becomes lifeless and humankind is faced with famine and annihilation. Zeus perceives the imminent disaster and sends the messenger goddess Iris to reason with Demeter. Her mission is to no avail and a succession of other envoys fare little better in their attempts at persuasion. Zeus therefore sends the messenger god Hermes to the underworld with orders that Persephone must be returned to the upper world. Hades seems to agree but, secretly, he gives Persephone a pomegranate seed to eat before placing her in his chariot and taking her back to Demeter. According to some traditions this is witnessed by Ascalaphos, son of the god of the underworld river Acheron, who relates what he has seen to Demeter. So enraged is she that she ungraciously turns him into an owl.

Demeter is overjoyed at the return of her daughter, but misgivings lead her to enquire of Persephone if she has eaten any food while in the underworld. When the truth about the pomegranate seed is confirmed Demeter accepts that Persephone has tasted the fruit of death and is now tied irrevocably to the underworld. The compromise settled with Hades is that Persephone may spend two thirds of every year in the world of the living, but for the remaining months she must return to the underworld as Hades's bride. In springtime Persephone will escape back to Olympus and after the harvest she will return to Hades to stay with him for the months of winter. During the time of separation Demeter will relinquish her responsibility for the earth and will mourn the separation from her daughter.

See also *Attis and Kybele*, page 224, and *The Birth of Adonis*, page 82.

THE DEPARTURE OF QUETZALCOATL

CULTURE OF ORIGIN: Aztec – classical Mesoamerican [Mexico]
PROVENANCE: probably worshipped circa 750 AD until 1500 AD and known from tradition in the Florentine and other pre-Columbian codices and detail on stone carvings.

There are many myths picturing the disappearance from the pantheon of the god Quetzalcoatl (the feathered serpent), who presided over the second of the five world ages. The method of his going also varies in that in some myths he goes east and burns himself to death. His heart survives and ascends to heaven as the morning star. This myth accounts his journey to Tlapallan, where he is to discover his destiny. It is reported that when the conquistador Cortez invaded Mexico, the emperor Motecuhzoma believed him to be an incarnation of Quetzalcoatl.

At a place called Temacpalco, Quetzalcoatl, tired and dispirited, supports himself on a rock and his hands sink in to the surface as if it were mud, leaving imprints. He gets up and journeys to Tepanoayan, where he reaches a broad river, laying down stones to make a bridge before crossing over. Onward he travels to Cooapan, where demons obstruct his path, demanding to know where he has come from and where he is going. They also wish to know who will perform the penances.

Quetzalcoatl responds that the demons cannot stop him and that he is going to Tlapellan to learn his fate. He tells them that the sun (Ehecatl) is calling him.

The demons agree that Quetzalcoatl should travel onwards, but they steal all his possessions from him. Only his jewels does he save and these he scatters in the river waters so that they are swept away. Quetzalcoatl still journeys, this time to a place where he is confronted by another demon who asks him the same questions and receives the same answers. The demon offers him a potion of *pulque*, which Quetzalcoatl drinks and falls asleep. When he awakens he tidies his hair and names the place Cochtocan.

He climbs the mountains between Popocatepetl and Iztactepetl accompanied by an army of dwarfs and hunchbacks, most of whom freeze to death. At this Quetzalcoatl weeps, but he sees in the distance another mountain, Poyanhtecatl. Again he sets off, naming villages along the way. He reaches the coast where he makes a raft of serpents and boards it. He is swept out on the current and, at last, he arrives at Tlapellan.

TELEPINU, THE MISSING GOD

CULTURE OF ORIGIN: Hattic and Hittite-Hurrian – Anatolian

PROVENANCE: cuneiform text derived from an oral tradition and discovered on a tablet at the site of Boghazkoy in Turkey [Ref. KUB xvii. 10 translated by Albrecht Goetze (*Ancient Near Eastern Texts* ed. J.B. Pritchard)].

This myth is not strictly a death and resurrection story, but it parallels the standard Mesopotamian accounts of the demise and regenesis of nature and there can be little doubt that it was recited during ritual celebrations. The name Telepinu first emerges in literature circa 1800 BC and, though carried into the Hittite-Hurrian pantheon, is of Hattic origin.

Telepinu, the god of fertility and vegetation, flies into a rage so great that he puts his shoes on the wrong feet and ceases to attend to his duties. Mist swirls about the windows and smoke fills the house because the logs no longer burn properly. Sheep and cattle become barren in the fields. Unpacified, Telepinu goes away to the steppes of Asia, taking the fecundity of nature with him so that the crops fail, the soil becomes sterile and famine settles on the land. Far from home the fertility god becomes lost and falls into an exhausted sleep.

Meanwhile, the crisis of nature deepens and the sun god arranges an emergency meeting for the thousand gods of Hatti. They start to eat and drink, but the meagre supply of rations is insufficient to satisfy their hunger and thirst. Telepinu has taken every good thing with him and his father Tešub, the storm god, voices an increasing anxiety about his son's angry disappearance. When the gods decide that Telepinu must be found, the sun god dispatches an eagle to search the mountains, but it returns without success. Next Tešub seeks the advice of the great mother goddess, Hannahanna, but she tells him to go and look for his son himself. Tešub accordingly sets out in search. He knocks on the gates of Telepinu's city and breaks them open, but the fertility god is not there. (See also the *Canticus Canticorum*, page 207.)

Hannahanna decides to send out a bee, a solution regarding which Tešub expresses some scepticism, but the goddess tells the bee that when it finds Telepinu it is to sting him awake and smear upon him the wax of purification. The bee searches far and wide, using up all its honey and wax, but eventually it finds Telepinu asleep in a meadow. As instructed it stings the sleeper, who awakens to an even worse temper than before. In his febrile state he dries up springs, diverts rivers, blocks clay pits and demolishes houses so that still more of life perishes.

The gods are at a loss to know what to do until the sun god instructs Kamrusepa, the goddess of healing, to pacify Telepinu and bring him back. When, finally, he returns to a more agreeable frame of mind and follows Kamrusepa home, a pillar is erected in his honour decked with the skin of a sheep to signify the fat of the land and the progeny for which Telepinu must take responsibility during the coming season.

YAMA AND YAMI

CULTURE OF ORIGIN: Vedic Hindu [India]

PROVENANCE: the first significant reference comes from the *Rg Veda* collection of 1028 hymns (Vedas), composed in Sanskrit and dating from circa 1200 BC, but based on an oral tradition which was in circulation among the Aryan immigrants to the subcontinent circa 1700–700 BC. Used as a hymn of praise at the time of religious sacrifice, this myth of Yama would be chanted during funeral rites to assist a deceased person on his journey to the otherworld. A more extended version of how Yama becomes ruler of the dead appears in the *Markandeya Purana*, composed circa 250 AD.

The god of death, Yama, was once a mortal man, the son of Vivasvan (Surya), the sun god. He was the first human being to discover and walk the paths to the heavenly otherworld so that others might safely follow. In the Vedic hymns Yama is invited to sit upon the sacred grass with the priests and to partake of the funeral sacrifice, including the sacred *soma* drink. The dead man is encouraged to go forth on the ancient paths and to unite with Yama, while demons are commanded to keep away. The deceased must pass between Yama's pair of four-eyed hounds who will watch over him until he reaches the highest heaven and meets with Yama and the guardian god, Varuna. Finally an oblation of butter and honey is offered to Yama.

In the Puranic myth Vivasvan has three godly children with his wife Saranyu. They include Manu and the twins Yama and Yami (also called Yamuna). So great is Vivasvan's burning energy, however, that Saranyu can bear it no longer and she goes away, leaving behind her shadow to foster the children. She lives in her father's house until he chastises her and sends her away; she then takes to asceticism in the form of a mare living in a remote part of the country.

The shadow does not extend the same affection to the children and Yama becomes very unhappy. He threatens the shadow, who promptly curses him. Yama, with his brother Manu, reports to his father what has taken place, telling Vivasvan that the shadow is very different in temperament and affection from his real mother. The sun god goes to the shadow of Saranyu and vents his anger, but when he visits his father-in-law, Visvakarman, the architect of the gods, Visvakarman points out that Vivasvan's energy is so great that no woman will be able to withstand it for long. Visvakarman reminds his son-in-law that Saranyu is practising asceticism in the wilderness and

Vivasvan is persuaded to place his burning orb on a lathe so that fifteen parts of its energy can be cut away. With these are made the holiest weapons of the other great gods. His energy lessened, Vivasvan becomes more approachable and takes on a new aspect, Martanda.

Discovering the whereabouts of his wife in her ascetic guise of a mare, Martanda takes the form of a stallion. Reluctant for sexual encounter she turns to face him, but as their noses touch she is imbued with his latent energy and conceives the twin horse gods, the Asvins. She also bears to Martanda the god of hunters, Revanta.

Vivasvan reveals his true form and Saranyu returns home with him, casting off her equestrian guise.

NOTE: according to some mythical sources Yami is not merely the twin sister of Yama, but also becomes his wife.

11

Myths of Immortality

This section of myths appears subtly distinct from that with the heading *Myths of Death and Afterlife*, since it specifically addresses the interest in immortality and its various elusive elixirs. The Chinese developed the idea of longevity being achieved through consumption of an esoteric fruit, the so-called Peaches of Immortality, although this romantic idea is closely linked with the notion that the boon of immortality can be won by perfecting one's earthly life.

Outside of Chinese Daoism, eternal life seems to prove impossible unless one is lucky enough to be transformed into a god or goddess. The Christian tradition argues that Jesus Christ and the Virgin Mary at different times ascended bodily into heaven, but elsewhere mortal beings have searched less successfully to break free from the bonds of finite mortal existence and the inevitable decline into old age. The best known saga concerning the quest for immortality is that of the Mesopotamian hero Gilgameš. His endeavours are typical in that he comes close to retaining the precious elixir, but each time it slips away from his grasp. It is as if the human mind has accepted the certainty that, even in the context of the wildest romance, death must surely follow birth.

ADAPA

CULTURE OF ORIGIN: Mesopotamian – Akkadian, probably derived from a Sumerian source

PROVENANCE: one of the less prominent of the Mesopotamian stories which recount the frustrated search for eternal life or potency, the myth of Adapa is known from two fragmentary tablet sources. Parts were discovered at Tell el-Amarna in Egypt (dating from the fifteenth or fourteenth century

BC) and also at Aššur, the Assyrian capital (late in the second millennium BC). Neither version is complete and it is difficult to assess the overall length of the work, but it is thought to be of about 120 lines, originally inscribed on two sides of a single tablet.

Adapa is not a deity, but the priest of the god Ea and the first of seven legendary sages who populated the earth before the great flood. According to tradition Ea endowed him with the boon of wisdom and gave him responsibility for introducing civilization and the proper rites of religious observance to mankind. Ea, the god of the primeval ocean, evolved in the Akkadian pantheon from the Sumerian god of wisdom, Enki, and was recognized as the tutelary deity of Eridu, by tradition the earliest Mesopotamian city. Its archaeological site lies in the marshy delta region of what is now southern Iraq at the head of the Arabian Gulf.

See also *Etana*, page 86, and *Gilgameš*, page 252.

Adapa spends a part of each day assisting in the baking of bread for the city and in catching fish at sea. One day the god Ea creates a storm and sinks Adapa's small boat, at which Adapa curses the wind and it is broken for seven days. The gods call him to task but, in an effort to assuage their anger, Ea makes Adapa dress in sombre clothes and wear his hair unkempt. Adapa's explanation is that he is in mourning for the gods Dumuzi and Ningis Zi Da (Giszida) who have disappeared from the earth (see *Inana's Descent into the Underworld and the Death of Dumuzi*, page 233).

When Adapa presents himself before the assembly of great gods he is offered the food and water of eternal life but, on Ea's instruction, he refuses these boons and is thus returned to the earth.

The meaning of the myth is ambiguous. In effect Adapa loses the opportunity, as do the other six sages who follow him, to seize eternal life. Possibly Ea tricked him out of the chance of immortality by instructing him to refuse the food and water of life, or alternatively Ea genuinely tried to guide him towards immortality, but the plan failed for some other reason. Perhaps the great gods were determined to punish Adapa for cursing the wind, or perhaps they felt slighted that he had contravened the laws of hospitality by refusing the celestial fare. In any event this myth bears a striking similarity to several others among Mesopotamian literature where mortal beings strive for the elixir only to lose it through some twist of fate.

AGNI

CULTURE OF ORIGIN: Vedic Hindu [India]
PROVENANCE: the *Rg Veda* collection of 1028 hymns (Vedas) composed, in Sanskrit and based on an oral tradition which was in circulation among the Aryan immigrants to the subcontinent circa 1700–700 BC. These hymns

were chanted at times of sacrifice. In subsequent Puranic literature the *Brhaddevata* arranges the hymnic dialogues into a more coherent narrative and the epic *Mahabharata* also contains a version.

Since, in Hindu philosophy, there is a conjunction between fire and water, Agni is identified as the apotheosis of fire but also as the 'Child of the Waters' (Apam Napat) who appears as lightning riven from the rain clouds. His home is deep in the primeval sea surrounded by minor female horse goddesses. Agni bears particular significance in Hindu ritual since it is he who carries the sacrificial offerings to all the gods.

The story is essentially one of death and resurrection to an immortal existence, the basis of the Indo–European concept of the phoenix, a bird which carries fire, the elixir of immortality, as it rekindles itself from ashes.

The brothers of Agni have suffered death running back and forth and carrying the oblation of fire in the service of the gods. Agni becomes fearful of a similar fate, so he flees from the other deities and hides in the primeval waters whence he was born (in later texts he enters the seasons, the waters and the trees and he is betrayed by a fish, which he promptly curses, warning that henceforth it will be killed whenever the fancy takes mankind). When Agni vanishes, however, a crisis descends on the pant'eon because the sacrificial fire is extinguished.

> *'I fled in fear of the task of the oblation-giver. I went in fear that the gods would harness me to the task, O Varuna. I went into various places; I, Agni, have ceased to consider the task.'*

The god Varuna (in some versions accompanied by Yama) discovers Agni inside the body of the demonic god of chaos, Vrtra, and entreats him to return; he also provides a discourse on the dangers of birth and life, since these experiences also involve old age and death. Agni asks for the boon of longevity (effectively that of immortality) and to this the gods accede. It is left to the weather god, Indra, to coax Agni back from his hiding place. He has secreted himself there with Varuna, a guardian deity associated with water, and with Soma, the deification of the sacred drink that bears his name. Agni returns and Vrtra is slain.

> *'Come, O Agni, to our sacrifice that has five roads, three layers and seven threads. Bear our oblation and go before us. For too long you have lain in darkness.'*

In the *Mahabharata* version Agni flees because he fears having to carry the seed of the god Šiva.

The myth is paralleled, obscurely, by a human tradition which offers inferences of the birth of a hidden child mingled with the rekindling of the sacred fire: having quarrelled with his king over the death of a male child, a priest leaves the kingdom and all the fires become cold. He eventually returns but blames the king's consort for hiding the fire. He swears an oath of truth and when the fire returns it burns the queen.

BA XIAN (PA HSIEN)
(The Eight Immortals)

CULTURE OF ORIGIN: Chinese Daoist (Taoist)
PROVENANCE: recorded in various texts and art from oral traditions.

Generally speaking an immortal or Xian (Hsien) is a Daoist devotee who has gained immortality either through an exemplary lifestyle or by learning the recipe for extracting the elixir of eternal life from the Peaches of Immortality. It is uncertain why the eight figures of the Ba Xian and their stories are grouped collectively. Three are apparently historical figures in as much as they are given dates and places identifying mortal existence on earth, though the implication is that all achieved immortality through their exemplary lifestyles. Each is from a different period, none lived contemporaneously, and frequently the myths surrounding them contain anachronistic elements. All are said to have gone to the island of Peng-lai (P'eng Lai), the easterly of the two paradise lands to which all earthly souls are destined. The first known reference to the Ba Xian dates from the Yuan (Mongol) Dynasty (AD 1260–1368).

It should be noted that the anglicized equivalents of Chinese characters vary considerably in transliteration. The official Chinese Pinyin system is applied here, followed, where appropriate, in brackets, by the more generally encountered Wade-Giles system.

Han Xiang-Zhi (Han Hsiang-tzu) is said to have lived during the ninth century AD, studying under the tutelage of the Tang philosopher Han Yu. When Han Yu is exiled to Guangzhou (Canton) for his religious and political differences with the Emperor Xien Jung (Hsien Tsung), Han Xiang-Zhi accompanies him, correctly predicting that the philosopher will in course of time be restored to office. Han Xiang-Zhi becomes a disciple of Lu Dong Pin (Lu Tung-pin), who guides him to the top of the Sacred Peach Tree, symbol of longevity, from whose branches he plunges into immortality.

He Xian-Ku (Ho Hsien-ku), said to have been born in Guangzhou during the Tang Dynasty in the reign of Empress Wu (AD 684–705), is the only female among the Eight Immortals and following her apotheosis she became the tutelary goddess of housewives. She is the daughter of Ho Tai and foster mother of Tai Sui, the god of astrology and time. She dreams that she must travel to the Mother of Pearl Mountains where she will obtain immortality. Following mystical instructions she finds a certain semi-precious stone, grinds it into a powder and swallows it to achieve eternal life.

Kao Kuo-Zhu (T'sao Kuo-chiu) is the brother of the Empress Kao, who reigned with Jen Jung (Jen Tsung) (AD 1023–1064). His story begins when, as a student, he is travelling with his beautiful young wife to sit his examinations in the capital. He is invited to stay at the house of Zhing-ji (Ching-chi), the Empress's younger brother, but Zhing-ji slays Kao Kuo-Zhu and tries to seduce his wife. When she refuses his advances he has her thrown into gaol. The shade of the murdered student appears and demands retribution and, to remove traces of guilt, Kao Kuo-Zhu now advises his younger sibling to have the girl thrown down a well. She escapes death and, not knowing the extent of her enemies, complains to Kao Kuo-Zhu about her treatment. He has her beaten and left for dead, but again she recovers and this time she takes her complaint to the Imperial Censor. He orders the execution of Zhing-ji but the Emperor extends an amnesty to Kao Kuo-Zhu. The latter goes away to lead a reclusive life in the mountains where he meets two other immortals, Zhong-Li Kuan and Lu Dong-Pin, who teach him the way to achieve self-perfection.

Lan Kai-He (Lan Ts'ai-ho) has a certain sexual ambiguity, being sometimes depicted in one gender and sometimes another. He (or she) wears ragged clothes and wanders the land as an itinerant beggar, earning money by singing and beating time with a stick. One day in a drunken stupor he is carried to heaven on a cloud, leaving his tattered garments behind. After his apotheosis he becomes a guardian deity of the poor and needy.

Li Thieh-Kuai (T'ieh-kuai Li) is the guardian god of the sick and infirm. His name means 'he with the iron crutch' and at least two differing stories account for this epithet. In one version, where he is known as Li Ning-Yang, he is instructed in the way to perfection under the tutelage of the shade of Lao-Kze, the founder of Taoism and one of the three San Ching deities whose images repose in every Taoist shrine. When the time comes for Li Ning-Yang to rise to heaven he instructs his student Lang Ling to cremate his mortal body if he fails to return to it within seven days. On the sixth day, however, Lang Ling finds that his mother is dying, so he cremates his teacher's corpse prematurely before going to her bedside. Li Ning-Yang returns to discover that his remains have disappeared, so he takes the body of a deceased mendicant instead. The body is deformed, however, and Li Ning-Yang is obliged to rely on an iron crutch for support.

An alternative version of the myth tells how the goddess of the Western Paradise, Xi Wang Mu (Hsi Wang Mu), gives Li Thieh-Kuai an iron crutch when he falls lame from an ulcerated leg.

Lu Dong-Pin (Lu Tung-pin, or Lu Yen) is said to have been born in Shansi in AD 755, the son of the governor of Hai Chou, during the Tang Dynasty (AD 618–906) and to have studied in Xi'an (Chang'an).

He became the patron deity of scholars. At Xi'an he meets with the immortal Zhong-Li Kuan, who is warming rice wine at an inn. While sleeping Lu Dong-Pin experiences a vision-like dream of the rest of his life in which he perceives that he is to rise to a position of considerable influence before being disgraced and exiled, and his family executed. It is this prophetic dream which makes him turn to Zhong-Li Kuan as a tutor in the search for perfection.

Zhang Kuo-Lao (Chang-kuo Lao) is also said to have been born at Shansi in the seventh century AD and to have become a hermit at Ping-Yang. According to tradition he died at the age of more than a hundred and, when his grave was opened subsequently, it was found to be empty. He is called to the court of Empress Wu, but collapses and seemingly dies on the steps of a temple. The body begins to decompose, but is then miraculously restored and Zhang Kuo-Lao retreats to a contemplative life in the mountains, travelling on a donkey which folds away like a map.

Zhong-Li Kuan (Chung-li Ch'uan) is said to have been born in Shensi and to have achieved the status of Marshal of the Empire in 21 BC, following which he retired to a contemplative life as a hermit. He possesses the power of alchemy, turning base metals into silver which he distributes to the poor. He learns the secrets of immortality when the wall of his hermit's cave splits, revealing a fissure in which rests a jade casket containing the formula. He then flies to Peng-Lai on the back of a stork.

GILGAMEŠ AND THE HALUB TREE

CULTURE OF ORIGIN: Mesopotamian – Sumerian

PROVENANCE: unknown, though it almost certainly dates back to pre-literate times when it would have been related and preserved as part of an oral tradition perhaps more than 5000 years old. The text of part of the myth has been known for many decades under the title *Gilgameš, Enkidu and the Netherworld*, since it constitutes the Akkadian text contained on the final Tablet XII of the Babylonian *Epic of Gilgameš* (see page 179). The material was for a long period considered enigmatic since it did not seem to tie in with the other eleven texts making up the Babylonian epic. In 1939, however, a broken prism from the diggings at Ur and inscribed in Sumerian cuneiform was translated and found to contain parts of a hitherto unknown poetic myth. Other fragments apparently belonging to the same story had been located at Ur and Nippur and in recent years the full extent of this epic narrative has been pieced together. The Akkadian section is now known to constitute only its final 'chapter'. The Ur fragments are tentatively dated to about 2000 BC, but are probably copies of an earlier written original.

The first six lines are unintelligible, but the story opens with a scene-setting prologue of creation mythology, typical of many Sumerian myths:

After heaven had moved away from earth,
After earth had been separated from heaven
After the name of mankind had been fixed
After An had carried off unto himself the heaven
After Enlil had carried off unto himself the earth,
After Ereškigal had been presented to the nether world, etc.

The text continues in this vein for some twenty-five lines to establish the era in which the action takes place. Then it introduces the first main theme, that of the halub tree. We are told a sapling has grown on the banks of the Euphrates until a mighty storm uproots it and carries it off on the flood waters. The goddess of fertility, Inana (Ištar), discovers the sapling and takes it to her garden in Uruk, where she plants and tends it as it grows towards full stature. There follows an enigmatic statement:

'When at last shall I have a holy throne that I may sit on it?' concerning it, she said.
'When at last shall I have a holy bed that I may lie on it?' concerning it, she said.
The tree grew large, but she could not cut off its bark.
At its base the snake who knows no charm had set itself up a nest.
In its crown the Imdugud bird had placed its young.
In its midst Lilith had built for herself a house.
The ever shouting maid, the rejoicer of all hearts,
The pure Inana, how she weeps.

The Imdugud bird referred to is a mythical bringer of mischief and Lilith is the demonic Sumerian goddess of desolation. In other words the halub tree is infested with harbingers of devastation in the natural world.

The hero Gilgameš appears on the scene wearing his armour and wielding his mighty axe. He attacks the Imdugud bird and the snake causing them to abandon the tree, and he despatches Lilith to the desert wastes. Gilgameš now hands over the restored tree to Inana, so that she may have her throne and her bed, having first removed part of the crown and the base of the tree for himself. From these pieces he fashions what are arguably a sacred drum and drumsticks, the *pukku* and *mikku*. The section may be a pictorial allegory implying that the tree is the living symbol of Inana's presence on earth, and that the portions taken by Gilgameš are in pursuit of his obsession with finding the secret elixir of eternal life – a drum and drumsticks often being of deep religious and talismanic significance (see also the *Epic of Gilgameš*, page 179). It is worth noting that in the myth of *Etana of Kiš* (see page 86), the king is encouraged by the eagle to visit Inana in order to secure the plant that will give his wife the boon of fertility.

NOTE: the text contained in Tablet XII of the Babylonian epic of Gilgameš fits into the Sumerian story at this point.

HUAI NAN TZU
(The Apotheosis of Liu An)

CULTURE OF ORIGIN: Chinese Daoist (Taoist)
PROVENANCE: recorded in various texts and art from oral traditions, but known chiefly from the *Shen-Xian Tung Zhien* (the Complete Mirror of Spirits and Genie).

Myths whose keynote is the search for the secrets of eternal life are legion in China and parallel those of many other cultures. Daoist philosophy argues, in essence, that there are two routes to immortality, either through an exemplary lifestyle on earth, or by learning how to distil the elixir from the celestial Peaches of Immortality. Since most deities in Buddhist and Daoist belief were once historical figures living on earth who subsequently received apotheosis, the route to immortality is of considerable significance. This myth, which involves the celebrated Eight Immortals of Daoist belief (see *Ba Xian*, page 250), is typical of the latter route and is set some time during the second century BC at the start of the Han Dynasty.

It should be noted that the anglicized equivalents of Chinese characters vary considerably in transliteration. The official Chinese Pinyin system is applied here, followed, where appropriate, in brackets, by the more generally encountered Wade-Giles system.

A young man, who announces himself as Wang Zhung-Kao, appears according to tradition before successive generations of the ruling classes, advising them that he is at least two thousand years old and is teaching the arts of immortality through his students. Shortly after he has made his appearance before one such local overlord, Liu An, eight elderly gentlemen arrive at his palace requesting an audience. Liu An refuses to see them unless they can offer him the boon of immortality, upon which they are transformed into youths and reveal themselves as the Eight Immortals. The ruler is informed of this miracle and insists that they are brought to him. They are, of course, students of Wang Zhung-Kao and they proceed to instruct Liu An in the arts of immortality.

Meanwhile Liu Zhien, the ruler's son, becomes involved in a duel with a rival, Lei Bei (Lei Pei), who manages to injure him. Fearing recrimination Lei Bei circulates rumours that Liu An and his brother, the ruler of a neighbouring fiefdom, are plotting treason against the

Emperor, Wu Di. The brother hangs himself, but the Eight Immortals persuade Liu An to follow them to the Eastern Paradise and to the court of Yu Huang Shang Di, the Jade Emperor. Liu An at first displays some arrogance before Yu Ti and is almost sent back to a carnate existence. The Eight Immortals plead, however, on his behalf and persuade him to adopt a humble attitude. He thus changes his name to Huai Nan Tzu (the Thinker of South Huai) and his brother is restored to life.

IDUNN AND THE APPLES OF IMMORTALITY

CULTURE OF ORIGIN: Teutonic – Nordic (Icelandic)
PROVENANCE: the *Prose Edda* (Codex Wormianus), composed by the Icelandic scholar Snorri Sturluson between 1178 and 1241 AD and dispatched in the seventeenth century by the historian Arngrimur Jonsson to a colleague in Denmark, Ole Worm.

The content is, effectively, a textbook, the first part of which is titled *Gylfaginning* (The Tricking of Gylfi) and constitutes an overview of Nordic mythology. It is worth comparing the concepts of this myth with those in Chinese mythology which describe the Peaches of Immortality owned by the Jade Emperor (see *Ba Xian*, page 250).

Three of the Aesir gods – Othin, Loki and Hoenir – attempt to roast an ox while on their travels, but they are unable to cook it properly. The giant Thiassi, disguised as an eagle, offers to have the meat properly served, providing they give him a portion as recompense. It transpires that the eagle demands the greater part of the ox, so Loki beats him with a stick for his temerity. The eagle seizes Loki and carries him aloft, refusing to let him go unless the goddess Idunn is presented to him with her apples of immortality. To this condition Loki agrees and, once released, he lures Idunn into the eagle's clutches.

The gods, prevented from eating their daily ration of apples, begin to grow old and eventually they learn of Loki's duplicity. They threaten to kill him unless he puts matters right, so he goes in search of Idunn. When he discovers her whereabouts he rescues her and brings her back to Asgarth with Thiassi in hot pursuit, still in the guise of the eagle.

The gods light a huge bonfire which burns the bird's wings and he falls to earth, where he is promptly slaughtered. It is his daughter Skadi who seeks revenge and the gods offer her the hand of one of their number in marriage as compensation. The identity of the bridegroom is concealed from her, though, until the final moments and she believes she is being wed to Balder. In fact her intended husband is Njord, the god of the sea, who is of less exalted pedigree: he was originally a Vanir god who was handed over to the gods of Aesir as a hostage during the war between the two godly races and became a pledge of truce between them.

NOTE: Richard Wagner used this incident as a major strand of the prologue to his Ring Cycle, *Das Rhinegold*. In his version two giants are called upon to build the fortress of Valholl. When Othin refuses to pay them for their work, they seize Freya in compensation and refuse to return her until the gods provide enough gold. It is their desperate theft of this ransom from Alberich as they begin to age, and his subsequent curse, which trigger the fatal chain of events that terminate in the *Götterdammerung*.

XI WANG MU (HSI WANG MU) AND HOU I

CULTURE OF ORIGIN: Chinese Daoist (Taoist)

PROVENANCE: recorded in various texts and art from oral traditions. One of the earliest is the *History of the Zhou Dynasty* (second century BC), which was probably compiled from earlier, but lost, written sources. Some of the detail surrounding the goddess, including the Peaches of Immortality, was committed to writing by the fifth century philosopher Lieh-Tzu.

It should be noted that the anglicized equivalents of Chinese characters vary considerably in transliteration. The official Chinese Pinyin system is applied here, followed, where appropriate, in brackets, by the more generally encountered Wade-Giles system.

Xi Wang Mu (Hsi Wang Mu) is a goddess, probably based on a historical queen somewhere in the west of China, who governs the length of mortal life and who may give the blessing of longevity. Represented by birds, both the mythical phoenix and the less exotic crane, she lives in a palace of pure gold ornamented with precious stones and with walls 333 miles in circumference. Her consort is Dung Wang Kung (Tung Wang Kung) with whom she has nine sons among twenty-four children. Tradition has it that she met with, and gave an audience to, the fifth ruler of the Zhou (Chou) Dynasty in 985 BC at the Lake of Jewels [location unknown] which lies adjacent to her palace. There she grows the Peaches of Immortality, each of which takes three thousand years to form and another three thousand years to ripen, at which time she celebrates her birthday by eating one of the peaches.

The heavenly archer, Hou I, who has shot nine of the ten suns from the sky, builds Xi Wang Mu a jade palace in the Western Heaven and when his task is complete she rewards him with a elixir, which glows with an unearthly light, and which is made from the Peaches of

Immortality. She instructs Hou I, however, to refrain from taking the potion until he has fasted for a year, so he hides it in the roof of his house. One day his wife discovers it. As soon as she has swallowed the potion, she feels herself float off the ground and through the window of the house. Angry, Hou I tries to follow her but she flies so far and so fast that she reaches the moon. There she turns into a three-legged toad and, beneath a cassia tree, meets a hare who has found another source of the elixir of life.

12

Myths of the Otherworld

Most cultures perceive the underworld or otherworld as a gloomy place to which the soul journeys after death, either directly or via an intermediate purgatory, and the journey itself is regarded as being full of pitfalls to trap or hinder those whose earthly lives have been found wanting. It is in this belief that death heralds a journey into the unknown that many societies provide their dead with the food and weapons needed to protect and sustain them on their final odyssey.

Generally speaking, once a soul has entered the otherworld it may not leave, particularly if it has been persuaded to consume the food of death. Thus Persephone may not return to her mother Demeter once she has eaten the pomegranate seeds offered to her by Hades. Even a deity consigned to the otherworld kingdom is trapped forever unless a special arrangement for release can be reached. Thus the goddess Inana, having been slain by the otherworld queen Ereškigal, may only return to the upper realms if a substitute is left behind in the form of her consort Dumuzi. Conversely, the ruler of the otherworld is unlikely to be able to leave it at any time except to snatch unwatchful victims at the interface between the worlds of the living and the dead.

This difficulty of movement between the upper and lower worlds creates problems of communication, for which reason messengers have to be employed who are provided with immunity from the perils of the other-world and death. In Greek mythology the god Hermes seems able to travel without consequence between the kingdom of Hades and the upper world of the living. Likewise the minor figure of Kakka in Mesopotamian myth travels freely between the kingdoms of the gods and of Ereškigal.

Otherworld deities are, despite their intimidating aura, attributed with normal human feelings and, in particular, those of sexuality. Hades thus needs the company of the beautiful Persephone as his queen, and Ereškigal demands the lusty services of the amorous Nergal.

On a separate note the route taken by the sun at night is often seen to pass through the realms of the otherworld. This concept is typified by the nocturnal journey of the Egyptian creator god Re. (See also *Myths of Death and Afterlife*.)

THE HORSE OF ABARTA

CULTURE OF ORIGIN: Celtic – Irish
PROVENANCE: recorded from oral traditions in the Fenian or Ossianic Cycle of myths which first appeared as a complete 'volume' in the manuscript known as *Acallm na Senorachul* (twelfth century). The central character, Abarta, is less a villain than a mischievous prankster.

Abarta, one of the Tuatha de Danaan (the Irish otherworld pantheon) and the attendant of Fionn Mac Cumhail of the Fianna (the royal guard of the early kings of Ireland) decides that by deception he will capture some of Fionn's forces. He brings his master an unruly grey horse which promptly attacks the horses of other guards. As many as fourteen soldiers, including one of their most formidable officers, Conan Mac Morna, attempt to control the beast and Abarta himself jumps on at the rear. The horse gallops off, exactly as Abarta has predicted, with many other retainers hanging on to its tail. It makes its way straight back to the otherworld with Abarta and his unwitting captives.

Meanwhile Fionn employs resources of his own. He commissions the craftsman Faruach, son of the king of Innia, to build a ship (which he does by striking three massive blows with his axe). Faruach's brother, Foltor, is also commandeered, since he has the magical ability to track anything which moves on land or sea. They follow Abarta to the otherworld and confront him. He agrees to release the prisoners, but Conan demands compensation by way of fourteen of Abarta's retainers, with Abarta himself hanging on to the horse's tail. Abarta feels obliged to comply in order to restore peace and good will.

BALDR'S DRAUMAR
(The Dreams of Balder)

CULTURE OF ORIGIN: Teutonic – Nordic and Germanic (Icelandic)
PROVENANCE: the *Codex Arnamagnaeanus* No. 544 (*Hauksbok*) [Copenhagen University].

Balder is the ill-fated god of Nordic mythology whose death presages the day of doom, Ragnarok. He cannot be compared directly with the dying-and-rising god images of Near Eastern mythology, since Nordic texts make no mention of a resurrection process.

The Aesir gods of Asgarth meet in their assembly, the Thing, to discuss the portent of Balder's dreams which seem to intimate his own doom. Othin mounts his magical eight-legged horse, Sleipnir, and rides towards the underworld of Hel. On the path he is confronted by a hound, its mask red with blood, but he avoids it and rides on until he approaches the eastern gate of Hel's realm. There he is met by a seeress who demands to know who it is that has awoken her from her sleep.

Othin identifies himself only as the Wayfarer and asks for whom Hel's hall has been decked out in lavish readiness.

The seeress replies that it is laid for Balder, Othin's favourite son.

'It is for Balder that the ale is brewed;
covered with protecting shield.
The sons of Othin are lost in their sorrow
and I was loath to speak, so let me end.'

Othin asks who the slayer of Balder will be and the seeress names Hoder, the blind god. Othin then asks who will avenge Balder and she replies that the god Vali will slay Hoder on the appointed day. There follows an obscure verse which speaks of girls waving their handkerchiefs in grief. This is thought to be a reference to the white-capped waves of the sea across which the ship of death will carry Balder's corpse.

At this juncture the seeress challenges the god that he is not a Wanderer but Othin. She tells him to go home because no further spells will raise her from her sleep until the day of doom when Loki's terrible offspring, the wolf Fenrir, is loosed from his chains to run amok.

NOTE: for a more comprehensive account of Nordic cosmogony see *Voluspa*, page 122.

DI YU and YEN LO
(The Earth Prison and its Judge)

CULTURE OF ORIGIN: Chinese Daoist (Taoist)
PROVENANCE: recorded in various texts and art from oral traditions.

The concept of the otherworld to which human souls travel after death is a complex one in Chinese belief. It involves the separation of the *po* (the life force of the mortal body) from the *hun* (the conscious soul), which may or may not reach the heavenly paradise. The *po* is believed to stay with the body for some time, eventually leaving it for a kind of purgatory. For this purpose it needs proper provisions, which is why traditional Chinese funerals are accompanied by the burning of paper models of houses, clothes, weapons and anything else the deceased might need to add to his comfort in the next world.

The otherworld is ruled by a supreme deity, Di-Kang Wang (Ti Tsang Wang), the King of the Earth Womb. Tradition has it that he lived a mortal life as a Buddhist monk during the Tang Dynasty (AD 618–906), died at the age of ninety-nine while seated in his coffin, following which his remains refused to decompose. He was then deified into his present role. Subservient to him are various figures, including Yen-Wang, the terrible Judge of the Dead, based approximately on the Hindu god Yama and depicted as a demonic figure with a green face and wearing crimson robes. The underworld staffing also includes the demons Ma Mien (Horse Face), Niu Tou (Ox Head) and the Wu-Zhang Guei (Ghosts of Impermanence), a pair of underworld messengers – Yang Wu-Zhang, who collects the younger deceased, and Yin Wu-Zhang, who collects all over the age of fifty. The following myth is one of many, sometimes of confusing or contradictory doctrine, which pervade Daoist belief.

It should be noted that the anglicized equivalents of Chinese characters vary considerably in transliteration. The official Chinese Pinyin system is applied here, followed, where appropriate, in brackets, by the more generally encountered Wade-Giles system.

When a person dies he or she sets out on a journey full of perils, obstacles and, for those who have led corrupt lives, an assortment of tortures with varying degrees of severity. At the entrance to the underworld demons attack the soul unless money is paid. It then passes into the hall where it is weighed in the scales of judgement. Souls which are light and free from the burden of guilt pass through unharmed, but those which are heavy are beaten again. The soul is now confronted by hounds which are able to distinguish the good from the bad and which respond appropriately. In the fourth stage of passage to the infernal regions the soul is allowed to look into a mirror of the future and see what it will become in the next incarnation. Then it is led to a vantage point where it may look back at those it has left behind and ponder on its earthly failings. The sixth ordeal is a bridge spanning a terrifying chasm. The good pass across a wide aisle fashioned in silver and gold, the evil must negotiate a path only an inch wide.

The soul has now almost reached the end of its journey and it enters the Wheel of the Law. When it is spun out of the wheel it is in the form it will take for its next incarnation. Finally it receives a drink which obliterates all memory of what has gone before.

EMMA O

CULTURE OF ORIGIN: Japanese Buddhist
PROVENANCE: recorded in various texts and art from oral traditions and based largely on Buddhist teachings. Emma O, the lord of the dead, is derived from the Hindu Vedic god of death, Yama.

After death the soul sets out upon a long journey to the Yellow Springs, the home of Emma O, in the underworld kingdom of Yomi. To provide for the journey the dead are accompanied by food and money. During Bommatsuri, the Festival of the Dead (13-16 July), lanterns are also lit to guide them on their way. When the soul reaches the dried-up bed of the river of the dead, the Sanzu no Kawa, the old woman who controls the crossing, Sodzu Baba, must be paid to allow it permission to pass.

The soul eventually arrives in purgatory, Gakido, the so-called 'Demon Road', where it is judged by Emma O and pays for sins committed during life according to the Law of Buddha. Purgatory is the lowest point in the existence of the soul. The benign and merciful guardian goddess, Guan Yui (Kuan Yin), modelled on the *sakti* of the Buddhist *boddhisattva* Avalokitesvara, may intervene to exonerate and raise it to a peaceful and immortal afterlife. If the person has lived a good mortal life and made pilgrimage to the thirty-three shrines of Guan Yin scattered around Japan, this intercession is more likely. Even if they have sinned she may still act on their behalf, ameliorating their penance. For those who have been truly wicked there is only the prospect of Emma O, who tosses them into a vat of molten metal. Guan Yin once threatened to turn the underworld into a kind of paradise, but Emma O insisted that it remain a sober place, so she returned to earth.

Jizo, the benevolent male counterpart of Guan Yin, also plays a role in the protection of souls. He is modelled on the Buddhist *boddhisattva* Ksitigarbha (woman of the earth) and is the guardian of the grave-yards. His responsibility is to keep *oni* or evil spirits at bay. These are demonic creatures possessing three eyes, horns and talons. Jizo hides souls in his clothing to prevent the *oni* from seizing them. He also ministers to the spirits of the dead in purgatory, saving them from the worst excesses of Emma O.

Sometimes souls may wander, seeking rest. These spirits are perceived as fiery glowing spheres called Shito Dama.

KITAMBA AND THE DEATH OF MUHONGO

CULTURE OF ORIGIN: Kimbundu [Angola, south–west Africa]
PROVENANCE: recorded from an oral tradition.

The myth appears to have several messages. Firstly it reinforces the global understanding of mankind that ordinary mortals, even those who assume mythical dimensions, cannot return from the underworld once they have passed through its portals. It also offers a typically confused view of many shamanistic societies about the powers of tribal priests. Certain select individuals may travel between earthly, upper and lower realms as messengers, but even they are not immune from death. This resignation is tinged, however, with the equally universal optimism that out of death in the natural world comes regenesis of life.

King Kitamba's wife, Muhongo, has died. The distraught king directs a celebrated herbalist and shaman known as a *kimbanda* to intercede for her in the underworld. First the *kimbanda* collects medicinal plants in the forest and then lays himself on his own hearth. He instructs his sons to cover him with earth and his wife to sprinkle him each day with water. Thus interred, he discovers a subterranean pathway leading to the underworld. Following it he comes across the hut of the dead queen and greets her, pleading that she shall come back with him to the upper world where her husband mourns her loss. Muhongo replies, however, that, like all deceased, she is a now a servant of the ruler of the dead, Kalunga-Ngombe, and can never return to the land of the living.

The shaman's wife continues dutifully to water the mound of earth under which he lies and eventually she sees her husband's nose sprout through the soil like a courgette. She can see that he begins to breathe again, so she harvests him, like a big sweet potato.

NERGAL AND EREŠKIGAL

CULTURE OF ORIGIN: Mesopotamian – Akkadian

PROVENANCE: two contrasting versions of the myth are known. The earlier account, which takes the form of a précis, was discovered at Tell el-Amarna in Egypt and dates from the fifteenth or fourteenth century BC. The later version, extending to some 750 lines, was found separately at both Sultanepe near Harran in the north of Iraq and at Uruk (Warka). These tablets date from the Late Babylonian period, about the seventh century BC. Although the myth is probably of Sumerian origin no independent Sumerian version of the text has been discovered. It may, according to separate literary evidence, represent an attempt to syncretize certain Sumerian and Babylonian traditions. In a very early literary composition Nergal is also described as the Enlil of the Netherworld.

The exact message of the myth is unclear. Ostensibly it recounts the transition of rule in the underworld from a single figure, the goddess Ereškigal, to a pair of deities when she is joined in her realm by Nergal. He is one of the élite band of gods in underworld mythology who is apparently able to travel between the worlds of the living and the dead and this may possess some other significance which now escapes us.

In the Sultanepe and Uruk versions the gods, headed by Anu, prepare a banquet to which all the deities in the pantheon are invited. For one goddess, however, attendance is impossible. Ereškigal, queen of the underworld, is obliged to remain in her dark realm. So Anu, the god of heaven, sends his vizier, Kakka, to speak with her to the effect that since the other gods cannot descend to her, and she is unable to join them for the feast, the least courtesy he can extend is to send some food down to her:

'In your year you cannot come up to see us
And it is impossible for us to go down
In our months we cannot go down to see you.
Let your messenger come
And take from the table, let him accept a present for you.'

Kakka descends the stairway of heaven and is permitted through the seven gates of the underworld, thus gaining entry to the dark city of Erkalla where Ereškigal reigns. He respectfully delivers his message before the throne of the underworld goddess and suggests, following instructions from Anu, that she may care to send her own vizier, Namtar, to collect the gift of celestial fare. The goddess treats Kakka with appropriate civility, agrees to the suggestion and Namtar ascends to the upper world.

At this juncture Nergal, the god of war, the son of Enlil and Ninlil, destined to reign with Ereškigal as co-ruler of the underworld, enters the saga. For reasons which are not made clear he behaves in a cavalier manner to Kakka. This constitutes an indirect slight against Ereškigal which cannot go unanswered. Nergal is, therefore, commanded to descend and face her wrath. In anticipation of his fate, he proceeds on a journey the object of which seems to be the construction of a throne which he will carry with him to the underworld and which will enable him to escape its deathly embrace. In this he is directed by Ea, god of wisdom. Armed with his insurance Nergal descends to Erkalla and presents himself, clearly with some reluctance, to Ereškigal. She, however, far from turning her anger upon him, seduces him by arranging that he catches sight of her naked body in the bath. He responds in energetic fashion and the pair engage in sexual intercourse for seven days.

She went to her bath
And dressed herself in a fine dress
And allowed him to catch a glimpse of her body.
He gave in to his heart's desire to do what men and women do.
The two embraced each other
And went passionately to bed.

After the passion Nergal makes his escape back to the heavens but, in doing so, he compounds the insult since Ereškigal is now pregnant. Deeply offended, she implores the great gods to return Nergal to her side since without him she is defiled and unable to perform her royal duties. She threatens terrible retribution in which the dead will rise up and consume the living and, once more, she sends Namtar up to the heavens to arrest her errant lover.

Anu has little alternative but to take proper notice of the potential consequences of standing idly by and he allows Namtar to search the ranks of gods for Nergal. In due course of time Namtar discovers him and Anu directs his enforced return to the arms of Ereškigal.

The myth ends on a positive note because Nergal smashes his way through the seven gates with sudden virile enthusiasm, striking down keepers as he goes. He seizes Ereškigal in a fiery embrace once more, beds her for a further seven days and thus begins his eternal reign as her consort and lord of the underworld.

THE THUNDERER

CULTURE OF ORIGIN: native American – Chinook [Columbia River, north-western USA]

PROVENANCE: recorded from oral traditions. Principal sources include *Chinook Texts*. F. Boas. Bulletin 20, Bureau of American Ethnology. Washington, 1895.

This complex myth provides an excellent illustration of a folk story designed to ameliorate fears of the otherworld by providing a tale of heroes who challenge the spirit forces and emerge unscathed. Portraying the spirit world engaged in rather ludicrous activities reduces its terrors.

Four brothers hunt elk while a fifth, the youngest, remains reluctantly in the camp. One day the boy is frightened by a terrifying noise and the sight of a gigantic figure in the doorway demanding food. The boy provides meat, but discovers that the giant possesses an insatiable appetite, eating all the food in the house. When the older brothers return to the camp they throw the day's kill into the store but, on the following morning, all the food has gone and the giant demands to know what he is to eat next, since there are only skins left – and, of course, the five brothers!

The brothers realize that the giant means to eat them too, so they boil up the skins to keep him satisfied through the following night and escape through a hole in the wall of the house, leaving a hound on guard with instruction to send the giant off in the wrong direction. At dawn the giant awakens and asks the dog where the brothers have gone, but the dog only nods in the wrong direction. When the giant returns empty-handed the dog repeats its dumb gesture and the game goes on for some time until the giant chances to catch sight of the brothers. He runs after them and slaughters them one by one until only the youngest is left, fleeing towards a river on the far bank of which is a fisherman called Thunderer. When the boy pleads for his life, Thunderer agrees to row him over the river and sends him away to the safety of his hut. The giant arrives at the river bank demanding to cross and Thunderer agrees, but only if the giant will use him as a bridge and walk upon his body stretched over the water. Thunderer is worried that a man of such size will capsize his ferry. The giant misses the obvious ruse and steps out, but when he reaches the legs Thunderer spreads them and the giant is swept away downstream, his hat floating after him. Thunderer announces that the giant shall be named Okulam (Noise of Tempest) and that, henceforth, when the weather is bad Okulam and his hat will be evident.

The boy grows up to marry Thunderer's daughter and one day he goes to the shore to watch his father-in-law trying to catch a whale. A mighty storm brews and Thunderer gives up the struggle. When the pair get home, the son-in-law climbs a mountain and blackens his face with coal to emulate the dark storm clouds. Immediately another storm arises and blows everything away, including Thunderer's house, so the daughter runs to find her husband and tells him that he is the cause of all the destruction. When he returns home and washes his face the storm abates and he helps Thunderer rebuild the hut. The next day the pair go to the shore, but this time it is the young man who casts the net and he drags in a whale with no trouble. Thunderer muses that his son-in-law is just as powerful as he was in his younger days.

The daughter gives birth to twin sons and the son-in-law is sent to capture two wolves which Thunderer played with when he was a boy. But when the animals are brought back they have forgotten Thunderer and they maul him. Amnesia also besets brown bears, grizzly bears and panthers, all of which are brought home with disastrous consequences and then returned to the forest. The next test for the young man is to split a hollow tree trunk and be incarcerated inside it. He frees himself with ease and again Thunderer reminisces on his own youth, seeing the skills he once had now in the hands of the younger generation.

Thunderer's grandsons grow up and the son-in-law is instructed to go to the Land of the Spirit People to obtain their playing hoop. When darkness falls he dashes in to the village and steals the hoop, but the Spirit People chase him with torches. Now the young man's wife realizes her husband's plight and tells her children to beat Thunderer. This causes rain to fall in Spirit Land and the torches are extinguished. The son-in-law hands over the hoop to Thunderer but he is told to go back and steal the shooting targets of the Spirit People. Again the same style of escape takes place.

After a while the young man becomes restless and sets out in search of adventure of his own. He comes to a village of the Spirit People with five rows of houses; inside the last house, which is very small, he meets two old women, the Mice. Blue Jay lives in the village and, being mischievous, he tells the chief that the stranger is demanding a shooting match. Blue Jay liaises between the two and the match is set up on the shore. The old chief wins the contest and Blue Jay leaps in, scalping the newcomer and dismembering him. The Mice, however, feed the head and keep it alive for many months until the victim's sons come in search of him. The old women warn the two boys of Blue Jay's treachery and relate the story of their father's fate. Three times Blue Jay attempts to set up another shooting match, but the grandsons decline the invitation and cast their gaze on Blue Jay in a way which sets his hair on fire.

Eventually the shooting match is agreed, but the two brothers insist on using their own targets. These are so brilliant that the old chief is dazzled, suffering defeat and so annoyed with Blue Jay are the villagers that they throw him in the river, turning him into a fish. The Mice they reward, telling them that they may, henceforth, eat everything that is good.

THE UNDERWORLD JOURNEY OF RE

CULTURE OF ORIGIN: Egyptian

PROVENANCE: various sources, but all in the form of hieroglyphic texts inscribed on the walls of pharaonic burial chambers constructed in the Valley of the Kings during Dynasties XVIII to XX in the New Kingdom period (circa 1492–1070 BC). In chronological order of composition they are the *Book of Am-Duat*, inscribed in tombs including those of Tuthmosis III, Amenhotep II, Seti I and Ramesses VI (not all of these compositions include the full account); the *Book of Gates*, inscribed in the tombs of Ramesses VI and Seti I; and the *Book of Caverns*, inscribed in the tomb of Ramesses VI.

According to the *Book of Am-Duat* Re sets out from the western horizon to begin his nocturnal journey through the underworld. He is to travel through the Twelve Hours by sailing the river of the underworld in his solar barque. He takes with him a crew of deities and as he enters the First Hour he takes human form, surmounted with the head of a ram. In the Second Hour, he provides fertile land for the gods of agriculture. In the Third Hour he revitalizes the underworld god Osiris. In the Fourth Re passes through the gates guarded by serpents. The Fifth Hour encompasses thoughts of resurrection. In the Sixth Hour, Re meets with the god of wisdom, Thoth, in the guise of a baboon who holds a sacred ibis. He also confronts his own corpse in the form of the scarab beetle, Khepri, engulfed by a serpent. The Seventh Hour finds Re guarded by three obscure deities, a serpent god identified as the 'Flesh of Osiris', a feline god with a knife and a third who binds opponents of Re with a rope. In the

Eighth Hour the demonic underworld god, Apophis, depicted as a huge serpent, is subjugated and wounded though never destroyed.

In the Ninth Hour the enemies of Re are destroyed by magical weapons. In the Tenth the symbols of Re's emergence for the start of the new day appear. The scarab beetle holds an egg from which Re will come at sunrise and the sun discs also appear in the scene. Twelve guardian deities act as a vanguard to check the safety of the eastern horizon. In the Eleventh Hour, the adversaries of Re in the underworld are consigned to a fiery pit. Finally comes the Twelfth Hour during which, within the body of a huge serpent whose bowel Re has entered, he transforms into his daytime form and becomes the scarab beetle which climbs from the snake's mouth. The god of the air, Su, closes the gates of the underworld and Re hovers above his head. Re sails in his solar barque up the legs of the creator goddess Nut and so begins his daytime journey.

The *Book of Caverns* offers variations on the above in which Re passes through a series of twelve caverns on his nocturnal voyage. The *Book of Gates* recounts a similar story in the course of which Re passes through twelve gates.

WATER GOD AND THE DROWNED CHILD

CULTURE OF ORIGIN: native American – Sioux, including the Iowa and Omaha tribes [north of the Arkansas River to Lake Michigan and up the Missouri Valley]

PROVENANCE: recorded from an oral tradition.

Comparison may be drawn with the death and resurrection tales stemming from classical Greek and other cultures in which the partaking of non-earthly food marks the frontier between life and 'permanent' death. It is significant that, in less sophisticated cultures, the notion of restoration rarely occurs. The dead are destined to travel on a one-way ticket to the otherworld, or to a state of nothingness.

A small child wanders away from his parents' house, falls into the river and is drowned. The family grieve deeply, especially the father, who goes outside and lies on the bare earth all night. Suddenly, however, he hears the sound of his child crying from deep beneath the ground, so he gathers his relatives and asks them to dig until the child is located. They are reluctant to tamper with the otherworld, but they offer rewards to anyone who will take on the task.

Two men who claim to have supernatural abilities agree to dig in return for all the father's possessions should they find the missing child. One paints himself black, the other yellow, and they dive into the river in search of the Water God. They discover that he has adopted the child since he has no children of his own, but when they ask to take the boy back to his rightful parents the Water God tells them they are too late. The child has eaten the god's food and will die if he is removed from the water (see also *Persephone and Demeter*, page 241).

The men return to the child's father and relate the sad tale, but still he is determined and suggests a white dog in payment to the Water God. The men dive down again with the offer and this time they return with the child. When he is put in his father's arms he is dead, but the father still pays his promised due by throwing a white dog into the water.

The end of the myth relates how the couple later lose a daughter to the river but they rescue her, on payment of four white dogs, before she has had an opportunity to eat at the Water God's table.

MISCELLANEOUS

FIJI: The snake god Degei awaits the spirits of the dead when they arrive in the other world. He judges each person on merit and each is cast into a great lake where it sinks down to the land of Murimuria. Those who have conducted lazy lives on earth, and whose nails are long, continue to fall into the dark places, where they are punished. Those whose lives have been worthwhile are lifted up to the land of Burotu, where they will rest in paradise.

POLYNESIAN (MAORI): Maui, the great Maori super-hero and the first man, is growing old, but he is determined to evade the goddess of death, Hine-Nui-Te-Po. He knows that he must be swallowed and enter the womb of the mother of death to fall asleep once more, as he was before he was born, unless he can creep stealthily through her body and emerge from her vagina. The goddess is asleep and he tries to pass without awakening her, but just as he thinks he has succeeded a little songbird twitters and disturbs Hine-Nui-Te-Po. She closes her legs and Maui is dead.

CELTIC (WELSH): While out hunting Pwyll, Lord of Dyfed, inadvertently insults the underworld god Arawn, in the guise of a huntsman with a pack of red-eared hounds. To compensate Arawn he offers to exchange places with him for an annual confrontation in which Arawn is obliged to fight his rival, Hafgan. To this Arawn agrees, but first it is necessary for Pwyll to *become* Arawn for a year of preparation. The two become good friends and Arawn reveals to Pwyll how he may overcome Hafgan with a single blow. If he strikes two blows the battle will be lost because Hafgan will revive.

Pwyll is victorious in the contest and, in gratitude for ridding him of Hafgan, Arawn gives Pwyll a prize of pigs. These animals originate from the underworld and are the only domesticated pigs in the Celtic realms. Ironically they become the spark that sets off a war between Dyfed and Gwynedd (see *Pryderi*, page 193).

13

Myths of Magical Powers

These are essentially animistic myths which endorse the notion that gods and their chosen representatives possess the whimsical and capricious ability to inflict on mankind various punishments and tribulations through the aegis of magic. This frequently involves such tricks as shape-changing and goes back to the primitive notion that every object in nature, humankind included, is merely a link in a constantly shifting chain.

THE HEAD OF FERGAL MAC MAILE DUIN

CULTURE OF ORIGIN: Celtic – Irish
PROVENANCE: recorded from oral traditions in the *Cath Almaine*, included in the so-called Cycle of Kings. The myth highlights the sacred significance of the human head in Celtic belief.

The fortress of Almu (Allen), constructed by Nuada, the chief druid to Cahir Mor, a forebear of Fionn Mac Cumhaill, is placed under siege by the army of Leinster. During the battle the hero Fergal Mac Maile Duin is decapitated, but the Leinstermen treat his head with great reverence. They wash it carefully, comb the locks and set it upon a pike over which Badb, the warrior goddess aspect of the Morrigan, hovers as a crow. A feast takes place in Fergal's honour, at which the head of the young minstrel, Donn Bo, also decapitated during the attack and set upon an adjacent pike, sings in tribute to Fergal.

THE NAME OF THE SUN GOD

OF ORIGIN: Egyptian
NANCE: Papyrus 1993 [Turin], inscribed during the XIX Dynasty
circa 1200 BC).

The myth has little substance, but underscores the concept that deities possessed secret names, knowledge of which afforded the recipient great power and advantage. In this instance, we are not accorded the answer!

Isis wishes to learn the hidden name of the sun god, since the knowledge will enhance her own status and that of her son, Horus. The sun god is depicted as an old and enfeebled character, dribbling saliva and dozing off to sleep. Isis collects the saliva, mixes it with dirt and concocts a serpent from the mixture which she deposits in the sun god's path. It bites him and he is consumed by a terrible fever. His pantheon, the Ennead, are summoned by his cries and demand to know what has afflicted him. In great pain he tells them the distress he is suffering and the other gods bewail the loss of his health and virility.

At this juncture Isis arrives to find the sun god with all the symptoms of serious snake-bite poisoning. He is alternately burning up, then sweating, then shivering and his eyesight is failing. Isis offers to cure him by using her special powers in exchange for the secret of his name and identity, but the sun god is wary, even in his parlous state, and tries to fob her off with many of his lesser titles. Isis is not fooled by this and, as if by portent, the fever increases.

In agony, the sun god capitulates, agreeing to reveal his secret on the understanding that Horus will be bound, on oath, to respect its confidentiality.

ISIS AND THE SCORPIONS

Culture of origin: Egypt
Provenance: Metternich Stela [New York].

This myth was probably intended to be recited as a protection against the dangers of scorpion bite. It has social class overtones as well as a moral message that kindness repays kindness. The essential implication is, however, that a victim of scorpion sting can be cured if the words of the myth, and in particular Isis's incantation, are recited.

The story opens with a short prelude which recounts elements of the myth of Isis, Horus and Seth and finds Isis weaving a winding cloth for the mummified body of Osiris. The narrative proper then gets under way.

Isis leaves her house in the evening accompanied by a retinue of seven scorpions who are to protect her from potential attack by Seth. Three of the scorpions, Matet, Petet and Tjetet, form a protective vanguard, two more, Mesetet and Mesetetef, accompany Isis, and the sixth and seventh, Befen and Tefen, bring up the rear.

When Isis arrives at her destination, the door of a prosperous family home is barred to her and her retinue because the lady of the house fears the presence of the dangerous creatures. The scorpions are enraged and, with revenge in view, six of them deposit their combined venom into the sting of the seventh, Tefen.

Isis finds overnight refuge in the humble home of a peasant woman and during the night Tefen wriggles under the door of the wealthy household and stings the lady's son. The aristocratic lady desperately seeks help from around the town, but no one responds. The myth, however, has a happy ending. Isis, herself a mother, is unable to stand by while the child dies, so she takes it in her arms, utters her magic over it and it is restored.

KIRKE (Circe) AND ODYSSEOS (Odysseus)

CULTURE OF ORIGIN: classical Greek, but subsequently adopted into Roman culture
PROVENANCE: recorded from an oral tradition by the Greek poet Homer in the epics *Odyssey* and *Iliad*. In the Roman derivation Odysseos becomes Ulysses.

During his homeward voyage to Ithaca after the siege of Troy, Odysseos sails his ship to the island of Aeaea, the home of the sorceress Kirke, daughter of Helios and Perseis and sister of Pasiphae. A reconnaissance expedition, headed by Eurylochos, comes upon Kirke's palace set deep in a forest. She appears to welcome the men and offers them a banquet, but almost as soon as they have sat down she touches each with a wand and turns him into a swine or some other beast according to individual human nature. Only Eurylochos, who has remained outside on guard, escapes her spell and is able to return to the ship and relate the incident.

Odysseos sets out to rescue his crew, but on his way he meets the messenger god Hermes, who warns him of Kirke's powers and offers him a herb which will render him immune. When the sorceress realizes she can do Odysseos no harm, and he threatens her, she agrees to release his crew from her spell. The swine are thus all returned to their original human form. Odysseos spends a season with Kirke and she bears him a son, Telegonos, and a daughter, Kassiphone.

TUIREANN
(The Children of Tuireann)

CULTURE OF ORIGIN: Celtic – Irish

PROVENANCE: recorded from oral traditions in an indefinite number of manuscripts, now lost, collectively known as the *Leabhar Gabhala* (the Book of Invasions). Much of the material survives in the *Leabhar Laighnech: Book of Leinster*, compiled circa 1160 by Aed Mac Crimtheinn [Dublin Institute for Advanced Studies]. It is also included in the work of the seventeenth-century Irish historian, Michael O Cleirigh (published 1643), the source which is generally referred to.

The *Leabhar Gabhala* includes, under modern convention, the so-called Mythological Cycle of stories which involve, by and large, the deities of the Side, the Tuatha de Danaan (people of the goddess Dana), who overcame the ancient inhabitants of Ireland, the Firbolg and the Fomorii, and whose activities took place largely in the valley of the Boyne.

The action takes place in the period of Irish mythological history between the First and Second Battles of Magh Tuireadh (see *Cath Magh Tuireadh*, page 187).

The god Lugh is preparing for the onslaught against the Fomorii for which he requires certain materials of magical quality. He sends his father, Cian, to Ulster to enlist troops but, en route, Cian is confronted on the Plain of Muirhevna [near Dundalk] by the three sons of Tuireann by the goddess Brigid – Brian, Iuchar and Iucharba. Recognizing mortal danger, Cian transforms himself into a pig and hides among a herd of swine. The brothers, however, perceive the ruse and Brian turns his two younger siblings into hounds. They sniff out the disguised quarry and Brian wounds Cian mortally with his spear. In his dying moments Cian returns to his human form, so that he can be recognized and avenged. Realizing the danger, the sons of Tuireann complete their murderous intent by battering Cian into unrecognizable form and burying his remains in a deep hole covered over with boulders. But the grave is discovered by Lugh and, as he re-inters the corpse, he swears to hunt down the slayers of his father.

A feast (to celebrate local victories against the Fomorii) is held at Temuir [the Hill of Tara] and the Tuireann brothers are invited, ostensibly as loyal allies. During the evening, however, Lugh announces his vengeful purpose, to find and execute the guilty ones. He declares that the killers are among those present at the feast and points his sword at the sons of Tuireann.

Lugh may not, according to strict laws of hospitality, take revenge on guests under his roof. He therefore demands payment by compensation, requiring of the brothers a number of seemingly innocuous items to give the Tuatha de Danaan advantages in the forthcoming battle. These items include three healing apples from the oriental Garden of the Light; the healing pigskin of King Tuis of Greece; the invincible burning spear of King Pisear of Persia; the chariot and horses of King Dobhar of Siogair which can outpace even the wind; the pigs of King Easal of the Golden Pillars which possess the power of regenesis; Fail-Inis, the terrifying young hound of the King of Ioruaidh; and the cooking spit of the women of Fianchuibhe who live far beneath the sea. When all these items have been gathered together, the brothers are to give three shouts from the Hill of Miodchaoin [to the north of Temuir], which belongs to a provincial ruler who was the foster father of Cian.

Brian, Iuchar and Iucharba set out on their quest. To obtain the apples from the heavily fortified Garden of Light they transmute themselves into hawks and seize the fruits from the air. Next they present themselves at the court of King Tuis in the guise of bards, singing his praises so elegantly that he offers them a reward. He declines to part with the magic pigskin, but suggests a gift in gold to match its volume. The brothers, however, seize the skin and battle their way out of the stronghold, killing Tuis but also suffering severe injuries themselves.

To obtain the fiery spear, which rests in an ice pit, they again present themselves as bards. This time the disguise is less successful, but, as fighting breaks out, Brian hurls one of the apples, smashing Pisear's skull. The brothers seize the spear from its icy rest and make their escape. Reaching the stronghold of Dobhar, they take employment as mercenary guards until such time as the king chooses to display his magical ordnance. While the chariot and horses are being driven around the stronghold, Brian leaps aboard, slaying the charioteer while his brothers jump up beside him and they speed away with the fourth of their items.

By this stage the renown of the sons of Tuireann has spread and King Easal hands over his swine without a fight, although to obtain the hound from Ioruaidh, their sixth item, they are once more obliged to engage in a ferocious combat. At this point, Lugh arranges for them to return to Ireland, where they surrender their trophies, thinking that their Herculean tasks may be at an end. Lugh, however, reminds them that two assignments remain outstanding and they set out to obtain the cooking spit from the ocean depths by seducing the women who guard it. Finally they climb the Hill of Miodchaoin but, unbeknown to them, the king has ruled that, in memory of the slaughtered Cian, no one may ever raise their voice from this sacred hill-top and he promptly engages them in combat. The king is slain by Brian and the onslaught continues until the three brothers stand triumphant but mortally wounded, raising their shouts to fulfil the blood debt.

The sons of Tuireann beg the use of the healing pigskin to restore themselves, but Lugh refuses and they die. Justice has prevailed.

14

Myths of Hunting

These stories constitute a special kind of animistic myths in that they explain the complex relationship between man and wild beast. In the world of the primitive hunter where the spiritual power of animals is of great significance, the hunting and killing of prey may bring down the wrath of the animal's spirit guardian. Providing the next meal thus involves more than a physical interplay between hunter and hunted. An intense reverence may be extended to dead animals. A slaughtered beast is treated as a dear and honoured friend with everything possible done to alleviate the appearance of premeditated murder. There is a sense that the killing of an animal is carried out after formal agreement between hunter and guardian spirit. This correct relationship is, to a greater or lesser extent, discernible in the myths of hunting.

THE HOUND OF FIONN MAC CUMHAILL

CULTURE OF ORIGIN: Celtic – Irish
PROVENANCE: recorded from oral traditions in the Fenian or Ossianic Cycle of myths which first appeared as a complete 'volume' in the manuscript known as *Acallm na Senorachul* (twelfth century).

Fionn Mac Cumhaill of the Fianna (royal guard of the Irish kings) owns a favourite hound named Adhnuall. One day it is captured by Arthur, the son of the British king, but Fionn's men chase him to Britain and rescue it. Arthur swears loyalty to Fionn and the hound continues in the service of its master until the battle of Leinster when it tracks around the battlefield three times and dies, howling, over the grave of some Fianna heroes.

LENDIX'TCUX

CULTURE OF ORIGIN: native American – Chilcotin [British Columbia in the region of Lake Anahem]
PROVENANCE: recorded fron oral traditions. The myth was related to Livingstone Farrand and recorded in the Memoirs of the American Museum of Natural History, 1900.

The virgin daughter of a chief awakens to discover a stranger in her bed, but he leaves before daybreak. The next night he visits her again and on the third night, anxious to discover the identity of the man, she places a pot of white paint by the bed. As the stranger leaves she dips her hand into the paint and presses her palm against his back.

In the morning she climbs to the roof and searches the village but sees no one with a white paint mark until she notices an old dog, Lendix'tcux, belonging to her father. The dog has a white handprint on its shoulder and she weeps with despair at the thought that this creature has become her lover. In due course of time, however, she becomes pregnant and delivers three puppy dogs.

The girl's father is very angry and orders the rest of the clan to abandon the village, leaving the hapless girl to starve. Only the old dog and the puppies remain. The girl builds a shelter and prepares some food which a magpie has kindly procured for her, but a malevolent raven hinders her efforts by covering the fires with dung to put them out.

Each day the girl goes out to dig up roots, but one day when she comes home she discovers children's footprints in the earth around the fire. The next day, out of curiosity, she leaves a substitute in her clothes to collect roots while she hides in some brushwood piled against the side of the house and peeps through a small hole in the wall. She sees three children playing around the fire with Lendix'tcux who, like them, is in human form. The dog skins are lying on the ground close by her hiding place. Lendix'tcux tells the eldest child to go and make sure that their mother is still gathering roots, but it sees the substitute and tells Lendix'tcux that all is well. The mother promptly tears a hole in the wall, jumps through and seizes the children's skins, tearing them into shreds and burning them. She tries to destroy Lendix'tcux's dog skin but he manages to rescue half of it and put it on, so he remains half man, half canine, while the children retain their human form. The mother shows the children how to hunt game.

Meanwhile the friendly magpie comes to see how she is managing and reports that the people who abandoned the girl are all starving. She gives him some food for his kindness, while the raven receives the reward of a pile of dung in his house! The magpie tells the raven that the food is obtained by burning a particular kind of wood but when the raven tries the trick he only burns his children's faces. Eventually, though, the magpie reveals the truth.

Lendix'tcux and the children become restless, wishing to visit the rest of the Chilcotin people, so the woman instructs them how to guard themselves against wild animals and how to persuade the animals not to harm mankind. On their journey they have many adventures, battling with a moose, an aggressive salmon fisherman, flood waters, eagles, marmot and even a tobacco tree. In each case they kill the animals, restore them to life and win them over, teaching them not to harm mankind. At a beaver dam Lendix'tcux spears the beaver, but is pulled under the water and when the boys hunt for the animal they find it dead. Inside the beaver's belly is Lendix'tcux who has killed it by eating its heart but it, like the other game, is restored to life. Finally they try to catch a chipmunk, but it eludes them and they turn to stone.

On that last day they were supposed to have met a bear and converted him, but they were distracted by the chipmunk – which is why, to this day, the bear of all wild animals is the most dangerous to man.

QUIKINNA'QU AND THE WHALE
(Big Raven and the Whale)

CULTURE OF ORIGIN: Siberian – Koryak

PROVENANCE: from an oral tradition among the Koryak whale hunters living in the vicinity of Penzhinskaya Bay on the Kamchatka Peninsula of southeastern Siberia. Modern authorship is that of the Swedish ethnologist Waldemar Jochelson, who recorded the tale during the Jesup North Pacific Survey of 1900, sponsored by the American Society for Natural History [Memoirs of the American Museum of Natural History, 10, 1905].

In the mythology of a primitive animistic society Quikinna'qu is the founder of the world, perceived not only as a deity but also as the first man and a powerful shaman. The myth incorporates several strongly held beliefs amongst primitive hunting cultures. It indicates the power of hallucinogens, in this instance those contained in a fungus, and it affirms the vital and reverential bond between hunter and hunted. It also identifies that saliva of the sky spirits (rain) has the property of a celestial semen.

Quikinna'qu (Big Raven) catches a whale but he cannot send it home to the sea because he is unable to lift the grass bag containing its travelling provisions. Quikinna'qu calls out to Tenanto'mwan (Existence) for help and Tenanto'mwan instructs him to go to a level place near the sea where he will find plants growing in the form of soft white stalks with spotted hats. These, he is told, are the embodiment of spirits, the Wapag men, who will help him if he eats some of them.

Quikinna'qu goes to the place which Tenanto'mwan has pointed out and while he is on his way, Tenanto'mwan spits on to the ground. From his saliva grow the strange plants [the fungus species *Amanita muscaria* – 'Fly Agaric']. Quikinna'qu eats the fungi as instructed and begins to feel happy. He starts to dance and hears the Wapag men deriding him: 'How is it that though being such a strong man, you cannot lift the bag?'

The taunt irritates Quikinna'qu and he tells himself that he is strong enough to lift the travelling bag of the whale. This he does and the Wapag men offer him a vision of the whale swimming home to its brothers and sisters. Quikinna'qu proclaims that the fungus shall remain on the earth, saying, 'Let my children see what it will show them.'

THE SACRED BUNDLE

CULTURE OF ORIGIN: native American – Pawnee [Oklahoma and North Dakota]

PROVENANCE: recorded fron oral traditions. Principal sources include *The Pawnee: Mythology* G.A. Dorsey. Carnegie Institution of Washington. No 59. 1906.

The myth accounts for the origin of the sacred bundles which were among the most important possessions of native Americans and brought out in times of need. It has a strongly animistic focus in that spirit beings inhabit the bodies of animals. The sacred relationship between the tribe and the buffalo is also underscored.

A young hunter who possesses an eagle feather with magical properties becomes separated from other members of a hunting party following buffalo and he comes across a young cow trapped in a mud hole. He is about to fire an arrow when the animal transforms into a beautiful young girl. Falling in love with her, he proposes marriage and she consents on the condition that they make their home by the water hole. He agrees and gives her a necklace of blue and white beads as a wedding gift. Then one evening he returns home to find his wife and his camp gone and with a great sadness he returns to his tribe.

Years pass until a small boy comes up to the hunter wearing a string of blue and white beads. The boy addresses the hunter as his father and tells him, 'Mother wants you.' At first the hunter takes no notice, but then he is persuaded to go with the small boy and, in doing so, he recognizes the beads. He follows a buffalo cow and calf which he realizes are his lost wife and her child on a long and arduous trek until they reach the home of the buffaloes. The bulls threaten to kill him.

They offer him a test, however, placing six cows before him and asking him to point out his wife. This he does, but the bulls now ask him to select his son from among a group of calves. Again he performs the task well, but the buffaloes set him another ordeal. He is to race against their fastest. On the day of the race, however, the ground is covered with ice and too slippery for the buffaloes to run properly, so the hunter wins.

Still the bulls are angry and the fiercest are ordered to charge at the hunter while he is seated on the ground. His feather floats into the air and they presume they have killed him, but when they retreat he is unharmed, protected by his magic eagle feather. The buffaloes now make him welcome on the understanding that he will bring presents from his tribe, so he and his buffalo wife return to his village, which they find to be starving. The wife produces some meat from her cloak and the pair take gifts back to the buffaloes.

The bulls agree to bring the herd to the hungry villagers and the hunter's son joins them in the guise of a yellow calf. The hunter warns the villagers not to harm his son because the yellow calf will return each year bringing more buffaloes. The child, however, tells his father that he is going to lead the herd away in the form of a young bull and that the villagers must kill the yellow calf and sacrifice it to the great god Atius Tirawa because each year another will take its place. They must tan the hide and wrap in it an ear of corn and a piece of the meat. Each year they must add a new piece of meat to the bundle.

In the future, when food becomes scarce, the elders of the tribe are to call upon the young buffalo bull and ask him to send the yellow calf with a fresh herd. The buffalo wife eventually disappears and the hunter dies, but the yellow hide bundle is preserved and added to year by year as a sacred talisman.

SISI'SAN AND TATO'LALAN
(White Whale Man and Fox Man)

CULTURE OF ORIGIN: Siberian – Koryak

PROVENANCE: from an oral tradition among the Koryak reindeer hunters living on the Kamchatka Peninsula of south-eastern Siberia. The myth was related by an unnamed shamanka in the hunting village of Qa'yilin. Modern authorship is that of the Swedish ethnologist Waldemar Jochelson, who recorded the tale during the Jesup North Pacific Survey of 1900, sponsored by the American Society for Natural History [Memoirs of the American Museum of Natural History, 10, 1905].

The sister of Sisi'san (White Whale Man), called Re'ra (White Whale Woman), suggests that they go hunting for reindeer. When a large buck runs past Re'ra wants to kill it, but Sisi'san refuses. He tells her that his arrows are too short and if the deer struggles it will lose fat. He must go back to the camp and collect larger arrows. He returns with the new weapons, as big as tent poles, but the buck is long gone.

The pair reach a river and Sisi'san uses his sister's clothes as a net so that they catch many fish. The morning after they retrace their steps homewards, carrying the bundles of fish.

After a while all the fish are used up and Re'ra suggests to Yine'ane'ut, the daughter of Tenanto'mwan, the creator being, that they set off in search of some edible roots. The two women come across a house occupied solely by men and they squabble over who will enter first! Re'ra jumps in quickly and is promptly claimed by Tato'lalan (Fox Man) as his wife. In her haste to follow Yine'ane'ut tumbles down the ladder (rooms in Koryak houses are below ground) and a ram amorously butts her in the face. She orders it away indignantly, saying that it is in no way fit to claim her as a wife. The same approach is made by a reindeer buck and a bear. When the bear squeezes her she wants to cry out but only breaks wind. Both suitors are likewise rejected.

Re'ra meanwhile gives birth to twin fox cubs and Tato'lalan slaughters the bear, the sheep and the reindeer, providing a supply of meat for his family. Re'ra eats the fattest of the food and, thus fortified, gives birth to a succession of fox cubs: first four, then thirty, then fifty, until her children are past counting.

Yine'ane'ut is very much put out over her lack of success in finding a husband and says she is going home. Re'ra, however, becomes lonely without Yine'ane'ut and asks Tato'lalan if she may also go home to visit her family. At first Tato'lalan is reluctant because he suspects that her people have been responsible for the wholesale slaughter of his reindeer bucks but he relents and Sisi'san rejoices at the news that his sister is coming home. He imagines that her husband is a wealthy Koryak reindeer breeder who will deliver a large herd and is therefore unpleasantly surprised when he sees a large pack of foxes descending on his home.

The foxes fight their way into the house, but there is insufficient space and the hungry animals eat all Sisi'san's food. They also gnaw the sleeping tents, the leather guy lines and the skins in the house. Then, in the night, they bite the noses and the ears of a number of people and, worse, nip off the end of Sisi'san's penis. At this juncture Sisi'san has had enough of his uninvited guests. He slaughters the entire pack and fills two storehouses with their pelts. He smears his damaged parts with oil and is restored to his normal state of health.

15

Myths of Charter and Kingship

This small section of myths is included to demonstrate that, in ancient civilizations, each centre of population, whether a small village or a major city state, was actively protected by one or more tutelary or guardian deities and the king was the earthly incarnation of the god. Thus whatever the ruler did was only a manifestation of the action of his personal deity. If he went to war against a neighbour, it was his god battling with another.

The gods overshadowed the very stuff of life and their temple administrations managed all that went on. Temples were built as living places to serve the needs of gods and their earthly retinue alike. Each complex had its administrative centre, its bakery, silversmith, brewery, carpenter and butcher. The votive inscriptions reinforce the picture that the tutelary gods and goddesses of ancient cities were held in enormous esteem and the myths of charter and kingship detail how these deities came to rule and to interact one with another.

ALALU AND ANU

CULTURE OF ORIGIN: Hattic or pre-Hittite and Hurrian – Anatolian
PROVENANCE: cuneiform text derived from an oral tradition and discovered on a tablet at the site of Boghazkoy in Turkey [Ref. KUB xxxiii. 120 translated by Albrecht Goetze (*Ancient Near Eastern Texts* ed. J.B. Pritchard)].

This is a myth typical of those which explain how a new national god (Taru) interacts with and supersedes one from an older culture (Anu) through an intermediate stage (Kumarbi).

The primordial being of the cosmos, Alalu, reigns for nine years with his attendant, Anu, standing before him to hand him his drinking cup. Then Anu slays Alalu and takes his place on the throne of heaven, employing as his own cup-bearer Kumarbi. Anu reigns for a further nine years until fate repeats itself and Kumarbi attacks Anu, dragging him from the sky and consuming his genital organs.

Anu informs Kumarbi that he has inherited a heavy burden because, in eating Anu's genitals, he has been impregnated with three awesome deities – Taru (Tešub) the storm god, the river god of the Tigris, and Tasmisu, the sibling attendant of Taru. After seven months Anu advises the unborn storm god from which orifices of Kumarbi's body he may best emerge. The first two siblings Kumarbi spits out upon the earth, but Taru comes to realize that being born from any one part of his surrogate father's body has disadvantages, so he threatens to tear it asunder when his time for delivery comes. Kumarbi becomes ill and he is brought a sacrificial meal to consume, in consequence of which Taru is born from the 'good place' (it is not made clear where this is).

Anu plans, with the help of Taru, to slay Kumarbi and although the ending of the myth is vague it is assumed that Taru vanquishes Kumarbi and takes on the kingship of heaven.

ENKI AND ERIDU

CULTURE OF ORIGIN: Mesopotamian – Sumerian
PROVENANCE: the earliest inscribed version of the myth dates from about 2000 BC, shortly after the collapse of the Third Dynasty at Ur, but it undoubtedly originates in an earlier oral tradition. The names of the deities appear on inscriptions dating from about 3500 BC. The essential purpose of the myth is to provide a eulogy on Enki's temple in Eridu.

In Eridu Enki builds for himself a magnificent shrine of silver and lapis lazuli; his messenger, Isimud, the god with two faces, sings its praises. It takes the form of a maze-like mountain floating over the primeval sea, the Abzu, and surrounded by a paradise garden, its streams filled with fish and its trees with birds. So magnificent is Enki's dwelling that even the sea and the River Euphrates are in awe.

Enki boards his boat and casts off from the moorings, using a snake as a punting pole and reeds as oars. He slaughters sacrificial sheep and cattle, and brings them to Nippur with an assortment of musical instruments. When he reaches Nippur he prepares a banquet of beer and cakes, and offers honey bread to Enlil, god of the air, in his shrine. The feast is laid out with a proper seating arrangement following a protocol in which An, the god of heaven, takes the high place, while

Enlil and Nintu, the mother goddess, sit on either side of him. Much drinking and feasting goes on before Enki's temple is blessed.

INANA AND ENKI IN ERIDU

CULTURE OF ORIGIN: Mesopotamian – Sumerian

PROVENANCE: the earliest inscribed version of the myth dates from about 2000 BC, shortly after the collapse of the Third Dynasty at Ur, but it undoubtedly originates in an earlier oral tradition. The names of the deities appear on inscriptions dating from about 3500 BC. This is essentially a charter myth, but it underlines a Sumerian concept that the cosmos is governed by standards, norms, rules and regulations.

In an introductory passage, the fertility goddess Inana visits the sheepfold and has intercourse with the shepherd demi-god Dumuzi while proclaiming the magnificence of her own genitalia.

Inana is covetous of the *mes*, or emblems of divine power, which belong to Enki, the god of wisdom, so she decides to visit his temple in Eridu. She sets out from her home city of Erech in her reed boat and, when she is a mile off the shore of Eridu, Enki sends his messenger Isimud to welcome her with certain instructions:

When the goddess Inana enters the Abzu of Eridu
Let her consume buttercake,
Have them pour out for her the cold water
which refreshes the heart.
Give her beer that she may drink before the lion.
Treat her generously, be towards her as a friend.

As soon as Enki and Inana meet they settle to a prolonged drinking bout and, in his inebriated state, Enki rashly insists on handing over all of his *mes*. Inana accepts the gifts, one by one, until she has amassed no fewer than ninety-four. Armed with these, she prepares to leave for home and Enki, still in his expansive mood, orders his messenger Isimud to ensure that she makes her departure in safety.

Too late, Enki sobers up and realizes what he has done. He now tries to intercept the boat and its precious cargo. Isimud manages to catch up with Inana just as she is departing the quayside and tells her that Enki wants his *mes* returned. Inana, however, flies into a rage, branding Enki as deceitful and ordering her maid Ninšubur to cast off the mooring rope. On five more occasions while Inana journeys home, Enki attempts to rescue his property, enlisting the help of fish, sea monsters, watchmen and others, but the efforts are in vain and Inana finally unloads her cargo on to the White Quay of Erech.

16

Moral and Doctrinal Myths

A short and disparate collection of stories which explain how the gods themselves need to pursue knowledge of the universe and its destiny. The quest of the Norse god Othin for knowledge of the fate of the world is typical. In oriental mythologies there may be a desire to explain metaphysical concepts in a simple fashion, hence the Daoist account of the five elements. Those which discuss moralities, such as that of Midas and the golden touch, underscore the belief that the sins of humankind do not pay! In particular, the gnostic story of the exegesis of the soul is worthy of careful examination as being typical of an idea which developed in the classical period that the soul could rise above the corruption of the flesh. This belief has seen its fullest expression in Christian beliefs.

THE EXEGESIS OF THE SOUL

CULTURE OF ORIGIN: gnostic Christian

PROVENANCE: the text is contained in tractate II,6 of the twelve codices which were discovered in 1945 at Nag Hammadi in Upper Egypt, where they were buried circa 400 AD [Coptic Museum, Cairo]. The manuscript, written in Coptic, probably during the third century AD, is considered to be a translation from an original Greek work. It takes the form of a short romance following mainly Valentinian philosophy (that put forward by Valentinius, an early Christian teacher who had been educated in the Platonist tradition) of the fall and restoration of the soul. It is also influenced by Greek and Jewish romantic traditions. Authorship is unknown and the title has been assigned in modern times.

The soul is a female entity who lives in virginal sanctity with her heavenly father until one day she falls into a mortal body and takes on human existence. In this state men abuse the soul and rape away her virginity until she adopts the mentality of a common prostitute running wilfully from one adulterous bed to another. Thus she remains, eventually becoming destitute and alone, having gained nothing except the contempt of those who have defiled her. The children she bears are feeble-minded and sickly.

Eventually she realizes what she has become, is deeply ashamed and begs her father in his mercy to save her. The writer then introduces an extensive homily on the subject of prostitution and its torments set beside the holy state of matrimony, delivering extracts from the Old Testament prophetic books of Jeremiah, Hosea and Ezekiel and from Greek Homeric sources.

The father performs two acts. He takes the soul's genitals, which are on the outside of her body like those of a man, and turns them inwards to guard them from further contamination. Thus, by analogy, he protects the soul. He also sends her brother down from heaven to be her bridegroom. She bathes and dresses herself and awaits the arrival of her husband. When he greets her, they consummate their marriage with passion. The soul is purified by this spiritual union and her children are born healthy and good. She is restored to her original state and ascends back into heaven.

THE FIVE DEVILS

CULTURE OF ORIGIN: Chinese Daoist (Taoist)
PROVENANCE: recorded in various texts and art from oral traditions.

Epidemics in China are considered to be attributable to the Five Plague Demons, the number five being based on the Five Elements of Chinese philosophy. There are several myths accounting for the origin of these devils, the following being the most comprehensive. It also introduces a significant figure in Daoist mythology, the Master Daoist Zhang Dao Ling (Chang Tao Ling), born in AD 35. He is said to have lived 123 years, having discovered how to distil the secret elixir of life from the Peaches of Immortality while living in the Cave of the Immortals. He argued the philosophy that sin is the root cause of all illness. Later he became known as Zhang Tien-Shih and the central monastery of the Daoist movement was established on Lung Hu Shan Mountain.

It should be noted that the anglicized equivalents of Chinese characters vary considerably in transliteration. The official Chinese Pinyin system is applied here, followed, where appropriate, in brackets, by the more generally encountered Wade-Giles system.

Five Demons are sent to earth by the Jade Emperor, Yu Huang Shang-Di (generally abbreviated to Yu-Di), where they become scholars of great repute. In the year AD 627 all the academics in the land are called to the capital by the Emperor Li Shih-Min to sit a special test. On their way the Five Demons are waylaid and robbed so that they arrive too late for the examination. They meet up in the shrine of San-i Ko and to provide themselves with an income they decide to become itinerant musicians. Their obvious talents in this capacity gain them an introduction to the imperial court.

Meanwhile the Master Daoist, Zhang Dao Ling, has refused to pay his taxes, for which the emperor wishes to punish him. The emperor invites the Master Daoist to a feast and hides the five musicians in a secret place beneath his state rooms, instructing them to play or cease playing on receiving a cryptic signal. When the musicians start to play the emperor complains that the row is being created by demons and orders the Master Daoist to exorcise them or die. After a few failed attempts Zhang Dao-Ling perceives the true identity of the Five Demons and gets rid of them using appropriate magic.

The emperor is unable to fault Zhang Dao-Ling. There is, however, a sting in the tail of the myth, because the ghosts of the Five Demons are told that the blame lies with the Master Daoist. They accordngly haunt him until he restores them to life. In revenge he offers each demon a special gift of torment with which to plague the emperor and the people until the five are elevated by the emperor to the status of immortals. To the first he gives the Fan of Chills, to the second the Fiery Gourd of Fever, to the third the Iron Band of Headaches, to the fourth the Wolf Tooth Stick of Aches and Pains, and to the fifth the Water Jar of Sweats. Eventually the emperor is obliged to own up to his behaviour and he reconsecrates the shrine of San-i Ko to the Five Demons.

THE FIVE ELEMENTS

CULTURE OF ORIGIN: Chinese Daoist (Taoist)

PROVENANCE: recorded in various texts and art from oral traditions, the theory of the Five Elements (wood, fire, earth, metal and water) is an essential feature of Chinese philosophy. Unlike the Greek notion of the Four Elements (earth, air, fire and water) in a state of balance, those of the Chinese are in a state of flux generally arranged into a productive or destructive sequence in which one generates or destroys the next. The Five Elements also contain astrological symbolism. They were all worshipped in their own right from the period of the Tang Dynasty (618–906 AD) although Earth, Tu Ti, was recognized as a deity from much earlier times.

It should be noted that the anglicized equivalents of Chinese characters vary considerably in transliteration. The official Chinese Pinyin system is applied here, followed, where appropriate, in brackets, by the more generally encountered Wade-Giles system.

Wood, Mu Kung, generates Fire and is itself produced by Water in the productive sequence. In the destructive mode Wood destroys Earth by drawing on its strength, but is chopped down by Metal. It is associated with the easterly direction under the rule of the deity Tung Wang Kung (Lord of the Eastern Paradise) whose attendants are Xien Tung (Hsien T'ung) (Immortal Youth) and Yu Nu (Jade Mistress). Wood is further identified with the season of spring and its colour is blue-green.

Fire produces earth (through its ash) and is generated by Wood. Fire conversely melts Metal and is extinguished by Water. It is associated with the south and with summer and its colour is red. Several deities are associated with Fire in Chinese mythology, including Chu Jung, Hui Lu and Zhih Jing-Tzu.

Earth produces Metal and is produced by Fire, while it contaminates Water and is weakened by Wood. Earth represents a central point from which the other elements radiate and its colour is yellow. It is presided over by the earth god Tu Ti, but is also recognized through innumerable local earth deities.

Metal generates Water (melting like ice) and is produced by Earth. In its destructive phase it cuts Wood and is melted by Fire. It is associated with the westerly direction under the rule of the deity Xi Wang Mu (Queen of the Western Paradise) and it is the element of the various gods of war. It is identified with the autumn season and harvesting.

Water, the final element, generates wood through plant life and is produced by Metal, while it extinguishes Fire but is itself contaminated by Earth. It is associated with the north, cold and darkness. Since China regularly suffers from inundation there is a celestial Ministry of Water and Floods controlled by the Dragon King, Lung Wang, and administered by the water gods, the Shui Fui. Lower orders of deities guard the seas and the rivers, particularly significant among which is the river Lo Yang, which gave up certain mystical diagrams upon the back of a tortoise.

MIDAS AND THE GOLDEN TOUCH

CULTURE OF ORIGIN: classical Greek, but subsequently adopted into Roman culture

PROVENANCE: recorded by the Greek author Plutarch and also by the Roman writer Ovid in *Metamorphoses*

The satyr Silenos, asleep after a bout of drinking, is caught by some peasants and taken captive before Midas, the King of Phrygia. Midas, however, recognizes his prisoner and, knowing the power of his master Dionysos, releases Silenos and treats him well. In return the satyr leads Midas before Dionysos, who offers the king a boon.

Midas requests that all he touches shall be turned to gold. The wish is granted and, at first, he is delighted with his new gift. But the euphoria evaporates when he discovers that even his food and drink turn to gold, so he begs Dionysos to release him from what he now perceives as a curse. Dionysos instructs him to immerse himself in a spring which is the source of the River Pactolos and when Midas does so the golden touch is removed from him.

OTHIN AND THE YGGDRASIL

CULTURE OF ORIGIN: Teutonic – Nordic (Icelandic)
PROVENANCE: the *Prose Edda* (Codex Wormianus), composed by the Icelandic scholar Snorri Sturluson between 1178 and 1241 AD and dispatched in the seventeenth century by the historian Arngrimur Jonsson to a colleague in Denmark, Ole Worm.

The content is, effectively, a textbook, the first part of which is titled *Gylfaginning* (The Tricking of Gylfi) and constitutes an overview of Nordic mythology. This incident, by which the god Othin loses his eye in pursuit of esoteric knowledge, is only alluded to in the *Poetic Edda* and Snorri's more detailed source is unknown.

At the centre of the world stands a mighty ash tree, the Yggdrasil, whose branches encompass heaven and earth and whose roots pass into different realms. One reaches to Asgarth, the realm of the Aesir gods, another goes to the land of the Frost Giants, and a third penetrates the place of the dead, Hel. Thus the tree forms a link between the different worlds.

Below the Yggdrasil is the Well of Urd where the gods assemble each day to discuss their affairs. The tree is tended by the Norns, the sisters of fate, and it is watered from the sacred spring of the god Mimir. These waters are charged with wisdom and knowledge and it is to the well of Mimir that the supreme god Othin comes, anxious to understand the destiny and fate of the world. He barters with Mimir to partake of the water of the spring and in exchange for its boon of knowledge he agrees to pluck out his right eye.

RYUJIN
(The Palace of the Dragon King)

CULTURE OF ORIGIN: Japanese Buddhist and Shinto
PROVENANCE: recorded in various texts and art from oral traditions.

Most of the cultures in the Pacific region acknowledge a god of the ocean. The mythology of Ryujin is typical. His festival takes place each year in June and he is worshipped extensively by farmers, particularly in times of drought.

Beneath the sea somewhere near the islands of Ryu Kyu lies the vast palace of the dragon god, Ryujin, built from coral and containing many rooms. Ryujin controls the thunder and rain and is the most powerful of the weather gods known as the Raijin. His kingdom, where a single day is the equal of one hundred mortal years, is guarded by water dragons and he is served by the fishes of the sea. On each side of the palace lie the halls of the seasons, not only of nature but of the mortal span. To the east is the Palace of Spring, where the nightingale sings its song and where the cherry trees are massed with butterflies. To the south is the Palace of Summer, filled with lush vegetation and the sounds of insects. To the west is the Palace of Autumn, where the trees are clothed in shades of red and gold. To the north is the Palace of Winter, a hall of eternal frost and snow from which there is no return.

17

Miscellaneous Myths

This final chapter includes a few short myths which did not find place elsewhere but which merit inclusion simply on the grounds of interest.

MYTHS OF CROCODILES AND HIPPOPOTAMI

These stories, associated with cultures where crocodiles and hippos play a significant role in local life and where people are found adjacent to rivers and swamps, are generally short and pithy. These animals are perceived to be incarnations of spirits who can do considerable harm to mankind, but who may also be seen as dispensers of summary justice, rewarding the good but punishing evil doers. Much of the ethos relies on the fact that hippos possess considerable strength while crocodiles have the ability to attack and kill with great speed. Both creatures, however, represent a source of food to societies living along river-banks, as the Biblical myth underlines. The dragon myths of Western and ancient Near Eastern cultures are scarcely comparable, since they are based on terrestrial creatures, including snakes and lizards.

BIBLICAL: Psalm 74 describes water dragons and the leviathan, both of which may reflect images of crocodiles.

Thou didst divide the sea by thy strength; thou breakest the heads of the dragons in the waters. Thou breakest the heads of leviathan in pieces and gavest him to be meat to the people inhabiting the wilderness.

Job 40.15–24 includes mythology of the hippopotamus, which it describes as the behemoth.

> *He eateth grass as an ox. Lo now, his strength is in his loins and his force is in the navel of his belly. He moveth his tail like a cedar; the sinews of his stones are wrapped together. His bones are as strong pieces of brass; his bones are like bars of iron . . . he lieth under the shady trees, in the covert of the reed and fens. The shady trees cover him with their shadow; the willows of the brook compass him about. Behold he drinketh up a river and hasteth not; he trusteth that he can draw up Jordan into his mouth.*

CHINESE: in Chinese mythology the crocodile is probably more often than not represented by the water dragons which inhabit lakes, rivers and the sea. Though the dragon lives in water it can also fly to the heavens and in this capacity it pulls the carriages of various deities, including Xi Wang Mu (Queen of the Western Heaven). The dragon also has the capacity to disgorge pearls and to make itself invisible.

The dragon kings of Chinese myth include Ao Kuang, Chung Lung and Pai Lung, the 'white dragon'. The latter was born of a mortal mother who lived in the fourth century AD. During a storm she takes shelter with an old man and becomes pregnant, upon which disgrace her parents disown her. In due course she gives birth to a formless, fleshy object that she tosses into the water. It is transformed into a huge white dragon which so terrifies the girl that she collapses and dies.

DAYAK (BORNEO): crocodiles are the spirits of the dead which assume reptilian form when they are sent back to the upper world at the behest of Jata, the underworld god and son of Mahatara, the supreme deity. Jata possesses a red face and a crocodile head. An alternative Dayak mythology places Djata as the queen of the underworld and therefore Mahatara's counterpart. She was originally seen in the form of a water serpent called Tambon.

EGYPTIAN: one of the most ancient crocodile gods is Chenti-cheti, who probably dispenses justice. Sobek, the son of the creator goddess, Neith, appears as a crocodile principally worshipped in the Fayum region. The god of chaos and adversity, Seth, is also depicted in certain circumstances as a crocodile and it is probably in this guise that he takes the body of his brother Osiris and rips it into pieces (see *Isis and Osiris*, page 235). In separate imagery he takes the penis of Osiris and throws it into the jaws of a crocodile to ensure that, even if Osiris should be restored through the magic of Isis, he will never again be able to father children (it is his son Horus who engages Seth in a desperate battle for the crown of Egypt).

The oldest Egyptian hippo goddesses are probably Ipet and Reret, though the goddess of birth, Taweret, is the best known. She is depicted as a hybrid with the head of a hippo who has a kindly nature and frightens away evil influences before and after childbirth. Her consort, Seth, by contrast, sometimes takes on the more destructive nature of the hippo.

JAVAN: crocodiles are controlled by benevolent spirits of ancestors which protect mankind from illness.

LESOTHO (SOUTHERN AFRICAN): a beautiful girl, Selekana, is thrown into the river by jealous rivals and is captured by the crocodile god, 'River King'. Selekana is forced to do menial tasks for River King's consort, River Woman, who has only one arm and one leg. River Woman is not unkind and lets her go, paying her with some precious stones from the river-bed. When Selekana returns to her village she receives the admiration of her friends, but the daughter of the chief is covetous of her reward and she too decides to go and try her luck in the river. She refuses, however, to work for River Woman, and River King eats her. So ends a tale of summary justice.

MALAYSIAN: various mythical notions are associated with crocodiles. A child which is eaten actually becomes a crocodile, beginning with the development of a tail and ending with the head, while the clothes of the victim are concealed in a special stomach within the crocodile's belly.

MALI (WEST AFRICAN): an enormous hippo lives in the rivers but plunders all the rice fields so that the people begin to starve. The local hero, Fara Maka, does his best to slay the monster with his spears, but the blades only crumple against the animal's tough hide. The hunter Karadigi brings his enormous hounds to join the attack, but they are all eaten alive. Finally, the wife of Fara Maka gets the better of the hippo by paralysing it through the power of a magical spell.

MYTHS OF DRAGONS AND FANTASTIC BEASTS

CELTIC (IRISH): at the festival of Imbolc, on 1 February, Brigit, the goddess of spring and the guardian of flocks, challenges the dragon of Cailleach Bheur, the hag with a blue face who symbolizes the dearth of winter and who devours human beings. Brigit advances with her lamb to fight against the dragon and the lamb of spring defeats the symbol of winter. Cailleach lays down her staff beneath a holly bush and, on 30 April, she turns to stone until the coming of winter again.

CELTIC (IRISH): every year at the festival of Samhain (31 October) a fearsome beast, Aillen, emerges from its cave and, through the magic of its song, puts the Fianna (royal guard) of the high kings at Tara to sleep. The hero of the Fianna, Fionn Mac Cumhaill, resists its soporific voice by pressing his spear against his brow and then attacks Aillen, decapitating him.

CELTIC (IRISH): a monster, Airitech, inhabits a cave at Cruachan, the fortress capital of Connacht. The cave is reputed to be the entrance to the underworld and from it the three daughters of the monster, in the guise of werewolves, predate on the neighbouring countryside. The only member of the Tuatha de Danaan able to resist them is the musician Cas Corach who, with the assistance of Cailte (a cousin of Fionn Mac Cumhaill), enchants them with his music and persuades them to assume human form. When they do so, Cailte impales them upon his spear and Cas Corach decapitates them.

CELTIC (SCOTTISH): a huge serpent-like monster, the Stoorworm, lives in the sea and causes tidal waves which inundate the land as it thrashes about. It can only be propitiated by the sacrifice of living virgins until the king offers the hand of his beautiful daughter, half his kingdom and the sword of Othin to the champion who can defeat the Stoorworm. The hero Assipattle attacks the serpent with burning blocks of peat which he forces it to swallow. As it writhes in its death throes it vomits its teeth and these become the islands of Orkney, Faroe and Shetland, while the lashing of its tail carves a channel between Norway and Sweden to form the Skaggerak. The monster finally knots itself into a ball and becomes Iceland, its burning innards forming the volcanoes and the thermal springs.

JAPANESE: the storm god, Susano-Wo, meets a beautiful young girl, Kushi-nada, who appears to be in great distress. He enquires of the weeping girl what is the matter and she explains that all seven of her sisters have been devoured by a terrifying dragon with eight claws. Susano-Wo offers to save Kushinada in return for her hand in marriage and to this her parents accede. Through his powers of magic Susano-Wo changes the girl into a comb which he places in his hair and he prepares to confront the dragon. He offers it a drink of *sake* and when it has succumbed to the effects he slaughters it.

MYTHS OF FIRE

POLYNESIAN (MAORI): the guardian of the sacred fire is Mahuika, the arche-typal mother goddess, whom people imagine as a terrifying and aged ogress who eats human beings. The hero, Maui, is bored with eating his food raw, so he decides to steal fire from Mahuika and goes to her house, telling her that she must not devour him because he is her own grandson. When Mahuika demands to know what he wants, he tells her that mankind needs the use of her fire. Reluctantly, she pulls out one of her flaming fingernails, but the moment Maui takes the nail it burns his fingers and he drops it in his canoe. The fiery nail also burns the boat but is finally extinguished by the water. Ashamedly Maui asks for another nail, but he is defeated once more by its heat and eventually the fire guardian loses her temper and throws all her fire at him so that he is engulfed by flames. He transmutes into a hawk to escape and then plunges into the ocean, becoming a fish. The entire world is now in flames and to control the conflagration Maui begs the gods of storm and rain to intervene. A great deluge commences and fire is only saved for mankind by keeping a small part of it dry inside a *kaikomako* tree (*Pennantia coymbosa*). Maui fashions fire boards and sticks from the sacred wood so that mankind may benefit from its latent power.

MYTHS OF THE SEA

JAPANESE: the daughter of the Sea Dragon King lives with her father in his palace beneath the sea near the Ryu Kyu Islands. One day she takes the form of a turtle, but she is trapped in the net of a fisherman, Urashima. When he has landed his catch, the daughter of the Sea Dragon King returns to her human form and the young fisherman falls in love with her. They return to her father's palace beneath the waves and marry. After three days Urashima wishes to go home and tell his mother and father what has happened, so the goddess releases him with her blessing. But when he arrives at his mortal home three days have become three hundred years and he dies.

SAMOAN: the god of war, Fe'e, lives beneath the sea in the form of a gigantic octopus whose arms encircle the world. His house is Bale-Fe'e and when he speaks it is with the voice of thunder. He falls in love with the daughter of a king in the town of Apia, but when he is spurned he rampages over the coral reef which protects the island of Upolu where the girl lives and breaches its protective ramparts.

MYTHS OF TEMPEST AND STORM

POLYNESIAN (MAORI): the god of thunder, Tawhaki, falls in love with the goddess Hine Piripiri, who is already engaged to another man. While he is bathing in a lake, the jilted lover and his brothers attack Tawhaki and leave him for dead, but Piripiri finds him and nurses him back to life. They marry and live happily in a castle on a hill-top until a cousin of Piripiri ascends the hill, intent on slaying Tawhaki. This time the thunder god is ready for his assailant and he raises his hands with bolts of lightning. The storm is unleashed and all Tawhaki's enemies are drowned in the ensuing deluge.

POLYNESIAN (TONGA): the sun god takes a mortal woman whom he discovers naked and catching fish; through him she bears a son, Sisimatailaa. When he has grown to manhood the son falls in love with a girl whom he wishes to marry and he seeks the consent of his father. On the advice of his mortal mother he climbs to the top of a mountain on the island of Tonga where he entreats the sun god's permission to take a wife. From the sky, in answer, come two wedding gifts, one of which he is encouraged to open, the other to leave untouched. Inside the first box he finds riches of gold and silver and he returns to Tonga to take his bride. Time passes until one day, while they are out on a fishing trip, the girl discovers the second box hidden in her husband's boat and she opens it while he sleeps. She releases tempests and storms into the world and the boat is sunk without trace.

MYTHS OF TROLLS AND OGRES

JAPANESE: an old peasant farmer, journeying in the forest, meets a strange woman whom he hears crying like a child and realizes that she is a demon who will try to devour him. As she approaches he seizes her by the hands and feet and takes her home. He throws the captive into his hut, making sure that every possible means of escape is blocked, and lights a great fire. At first the trapped demon tries to intimidate the peasant by baring her huge fangs, but then she vanishes and the old man realizes that the statue of his benevolent guardian house goddess, Kwannon, has developed a 'twin'. The question poses itself – which is the goddess and which is the demon? To test the statues he prepares the traditional offering to Kwannon of rice and beans. Only one statue responds and so he hurls the other into a pot of boiling water. When he opens the container all he finds inside it is sticky black tar.

PAPUA NEW GUINEA: a mortal woman is travelling on a journey with her child, laden with firewood and sweet potatoes, when a strange woman appears and offers to carry the infant. The stranger is, however, an ogre and after a while she wrenches off one of the child's limbs and devours it. The baby cries out, but the ogre assures the mother that it is only crying in its sleep and tears off another limb. As the nightmare journey continues the ogre consumes the whole of the child and, when the mother asks to take it back, replaces it with a piece of wood.

Only now does the woman realize the horrific nature of her travelling companion and she flees to her house. The ogre rips at the walls with her talons, but then transforms herself into a flying fox, retiring into the trees where she begins to eat fruit. The husband of the distraught woman returns home and learns of what has happened, so he builds a fire and lures the ogre indoors with the promise of roasted nuts. As she bends to take the food he spears her and holds her in the fire until she is burnt up. When the fire goes out he discovers that the evil influence has been transformed into wholesome vegetables by the purifying flames.

Appendix
Myths of the World by Culture

Index